The Perverted Priorities
of
American Politics

THE
Perverted Priorities
OF
American Politics

by Duane Lockard

The Macmillan Company <small>NEW YORK</small>
Collier-Macmillan Limited · <small>LONDON</small>

COPYRIGHT © 1971, DUANE LOCKARD

PRINTED IN THE UNITED STATES OF AMERICA

THE MACMILLAN COMPANY
866 Third Avenue, New York, New York 10022

COLLIER-MACMILLAN CANADA, LTD., Toronto, Ontario

Library of Congress catalog card number: 76-122297

First Printing

Dedicated to my students
who are determined
not to comply with
Shakespeare's
"You'll be rotten ere
you be half ripe . . ."

Preface

FOR twenty years I have been privileged to share the often exciting company of perhaps as many as a thousand college students whom I have come to know reasonably well. Those among them who remember my teaching will recall that I complained about things I found wrong with American public policies and politics, but the most reflective of them remember me as a stanch defender of the American political system and its overall "success." In the last few years, however, my own children and many of my students have forced me to reopen a great many questions that I had hitherto thought were satisfactorily answered. In their defiance of tyranny—whether in Mississippi, Chicago, or on a college campus—they have forced me to reconsider many issues such as the implications of a relentless racism, a national policy of murderous imperialism, and the blind pursuit of economic advantage whatever its consequences.

Those issues provide some of the reasons why this book was written. I wanted to search for the reasons why this society consigns black people to be "Invisible Men," in Ralph Ellison's phrase, while rewarding the scions of established families with automatic preference. I sought some kind of explanation for why we condemn thousands of coal miners to sudden or lingering death in our pursuit of "competitive" fuel prices. I asked myself why we pay billions of dollars to wealthy farmers not to produce food while millions of poor people go hungry. Why are we so enthralled with "national security" that we find it excusable to dump more explosives from our aircraft onto Vietnam than we used in all of Europe and Asia in World War II? How can one explain a national commitment to spend countless billions to send men to the moon or to build anti-ballistic missiles while we ignore the very real possibility that we may be creating an environment that will no longer sustain life on this planet?

In other words this book is a critical examination of the perverse ways in which we determine the priorities of American politics.

And like most such books this one owes much to those who looked over the author's shoulder and said that won't do. My Princeton University colleagues Walter Murphy, Jameson Doig, and Richard Falk helpfully criticized early drafts of parts of the manuscript. Stanley

Husid and Ralph Dupont, busy practitioners of politics, gave me their critiques of chapters of interest to them. Professors Nelson Polsby and Ted Lowi of the University of California at Berkeley and Chicago University respectively did painstaking critiques of the whole manuscript, and happily I found I could ignore some of what they said because they canceled out each other's criticisms. My daughters Leslie and Jay were also helpful readers. Ted Tedeschi and Elliott Moorman aided me as diligent research assistants, and David H. Tiffany and Jay Carroll of Macmillan were unfailing sources of encouragement in my moments of doubt. The greatest debt of all I owe to Beverly, who not only served again as my best editor but bore with me and collaborated as I thought aloud about every idea in the book.

D. L.

Princeton, N.J.

Contents

The Perverted Priorities
of
American Politics

The Times Are Out of Joint

THE TIMES are out of joint. Things sacred are no longer respected; long-accepted verities are harshly challenged. Normally law-abiding Roman Catholic priests join others invading a Selective Service office and help destroy files, openly inviting arrest in order to publicize their dissent. The staid are shocked by assertions that the behavior of the United States in Vietnam is not essentially different from that of the Nazis. Middle-aged parents, who recall World War II as a time of sacrifice and struggle for objectives that seemed eminently justified, now find their children denying the morality of World War II or any other war. Many of those sons and daughters are freer of the cant of nationalism than any generation since the full emergence of the nation state.

So it is a generation asking where the Emperor's clothes are. Because the Emperor is nearly naked the question is appropriate, but it is shocking to hear nonetheless. For all men live to some extent with their own little lies—lies that cushion unkind truths. Indeed it is when men face the uglier truths and can no longer accept any lies about themselves that they commit suicide. But there are lies and lies—some are cushions and some are weapons. Whichever type the lies (myths, if you like a softer word) may be, the probing honesty of this generation of young adults is shattering some profound beliefs of the only recent past, and the consequences are incalculable.

No better illustration of this can be found than the actions of a small group of black college students in North Carolina in 1960. Fed up with being categorically and constantly placed in a second-class status, they rebelled. The rebellion was insistent but peaceful; it broke occasionally into violence later in response to the massive violence turned upon them. In the beginning it was no more than an insistence that the white community face the glaring lie that whites had learned to live with so comfortably: namely that the black American was satisfied to put up with repression and discrimination forever—that Negroes would go on and

1

on being willing to wait till next year, next century before their legal rights became social reality. Black students by sitting down at a dime-store lunch counter and demanding service opened the way for all manner of question asking and demand making by white and black alike in the decade that followed the first sit-in. In part, white students joined black students and helped them seek their liberation, but the questions raised by the black students opened the eyes of their white allies to other basic lies and truths about American society. Gradually youth turned into the nagging conscience of the society, thereby winning the genuine hatred of many but at the same time shaking awake others for reconsideration of accepted ideas.

Then the war in Vietnam gave new reason for reevaluation of norms hitherto accepted without thought. As doubt about the morality of our involvement in that war grew, so did the sympathy for the young who were being asked to serve and die in that futile effort. The young, subject to the draft and forced to give up all right to object or even to have a minimal control over their lives, were compelled to participate in a war to which many, probably most, had no sense of commitment whatever. And the ultimate irony was that the well-to-do could evade the draft by remaining in college whereas the poor had no option but to go —and be paid a substandard wage for the most odious activity a nation can demand of its citizenry.

Yet the war was not the only fundamental source of widespread dissent. Vietnam is an attack of a recurrent fever produced by a deeper malady that will continue to plague us long after we have extricated ourselves from that morass. The establishment "explains" our presence there by pointing to a "commitment" to the people of South Vietnam, but the commitment is an afterthought, a rationalization for a series of egregious blunders that led to losing a military involvement that vanity and internal political rigidity would not permit us to escape. The Vietnam involvement, however, has struck deeply at the superficial consensus that characterizes American society. It turned the presidential politics of 1968 upside down. That was the campaign when an incumbent president—who by all logic of past performance would probably be unbeatable in the election and absolutely sure of renomination— withdrew from the race when he was defeated in the New Hampshire primary by Senator Eugene McCarthy, who lacked a real organization and had little more than a band of determined college students to carry his campaign to the people; it was the year the President of the United States dared not go to the Democratic National Convention for fear of inciting a riot by his presence or at the very least of inviting insult to himself and to the office he held; it was the year when a shocked nation looked on in amazement as the berserk police of Chicago pounded demonstrators, priests, reporters, and nearly anyone in sight—an action called in an official report "a police riot." [1] This then was the year when virtually every major political figure in the country admitted implicitly or explicitly that the time had come to cut our losses and leave Vietnam, but few of those politicians were willing to take the next step and ask why and how we had got there in the first place. As the sage historian Henry Steele Commager has said, "We will have learned from this tragic conflict a few practical lessons for the immediate present, but no moral lessons to guide our future." [2]

But Vietnam has not been the only trigger releasing expressions of discontent; other issues have invited similar probing questions. How is it that the nation can blithely spend billions in order to race the Russians to the moon, while people starve and lead lives of the most abject deprivation within the borders of this country and far worse conditions prevail in most other nations. This is not to say that the billions merely given to the poor would have solved the problem, but it is to ask why our ingenuity can be harnessed to finding a way to the moon whereas it cannot be directed to the resolution of the problem of a shortage of decent food. Why did many Americans think former Secretary of State Dean Rusk to be a great humorist when he said that one right small nations should have is not to be molested by their large neighbors? (Some didn't enjoy the joke for choking on the tragedy of it.) Why is it that we spend billions on antimissile missiles while our cities sink into the muck of their own degradation: ugly, decaying, deserted by those able to escape, and occupied by the alienated, the angry, and the trapped. Why does a nation placidly put up with a Congress that discharges from its ranks a black Congressman who cheats and flouts conventions while it accepts and condones the same behavior—more surreptitiously engaged in—in other colleagues who are not black and outspoken? Why does the nation not react when a United States Senator asserts that it is necessary to have an antiballistic missile system in order that the Adam and Eve who emerge after a "nuclear exchange" (how antiseptic it sounds!) shall be "Americans and not Russians." How can ostensibly sane men talk about the obliteration of hundreds of millions of persons and produce no more than a ripple of public reaction?

These and thousands of other questions are asked. Who runs the university and how and to what end? Why is the university involved in secret research, including ghastly ways of annihilating life? Why must

1. See Daniel Walker, "Rights in Conflict," a report to the National Commission on the Causes and Prevention of Violence, excerpted in *The New York Times*, Dec. 2, 1968, and subsequently published as *"Rights in Conflict"; Chicago's 7 Brutal Days* (New York: Grosset and Dunlap, 1968).
2. "Common Sense," *New York Review of Books*, Dec. 5, 1968, p. 4.

black people put up with discriminatory hiring practices and why are black unemployment rates twice those for whites? Why is this one of the last major nations in the world that does not have a governmentally supported health plan for all? Why have an average of a hundred coal miners died in accidents every month for a hundred years? Why are the water and air so polluted that we sometimes endanger our lives by taking a drink or breathing? Why is the death rate from tuberculosis so high in slums? Why is the infant mortality rate for black children twice as high as for white ones? And why do black mothers die in childbirth at a rate three and one half times that for whites?

Every one of these questions rests upon certain moral judgments or assumptions, and most of them also involve matters of economics (in the sense of the availability and allocation of resources). They are also without exception political problems. That is to say they concern matters of influence and power. The processes by which the influential attempt to make decisions, allocate values, determine what others shall do (or even think or not think)—such acts are the essence of politics. My purpose in this book is to examine the politics of American government—with emphasis on national government, but not exclusively so— to see how our institutions establish priorities on a wide range of important issues. We shall look at the *myths* apparently believed by leaders that make them act as they do. We shall examine some of the *constitutional verities* and compare them with *political realities*. We shall deal with the question of whether or to what extent the institutional framework is at the root of why the system produces the policies it does. And we shall try at all times to be as free of cant and as open about prior assumptions as we can be. This is difficult and no doubt we shall at times fail, but we intend to keep the deck fair and deal an honest hand. Obviously my personal values partly control what gets through the typewriter and onto the page. There is no such thing as scientific neutrality when dealing with moral and political issues of the kind set forth here. One can be neutral about governmental matters only by ignoring the morality of moral issues! That is, one might assume the "fact" of the powerful military-industrial complex and simply put it down as an actor in the political process—that is, consider it a "given" —and try to refrain from all evaluating. But one has to choose examples to illustrate points, one must work with a language that is filled with nuances and shades of meaning, and both these factors can subtly weave into the picture a set of moral judgments. (As E. B. White said long ago, "All writing slants the way the writer leans.") Anyone who can calmly and completely dispassionately discuss the prospects of the annihilation of hundreds of millions of human beings and feel or express no emotion about it is either a moral idiot or worse.

This then will be the aim: to keep the assumptions out in the open. But a writer's bias is served by his subtleties, and the reader is therefore duly forewarned. Not that I intend to take liberties with the canons of scholarship: when I quote I will try to be fair and when I represent a position I shall do so with care. Anyone who tends to agree with the obvious moral commitment that colors this writing should, however, be as skeptical as possible as he reads; others, I dare say, will have no problem. Fair warning given, let us proceed to show what the approach is going to be.

The chapter that follows presents an analysis of contemporary politics in the United States, stressing the distribution of power and the general methods of implementing policy. That discussion will serve as an introduction to ensuing chapters by setting forth the political context of this country as I comprehend it. In particular, the different approaches to politics of various groups and individuals will be assessed, and an argument will be offered concerning how widely distributed or how narrowly · concentrated political authority is in this country. And we shall raise some of the implications that follow from the failure of the political system to deal with certain critical issues.

Then, on the basis of this introductory analysis, we shall in turn discuss the "rules of politics," the party system, federalism, Congress, the judiciary, and finally the Presidency and the bureaucracy. Each chapter will analyze specific policy problems and each will illustrate the operations of the institutions by showing how they deal with them. The concluding chapter will ask essentially these questions: Is this adequate? Are these responses to grave problems morally acceptable? Why does the governmental system generate these particular answers? Is there any way to change the kinds of answers that the system provides? Or is the system already giving democratically responsive answers to the problems? That is, does the fact that the government builds extensive highway networks and concentrates on subsidizing middle-class housing instead of feeding the hungry and caring for the ill indicate that the government is merely being responsive to majority wishes? Do we reject the needs of the poor, the black, and the aged because the poor, black, and aged are inherently minorities, whereas the white, comfortable, and not-yet-aged—constituting the vast majority—are getting from a "democratic" government exactly what *they* want?

These are disturbing thoughts, raising doubts about the whole firmament of American society and politics. I make no pretense of knowing the "answers" to these disturbing questions, but I insist the questions need to be asked and their implications faced. This then is one person's attempt to grope toward some answers.

CHAPTER ONE

American Politics: The Way Things Are

D EEP beneath the hills and valleys of north central West Virginia runs a seven-to-eight-foot seam of bituminous coal. This shiny black, high-grade coal is enormously profitable for its producers and indispensable for stoking American industry. Mining coal is an expensive process, but it would be costlier still were it not for hidden costs that are never entered on the accounting sheets. Part of that hidden cost is human suffering, as revealed during the week before Thanksgiving, 1968, while the drama of seventy-eight men trapped in the stygian blackness of Consolidated Coal Company's mine near Farmington, West Virginia, ran its course. At 5:40 A.M. November 20, 1968, the "cat eye shift" was near the end of its day's work when a methane explosion ripped through the mine. A volcanic torrent of flame blew the massive hoist out of the mine shaft like a rocket. Some workers escaped, but for days it was not certain whether the remaining seventy-eight had any chance to survive. Rescue efforts continued until an inevitable decision had to be made: the mine became the workers' tomb because the only way to extinguish the fire inside was to seal off all air. The seventy-eight were among the 120,000 who have died violently in American mines— *an average of 100 men per month* during a century of operations.[1]

For a fleeting moment the nation had the opportunity to know something about the untabulated costs of coal production, but the public, although it will watch any life-and-death drama on television for a few days, cannot long be bothered with such remote matters as coal mine safety. Who in the general public knows that the accident rate in coal mines is 4.5 times higher than the average industrial accident rate? Neither the public nor Congress knows or cares about the lethal dust that collects in miners' lungs, the coal dust that gathers in explosive quantities inside mines, or the slate falls that annually bury hundreds of

1. See the excellent review of coal mining nonsafety by Ben A. Franklin, "The Scandal of Death and Injury in the Mines," *The New York Times Magazine*, March 30, 1969, pp. 25ff.

miners. It is true that the accident rate is slightly lower now than it was thirty years ago. The actual number of fatalities is much lower, but that is because 135,000 miners now produce as much soft coal as did nearly half a million thirty years ago—owing, of course, to the mechanization of mining. It remains true, however, that every year hundreds of miners die in accidents and hundreds more succumb to diseases caused by mining—such as "black lung," which results from years of breathing coal dust.[2]

Central West Virginia has known many mine disasters. In Monongah an explosion killed 362 miners in 1907. (And one pathetic immigrant bride spent the rest of her confused life searching the Monongah slag heap, hunting, presumably, for some memento of a deceased husband.) That catastrophe led to the establishment of the U.S. Bureau of Mines in 1910, but its powers were negligible. Bureau inspectors could enter a mine only with the permission of the mine owners. The industry (pleading states' rights) insisted that only the states should be responsible for mine safety, and Congress agreed. (It hardly need be said that complaint state governments, as expected, did little to regulate the industrial giants in their states. In my youth I worked as long as twenty-four hours on a weekend in a mine, preparing it for the visit of a state mine inspector, because the company had been forewarned the inspector would arrive Monday morning. In the meantime, anyone with good sense trembled at the thought that a fire might break out, because explosive coal dust lay inches thick over parts of the mine.) Not until 1941, after 12,000 more deaths by explosion had revealed the need for more stringent laws, was the Bureau given authority to enter a mine on its own initiative. Even so, the only power the Bureau had was to publicize violations of safety rules; the law was unenforceable!

Then in the winter of 1951 another mine exploded—this one in West Frankfort, Illinois—taking the lives of 119 miners. Within six months Congress passed the first federal mine safety law with any enforcement powers. The 1952 law still had gaping holes in it, holes punched out by coal-industry–oriented Congressmen. So between the enactment of that law and the 1968 explosion 5,500 more miners died in accidents and as many as a quarter million suffered serious disablement.

Although the 1952 law provided authority to close mines found to be in dangerous condition, few mines were closed. Indeed the Consolidated Coal Company's Mine Number 9—the one that killed the seventy-eight men—had been reported for more than twenty-five serious violations of the code in the seven federal inspections that had been conducted in the previous two years, but not once had the mine been shut because of the

2. See Robert Coles and Harry Huge, " 'Black Lung,' Mining as a Way of Death," *New Republic*, Jan. 25, 1969, pp. 17–21.

infractions. Senator Gaylord Nelson of Wisconsin pointed out that these violations included inadequate coal dust suppression and unsafe electrical equipment. Considering the fact that the mine was located over a gas field and that methane gas constantly leaked into it, these violations would on their face appear to be dangerous. The Senator went on to say that the Bureau of Mines "appears to be little more than a coal industry mouthpiece, failing to foster safety studies, failing to take the initiative in recommending stronger legislation to the Congress, and failing to enforce existing laws." It is significant that when the Bureau brought proposed legislation to the White House in 1968, President Lyndon Johnson sent it on to Congress only after considerably strengthening its provisions.

Isn't it appropriate to ask why this human sacrifice goes on year after year? Why does our economic and political system allow this to continue, if, as many experts believe, there are ways to stop it? In the first place one obvious reason is that it would be costly to make mines safer. Coal competes with other fuels and mine owners claim that extra cost would ruin their competitive position. Oddly enough this is the United Mine Workers position also. For example, the union's marketing expert is reported to have testified that steps to eradicate "black lung" would be so expensive as to affect the industry's competitive position.[3] The claim is that more stringent safety laws would merely mean more unemployment because of the loss of markets to other fuels. And to be sure this is an argument that strikes fear into the hearts of people in the coal mining country, for mechanization of the industry has reduced employment drastically over the last thirty years; as noted above 135,000 men now turn out as much coal as did half a million in the past. The consequence for tens of thousands has been abject poverty and hopelessness.

The argument is that preventing these deaths would be prohibitively expensive. It is parallel to the gambit of some economists who point out that complete removal of all rail-highway grade-level crossings would save some lives. But to do so would either require a government subsidy or bankrupt the railroads, and therefore we consciously risk lives—and lose some every year—by eliminating only the most dangerous crossings. How apt is this analogy for the coal-mine safety problem? It applies to a degree. Complete coal mine safety is unattainable; mines are inherently dangerous, and a lower accident rate would be costly. But the question can reasonably be asked as to why we allow mines to be in unsafe condition where only remote, unseen miners are risked, whereas the United States government readily spends millions to see to it that

3. "Mine Safety Law Held Inadequate," *The New York Times*, Nov. 22, 1968.

there is no repetition of the fire that took the lives of three astronauts. The question, that is to say, is whether the accidents at the grade crossings occur with undue regularity to certain groups of the disadvantaged and not to others? In short, what we are facing is not the *logical* problem posed by the economist so much as the *moral* problem that is rarely posed by anyone.

But it is apparently not impossibly expensive to protect miners; other nations do so. The International Labour Office's statistics show that, for the twenty-two nations on which it has mine accident data, only Canada, Taiwan, Korea, and Turkey have rates as high as ours. Morocco and Southern Rhodesia have rates only half ours, whereas India, Czechoslovakia, Poland, Great Britain, and Yugoslavia have still lower rates. In the United States the number of fatal accidents per 1,000 underground workers per year has never gone below 2.10 and has been as high as 2.73 in the 1960's. In Britain the number has never gone over .67 in recent years and has steadily declined.[4]

The following table of averaged rates for selected countries (for 1960 through 1967) makes the American record a sad story.

TABLE I-1.

UNDERGROUND MINING: AVERAGE ANNUAL FATAL ACCIDENTS

Rates per 1000 Workers
(1960–1967)

Canada	2.48	Hungary	.64	Netherlands	.34*
U.S.	2.49	Poland	.59	United Kingdom	.57
Turkey	3.54	Yugoslavia	.71	Czechoslovakia	.62**

* No data for 1966 and 1967.
** Data available only for 1965, 1966, and 1967.

SOURCE: International Labour Office, *1968 Year Book of Labour Statistics* (Geneva: ILO, 1968) pp. 682–83. The ILO data compare favorably with accident statistics tabulated by the U.S. Bureau of Mines in a mimeographed report the Bureau prepared on the United States and five West European countries. Their table is entitled "Death Rates per 100,000 Manshifts Worked Underground at Hard Coal Mines in Selected Countries, 1946–1965." There are also data in that table for United States soft coal mines, and they are not significantly different from United States hard coal rates. The United States rates average out about two to four times higher than for Belgium, France, Great Britain, Netherlands, and West Germany.

Perhaps, however, American mines are inherently less safe for physical reasons having nothing to do with safety rules or enforcement. I

4. It is revealing—and shocking—to compare mine accident data reporting for the United States and Great Britain. Compare our monthly "Coal Mine Injuries and Worktime" issued by the U.S. Bureau of Mines (the issue of May 14, 1969, covers a survey for 1968), and the (British) National Coal Board's "Safety Branch Annual Report" for 1967–68.

put that question to an experienced British mining official and this was his reply:

British mines are inherently more dangerous than yours and therefore our safety standards have to be all the higher. . . . Our rock dusting standards are very high and rigidly enforced [to reduce the explosiveness of coal dust] I believe our standards of electrical safety are higher than in the U.S. Indeed, most American machinery—if not all—that has been installed over here has had to be redesigned [for] electrical [safety].

It sounds as though I'm being beastly and critical of your mining people and I would hate to be so, because we have a lot to learn from them in some matters while still trying to retain our safety standards. We have learned by experience, much of which has been bitter, and I am quite sure that it is the inherently greater danger in our mines that makes us more careful and creates our higher standards.

But why do miners continue to take such risks? They are not slaves and can always refuse to enter an unsafe mine. True, but if one has seen the destitution that prevails in many parts of Appalachia where mines have closed down, then the answer may not appear so obvious as it might seem on the surface. If one knows those places and has seen proud, hard-working, former miners reduced to humiliating poverty because other sources of employment are hard to find, it may be easier to understand why miners continue on the job at over thirty dollars a day, risk or no risk. These words of an unemployed miner, aged forty-one, father of nine children, and now reduced to any part-time work he can find, will help explain.

I had a bad cough all the time, like you do when you work down in the mines. After a while you stop thinking about it. You cough like you breathe, on and off all day. Then the cough got real bad and I saw a couple of doctors, company doctors. They gave me medicine to keep the cough down, and I stopped worrying. You can't be a coal miner and worry about what it looks like inside, in your lungs. Then I got hurt, my back. That happens a lot, too— and you either can go back to work or not. I wanted to go back, and I was lucky because I could. I'd still have trouble, but like with the cough, I could keep going. I took some pills when it got bad, but most of the time I showed up first thing in the morning and stuck it out to the end. And I miss those days. They went fast, and there was money around, enough to pay the bills and live real decent-like and feel like a man, like somebody who was doing at least something with his life.[5]

Many miners know no other occupation and dread moving to a hostile and confusing city—even assuming that an unemployed and often ailing miner can find a city job. Moreover the risks of the mine are ones that miners learn to live with. Like all persons who face risks, miners simply do not expect the worst. Why do individuals drive at seventy-five miles an hour when they know the risks of death in an accident at that speed are infinitely greater than at forty? If one drives at unsafe speeds merely to arrive a few minutes sooner, so might a miner choose risks rather than forfeit $150 a week. Indeed, if all the obligations for such risks are to be assigned to the miner, then why should we make efforts to protect individuals from cancer, when, after all, many prospective victims of cancer do not stop smoking, do not have regular physical examinations, and do not do other things to reduce the risk? Clearly a case can be made for protecting individuals even where they do not take full advantage of opportunities to help themselves. In the last analysis miners have heard from childhood on about the risks of mining, and they take their chances rather stoically; indeed they take a certain pride in the remarks made to them about how much guts it must take to work below the ground. Since when has bravery been without psychological value?

Why doesn't the union demand safety when it negotiates contracts? Union leaders claim they do stress safety, but the best evidence of their seriousness comes at the bargaining table. Union negotiators are more likely to battle for wages and fringe benefits, such as retirement pay, hospitalization, and paid vacations. To an unusual degree the United Mine Workers has developed a "buddy" relationship with the coal industry. Under John L. Lewis the union made so fraternal an accommodation with the operators that a U.S. District Court in Kentucky handed down a finding of conspiracy between the operators and the union to restrain trade. The Court awarded $7 million in damages to a marginal coal producer squeezed by the big operators with the union's cooperation.[6] So it is that the union no less than the industry takes an economic—and fatalistic—view of mine dangers. The chief of the UMW, W. A. Boyle, went to the scene of the West Virginia explosion not to condemn the

5. Robert Coles, "Appalachia: Hunger in the Hollows," *New Republic*, Nov. 9, 1968, pp. 16–17.

6. The history of this cooperation is told by T. N. Bethel in "Conspiracy in Coal," *Washington Monthly*, March, 1969, pp. 16ff.

Consolidated Coal Company for its neglect but to praise it as "one of the better companies, as far as cooperation with our union and safety is concerned." He went on, "I share the grief. I've lost relatives in a mine explosion. But as long as we mine coal, there is always this inherent danger of explosion." Many of the miners who survived the disaster did not agree. One of them said, "It's been filled with gas . . . something was bound to happen." He called conditions inside the mine "lousy." Another miner told a hearing conducted by the West Virginia Department of Mines that he had complained of unsafe conditions a few days before the blast, particularly failure to "rock-dust" adequately in order to reduce the explosiveness of coal dust. He said he expected to have trouble finding another job as a result of his testimony, but he said, "I had to tell the truth, didn't I?" [7] It is true that later, when others were demanding safety legislation, and when Boyle was seeking reelection as UMW president, Boyle *then* demanded safety legislation. His earlier remarks, alas, are more characteristic.

Why don't Congressmen from coal mining regions make a great issue of mine safety? To account for some of them, they are so much in the vest pocket of the mining companies that they prefer to say nothing. Other legislators, like the union leadership, tend to take the position that unemployment is the real problem, and that anything endangering the competitive position of the industry would risk jobs. Still others just don't care.

It is true, however, that in late 1969, after the previous paragraphs were originally written, Congress passed and the President reluctantly signed a new piece of mine safety legislation. It came partly from the drama of the West Virginia explosion and the attendant publicity, kept alive by wildcat strikes and other strident demands from coal miners. A challenge within the union also changed the role of the United Mine Workers leadership, which now demanded, instead of soft pedaling safety legislation. For when Jock Yablonski opposed Tony Boyle for the UMW presidency, and the safety issue became a prominent one in the campaign, the incumbent leadership had to change its tack. The law was an improvement over the previous one, but a great many issues were omitted and the victims of black lung (or their survivors) are to be paid the princely monthly compensation of $136 per month. And a tax on coal of an insignificant amount to finance that compensation was stricken from the legislation. Whatever its improvement over the old law, the real test will come in the enforcement stage. If once again the

7. "Worker Critical of Mine's Safety," *The New York Times*, Dec. 6, 1968; also "Mine Hearing Told . . . of 'Too Much Gas,' " *The New York Times*, Dec. 7, 1968. On the nepotism and strange finances of the UMW, see *The New York Times* report on Ralph Nader's attack on the union, Apr. 28, 1969.

Bureau of Mines plays the game as it has in the past, the new rules will continue to permit very high death and injury rates.*

The miners' plight is but one example of the moral blindness of this political and economic system. Many other kinds of unconcern and injustice could have been cited. One could point to the curious anomaly of paying farmers $4 billion a year not to produce food when more than twenty million Americans are unable to purchase enough food to stay healthy. Or one would cite the pious protestations of intent to protect consumers of food and drugs while producers go on endangering life with filthy and adulterated products. Or there are our constant promises of equal job opportunities to minorities while means are found to exclude them from the available and lucrative building trades. And there is the supreme blindness of all: the systematic pollution of our atmosphere and earth to a point where many able ecologists now believe that the existence of life on the planet is threatened. For one thing we poison ourselves with the wanton use of pesticides. Rivers and oceans contain dangerously high levels of DDT, which fish either die from or, if they build a tolerance for it, in turn kill the birds that eat the contaminated fish. Penguins in remote Antarctica are found to contain dangerously high concentrations of DDT in their bodies. Not just penguins, however: mothers' milk is discovered to have DDT concentrations above the safety levels set for cows' milk. Coal mines and strip mining pollute thousands of miles of streams, killing every living thing in them. The Cuyahoga River in Cleveland became so loaded with flammable industrial waste in the summer of 1969 that the *river caught on fire* and burned two railroad trestles. It will cost billions a year to stop the pollution of the air we breathe and the water we drink, if indeed the damage is not irreversible. In the years of the sixties, the United States spent $30 billion for farm price supports and $35 billion on space programs, and about $3 billion on the control of air and water pollution.

The examples could go on and on. The point is, why do we set such mad priorities? Why is it unimportant how many miners are sacrificed for profit? Who decided that the regulation of food processing would be so hedged about in legal boobytraps that the regulations are stifled? How is power used to raise some priorities and to squash others? What collective wisdom decides? How do the poor and the unorganized participate? Indeed do they participate at all?

Many writers have commented on these questions, some of them with weighty scholarship, some with muckraking, some with political axes to grind. One school of commentators on power in American life

* It appears that the past is to be repeated. Before the new law took effect the enforcement-minded Director of the Bureau was removed and replaced by a person more acceptable to the coal companies.

has located a "power structure" at the top, finding that a definite pattern of interrelationships exists among key figures in industry, finance, government (especially the military), and politicians. This "power elite," as the late C. Wright Mills called it, may be in internal dissension from time to time, but he contended that they pulled in harmony together when crises arose.[8] He observed that military and corporate leadership groups were the most powerful elements, but that political leaders played a cooperative role. He says:

> Of the three types of circle that compose the power elite today, it is the military that has benefited the most in its enhanced power, although the corporate circles have also become more explicitly intrenched in the more public decision-making circles. It is the professional politician who has lost the most, so much that in examining the events and decisions, one is tempted to speak of a political vacuum in which the corporate rich and the high warlord, in their coinciding interests, rule.[9]

He goes on to show that these leaders occupy key positions in the corporations, in government, and in the military, specifically, and thereby influence policy enormously. They share a common social background, an ideology, and an interrelated set of interests. And in Mills's view they essentially "rule" the nation. Others have presented variations on this set of propositions, but the Mills position remains a basis for comprehension of the nature of American politics for a great many observers.[10]

But that does not include me. I am unconvinced by the elitist argument; it seems too simplistic and too limited in its capacity to explain how the "wrong things" happen to the powerful ones who supposedly are "ruling" the nation. There are some shaky assumptions and unproved conclusions in the argument. The evidence is very thin to demonstrate that these rulers do in fact rule. Specific evidence is lacking to show how these leaders constitute an unfailing and ever collaborating clique. Critics have shown numerous instances where the elite do not prevail, and they have raised the question of how evidence of the collaboration can be shown when the power-elite analysts refer to secret

8. C. Wright Mills, *The Power Elite* (New York: Oxford University Press, 1956), p. 276.

9. *Ibid.*, pp. 276–77.

10. See, for example, Floyd Hunter, *Top Leadership, USA* (Chapel Hill, N.C.: University of North Carolina Press, 1959); and G. William Domhoff, *Who Rules America* (Englewood Cliffs, N.J.: Prentice-Hall, Inc., 1967). Domhoff modifies the Mills argument considerably and places great stress on the common social class backgrounds of the elite that he sees as a "governing class."

cliques that meet clandestinely to decide the big issues. If another re-
searcher found one supposed circle of influentials did not in fact collaborate, there might then be claimed to be a still more secret and
obscure power structure that prevailed from behind the next veil of
covert authority.[11]

This is by no means to deny that these interests have a grossly disproportionate amount of political authority; they certainly have and
they clearly use it to their own ends. Their control of wealth, to use a
single example, can be turned into an inordinate potential source of
power.[12] Politicians running for office need ever-increasing sums of
cash to conduct their campaigns, and the controllers of corporate wealth,
although ostensibly forbidden to use corporate funds for campaigning,
can always find ways of getting the money to a compliant candidate.
This is not to say that the politicians are necessarily "bought" by this
process (in the next chapter I shall attempt to demonstrate that they are
not), but it is to say that as in comparison with other elements in the
society who have no great sums to contribute the corporate leadership
has a lopsided advantage in getting the ear of the man they aided in
gaining office.

And "access" to those with formal authority, as David Truman points
out, is a universal objective of the groups that participate in the political
game.[13] Access, of course, involves far more than willingness to make
campaign contributions. It depends upon the interest's having the right
lobbyist to appeal to Congress, for example. Thus it is that former Congressmen and persons who have held high administrative jobs are often
employed by huge corporations as lobbyists. (A foremost example of
this is the ex-military officer who goes to work for industrial suppliers
of military hardware.) Also the very prestige of an industrial giant can
open doors that would be closed to others. The possession of cash for
conducting a campaign for or against a certain legislative goal can be a
decisive factor, as for instance in the long and successful publicity war
by the medical fraternity to defeat a governmentally supported health
insurance program. They finally lost the battle where the elderly are
concerned, possibly because of the sympathy that can be aroused for

11. See, for example, Robert A. Dahl, "A Critique of the Ruling Elite Model." 52
American Political Science Review 465–69 (1958); Daniel Bell, "The Power Elite
Reconsidered," 64 *American Journal of Sociology* 238–50 (1958); Talcott Parsons,
"The Distribution of Power in American Society," 10 *World Politics* 123–43 (1957);
Nelson Polsby, *Community Power and Political Theory* (New Haven, Conn.: Yale
University Press, 1963).

12. An excellent illustration of this is Robert Engler's *The Politics of Oil* (New
York: Macmillan, 1961).

13. David B. Truman, *The Governmental Process* (New York: Alfred A. Knopf,
1951), pp. 264–70.

the aged poor, but the general provision of health care, which most modern governments have long provided, has consistently been turned back in Congress, not entirely because of skillful propagandists, of course, but with much use of that tactic. Money counts in other ways too. It can buy the best legal talent available, an important consideration in a governmental system that vests so much authority in the judiciary. It can buy influential "experts" to testify in courts and in all manner of forums (Congressional committees, the public media of communication, and regulatory agencies, for example). And many academic figures vastly supplement their salaries by telling what the powerful interests want told about the benign effects of corporate mergers, the harmlessness of cigarettes, or the necessity for sky-high drug prices. James Ridgeway exposes this practice, saying:

> Most often the professors are simply lobbyists for corporations, advancing the interests of their clients at the rate of $400 a day. . . . They are seldom taken for such, moving as they do beneath the cloak of distinguished degrees and university titles. Where the newspapers would rarely make note of the remarks of a registered lobbyist in the Capitol, a learned economist from an Ivy League university might well get two paragraphs for his views, even though they are not his opinions at all but those set out for him by some public relations man.[14]

Without belaboring the point further, suffice it to say that the combination of the corporations, the military, and the politicians is exceedingly powerful, but it does face some elements of counter force. Indeed it is this countervailing power that greatly impresses those analysts of American politics who espouse what is called "pluralism." They are unimpressed with the argument that an elite rules, but rather find that power is enormously dispersed. Ready in varying degrees to concede that there are elites and that they have far more power than other ordinary citizens, they still are impressed with the openness of the political system and the opportunity for any and all elements to get into the act.[15]

14. See *The Closed Corporation, American Universities in Crisis* (New York: Random House, 1968), pp. 84–85.
15. The literature of pluralism is extensive, but the chief protagonist of it is Robert A. Dahl. See particularly his *Who Governs?* (New Haven, Conn.: Yale University Press, 1961) and *Pluralist Democracy in the United States, Conflict and Consent* (Chicago: Rand McNally, 1967). Without specifically calling his theory pluralist, David B. Truman takes that position in his *The Governmental Process* (op. cit.): his patient and extensive portrayal of the myriad ways in which various political interest groups and potential interest groups act and interact provides fundamental and important background for analysis of contemporary politics— whether one agrees with his theory or not.

The pluralist notes that our political history is marked with constant effort to assure that no single element shall seize power, to balance all centers of power with countervailing opposition. Thus the Constitution is devoted to nicely balanced governmental authorities—federalism balancing the states and the nation, separation of powers balancing the branches of government, the veto empowering the President against Congress, the power of the purse empowering Congress against the President, the power of judicial review setting the Supreme Court up against all other elements—and so on throughout American politics. For we not only established formal Constitutional rules that require unusual majorities to get anything done, we further elaborate those formal rules with informal understandings that further the same end. Thus the filibuster becomes part of the Constitutional system, which is dedicated to the proposition that no action will be taken unless there is very widespread agreement upon it. (Or if no wide agreement, then wide unconcern, for if there is a significant minority that objects, any proposal will be either delayed or defeated, but if there is no great interest in the matter it may become law without resistance.) Other aspects of political procedure provide the same kind of opportunity for delay: the decentralization of American political parties, the power of the Rules Committee to waylay legislation, the opportunities for committee chairmen in Congress to cause the delay or defeat of what they personally dislike, the universal deference to strongly felt opinions that characterizes Congress, the infinite ways in which the judiciary can be used to achieve political delay or defeat—and so on.

Robert Dahl puts all this very well in his *Pluralist Democracy in the United States:*

> The theory and practice of American pluralism tend to assume, as I see it, that the existence of multiple centers of power, none of which is wholly sovereign, will help (may indeed be necessary) to tame power, to secure the consent of all, and to settle conflicts peacefully:
>   • Because one center of power is set against another, power itself will be tamed, civilized, controlled, and limited to decent human purposes, while coercion, the most evil form of power will be reduced to a minimum.
>   • Because even minorities are provided with opportunities to veto solutions they strongly object to, the consent of all will be won in the long run.
>   • Because constant negotiations among different centers of power are necessary in order to make decisions, citizens and leaders will perfect the precious art of dealing peacefully

with their conflicts, and not merely to the benefit of one
partisan but to the mutual benefit of all the parties to the
conflict.[16]

Granted, the prevention of tyranny is not one of the lesser goals of
any group of statesmen, and surely the lessons of the past warranted
the attention the framers of the U.S. Constitution and their successors
gave to the prevention of despotism. But the argument that prevention
of tyranny is the key to good government can be carried too far. For the
framers of the Constitution and the men who molded and shaped it in
succeeding generations were also concerned with some other very specific political objectives. If they were anxious to prevent tyranny, they
were also very anxious to see to it that the public did not gain an undue
amount of influence. The framers were men anxious to provide a stable
government that would survive its infancy, but it is also true that the
men at the Constitutional Convention were—most of them—more than
a little frightened at the possibility of democratic power. They made a
Constitution that has been more a means of curbing power, preventing
action, and restraining programs than it has been a fountain of authority
to cope with critical problems.

So the contention that there is considerable dispersal of power in our
politics makes more sense than the proposition that we are ruled by a
conspiratorial elite. But it remains true that *the dispersal of power in
combination with the great power that nearly all admit is clearly in the
hands of the most powerful groups leads to some very harsh consequences for the have-not's in the United States.* The migrant farm
worker has an exceedingly difficult time of getting into the grand political veto system that American politics is supposed to be. Sometimes it
is made to appear that the pluralist model provides a kind of equal opportunity for all to get into the act, suggesting that there is some "slack"
in the system that leaves to all an opportunity to affect policy. But this
fails to take account of the handicaps of some players in the political
game.

Many miners, to return to the original example, may want to reduce
the element of risk in their daily work, but they will face difficulty in
achieving their goals. They are in an organized union, admittedly, and
if the vast majority of them rose up and demanded that the union fight
for safety presumably there would be some response at least. But for
the vast majority of any group to participate in a social action is ab-
normal. Men are not activists by nature; their natural state is social
motionlessness rather than social action. And this is especially so for
men who are not highly educated and whose experience with participa-

16. Op. cit., p. 24.

tory democracy is at best limited. Collective action by miners to achieve mine safety through union pressure or legislation is extremely difficult —although not impossible, obviously.[17] There are too many catch points, too little opportunity to publicize the needs of miners, too much easy ignoring of the crises of these people shunted off into the hollows of the back country. In short we have an example of the universal problem of the responsiveness of government: *he who is obscure will have little opportunity to force the political machinery to redress his grievances.*[18]

As miners are comparatively obscure, so are migrant farm workers, the aged poor, Negroes, Mexican Americans, Puerto Ricans, prisoners, the mentally retarded, slum dwellers, draftees, victims of police brutality, and many more "minorities." Now to be sure, each one of these groups has had *some* public attention at some point, and they have formed (or been aided by other) groups that sought, sometimes with marginal success, to do something about their problems. But the harsh fact remains that the pluralism of American politics works primarily for those who have levers to pull, those who are in positions to delay or veto an action unless concessions are made, those who have the cash to produce public support and official attention. What is sometimes not understood about the veto system that pluralism endorses is that the power to say no—or even the power to delay—is often the power to decide. In the difficult process of making policy anyone with opportunities to stop the program until his demanded ransom is paid is a person with real power. And, as will be amply demonstrated subsequently, there are innumerable places for such piracy, and it takes place constantly in the process of public decision-making in this country.

A further problem is that some elements have a ready opportunity to force their special questions upon the public agenda whereas others have not. If the military-industrial complex decides that an antimissile missile is imperative, they have most effective means of getting the question considered.[19] There is a phalanx of Congressmen who are

17. In the spring of 1969 wildcat strikes in West Virginia forced the state legislature to enact a law providing compensation for black lung, but this kind of pressure has not been organized elsewhere.

18. E. E. Schattschneider in *The Semi-Sovereign People* (New York: Holt, Rinehart and Winston, 1960) makes a somewhat similar point.

19. For a good summation of the power and glory of the military see Richard F. Kaufman, "We Must Guard Against Unwarranted Influence by the Military-Industrial Complex," *The New York Times Magazine*, June 22, 1969, pp. 10ff. The title comes from Dwight Eisenhower's farewell address as President. See also the well-argued case by John Kenneth Gallbraith, *How to Control the Military* (New York: New American Library, 1969).

utterly convinced that the military can do no wrong and who are as devoutly militaristic as any "man-on-a-horse" ever was. They can be depended upon to urge inordinate expenditures to achieve this "safe-guard" as soon as possible. The politico-economic significance of defense industry is revealed by the fact that it employs four million persons, and the one hundred largest firms shared $26 billion in contracts in 1968. Congressmen therefore work in constant collaboration with both the corporate interests that want to build the hardware and the military men who want to command it. A stream of propaganda supports this game of "overkill." Not all of it is recognizable as propaganda for there are hack writers who will, for a fee, write (or copy) nearly anything and peddle it to reputable magazines as their own work. The public has no evidence of its actual source. The "defense" budget (as we now choose to call it, whatever the offensive and defensive elements of the military budget) likewise gets undeviating attention, whereas a call for money for slum problems will not only get intense scrutiny but may be chopped to pieces. The industries concerned with gasoline, automobiles, and road construction had little trouble in getting through the Eisenhower Administration (not one devoted to new large civilian ventures, to say the very least) the hugest peacetime spending program in the history of the nation: the Federal Aid Highway Act of 1956, which provided for the interstate highway system and was to cost some $75 billion. But when farm workers seek—as they have for decades—to delete the exclusion of farm workers from the protection of the National Labor Relations Act, they get nowhere.

The reasons for these variations are not too difficult to ascertain. Some kinds of issues are quietly suppressed—or ignored—whereas others have access from the moment of their instigation. To say the issues are suppressed may suggest too much of the air of conspiracy, for it is not by any means always an act of squashing the plea that keeps it off the agenda. (Although it may be, too; in Congress the plea of the farm worker for the protection of the law allowed to other workers has been buried year after year.) In many cases the group that needs redress has little or no means even to raise the issue of the evils they face. Let us take the prison system for an example. Very likely there is nothing else in the whole of society that represents more concentrated evil than our prison system. It serves only one useful purpose (the detention of the hopelessly violent and aggressive criminal); it is a sinkhole of burning hatred, provides education in crime, and promotes sexual perversion and sadism. Even assuming that only a small part of what I have asserted is true, what chance is there for the imprisoned inmates to do anything at all about correcting the situation? Perhaps that is an extreme example, but it illustrates the point of obscurity: few in the public are even remotely aware of the culture of the prison and fewer still are willing to make any effort to correct the abuses that it harbors. But is that example very much different from the situation in the center of our largest cities? In communities where the middle or upper classes live would they permit government to allow death rates from almost completely controllable diseases to run at nearly nineteenth-century rates? How long would "visible" communities tolerate rats attacking babies? But when Congress was presented a bill in 1967 to do something about the growing menace of rats in the central city, the House laughed it down. One witty member of Congress after another rose to make ridiculous comments about the possible appointment of a czar of rats under the "Civil rats bill." True, the bill was later resurrected when the news media played up that disgraceful debate, but that further demonstrates the validity of the obscurity point: if the Congressmen had been canny enough to murder the bill quietly it would probably have expired peacefully.

Conceivably some will argue that the groups I have cited as obscure are not really obscure today. It might be contended that the Negro is no longer out of sight but, as a consequence of his long campaign for equal rights, has come very much into the spotlight of publicity. So also it might be said that the media have presented evidence that Cesar Chavez and the California grape strikers are active, that the Puerto Rican community exists, that Medicare is evidence of recognition of the aged, that draft resistance betokens public awareness of the unpopularity of the war and the inequity of the Selective Service system. Similarly riots have alerted the public to the plight of the Negro and various forms of publicity have underscored the problems of other disadvantaged groups. But such publicity is evanescent. Even in the case of the central city riots it is so easy for the public to push the ugly realities out of mind that apparently the public retains no sustained impression of the problems that underlay the riots. In a public opinion poll taken in Newark four months after the July, 1967, riots no fewer than two thirds of all whites (both in the central city and in the suburban towns around Newark) asserted that Negroes have the same job opportunities as whites. Whereas half the Negroes asked believed the police were brutal in dealing with Negroes, only 5 per cent of the whites inside the city agreed and *only 1 per cent of those out in the suburbs* so believed. White and black opinions as to the causes of the riot were not even remotely similar; indeed the conditions of the ghetto that seemed to Negroes to be at the root of the trouble were not ones mentioned by whites. In general the black respondents emphasized the despair and deplorable living conditions of the slum, whereas few whites cited these causes and tended instead to place the blame on outside agitators or criminals or even a Communist conspiracy.[20] If white persons inside the city of Newark, relatively close to the physical and spiritual degradation that is the slum, were unaware of the conditions within the ghetto how can others be expected to know? Those who occupy the adjacent suburbs are even less aware of those conditions than are center city whites and for the very good reason that they never see, nor want to see, the ghetto. And if the suburbanites do not know how shall we expect persons living in the Midwest or in the Rocky Mountains to know? They do not know, by and large, anymore than they know about the conditions of the striking grape pickers in California or the starving poor up the desolate hollows of Appalachia or in the red clay country of the remote South.

But surely there are not actual cases of starvation in such an affluent nation as this? Although there is debate on the subject there is no denying that severe malnutrition is extensive and that people die because of it.[21] Of course, it is regularly denied, and the Congressional establishment has made every effort to controvert the evidence of chronic malnutrition, but the evidence remains: depressing but firm. A South Carolinian, Dr. Donald Gatch, has made a systematic effort to deal with the medical problems of the indigent of his area, and for being outspoken about these conditions he has been vilified repeatedly. In the summer of 1968 a team of medical doctors accompanied Dr. Gatch on a tour of his county, and Dr. Robert Coles reported on their findings. They are dramatic enough to bear quotation to underscore the conditions that few are even aware exist. A man speaking to the team of physicians said:

> Well, no sir, there just isn't no work for me. There isn't. So, I don't have any money coming in, none. I have my neighbors and my brothers and they help. And I hope maybe soon I can get some work. Now my wife she's sick, real bad sick, and I don't know

20. See "Negro and White Attitudes Toward Problems and Progress in Race Relations," a study by the Opinion Research Corporation for the Governor's Select Commission to Study Civil Disorder, Jan., 1968 (mimeo).

21. The literature on this subject has blossomed in the period since 1967 when a Senate investigation publicized conditions well known to the hungry. A survey of this evidence appears in "Hunger in America, Chronology and Selected Background Materials," Subcommittee on Employment, Manpower, and Poverty of the Senate Committee on Labor and Public Welfare, 90th Congress, Second Session (Washington: U.S. Government Printing Office, Oct., 1968). See also Citizens Board of Inquiry *Hunger U.S.A.* (Boston: Beacon Press, 1968), which is summarized in the Senate Document cited above, pp. 72–83. An excellent and haunting essay on this scandalous condition is Robert Coles's *Still Hungry in America* (New York: World Publishing, 1969). It is illustrated with a remarkable set of photographs by Al Clayton.

what I can do. What can you do if you don't have a dollar and your woman, she's bleeding, and your kids they seem sickly a lot of the time? [22]

This white father was like many of the black fathers in the area, desperate but unable to help prevent the hunger and diseases of their children. But are there no food-stamp programs to help out such cases? Food stamps can only be obtained by the payment of a percentage of their value, and families without income cannot even afford to buy stamps, assuming that the county in question has established a food-stamp program—which four hundred counties have not. After protestations that there were numerous cases in which the family could not afford even a few dollars to get their stamps for the month, a rule change permitted a penniless family to have the stamps if they were certified to be completely without funds. But such information seeps down slowly to families that haven't bought a newspaper in years, and county officials do not go out of their way in many areas to supply information about new opportunities. Getting to town from the remote hollows or isolated farms is expensive or nearly impossible because public transportation often does not exist. Here a mother of nine children comments about her inability to acquire the all-important stamps:

Sometimes we can just raise the money, so we can buy the food stamps, and get about $100 worth of food for the month. But we are eleven of us, and it's expensive to buy food here as any place else. By the third week we're down to nothing and I'm desperate. They take up collections at the church, and we go borrowing, and with your kin you don't starve to death, no sir. But it's not very good either. . . . For breakfast there's not much I can give the kids. In the winter I have to warm them up. I just have to. So I give them tea, real piping hot. Sometimes they have oatmeal, if there is some, and some biscuits, hot biscuits. Then for supper it depends—if the chickens have left us a few eggs, and if I have some preserves left. The worst time is around January, thereabouts. There's no work. There's no garden. There's nothing but those stamps, if we can raise the money. Then we'll go without supper sometimes, and breakfast too. Then it's tea and cornbread and oatmeal if we're lucky.[23]

22. Robert Coles and Harry Huge, "Strom Thurmond Country," *New Republic*, Nov. 30, 1968, p. 18. On Dr. Gatch's campaign, see also Bynum Shaw, "Let Us Now Praise Dr. Gatch," *Esquire Magazine*, June, 1968, also reprinted in the Senate Document "Hunger in America" (op. cit.).

23. Robert Coles, "Appalachia, Hunger in the Hollows," *New Republic*, Nov. 9, 1968, p. 17.

Secretary of Agriculture, Orville L. Freeman, late in his tenure did widen eligibility for food stamps and extended it to some 500,000 persons previously ineligible. But Mr. Freeman opposed free issue of the stamps on the grounds that the purchase of the stamps "provided an incentive to the poor to upgrade their diets." What does it say about the priorities of a society that can—apparently without intended grim humor—talk about upgrading the diet of a family of four with an income of less than thirty dollars a month by forcing them to spend two dollars of that pittance to buy surplus foods that the country's farmers produce and cannot sell? But Freeman expressed "little hope" that Congress would authorize free stamps; the opposition in Congress was too strong.[24]

But surely there are welfare payments for families so poor they cannot even afford a few dollars to buy perhaps seventy dollars' worth of food stamps? By no means is that true universally. At times getting a welfare check depends upon the political reliability of the potential receiver of aid. At times it is denied because of racial discrimination. At times it is not given because of bureaucratic confusion and endless delay. Or because an "employable" husband is in the home, thus rendering the family unable to get aid, even though the father has been unable to find work. As Coles and Huge point out, Beaufort County, South Carolina, has over seventeen thousand families earning under three thousand dollars a year, eleven thousand families earning less than two thousand dollars a year, and over one thousand families earning less than one thousand dollars a year, and yet "only 898 people receive public assistance."

The infant mortality rate in such areas approaches that of the most underdeveloped nations of the world, and the toll of diseases—many of them believed no longer to exist in this country—is fantastic. "Dr. Gatch," Coles and Huge go on, "can show his visitors X-rays in which long worms are seen happily and snugly rooted in the intestinal walls of both young and old, black and white American citizens. He estimates that over 90 per cent of his patients suffer from round worms." [25] The worms further weaken individuals who often have to subsist on grits, more grits, and grits with gravy, and then pneumonia comes as the wind whips through gaping cracks in the cabin walls. And the toll grows, as a direct and unmistakable consequence of malnutrition.

The 1968 presidential campaign featured much talk about the "for-

24. See "Food Stamp Plan to Be Liberalized," *The New York Times,* Dec. 12, 1968.

25. Robert Coles and Harry Huge, "The Way It Is in South Carolina: Strom Thurmond Country," *New Republic,* Nov. 30, 1968, pp. 17–21. See also Robert Coles, "Life in Appalachia," Transaction, June, 1963, pp. 23–33.

gotten American" as Richard Nixon and George Wallace denounced efforts to deal with the problems of people like those described by Coles and others. Their forgotten American was not these pitiful people who are indeed forgotten in their obscure misery, but the taxpayers of middle- and lower-middle-class rank who are beginning to have to pay some of the marginal costs of having ignored the problems of the truly forgotten. Riot and civil disorder, incredible welfare costs, alienation and racial separatism, street crime, and drug addiction, which invites more crime to support the habit born of alienation and self-hatred—these are but a few of the costs of sloughing off the problems of the obscure.

So the question of leaving out the obscure—letting them suffer while the system goes its way and tries to prevent tyranny from any one group from growing too strong—may begin in the years ahead to have more than a moral implication. The problems could get so chronic that two kinds of developments could occur—simultaneously in all likelihood. On the one hand the rebellious mood of the dispossessed and alienated will mount and tensions will invoke violence, counterviolence, and destruction. Past riots are a hint of what could come as the desperation grows. The other probable development is a fascistlike suppression of the rebels. John A. Williams, in his novel *The Man Who Cried I Am*, pictures such a program of systematic suppression: it sounds fantastic and unbelievable until one reflects that only three decades ago the United States, in its fear and hatred of the Japanese, hastily built concentration camps and indiscriminately placed all Japanese in them, regardless of whether they were citizens, aliens, landowners, children, storekeepers—all. The Japanese were not murdered as were the Jews by the Nazis, but in other respects the concentration camps were sadly similar. And who is to say that white hatred and fear of blacks will not rise to the same pitch of frenzy that it has before—and with consequences, not only for the black population but for the whole population, that are incalculable? [26]

That such consequences will follow the ignoring of the chronic problems of the obscured ones is by no means certain. Those without money, without organizing skills, without experience in political activity, and often with weak, divided, or perhaps no real leadership, are in no easy position to mount campaigns—whether rebellious or political—to rem-

26. Note that under the Internal Security Act of 1950 there are provisions for concentration camps for "subversives." Six such camps were established and are available for use upon a presidential proclamation. Title II of the Act provides for the camps, to which persons could be sent without trial. See the analysis of the issue by Michael Meyerson, "Concentration Camps: Whose Fantasy," *Civil Liberties*, Feb., 1969, pp. 8–11.

edy their ills. It is also a sad but undeniable fact that mankind is capable
of putting up with incredible circumstances if the situation inescapably
demands it. Men survive Russian prisons in Siberia, they did survive
Nazi concentration camps, and they will survive the rigors of urban and
rural deprivation in the United States. The cost will be high to families
whose young die before their eyes, to the ambitious who cannot get an
education to escape, to all who decline into a deprived old age. But as the
obscure they will have to suffer whatever consequences come their way.
For this is a political system and an economic system that responds to
those who have, which plays down systematic planning to cope with
social evils rather than facilitating focused public effort on their amelio-
ration. It is a political system that responds to power, to pressure, to
vetoes, to money, and to authority. It will be the objective of the re-
mainder of this volume to illustrate some of the ways in which this
political system responds to various kinds of political initiatives, how it
complies with some and suppresses or ignores others. And in the end
we shall ask the question: Is that enough?

CHAPTER TWO

The Rules of Politics as Determinants of Power

ISCUSSING political decision-making, Charles E. Lindblom has said that ". . . the power of various social groups like the rich or the whites is less a determinant of policy outcomes than itself a result of the rules that men have made to govern the policy-making process." [1] In view of the other sources of muscle that the rich and the well-placed have at their command, this may exaggerate the importance of the rules for the political effectiveness of the advantaged, but it nevertheless gives appropriate emphasis to the ways in which the rules can be utilized by those who have the advantages. The rules of the political process were not written by the have-not's and the severely disadvantaged, after all, but predominantly by the politically well-off. It is no surprise to find that the rules serve best the interests of the kind of people who write them. As we shall argue, a vitally important aspect of those rules is the opportunity to say no to policy initiatives, and to those who have advantages the opportunity to say no with impunity is a major source of strength. As many observers have noted, the American Constitutional system is notoriously warped in the direction of weakness and delay—inaction in a word—and the rules contribute mightily to that result. This makes it imperative, when analyzing the way the system fails to meet the minimal needs of the disadvantaged, that we look at the rules, how they were made, by whom, and to what ends. This implies a much more complicated analysis than that implicit in the elitist theory, in which—to oversimplify—the suspected conspirators are sought out and the accusations made. To get at the subtle ways in which the rules distribute handicaps and advantages, however, one must look to history, mythology, and the evolution of Constitutional law and political rationalization.

1. Charles E. Lindblom, *The Policy-Making Process* (Englewood Cliffs, N.J.: Prentice-Hall, Inc., 1968), p. 34.

Handicaps and Advantages

The rules that prescribe the way politics are to be conducted are never neutral; inevitably they give advantages to some and place handicaps on others. The handicaps and advantages are allocated not by the gods from Olympian objectivity, as the mythology surrounding the Founding Fathers would suggest, but by active and deeply concerned political operators with interests to protect. So it is also with subsequent formulators of the Constitution, both those who amend the Constitution formally and those who amend it informally by altering interpretations of it. They are men trying to formulate rules for future political conflict while battling furiously at the same time to further ends they consider vital. This is not to attribute evil intent to either eighteenth-century landowners, nineteenth-century industrialists, or twentieth-century corporate tycoons—or their adversaries—but merely to point to reality: the rules are never the product of purely objective contemplation (even though that certainly is involved too) but of calculations about the self-interest consequences of any change.

Consider, for example, the fear most of the Founding Fathers had of popular power. Although historians have painted us a portrait of "democrats" drawing a "democratic" Constitution, their picture is a distortion. The delegates came to the Convention frightened of what they considered democratic excesses in the states; to have universal suffrage and a majoritarian government was the last thing they desired. Alexander Hamilton, bourgeois lawyer and advocate of a powerful mercantilist government, deeply distrusted the mass of people. He is supposed to have said, "Sir, your people is a great beast." Others were more receptive to popular power, and some even went so far as to suggest that the President be chosen by direct popular vote. Some found that idea monstrous. George Mason expressed the opinion that "it would be as unnatural to refer the choice of the proper character for chief magistrate to the people, as it would be to refer a trial of colors to a blind man." [2] Others favored leaving the choice to the legislature, a natural suggestion in view of the prevalence of that practice for choosing governors of the states. Those, however, who desired a strong executive branch thought this unwise, and in the end the electoral college system came out of the process of compromise. The college turned out to be one of the least auspicious works of the Convention, but it is clear enough what the framers of the Constitution sought: an elite group who would in some rationalistic fashion choose the "best" man for President. In reality the party system shattered this indirect election system, by soon making

2. James Madison, *Journal of the Federal Convention* (New York: G. P. Putnam, 1908), Vol. I, p. 377.

it heresy for any elector to vote in any other way than the voters of his state had.

But there is no doubting the proposition that the landed gentry of the late eighteenth century and their gentlemen-of-commerce colleagues were in agreement that universal manhood suffrage was dangerous business. (This assumes, of course, that nearly any proponent of suffrage meant only white males, for none was so out of touch with American reality as to advocate Negro or female suffrage.) In the Convention, however, it proved impossible to reach an agreement on what to say about suffrage, and it was left to the states to decide. As things stood this must have seemed a safe choice for the antisuffrage men, for the states placed sharp restrictions on voting—by requiring possession of property, for example, or the payment of taxes, or affiliation with a church. This reluctance to permit popular participation is illustrated by the fact that in 1796 half of the states provided that the legislatures would choose presidential electors. But the tide was running against the gentry in this respect, for by 1820 only one third of the states chose electors that way. And by the election of 1836 only two states retained what had become an anachronistic way of choosing electors: South Carolina and Georgia. Opponents of broadening suffrage or involving the people in the choice of President were quite clear why this was dangerous. If property restrictions were removed from the privilege of voting, it only followed, they contended, that the privileges of property could no longer be protected. If those who paid no taxes acquired the vote, then no man's property would any longer be safe. He who paid no taxes would ruin those who did. In truth the danger was negligible, but the rationale that supported the opposition to suffrage was the same that backed the other limiting rules: that government is best which has the greatest difficulty in doing anything.

And the restraints that were explicitly written into the rules, or were informally added or interpreted into them, were great indeed. Separation of powers set one branch of the government in natural opposition to the other, for each was armed with certain devices to defend its position. The Congress had the initiative in many matters and especially in finances. Potentially the President had a broad range of authority, but he still needed the acquiescence of the Congress to do many things—to inaugurate new programs, to enter into treaties, to appoint subordinate officials, or to declare war. It is true that presidents have found ways around many of these barriers—even including the declaration of war (e.g., simply announce that the war is on and do not bother to declare it, or, as I. F. Stone said of President Johnson's inauguration of his air war on North Vietnam: he had it announced by a State Department press officer, "Declaration of War by the office boy"). But at first these were important barriers, and to some extent they remain so. Power in

Congress has declined greatly in this century, but no President can afford to trifle with Congressional authority unless he is on strong political ground. For members of Congress of the opposite party or of different persuasion from the President can hobble any incumbent in many ways.

The presidential veto is part of a constant game of pressure and counterpressure that the executive and legislative branches play in a system of separated powers. Likewise the two-thirds vote provisions in the Constitution concerning treaties and amendment of the Constitution are bulwarks against easy change. Even the fact that there are two houses of Congress works toward the same end, for what survives in one chamber may die navigating the shoals of the next house, or because time is vital in the legislative process it may be possible for opponents in either house to delay proceedings long enough to kill a bill merely by having the clock run out as the adjournment date arrives. The fact that there are double committee systems, double agendas, double leaderships, and institutional jealousies that attach to each chamber—all this contributes often to killing legislation. The framers of the Constitution put this forth as a matter of permitting due consideration of all measures, time to reflect and turn back or modify. How much they foresaw that this would become a major instrument of preventing action one can only guess, but whatever the intent that has been the consequence. (As will be more fully demonstrated in the chapter on Congress.)

Judicial review and federalism have similarly provided prime barriers against action to resolve problems—both at the state and at the national level. Justices of the Supreme Court have often pretended to be doing no more than reading the strict language of the Constitution and applying it as logical necessity required, but this is sheer fiction. No doubt some justices did believe themselves to be doing no more than solemnly weighing a statute against a principle of law, but many "principles of law" were anything but logically necessary derivations of the Constitution. What was happening, as some dissenting justices ungraciously told their brethren from time to time, was that the rules of the political system were being interpreted so as to serve the interests and philosophies of the judges who were a majority vote of the Court. Permit me a brief illustrative digression showing how the Supreme Court modified its interpretation of federalism over the years. It perfectly demonstrates how mythology grips the minds of decision makers, how rhetoric displaces logic, how self-interest (however disguised) plays a key role in the day-to-day process of shaping the rules of political engagement.

Federalism was only partly a product of the Convention; it grew and developed from only the sketchiest beginnings in the Constitution. Nothing like federalism strictly speaking had ever existed to serve as model for the members of the Convention; instead they politicked with each other and groped toward some kind of arrangement that would create the strongest central government that could be achieved, although not going so far as to cause the Constitution to be rejected by the states. It was a difficult line to walk. Some of the key moves in keeping to the narrow chalk were these. First it was to be a national government of limited and delegated powers, with the states guaranteed existence and protection in various ways (through equality of representation in the Senate, and by providing that the Constitution could not be amended on that issue); the new government would be one that could act on the citizens of the nation not just on the states as had been true under the Articles of Confederation; and finally there was the "supremacy clause," which asserted the supremacy of the national government. The more detailed provisions about the interrelations of the states were not particularly significant aspects of the federal system—such as the interstate rendition of prisoners or the full faith and credit clause; more important were the broader rules setting up the powers of the federal and state governments. Inscribing these lines on parchment was but a beginning: national-state relations have ever since been one of the most contentious aspects of our politics. Indeed that controversy invited the Convention itself; it contributed to nearly a century of conflict that ended in the Civil War; and it has been a source of legal and political contention ever since. It would be foolish therefore to consider federalism as solely the product of the Convention; it may have formally emerged there, but it had a previous history and subsequent developments have contributed more to the shaping of the federal system than the original words.

Chief among the shapers of the federal arrangement has been the Supreme Court. One of the most significant of all the interpreters of federalism was Chief Justice John Marshall, who, although his ideas went into a long eclipse in the era of laissez-faire, was nevertheless a formidable architect of federalism. A strong Federalist and an ardent believer in the need for a powerful central government, Marshall had to move with caution because he faced political adversaries with states' rights views; he still managed to set the rationale for a strongly pro-central government interpretation of the Constitution.

One of the best illustrations of his powerful argument for a free interpretation of potential Congressional authority came in his reading of the controversy between the United States Bank and the states, which desired their own banks and the easier currency that numerous state banks facilitated. It can be argued that Marshall was merely supporting the Philadelphia bankers and the safe money advocates in opposition to the debtor farmers, who needed money for expansion and development, rather than rendering a solemn reading of the necessities of the Constitution. But whatever Marshall's sympathies with the bankers, there can be no doubt that his fundamental philosophy of government led him to a centralist position. He genuinely believed that the Constitution intended Congress to have wide authority in fiscal matters (and in other similar cases). He wanted a *national* set of rules rather than to allow the states to go their separate ways. And he was a powerful logician: one who grants Marshall his assumptions will find it difficult not to accept his logical development from them.

There is no space to go into the full argument of the banking case— *McCulloch v. Maryland*,[3]—but a brief sketch of it will show how critical interpretation of the rules can be, as well as some key aspects of federalism. Maryland, seeking to sustain its own state bank by attacking the United States Bank, levied a tax on all bank notes issued by any bank in Maryland not chartered by the state, and the United States Bank, being a creature of Congress, was not. The case came to the Supreme Court after the state's highest court had upheld a ruling against the cashier of the United States branch bank in Baltimore for failure to pay the tax. Marshall dealt with two questions: did Congress have the power to charter a bank, and if so did Maryland have the authority to levy a tax upon it? His response to the first question rested upon his reading of the eighth section of Article One of the Constitution, which sets forth the powers of Congress. This section sets forth many specific powers and then in the final clause (sometimes called the elastic clause) it adds that Congress has authority:

> To make all laws which shall be necessary and proper for carrying into execution the foregoing powers, and all other powers vested by this Constitution in the government of the United States, or in any department or officer thereof.

Marshall's first reliance was upon what came to be called the doctrine of implied powers. That is the idea that because Congress has a number of specific powers granted to it, then it also must be understood to have acquired the normal and appropriate means to carry out those powers. Because there is need to raise taxes, provide for a military and a government, Marshall reasoned the elastic clause conferred authority to establish ordinary means to carry out those objectives. And the chartering of a bank, he held, was a reasonable exercise of that discretion. He would have nothing of petty limitations on the potential power of Congress; he asserted that the "government of the Union, though limited in its powers, is supreme within its sphere of action." The latter doctrine was decidedly not the means of interpreting federalism in a later time, al-

3. 4 *Wheaton*, 316, 1819.

though later judges never dealt with the master's logic—for good reason. In the course of his discussion Marshall had said, ". . . We must never forget that it is a constitution we are expounding." To him that meant a constitution was not intended as a set of iron bands to prevent government from functioning. Some of his successors, however, came close to taking that view of a constitution's purpose.

Counsel for the state read the word *necessary* in the disputed section of the Constitution to mean "indispensable"—something that was absolutely vital for the Congress to do in order to meet its other obligations, but Marshall read it the opposite way, holding that *necessary* could also mean "convenient, or useful, or essential to another" objective. The writers of the Constitution obviously intended in this section not to restrain Congress but to permit it to undertake things it could not otherwise do; therefore, it followed, Marshall argued, that the broader definition of the word *necessary* was appropriate. Then he stated a permissive interpretation of Congressional authority that later was to be silently scuttled by judges devoted to laissez-faire ideas. Marshall said:

> Let the end be legitimate, let it be within the scope of the Constitution, and all means which are appropriate, which are plainly adapted to that end, which are not prohibited, but consist with the letter and spirit of the Constitution, are constitutional.

Nor was the Chief Justice impressed with the argument of counsel for the state that the states could assert authority to tax any instrument of the national government. Having arrived at the conclusion that the bank was legitimate, he wasted little time in disposing of any power of the states to hamper the national bank. If one state could impede the functioning of the national bank, he argued, would that not imply a power to curtail the functioning of the government of all the people on the action of only one state. The power to tax, he went on, in the famous phrase is the power to destroy and no state can in such a way interfere with national government operations. Therefore the action of Maryland was unconstitutional.

In other cases Marshall similarly gave a very broad interpretation of potential national authority, as for example in his reading of the .commerce clause. In *Gibbons* v. *Ogden* [4] Marshall dealt with the question of the scope of Congressional power to regulate coastwise shipping. To reduce the case to its briefest elements, the question was whether the states could regulate shipping on the lower Hudson River or whether

4. 9 *Wheaton* 1, 1824.

Congressional law would apply. Counsel favoring state regulation held that *commerce* as used in the interstate commerce clause was meant to include only the direct dealing in commodities and not broad matters like navigational rules. But Marshall found that the term *commerce* was intended to be very inclusive; to him the term encompassed all general commercial activity. "This power," he said, "like all others vested in Congress, is complete in itself, may be exercised to its utmost extent, and acknowledges no limitations other than are prescribed in the Constitution." And he went further to suggest that conceivably when Congress had asserted its powers in a specific area of commerce that the states may have no power to act concurrently, although he did not have to and did not decide that question.

Marshall's reading of the Constitution in these two cases was politically significant. Whether Congress or the states had certain authority within their respective domains meant much to the commercial, banking, and other interests battling before the court and elsewhere. Marshall tended consistently to take the position that the Constitution had intended to grant broad authority to the national government, that indeed the national power was plenary wherever specified in or reasonably inferred from the language of the Constitution. That was consistent with Marshall's political predilections and he expounded a Constitution that sustained "reality" as he saw it.

Oddly, Marshall's decisions did more to set the rationale for future exercise of authority than to determine actions he would see in his own time. For he was much ahead of his time (or after it, if one thinks of the early Federalist position) in advocating broad national powers. Most national leaders during the three decades when he dominated the Supreme Court were uninterested in taking advantage of the regulatory power he asserted the Congress possessed. Much later, when some of the potential power that Marshall asserted to exist was exercised, the Court, after some years of stalling and reluctance to step into a bitter political battle, stepped in with force to curtail not only the incursions of federal law in the regulation of business interests (rare as they were) but also the more numerous state actions in behalf of the worker, consumer, or general public. From this there developed what students of the Court came to call "Dual Federalism," which involved the most negative possible reading of federalism, restraining both national and state efforts to deal with some of the consequences of the industrialization. The Court held that the states could not enter areas where the United States possessed authority and further could not act so as to deny a businessman a fair profit because this would be denying him "due process of law" under the Fourteenth Amendment. The doctrine of due process of law as originally developed in British practice and as stated in the Fifth Amendment to the Constitution was never intended to protect a business from public regulation, but that did not inhibit the Court. Similarly the United States could not regulate, for example, child labor because that would invade the states' domain of reserved powers under the Tenth Amendment. Despite Marshall's assertion that the commerce power was very broad, the Court after 1890 trimmed that power sharply in order to restrain the regulatory efforts of the national government. And repeatedly the Court found that Congress was invading states' rights even when Congress purported to be acting under the commerce or taxing powers. The restraint imposed by the "reserved powers" doctrine the Court manufactured from the vague language of the Tenth Amendment, for nowhere is there any list of powers specifically reserved to the states. Thus a twilight zone of business activity won protection from both state and federal regulation as the Court made law to suit their economic and political doctrines.

There is neither time nor necessity to go into detail about the cases that sustain the assertions of the previous paragraph—a schematic presentation of the evidence will suffice. First consider the commerce clause and the successive limitation of it in order to curtail federal regulation of business. One begins with the broad reading that Marshall gave the commerce clause: it was broad and plenary, and specific Constitutional restrictions were placed upon it. When, however, the Congress passed the Sherman Anti-Trust Law and began enforcing it, the Court obviously sought a way to limit the impact of the law. One tactic, as noted, was to constrict the by then well-established meaning of the commerce clause. Thus in the case of *United States* v. *E. C. Knight Co*,[5] the Supreme Court found that a contract among a group of sugar-producing companies that would give them control over *98 per cent of all the sugar refined in the nation* did not create a monopoly within the meaning of the Sherman Act. This curious result followed from the Court's conclusion that the *companies were not engaged in interstate commerce* but in the manufacture of sugar. Why the companies produced the sugar unless they had some notion that it might enter the channels of commerce is a little difficult to comprehend, but the Court was seeking an out and the fiction that manufacturing was one thing and commerce another served the purpose. It made a mockery of the generally accepted Marshall interpretation of the commerce power, but it achieved a political objective. Similarly the Court was later to discover that an attempt by Congress to regulate the widespread use of child labor was an improper use of the interstate commerce power. Congress had forbade the shipment in interstate commerce of the goods produced

5. 156 *U.S.* 1, 1895.

by child labor, but the Supreme Court held that this was not really an exercise of the commerce power as it appeared on its face, but a regulation of labor conditions that was within the realm of state government by their reading of the Tenth Amendment's invisible radiations.[6] Presumably the Court did not find child labor an admirable practice, but they rose above principle in order to defend business from other legislation that might have to be sustained by reasoning established in ruling favorably on child labor laws.

The curious thing is, however, that the Court did not always hold to its antiaction reasoning. It found that several other federal laws, roughly similar in intent and legal formulation, were valid. It agreed, for example, that Congress had the power to bar from the channels of interstate commerce such items as lottery tickets [7] and prostitutes [8] and impure foods.[9] Without exception the goal of these statutes (like child labor) was regulatory of the practices behind the commercial element, yet the Court found no fault. This led some observers to say the Court made a distinction between things that were evil in themselves (*malum in se*) and therefore subject to Congressional ban, whereas others were evil only by Congressional pronouncement (*malum prohibitas*) and therefore not subject to restriction. But this doctrine became a shaky one when in 1925 the Court upheld a Congressional act making it a crime to ship a stolen automobile across the borders of a state.[10] What was there more intrinsically evil about a stolen car than an unstolen car—or even a chair made by the hands of a child? Clearly the Court was ruling according to its political and moral predilections and not by any standard it or anyone else could defend. In the *Brooks* case, the Court admitted there was a problem to be overcome concerning the child labor cases, but it avoided the issue by saying, "It is known of all men that the radical change in transportation of persons and goods effected by the introduction of the automobile, the speed with which it moves, and the ease with which evil-minded persons can avoid capture have greatly encouraged and increased crimes." But were not the evils of child labor also evident, if, as the Court seemed to be suggesting, the constitutionality of a law depended upon the gravity of the issue?

The Court got itself into equally peculiar situations as it struck down by the dozens state acts intended to deal with labor and other problems arising out of rapid urbanization and industrialization. When the due process clause of the Fourteenth Amendment was first suggested as a

6. *Hammer* v. *Dagenhart*, 247 *U.S.* 251, 1918.
7. *Champion* v. *Ames*, 188 *U.S.* 231, 1903.
8. *Hoke* v. *U.S.*, 227 *U.S.* 308, 1913.
9. *Hipolite Egg Co.* v. *U.S.*, 220 *U.S.* 45, 1911.
10. *Brooks* v. *U.S.*, 267 *U.S.*, 432, 1925.

barrier to the state's regulating businesses, the notion was rejected, and one justice even offered the poor prediction that the Amendment would never be used for anything but the purpose for which it was originally intended: the protection of the newly freed slave. How wrong he was was amply demonstrated in time, although it took a minority of the Court some fifteen years to persuade their colleagues that the clause should be so used. One of the state efforts that led business to seek relief at court was the attempt to regulate hours and conditions of labor. Although the Court accepted a state law providing an eight-hour day for miners—on the grounds of safety—it otherwise did not find that argument persuasive. The justices conjured up something they labeled "liberty of contract" based upon a theoretical contract that employer and worker entered into and that the state had no right to interfere with, except under some unusual circumstances, like the safety of miners. In general the Court defended liberty of contract as it did when it decided against a ten-hour-day and a six-day-week maximum for bakers that the New York legislature had prescribed.[11] The majority doubted there was any sound social or health reason to restrict a baker's working hours. Then the Court asked, if bakers and their employers could be subject to such restraint, what other laws might then follow in trail? Some labor may be unhealthy, "But are we all, on that account, at the mercy of legislative majorities? A printer, a tinsmith, a locksmith, a carpenter, a cabinetmaker, a dry goods clerk, a bank's, a lawyer's, or a physician's clerk, or a clerk in almost any kind of business, would all come under the power of the legislature, on this assumption." Here was the Court deciding a case not on the basis of any sense of constitutionality per se but on their sense of what was and what wasn't good policy.

Mr. Justice Holmes in a dissenting opinion told the majority they were in effect legislating according to their own prejudices, that liberties are never absolute but subject to restraint by law on behalf of what legislatures feel to be in the public interest. "The Fourteenth Amendment," he went on, "does not enact Mr. Herbert Spencer's Social Statics." He then cited a number of state statutes that the Court had accepted (mandatory vaccination, regulations of the sales of stocks, and others). "Some of these laws embody convictions or prejudices which judges are likely to share. Some may not. But a constitution is not intended to embody a particular economic theory, whether of paternalism . . . or of laissez faire." But his was the dissenting, not the prevailing, view of the matter; clearly the prejudices of the judges were more determinative of what would and would not get judicial blessing.

11. *Lochner v. New York*, 198 *U.S.* 45, 1905.

Without going further into detail on matters such as minimum hours and wages for women employees (which the court rejected until 1937), suffice it to say that during the nearly 50-year period from the late 1880's until 1937 the court used the whipsaw of dual federalism to restrain the hand of government as it attempted to deal with growing social problems. The great reversal in 1937—after the Supreme Court had turned down numerous New Deal ventures intended to deal with aspects of the Depression—was a fundamental shift in policy. Now opportunities developed to deal with critical issues that had been beyond the reach of public agencies. No longer were the wages and working conditions of men engaged in interstate commerce (even if only remotely so) beyond the regulatory power of Congress. No longer would the Supreme Court sit as a superlegislature to determine whether a particular economic policy of the states or Congress was acceptable as wise or unwise social policy. Ultimately the Court would say that the Tenth Amendment was no barrier to enacting otherwise valid national acts, and similarly that the state could enact legislation to deal with social and economic problems as long as there was some relationship between the public welfare and a regulatory law.

This does not mean that either (1) the Supreme Court is no longer involved in formulating the broad rules of politics in important ways, or (2) that the subject of economic regulatory policies is no longer significantly affected by court interpretation. In fact, as the Supreme Court ceased prohibiting the states' effort to set economic policy, it began, sometimes on not much stronger grounds where any "absolute" constitutional factors are concerned, rejecting state policies in the area of civil rights and liberties. (In one generation the Court has changed friends and enemies: its once conservative friends are now its enemies and the liberals vice versa.) On the subject of Supreme Court involvement in civil rights and liberties more will be said when we consider federalism and later the judiciary. About the regulation of the economy it may be said summarily that although the Court does not much involve itself in determining whether or not policies now come within the scope of the Constitution, it remains a significant force for determining what the law means. Thus the Court decides, for example, what powers Congress meant the Securities and Exchange Commission to have. The Court reviews, on challenge, the rules and procedures of all the regulatory bodies and makes decisions of the highest importance to business. Or consider another example. A group of homeowners may bring suit against an airline claiming that their property has been seriously damaged by the noise created by huge planes that pass directly overhead. (And when the SST, the federally financed supersonic transport goes blasting through the sky creating a sonic boom fifty miles wide, it is certain the damage issue will ultimately land in the chambers of the Supreme Court.) At once the case becomes one of federal policy; what is the scope of potential public authority, the actuality of the rules, the consistency of those rules with the governing statutes, and the relationship of any of these to the private property rights of the homeowners? What is true here is in varying ways true of most significant areas of public policy, including such things as the regulation of the safety of drugs, tax policy, tidal oil lands, the equity of welfare policies, the application of the full faith and credit clause to divorces and wills—the list is nearly endless. In short, let it not be concluded that because the federal judiciary has largely withdrawn from consideration of whether federal or state statutes are "reasonable" regulations in terms of some laissez-faire norm, that therefore the courts ceased to be important in economic matters. On the contrary, they can be all important to all kinds of interests in innumerable situations.

But the judiciary is not the agency that makes all the rules of the game. When Congress establishes an Un-American Activities Committee or a Federal Trade Commission, or lays down rules on automobile safety, it thereby determines some basic rules. It not only asserts that such a power exists for Congress to exercise, but it also gives someone an official capacity to give orders to others and sets the standards for compliance, the procedures for raising objections, and the like. Each of these decisions establishes rules by which questions of subversiveness, competition, or safety are to be decided. Those empowered to act under these resolutions or statutes make the next set of determinations of the rules, often establishing subordinate codes that are just as much binding rules as the statutes to which they owe their origin. And so, down the line of political decisions, there are many interests significantly involved in setting the rules: the President or cabinet member who pushes for legislation in a specific form, the interest groups themselves who battle to defend their positions, even marginally political parties that may take positions on issues and perhaps help round up the necessary votes for passage of a bill in a certain form.

In short the basic rules influence or determine who shall have formal authority; they partially decide what recourse any person involved may possess (whether he is a beneficiary or a person disadvantaged by the decision in question); and they facilitate participation in determining policy for certain elements or prevent others from participating. For example, it was, as it turned out, important that the Anti-Poverty Law said there should be "maximum feasible participation" of the poor in the conduct of local programs. The clause in the statute appears to have gone unnoticed in the legislative stage by those who subsequently objected bitterly to its application, but, however it got there, it helped decide power allocation under the law. If the Office of Economic Opportunity (which administers that law) had been rigid about it, there might have been more opportunity for actual participation of the poor, but the OEO was flexible in applying the rule. As a consequence the opportunity for the affected clientele to participate in any meaningful way in the making of policy was much weakened.[12]

A good illustration of the point is to be found in the controversy that broke out during the last months of the Johnson Administration concerning the administration of federal highway grants to the states. Federal officials wanted to require two public hearings to be held by state highway departments before all federally supported highways could be constructed. One hearing would announce tentative alignments of the road and invite public comment; the second hearing would present the finally determined route and permit the public a second round of (inevitable) criticism. State highway commissioners bitterly objected to these requirements. In their view it was an invitation to trouble, and insofar as it facilitated the opportunity for affected parties to muster opposition to highway locations it no doubt would involve difficulty for highway men, who feel a compulsion to build roads as cheaply, efficiently, and expediously as possible. And inviting local opposition is no way to simplify road building. These requirements, finally adopted in the last days of the Johnson Administration, do significantly affect the way the highway location game is played. Those who oppose the location of a highway in their backyards use publicity as a prime means of attack, and there is nothing like a rowdy, emotional hearing to arouse wide antipathy to the highway bulldozer and its tendency to plow furrows eight lanes wide. In short a simple administrative ruling can have a tremendous impact on the way the actors in a controversy will be able to use their resources.[13]

The rules can alter power relationships completely. Thus, to use the antipoverty program as an example again, the mayors of the major cities of the country and the leaders of big-city political party organizations insisted in 1967 that Congress repeal the option the national OEO had of funding local independent groups to carry out OEO programs. Urban leaders insisted that only city agencies should be funded. Because the OEO could choose to work with privately organized groups concerned with welfare, manpower training, legal services to the poor,

12. See John C. Donovan, *The Politics of Poverty* (New York: Pegasus, 1967), especially Chapter 3.

13. Significantly the pressure of state officials forced the removal of a provision for appeals from decisions and released the highway departments from an obligation to consider alternative means of transportation, such as mass transit systems. See *The New York Times*, Jan. 17, 1969.

and the like, city hall politicians saw a real threat. The mayors' reasoning was perfectly clear: if we lack control over the patronage and operations of these private groups, they may become a challenge to our political hegemony. Of course, that was not the argument they used publicly—the announced reasons concerned proper coordination of agencies and their programs and other such sublime rationalizations, but at the heart of the matter was power. The rules decided who could have cash to spend on programs, and he who has cash can fill jobs and gain community standing for services offered—can, in short, gain some power. In the ultimate struggle over whether the mayors would force Congress to grant them authority to require that only public agencies receive OEO money, the inevitable happened: those who had the greater pull prevailed. Thus the Edith Green Amendment became law in 1967: it did not prohibit funds from going to a private group but permitted a local administration to rule that only public bodies could participate in the program.[14]

It is important to note that the rules of politics not only allocate power but also create understandings of what is right and what should be accepted, like it or not. To be sure in this political system there is much objection—in various forms from pickets to lawsuits, riots, and referenda, to mention but a few—but there is also a strong inclination to accept the official edicts of government. The regime has legitimacy, to use a term much favored by political scientists. The public, that is to say, respects the right of those in official positions to issue rulings: social norms endorse compliance not resistance, and if there is objection it is almost always to the particular rule and not to the general rightness of the authority issuing the order. It is obvious that the legitimacy of the system serves well those who have the greatest political influence. For acceptance of decisions without organized objection—partly on grounds of legitimacy—obviously aids most those who have the best resources for persuasion. This is a logical necessity, for if they prevail most often then they are pushed least often to have to organize dissent.

The tendency to accept government as legitimate on the part of the disadvantaged is reinforced by their sense of defeatism about using government to achieve their goals. That is, those who are only marginally or not at all involved in government, who are unskilled in the use of political techniques, and who also lack confidence in their capacity to win justice for themselves have developed apathy toward politics. A comparative study of political attitudes in five nations, done by Gabriel Almond and Sidney Verba, does show that the American lower class

14. See the article reviewing the legislative history of the Green Amendment, *The New York Times*, Dec. 25, 1967. Significantly the Amendment also bars use of OEO money for voter registration drives!

feels somewhat more confidence in its ability to affect government than the lower classes in other nations, but the difference between the top and the bottom groups in this country are also significant. Among United States citizens in professional and managerial occupations 96 per cent expressed such optimism. And of those with the least education in the United States only a third expected that they would be given serious consideration in a government office or from the police if they made complaints; among those with higher education no less than 85 per cent expressed confidence in their capacity to get attention.[15]

There is much in our culture that encourages the feeling that equitable treatment might be expected and that any citizen has a right to a hearing and due consideration. But there is also much that would discourage the lower class from taking advantage of what the beliefs and propaganda tell him is available. The literate and informed person has no qualms about going to a public official and making a complaint or request. He will have no fear that his attire, speech, demeanor would result in his own humiliation; he will not suspect that the police will take a jaundiced view of him because he makes an appeal; and he will know the relevant rules and procedures—or can readily find out what they are. From experience, either his own or that of others, he will expect a reasonable response. The poor, the undereducated, the chronically disadvantaged have none of these expectations. The poor are aware of the clear difference between themselves and those who work in government offices—in contrast to the middle- or upper-class person who may look down upon them as mere civil servants. The language of the poor is usually markedly different and so is their attire; they are ignorant of procedures and suspicious of officials. They feel less like equals and more like supplicants. If they have had to go to a hospital clinic or a welfare office or most any other kind of public institution dealing with the poor, they know the kind of neglect and rudeness that characterizes relations between the "public servant" and the client. (If this is doubted, dress in untidy clothes, sit in a welfare office for an hour, and observe the treatment the indigent routinely get.)

Not only this prevalent sense of "being out of it" restrains the poor and the uneducated from trying to use the government more effectively in their own behalf. There is also the set of myths that convinces many victims of these conditions that in some subtle way they are personally responsible for the troubles they are experiencing—that, indeed, government should not involve itself in personal problems of individuals, for some of the older, isolated poor are among the few who still have any belief in laissez-faire ideas. (Business tycoons believe in it only to

15. Gabriel Almond and Sidney Verba, *The Civic Culture* (Princeton, N.J.: Princeton University Press, 1963), pp. 210, 219.

get the government off their backs; laissez-faire is the farthest thing from their minds when they want a subsidy, contract, or government service.) Mockery though it is, many of those who need help feel that any man who cannot make his own way independently is not indeed a real man at all; this despite the rapacious behavior of coal, timber, and other extractive interests that raise the hopes of people today and smash them to despair tomorrow because the resources are depleted or have become uneconomical to exploit—or can be exploited in some simpler way that needs the work of one man, not ten. (Perhaps this contention is supported by the persistent attacks on the public welfare system—for reasons of wastefulness—by Senator Robert Byrd of West Virginia. Although he has had ample opportunity to learn better, he persists in wanting to restrict welfare payments to the bitter minimum and to insist on the maximum of humiliation in exchange for aid. This conforms with the Protestant ethic: anyone worth his salt would rise from poverty—as Senator Byrd did. Unhappily there are some to whom hunger is preferable to the humiliation of admitting the need for assistance.)

This then offers some reasons why the rules—constitutional, judicial, statutory, and administrative—can have an enormous effect on political contesting. Unhappily one of the fundamental consequences of the rules, as they now exist and tend to be interpreted, is that those without prestige and power tend to be even more pushed outside the comfortable gambits of American life by the character of those rules and their interpretation.

CHAPTER THREE

Parties, Politics, and Power

RADICALS of the right and radicals of the left are agreed on one thing at least: the two major political parties are an abomination. Their indictments are remarkably similar. Parties, they say, are a case of Tweedledum and Tweedledee, with no noticeable difference between them except for their names. Both are committed to essentially the status quo and they present similar programs—to the disgust of the left radicals because the government does not do enough about human problems and of the radical right because the government interferes too much. They also indict the parties as instruments of compromise on fundamental (but different) issues that should not be compromised. They point to the tendency for the party faithful to accept candidates or policies that are nearly intolerable for the sake of party victory. And they finally say that the parties become a barrier to any significant change, opting at all times for the middle of the road and actively stifling any fundamental change.

There is at least some truth in each of these charges. That may not mean that others would accept what radicals see as dysfunctional about parties; indeed the contrary is true—most American citizens seem to approve of the idea of a two-party system that results in the parties' coming to a middle ground, for compromising, and stifling radical change. And from the point of view of the stability of the regime no doubt these traits are beneficial. That is to say that *insofar as the party is an agency that takes the place of force in the selection of political leaders, tends to leave antagonists tolerant of each other, and induces compromise to let something be done rather than stifling political interests completely, the party system no doubt thereby helps make the political system stable.* Today stability is often derided as irrelevant, but in combination with other values (such as justice and equity) stability is important for any society. For we seek in government, as we do elsewhere, for certainty, for security against the winds of change that frighten most people. It appears that one of the basic things that all men have sought in developing government is to reduce the terrors of uncertainty and to maximize regularity and dependability. One need not go into a comparison of advanced and primitive societies to see that there are similarities between primitive societies' myths, councils, and chiefs and the development of constitutions, rules of law, and norms of nonarbitrary treatment of citizens in the more complicated societies.

The left radicals say, however, that stability can be worshiped too fervently. The last word in stability is found in prison or a concentration camp. Rightists are adept at scaring people by shouting for law and order. A stable, unthreatened existence is after all highly valued, especially when tension and turmoil seem to threaten stability and order. And the more rapid social change becomes, the greater the probability of tension and conflict. Hitler knew this and used it as one means of achieving power as have countless other demagogues and usurpers. Frightened people are more likely to opt for something to restore stability, and repression thus wins backing—as it has in the United States in recent years. Vice President Spiro T. Agnew's rhetoric and the "hard hat's" violent attacks are totally congruent.

The radical is saying that an emphasis on stability that stifles dissent, or that prevents any significant change (as distinct from changes that do not fundamentally affect the status quo or the basic order of things), can be dangerous in its own way. Without trying to settle the dispute between the advocate of status quo and the proponent of revolutionary change, let it be said that the party system has been a major contributor to the stability of the United States, including the apparently false sense of "national unity" or "consensus" that has been so often sought in recent years. That the consensus was in good measure superficial has been demonstrated by the rifts that now appear in the society, for it can hardly be contended that the black-white division of our time is a new development: it is merely the surfacing of antagonisms that have existed, in this case, for centuries. (One is reminded that President Richard Nixon and former Vice President Hubert Humphrey on the morning of November 6, 1968, when the election was determined, sent friendly messages to each other, each appealing for the healing of the differences in society, for bringing us all together once more. Neither seemed to sense that the divisions were true rifts and not superficial differences that could be swept away with words.)

Whatever else, it can be said that political parties in this country have contributed to the orderly process of contesting for the big prizes of politics, have facilitated compromise, have contributed to the stability of the regime by smothering dissent or buying it out, and have helped to blur beyond all recognition some basic problems of our time, and they are, for all their infirmities, very persistent and long-lasting institutions. Thus the argument of the radical left is certainly true: American major parties are anything but revolutionary parties—they are very

near the opposite of that. For revolution and political parties are opposite phenomena. That is, a party, prior to its becoming a governing institution, may espouse and even be a catalyst of revolution, but once the
party becomes a political arm of a regime in a postrevolutionary situation, the revolutionary qualities recede and the emphasis is upon stability and control, program support and unity, rather than on ferment
and change.

The present purpose is to assess the role of the parties in a very non-
revolutionary process: namely, their role in facilitating or frustrating
the application of governmental capacities to those most in need of it—
the obscure ones. To do so we shall briefly assess some attributes of
American parties—their characteristics, operation, and historical development, for example. For the party is a complicated phenomenon in
many ways; it serves at once to stifle and to respond to the needs of the
people. Sorting out the whys of each is not as simple as demagogy
makes it appear.

Popular Participation in Parties and Government

Not for any altruistic reasons but for practical ones, the parties have
to their credit a role in promoting the opportunities for public participation in politics. To be sure the parties' role here has involved duplicity,
with one faction fighting to prevent while another seeks to provide
wider public participation. And in every one of these democratization
battles, the lines have been drawn for the most part according to expectations of return. Although one must admit there are cases where party
factions sought reforms to widen opportunities for participation on the
basis of democratic ideals, even in those cases a motivating factor is the
hope of a favorable response from those who gain the opportunities.
Numerous party reform groups around the nation have over the years
played a large role in extending the party primary, and one has only to
hear the rhetoric of these ardent reformers to know that the ideology
of participatory democracy is a strong motivation for them. But one
learns too, when one joins them or listens long enough, that these protagonists of the people expect (rightly or wrongly in their prediction)
that the people will surely see things *their* way, once given the chance
to participate.

Another example is the advocacy of extended suffrage by the parties
in the nineteenth century. Party leaders in various states lined up for or
against expanding suffrage depending upon whether they expected to
be reaping a larger share of the new vote than their opponents. But in
their continued advocacy of wider electoral participation party leaders
also helped further and solidify a set of democratic norms in the Amer-

ican value system. Listen to these words of Herman Melville, himself a party hack and patronage seeker from time to time, but more importantly an ardent convert to the virtues of democracy. He says in *Moby Dick*:

> But this august dignity I treat of, is not the dignity of kings and robes, but that abounding dignity which has no robed investiture. Thou shalt see it shining in the arm that wields a pick or drives a spike; that democratic dignity which, on all hands, radiates without end from God; Himself! The great God absolute! The centre and circumference of all democracy! His omnipresence, our divine equality!
>
> If, then, to meanest mariners, and renegades, and castaways, I shall hereafter ascribe high qualities, though dark . . . then against all mortal critics bear me out in it, thou Spirit of Equality, which has spread one royal mantle of humanity over all my kind! Bear me out in it, thou great democratic God! . . . Thou who didst pick up Andrew Jackson from the pebbles; who didst hurl him upon a war-horse; who didst thunder him higher than a throne! Thou who, in all Thy mighty, earthly marchings, ever cullest Thy selectest champions from the kingly commons; bear me out in it, O God: [1]

There was also resistance to the growing popularity of democratic participation, and to many, egalitarian ideas were more a threat than a bright promise. Thus a South Carolina plantation owner wrote on the Fourth of July, 1856, "Today is the anniversary [sic] of American independence. I have no doubt in many parts there will be pretensions of great rejoicings, but I cannot really rejoice for a fredom [sic] which allows every bankrupt, swindler, thief and scoundrel, traitor and seller of his vote to be placed on an equality with myself . . . [T]he demon democracy by its leveling principles, universal suffrage and numerous popular elections, homestead laws and bribery are sapping the foundations of the rights of property in every thing." [2] Resistance even produced one small-time insurrection—Dorr's Rebellion in Rhode Island—but the chances of holding back general suffrage of white males was doomed. The parties became an agent of change because there was something for the parties to gain from extending the vote—or something to be feared if they resisted and the opposition won credit for the extension.

1. Quoted by John William Ward, *Andrew Jackson: Symbol for an Age* (New York: Oxford University Press, 1955), p. 98.
2. Quoted by Kenneth Stampp, *The Peculiar Institution* (New York: Random House, 1956, Vintage edition), p. 419.

The idea of popular participation in government was not a new idea in nineteenth-century America, for there had been varying degrees of opportunity for the people to become involved in government during the colonial period, and the party system itself had begun in the 1790's. But the parties in their early stages were not by any means what they were to become; they were in fact little more than cliques of office-holders and leading political figures who met in caucuses or formed cabals to promote their goals. The presidential nomination, for example, was decided by a caucus of the members of each party in Congress, and the state political parties similarly tended to be guided by the aristocratic and powerful few. This was particularly so in states where the suffrage was limited by law, and where interest in participation may have been low (as some historians suggest). In any event it has been estimated that fewer than 10 per cent of the adult males participated in the first Congressional elections, and even the presidential elections in the early part of the nineteenth century—when the constitution of the parties stirred some interest—usually drew about 25 per cent of the vote. Contrast this, however, with elections of the Jacksonian era, in which from half to three quarters of the white adult males voted.[3]

Gradually the parties ceased to be cabals of the leading few and began to become mass-based parties. That does not mean that the parties became the instruments of the mass of the electorate; rather the parties developed a following in the electorate and increasingly depended on that attachment as a means to power. The Jacksonian movement, seeking votes as well as responding to ideology, did much to popularize government and to expand the base of the party system. Turning out upper-class "career" public servants, the Jacksonians used the spoils system both to encourage support for the party and to provide a turnover in personnel, thereby permitting "the people" an opportunity to govern themselves through the holding of offices. Frequent elections and long ballots served the same ends. Similarly the Jacksonians abandoned the caucus and substituted the convention as a means of making nominations, emphasizing the role of the party follower rather than the elected officials in choosing candidates. It is true that the people exerted little actual control through the convention, but it was at least a more open process than the caucus.

Parties, having become spokesmen for the demos, became powerful institutions. Key leaders of the parties could and did dictate many decisions of those whom they aided in getting into formal office. Thus Abraham Lincoln, not being present at the Republican National Convention of 1860, wired his lieutenants to make no deals about the cabinet or other offices, whereupon they saddled Lincoln with a cabinet, complete

3. See William N. Chambers, *Political Parties in the New Nation* (New York: Oxford University Press, 1963), pp. 32–33.

with some notorious boodlers.[4] This became more important when party connections became the source of big money. As economic giantism developed in the last half of the nineteenth century and as large-scale urbanization developed, there were rich opportunities for plunder. Franchises for transportation systems, public utility development, and public construction threw business and politics together as never before. A natural alliance resulted between the rising economic interests and the leaders of urban (and even rural) machines. The allies then developed the cities badly from an aesthetic point of view, and sapped public treasuries with graft and corruption. Local governments were suspended by state legislative acts—passed by corrupt legislators bought by the business interests in alliance with the machines—and to replace these local governments the legislatures even went so far as to name specific persons to a governing body. At times they designated specific streets for transportation systems and specific developers for the projects. But "ripper legislation," as such laws were called, was not the whole story of the decline of party prestige in the latter half of the nineteenth century. There were also strong reactions to open bribery, protection of crime, dishonest elections, purchase of votes, herding of illiterate immigrants to the polls to do the bidding of the bosses, corruption of the judiciary and the police, patronage rackets that put the utterly incapable in all kinds of jobs—and so on. The whole unsavory mess that developed in state after state and city after city was duplicated in Washington, where the agents of the trusts, the boodlers, and the patronage hunters competed with each other to see who would be the most notoriously successful in turning the national government to their own advantage.

Thus the inevitable happened: reform movements sprang up, manned by an odd lot of strange allies. The reformers included some men from the upper class who, distressed over the decline of political morality, leaped into the reform movement with a mixture of disdain and abandon. (Theodore Roosevelt in his service as police commissioner of New York City was an example.) Others were radical reformers who used every device they knew to uncover the plunder and to arouse the populace to action. (Lincoln Steffens is the best example of this muckraker type.) Some businessmen entered the lists as reformers and some (like Tom Johnson, a wealthy Clevelander who became a reform mayor) achieved a certain success. Even some academic figures (like Woodrow Wilson) became involved in the reform movement. It must be said, however, that the reformers often showed an incredible naïveté. They believed that if the organization was once routed, the "good government" element could hold its gains—which proved wrong, for repeat-

4. William Barton, *Life of Abraham Lincoln* (Indianapolis: Bobbs-Merrill, 1925), Vol. 1, p. 433.

edly the permanence of the machine was demonstrated as it lasted long enough to take over again when the reform movement wasted away of inertia. And they were naïve too when they wrongly assumed that striking blows at the party machines would open the way for the people to supplant the machines and thereby do something decisive about the situation. Hence the reformers campaigned for the direct party primary to get the party machine out of and the people into the business of choosing nominees for office.[5] They also promoted nonpartisanship as a way of ridding the local scene of bossism. They backed such reforms as the "commission plan" of local government, but the ultimate adaptability of the machine to such devices was well illustrated by the success of Boss Frank Hague of Jersey City, who began his long career as dictator of Jersey City by winning election as a candidate with a "reform" group backing the commission plan. And they promoted a civil service system that they hoped would raise the caliber of public personnel and hurt the machines by denying them patronage. But none of these objectives was fully attainable. The primary did not turn over to the people power to nominate candidates. The machines frequently found ways to evade nonpartisanship. And the civil service system may have curtailed patronage greatly but never enough to eliminate the machines.

As we note later these reforms may have achieved fully none of their proponents' objectives but in combination with other forces they undoubtedly helped in altering fundamentally the place of parties in American government. Thus the party primary election did not turn over the nomination process to the people, but it remains a significant development. The people did not take over nominations because they could not and would not. Their level of interest in the fluctuating fortunes of politics is too low, and their capacity for collective action is too limited. Masses of people may influence or they may ratify decisions, but "control" they do not. Thus one finds that the proportion of the electorate who vote in primaries is markedly less than in the general elections—often amounting to as little as 10 per cent of those who come to general elections. In about three quarters of the sample of elections that V.O. Key studied to test voter turnout in primaries, a third or less of the voters participated.[6] And less than one primary in ten

5. On the early development of the primary see Robert LaFollete's *Autobiography* (Madison: University of Wisconsin Press, 1960, paperback edition), and also V. O. Key, Jr., *American State Politics: An Introduction* (New York: Alfred Knopf, 1956), pp. 87–97.

6. His sample did not include Southern states, which would have inflated the figure because the primary there—at least until recent years—was *the election*, there being no noticeable competition. See his *Politics, Parties, and Pressure Groups*, 5th ed. (New York: Thomas Y. Crowell, 1964), p. 582 (Table 21.2).

drew as much as half the potential electorate. It is easy to see why the levels of participation are low; for one thing the primary is not as widely advertised. The national channels of communication, from which inevitably many citizens get their political news, give little attention to primaries unless they have become key races for some particular reason and even then the amount of coverage, compared with general elections, is small. But it might be argued that even if turnout tends to be low, those who are interested do participate and therefore take the reins from the party leaders. But the leaders and self-propelled candidates are clearly more "in charge" than the electorate, whose choices are greatly limited by the activities of leading contestants and the organizations that back them. At best therefore the electorate in primaries have marginal influence and not much "control" if the latter word is to have much meaning.

The primary may not have done the impossible by giving the inchoate public the capacity to pick its own candidates, but it has nevertheless had some profound effects on our politics. It has fundamentally altered the once clear hegemony of the bosses, who could much more readily control the delegations to conventions than they can manage primaries. Again that does not say that the bosses have been rooted out of the political thicket; they have had to adapt, but are not thereby forced to retire from the field. Thus the Democratic leaders in Massachusetts changed their antagonism toward a candidate to great partiality toward him when he won a primary election—apparently by confusing the voters by the fortuitous chance that he happened to be named John F. Kennedy. (Chided for trading on the name of the then junior Senator from Massachusetts, Kennedy said that, being the older of the two, he had the name before the Senator did.) But the Democratic leaders took their defeat and backed the insurgent, saying that he had caught the imagination and interest of the voters and that his election would "afford proof that in Massachusetts democracy works and that Americans invariably draw their best talent for leadership from the rank and file of the people." [7] (A good question is what loss of the party's prestige such mendacity entails.)

The party primary may thus be said to have had these general effects. First it has made it possible for insurgents to win office without adapting to the demands of the key leaders of the party. Like the maverick Mr. Kennedy of Massachusetts, many of what the late Professor V. O. Key used to call the "left handed banjo players" can afford to ignore the party leadership and make their own appeals to the public; if they can provide enough drama they may be able to beat the organization. That such maneuvers have been successful with some regularity appears to

7. V. O. Key, Jr., *American State Politics* (op. cit.), p. 216.

have produced a second consequence of the existence of primaries: namely the atrophy of the party system. It may be exaggeration to attribute to the primary the basic responsibility for the decline in power of the parties, but to some unknown and unknowable extent the primary must certainly have made a contribution. This only stands to reason. If the leaders of a party can control access to important nominations and generally control the ladder of political ascent, then clearly those leaders will be deferred to by anyone with political ambitions. But if an alternative course to elective office is provided through the primary, the leadership will be less important and will have to do such second-takes as the Massachusetts Democrats did in the double Kennedy case. Or the leadership will be reduced literally to the position of withdrawing itself entirely from primaries and entering the scene after the decisions on candidacies are made; which is somewhat like arriving at the picnic after the food is gone—it may still be possible to join the crowd but, as a picnic, there is something lacking.

The primary has also had the distinct effect of facilitating the candidacy of the man with heavy financial support. Campaign costs are incredibly high in general, and a primary before a general election adds an enormous financial burden. And that may put some candidates out of the race in the beginning; in some states a gubernatorial or senatorial primary race may cost in excess of a million dollars. Few candidates can afford such sums on their own—and even if they can are not supposed to spend so lavishly according to the little-observed campaign finance laws. So the inevitable consequence is that those with money to invest in candidates will at least acquire ready access to candidates if and when they win.

The primary, because it facilitates the candidacies of insurgents or independent candidates, has also affected the capacity of the party leadership to exert discipline within the ranks of its elective officials. One consequence of the greater independence of candidates is that party leaders find it more difficult to pressure legislators into voting a party line.

Other things have been at work too; the availability of media of communication that permit independence on the part of candidates because they can reach the public without resort to the party organization, the changing character of politics with the development of the suburb and the increasingly educated and politically sophisticated public, and (for various reasons) a generally declined prestige of political party leaders. Hence the effort to democratize politics through the primary may not have gone far toward providing popular control over parties, but it has encouraged independent candidates and officials and assisted in reducing the significance of parties.

Have parties facilitated public participation in politics in general? No doubt they have. The competition of parties in major campaigns arouses voters' attention and obviously encourages voting participation. The greater the campaign publicity and the more civic pressure to vote—to which the parties contribute heavily—the higher the level of voter participation. Also some citizens are led to participate in politics by acting as agents of the party—to get out the vote, to assist campaigns in various active ways (from distribution of literature and door-to-door campaigning to voluntary secretarial work and campaign management). But the number involved is small. Even if all forms of participation are included (such as wearing a campaign button or putting a bumper sticker on the family car) the proportions are still small. By one calculation only 14 per cent of the public participates in active campaigning work—including those who participate in some of the following five activities: holding an office, being a candidate, soliciting political funds, attending caucuses or strategy meetings, and becoming active as a party member.[8]

Do parties educate the public on political matters? No doubt campaigns do contribute to public awareness of both candidates and issues, although one is tempted to say that if they do, it is in spite of the confusion they sow. For campaigns are contests for power and the objective is anything but educational. Every candidate is tempted to come close to saying something he doesn't dare say aloud and clearly—because he wants partisans of one point of view to see that he is with them on the issue while at the same time not being so unequivocal about it as to alienate others who disagree. The mendacity and intentionally misleading statements in campaigns place them on a level with commercial advertising, of which the less said the better. In 1968 for example, the major candidates raged about crime in the streets and law and order; no one came up with interesting or particularly relevant suggestions toward meeting the problem. The reasons for that were clear. To many persons "crime in the streets" was a general euphemism for black violence; and even the right wingers were careful in their choice of language about Negroes, because overt racism was taboo. Moreover when candidates used the term it was obvious that their purpose was less to discuss a serious problem than to ring in a favorite term of the white middle and lower-middle class, who were so apprehensive about Negroes. Hence the objective was to stir up the appropriate response rather than to enlighten or educate anybody. Candidates came out on all sides of the matter, absolutely defying anyone to tell what their position was. An advertisement for Hubert Humphrey, for example, stressed that "every

8. Lester W. Milbrath, *Political Participation* (Chicago: Rand McNally, 1965), pp. 18–20. See Milbrath generally about various aspects of participation.

man has the right to a decent and safe neighborhood. And on this there can be no compromise." This is followed by a stern voice saying that for every jail or policeman his opponents would provide Mr. Humphrey would match it and *also* build a house and hire a teacher. Exactly how that elucidates the problem of crime is difficult to perceive; how it suggests things favorable to Humphrey is somewhat easier to see, especially in view of the fact that it is all said while a mother hums a lullaby to her baby and after she worries aloud about the threat violence poses to her little one.[9] Thus Richard Nixon on one day war-hawked for greater armament to surpass the Russians in missiles. The next day he favored a disarmament program. (It used to be said in the day before modern communications systems developed that candidates said one thing in one area and another in others, hoping to please all; it sometimes seems that we have gone that one better now and the candidates say one thing one day and another thing the next to *everybody*.) Or the candidates pick on an issue that they think is good ammunition, but on which they have inadequate information or perhaps even know is not relevant. President Nixon is familiar with that routine, for it was used on him by John F. Kennedy in 1960, when he proclaimed a supposed missile gap, which, once Kennedy reached office, he dismissed from his agenda as quietly as possible.

But with all that speech making and television coverage it must follow that *some* public education takes place? No doubt some people do become more informed by campaigns, but if the rationality of the voter had to rest primarily upon the information derived from campaign speeches there would be little case to make for the good sense of the American voter. But as V. O. Key showed in his book *The Responsible Electorate* the average citizen is not the fool he is sometimes portrayed to be.[10] Voter comments that pollsters gather admittedly reveal a distinct lack of political knowledge on the part of many citizens.[11] This has led some people to the conclusion that the average voter might just as well not vote because he must vote from relative ignorance. The argument goes this way: when asked how many members there are in the Senate from each state, or what the name of the Chief Justice of the United States is, or what NATO is, a great number of voters either confess ignorance or answer wrong. Thus if the potential voter doesn't

9. See Thomas J. Fleming, "Selling the Product Named Hubert Humphrey," *The New York Times Magazine*, Oct. 13, 1968, p. 45. See also Joe McGuinnis, *The Selling of the President, 1968* (New York: Trident Press, 1969).

10. (Cambridge, Mass.: Harvard University Press, 1966), pp. 7–8.

11. A poll in the spring of 1969 showed almost a third of all respondents had never heard of the antiballistic missile controversy then raging, and only 40 per cent of the sample had formed an opinion. See *The New York Times*, Apr. 6, 1969.

read a newspaper or keep abreast of issues, why is there anything useful about his voting—because clearly it cannot be a rational process?

There is a deceptive simplicity about this argument that deserves to be examined. It seems to say that one can vote intelligently only if one comprehends the major policies of government. But the process of voting may not rationally require anything of the sort. Let us hypothesize a Negro farm worker in Mississippi, one who has never voted because he has been kept from doing so by the formal and informal power of the master race. Let us further assume that the potential voter is acutely aware of what he doesn't like about the regime in power: he dislikes everything about it that has kept him in a state of absolute subordination. He may be illiterate and utterly untutored in the nuance of politics, and wouldn't know NATO from the NAM, and he may not even know how many Senators Mississippi is allowed under the Constitution. But he knows where he hurts and he knows the traditional white officials have not been on his side. In short this hypothetical voter perceives the situation accurately and wants to express his antagonism to the incumbent regime and his approval of an alternate slate. If we take as the norm of "rational" voting a prior knowledge of the sophisticated facts of the political realm, then this Mississippian must be excluded from participation.

But not only he. Consider an alternative case, a cultivated scholar of medieval literature, a person of great learning and erudition. As a preoccupied woman with little else on her mind but her scholarly pursuits, she could still remember from her youth enough about the U.S. Constitution not to make obvious errors, if she were put to the test by a pollster. But she would have little notion of what the OEO was or what the letters *SEATO* stood for. Still she has either a generally liberal orientation, let us say, and wishes to be among those responsible citizens who express that attitude in the polling place. Should she be excluded for lack of sophisticated knowledge because she has not used her undoubted skills to find out more? The medieval scholar and the Mississippi sharecropper may seem to be worlds apart in the political sense, as in other senses, but they may not be so dissimilar as they superficially appear. Each has a sense of what's right and what's wrong and wishes to express it.

Or consider an alternative possibility. Imagine a person who is knowledgeable about politics and who reads about and discusses the subject regularly. But he lives in a Congressional district with an incumbent Representative who takes the liberal's position on domestic matters and a very hawkish position on defense and is ready to escalate foreign engagements in nearly any situation if it is suspected that Communists are somehow involved. This would pose a difficult situation for either a dedicated conservative or a liberal—either way they would be caught on half of the man's record. (As it turned out a good part of the country was caught on the horns of that dilemma in 1964 but were not fully aware of it until after the election when the full implications of President Johnson's Vietnam policy became apparent.) But assume a situation in which it is known well before the election that a member of Congress takes this schizoid position—and this is no figment of the imagination, many such Congressmen exist. What then is the rational voter to do? If the potential voter feels strongly that the really critical issues are international, should he ignore his preferences in domestic matters—and thereby perhaps promote policies to which he wishes to express bitter opposition, not seeming approval? It might be argued that the rational course would be to consider the partisan affiliation of the Congressman and decide on the basis of party, assuming that aiding one's own party in a marginal case would be advantageous. But given the flexibility with which many members of Congress vote, that may or may not be a rational decision. (In some cases it might be better to choose the candidate from the opposite party—but to require anyone to know that much about the candidates as a prerequisite of rational voting will be to limit the electorate to a decided minority.) Or perhaps the candidates' positions can be measured in some way to arrive at a decision, weighting the candidates' various positions—known ones only, remember, for all candidates fudge some issues or find them irrelevant and ignore them. How is one to compare such noncomparable things as the risk of war and a poor policy on housing or welfare? Or suppose one considers a knowledgeable black voter to whom, understandably, the cardinal issue is race. He may feel so strongly about race that nothing else matters much to him. The point is that in such situations there is no calculus that will permit the use of reason in an untrammeled way. The cross currents and the blinding confusion of political campaigns incline men to vote according to their prejudices, their emotions, their fears and resentments. A purely rational decision is unlikely, or if there is a rational element it occurs at a superficial level and may involve nothing more than perceived self-interest.

But the emphasis on rationality of choice is probably a misplaced emphasis anyhow. Indeed the concept of "choice"—in the sense of the voter's truly having a say in who will be the next incumbent—may be out of place. Perhaps the true importance of voting is not to be found in the act of choosing but in the expression of a political point of view. That is, the parties or the factions within parties make the most important decisions about who will be the next incumbent in an office, not the voter. By the time the voter arrives on the scene the alternatives have been narrowed, usually to two, and the chances that any individual's vote will be of marginal and therefore critical importance in deciding the election are slim indeed. But casting a vote does more than pick one candidate over another; it also tells all politicians how strongly a public felt about a party, program, or candidate. It is an erratic indicator, but politicians are always apprehensive about their future and the voters' expressions are key signals for them. The repudiation of the Goldwater candidacy in 1964 is an illustration. The advocates of genuine conservatism within the Republican party had been asking for an opportunity to show how well the public would accept a frankly conservative ideological presentation, and they got their chance. Nearly all politicians read the results as a broker reads the stock ticker: bad news, clearly expressed. In short, politicians are always apprehensive about the chances of defeat in an election. They take certain chances and refuse to take other chances in the light of the probable consequences at the polls. It is safe to say that leading politicians readily play games with the lives of millions because of their sense of how voters might react to their behavior.

The anticipated reactions of voters on election day do have some significance for politicians. It is easy to exaggerate the politicians' fear of voter retribution, but it should not be summarily discounted—as some tend to do in assessing the political process. One may grant that legislators know they have a wide range of latitude in their behavior. They know, for example, that there is a fairly narrow range of subjects that any large segment of their constituency will be aroused about. And they are aware that most voters, short of outrageous conduct by a legislator, will never know (or care) what their legislator does. Legislators realize that they can safely follow their own predilections on many issues, and without fear. Yet at every election there are some politicians who dare not run for reelection (President Johnson in 1968 is a prime example), or who are defeated in primaries or general elections. Although it is true that both of these categories are small as compared with the whole group seeking reelections, the point is that some do meet their political deaths and thereby make a profound impression on the survivors. Analysts may show that only x per cent of all incumbents were defeated for reelection over a given period of time, and deduce therefrom that election defeat is irrelevant to any knowing legislator. Granting that the defeats mean little to those in completely safe districts, to others it will mean a great deal. For if an infantry company loses only five of a complement of one hundred in a major engagement, that is not a negligible number to the remaining ninety-five. It does not take many deaths in battle or politics to be enormously impressive to the survivors. An interesting test of the concerns of legislators about constituent views comes when districts are altered or a House member goes to the Senate. An essentially urban House member who through reapportionment acquires some farm constituents suddenly shows new-found interest in things agricultural. And when Charles Goodell of New York represented an upstate rural district in the House he was relatively conservative; as Senator for the whole state he became an outspoken advocate of liberal causes.

But that is not to say that elective politicians are alert to all the desires of the constituency and are poised to respond to every nuance thereof. Such an argument is naïve. The representative lacks any effective way of finding out what those opinions are, and even if he knew he would find often that 30 per cent of his people are for a proposal, 30 per cent against, 20 per cent have no opinion, and 20 per cent never heard of it—which is less than a clear sign of what a representative is supposed to do. Moreover, even when the signs can be more readily interpreted, it is not always clear what a representative will interpret the signs to mean. Some will feel pressures and resist them as not truly representa-tive, not wise, or just dangerous politically. They may therefore evade the issue rather than face it—and all because of fears of repercussions in a future political contest. Likewise a political leader may fear *not to* act (Kennedy in Cuba, both the Bay of Pigs fiasco and the 1962 crisis). In short it isn't a dangling sword but neither is it an irrelevancy. It may embolden some political leaders to do what they feel otherwise they couldn't do; it may lead others into timidity and evasion. Which it will do in a given situation depends on many factors apart from the voters' anticipated pressure, but the analyst ignores it at peril of misunder-standing.

Political Parties: Organization and Operation

It is commonly said that political parties are outmoded and declining in significance, that they are creatures of the past that either need drastic reorganization or replacement. Critics of parties denounce them for poor organization, inadequate leadership, and general weakness. Thus James MacGregor Burns says that really strong parties at the state and local levels are rare today:

> At no level, except in a handful of industrial states, do state parties have the attributes of organization. They lack extensive dues-paying memberships; hence they number many captains and sergeants but few foot soldiers. They do a poor job of raising money for themselves as organizations, or even for their candi-dates. They lack strong and imaginative leadership of their own. They cannot control their most vital function—the nomination of

their candidates. . . . Most of the state parties are at best mere jousting grounds for embattled politicians; at worst they simply do not exist, as in the case of the Republicans in the rural South or Democrats in the rural Midwest.[12]

Is the party at the state and local level moribund? I think Professor Burns is burying the body prematurely. There can be no question that the political party today is not the effective organization it was fifty years ago. We have mentioned the reasons for this and would not deny it. But blowing taps now is another question, for many an aspiring politician or political group have had their respective hopes bashed by the remaining power of these supposedly moribund organizations. Consider the 1964 and 1968 presidential contests for nomination. There seems to be unanimous agreement that Senator Barry Goldwater consciously imitated President Kennedy in beating the bushes to win local organizational support for his candidacy—and won the nomination partly because he did muster a solid phalanx of organizational support in the convention. Granted, he had an ideological commitment that stirred a passionate enthusiasm among his followers, but enthusiasm alone is not enough, as the supporters of Eugene McCarthy discovered four years later. Presidential nominations are not won in primaries or in the opinion polls, although both are helpful. Many party organizations are still strong enough to be significant aids in the conduct of state presidential primaries, and an aspiring candidate has got to have numerous contacts and alliances with these organizations to get far. Goldwater, it should be recalled, had very little support in the public opinion polls and largely avoided primaries, except when he was forced into one. His continuing efforts to cement firm relations with local and state leaders proved his most reliable source of power.

In 1968 much the same thing was repeated in the Democratic party —and again in the Republican party. In the latter Nixon had gained the kind of state and local organizational support that Goldwater had won in 1964—and he did it the same way: he worked tirelessly at meeting these leaders, giving speeches for them, and helping them raise funds by appearing at their rubber chicken dinners. No other Republican contender gathered very much organizational support. On the Democratic side the organizations were hostile to both Eugene McCarthy and to Robert Kennedy because, at first, no one is supposed to challenge a president in office, and later both were considered unlikely to fit into the easy party molds as both Johnson and Humphrey had shown they

12. *The Deadlock of Democracy, Four Party Politics in America* (Englewood Cliffs, N.J.: Prentice-Hall, Inc., 1963), pp. 236–37.

could. Whatever their showing in the primaries, they were doomed to gain little organizational support. They won primary after primary only to have the organizations begin to play the "property" game, as Norman Mailer called it, when they arrived in Chicago to slaughter the opposition and pick a loser. Let me quote Mailer on the concept of "politics as property":

> Mark it: politics is the hard dealing of hard men over properties; their strength is in dealing and their virility. Back of each negotiator is the magic of his collected properties—the real contention of the negotiation is: whose properties possess the more potent magic? A good politician then can deal with every kind of property-holder but a fanatic, because the fanatic is disembodied from this property. He conceives of his property—and his noble ideal— as existing just as well without him. His magic partakes of the surreal.[13]

So the chief property holders of the convention—those who had organizational stakes back in their respective states—beat the insurgents as soundly in Convention Hall as the Chicago police crushed the dissenting fanatics in the streets. Insurgency was without property value to the brokers playing the game in Chicago—even if rejection of insurgency amounted to conceding the national election to Nixon. For victory with the insurgents would be of no value to organizations that had never trusted the insurgents. (The feeling was mutual.) They gathered in Chicago to pick an almost certain loser who would not jeopardize their property rather than a possible winner who would gain them nothing. As E. E. Schattschneider pointed out nearly thirty years ago, the local or state machine would rather sacrifice a general election victory than to suffer a serious challenge of control in its own bailiwick.[14] In short, the political party may have atrophied considerably in recent decades; in many places it amounts to little and in some places the reformers have nearly taken control; but to conclude the party has no significant effect on the making of key decisions in American policies would be to anticipate something that may but has not yet come to pass.

It is in fact arguable that the national parties have grown somewhat in significance over recent years. There is more conscious organizational effort at the national level, and there is coming to be more and more professionalism in the staffing of a permanent headquarters. As each

13. Norman Mailer, "Miami and Chicago," *Harper's Magazine*, Nov., 1968, p. 81. Subsequently published as *Miami and the Siege of Chicago* (New York: World Publishing, 1968).

14. *Party Government* (New York: Rinehart, 1942), Ch. 7.

presidential election makes one or the other an out party, there is renewed talk of (and some effort toward) creating a more unified central
party apparatus. This always appears as a threat to the Congressional
leadership, and as a consequence the growth of the national organization is always minimal, but there are some signs that gradual growth is
taking place in both parties. At least we are no longer in the situation
where the national party truly exists for only one year in four.

But the real backbone of the party in the United States—unlike most
nations of the world—is not found in the national but in state and local
party organizations. In most political systems of the world it is possible
for the central party organs to assert a considerable amount of discipline over not only local organizations but legislators chosen in regional
districts for the national parliament. This, of course, is not true here. If
there is one trait that sets off American from all other parties it is the
unusual degree of decentralization. Again to quote Schattschneider:

> Decentralization of power is by all odds the most important
> single characteristic of the American major party; more than any-
> thing else this trait distinguishes it from all others. Indeed, once
> this truth is understood, nearly everything else about American
> parties is greatly illuminated.[15]

To say that anything is decentralized in the United States will raise
suspicions, for having heard innumerable dire warnings against the
rising tide of centralization one can hardly believe anything has escaped.
But to a much larger degree than the government itself the parties have
resisted centralizing trends. (Not entirely, as previously noted, but to
a very large degree.) What evidence indicates this? One convenient
place to look is the national conventions. No aspiring presidential
candidate would seek support from his national committee—as a committee it would be irrelevant to his quest. (As powerful local individuals,
the *members* of the committee might merit some deference—but not
because they were on the national committee.) The national chairman
may play the game of an incumbent president and manipulate some
aspects of the convention to favor one faction or another—such as
seating and convention facilities—but this has at best a marginal effect,
and so strong is the tradition that the national chairman and committees
do not involve themselves in substantive issues, that any such manipulation would be done under cloak of absolute denial of any but the most
innocent intent.

The national convention is preeminently a ground for operations of
the individual state and local leaders. One has but to watch a few hours

15. Ibid., p. 129.

of the conventions on television to see the key positions assumed by prominent leaders of state and city organizations. Clearly the agents of all presidential contenders play to these powerful figures—governors, party chairmen, and other prominent local figures. The news media turn to these key leaders and not to the national chairmen for inklings of what the outcome on various issues is likely to be. Delegates are often at the convention only because they were selected to come by local or state leaders and are therefore not likely to respond to any other than those masters' voices. As a scene of serious compromising in pursuit of sufficient unity to win an election, the convention features the give and take of these nonnational leaders. Candidates and their staffers, being aware of the dispersal of power in the convention, are duly respectful of the position of the delegation leaders and therefore treat them gingerly and plead with them for support—or covertly bargain with them for it. At times, insistence on a particular point will lead to some delegates' departing the convention in a huff—notably on the race issue—but usually the differences, however great, can be plastered over somehow in the holy name of victory.

Also indicative of decentralization is the fact that state and local organizations assert whatever control is exerted over the choice of candidates for Congress; this prerogative the central party never assumes. At times the national party will by one means or another encourage a candidate in challenging an incumbent of the opposite party, but they virtually never dare to invade the constituency of an incumbent of their own party to challenge him. For any outside interest to challenge a candidate is to invite a countercampaign charging interference. The late Congressman John E. Rankin, a Negro-baiting haranguer from Mississippi, always made the most of attacks on him by Northern newspapers, and he claimed that they finally beat him by ignoring him in a close primary, thus depriving him of his favorite whipping boy. National party organizations do not enter local contests even when a party member like Rankin causes them much embarrassment; they would like perhaps to be rid of him, but dare not challenge the firm rule that nominations are local matters. Even when Franklin Roosevelt tried to purge some undesirables, from his point of view, he was successful in only one of half a dozen instances, succeeding only in dumping a Democratic Congressman from Roosevelt's own state. (Even so his national chairman, James Farley, thought the purge attempt was against the "rules of the game" and did nothing to help the project along.) [16] Note that this was much more a campaign by a popular chief executive than it was of the party per se.

16. See V. O. Key, Jr., *Politics, Parties, and Pressure Groups* (op. cit.), pp. 443–44.

The national and state and local organizations distrust each other. Financing is part of the trouble, for each needs to reach the same potential contributors. When the Democratic party in the past has tried to make an appeal for small sums of money through peddling "shares" in the Democratic party at campaign time—or related gimmicks, like "Dollars for Democrats"—the local organizations have been suspicious —and in some cases frankly unwilling to participate, even though assured a percentage of the take. Recently when there appeared to be a chance that Congress would pass a statute authorizing federal appropriations to help finance presidential campaigns, it was defeated, in part at least, by fears that the national committee would become too strong and dictate policy to the state organizations. And with some validity, the national organization staff people say in private that many of the state organizations are not to be trusted—either with money or with the responsibility for carrying out a campaign. This mutual distrust arises in part from the basis of power that the local party minions feel they have to protect and the attitude of the national organization toward deviant or independent organizations. When the battle lines are drawn, each sees what is vital to its own interest: the national staff sees as all important the presidential campaign, whereas to state and local organizations the national campaign is important only insofar as it will help elect local and state candidates. More than one presidential candidate has lost and harbored bitter feelings toward state organizations because they not only refused to help but even disassociated their local campaigns from the presidential ones in order to keep from going down with a sinking ship.

The decentralization phenomenon applies not only to the separation of the national party from state and local organizations, but equally the local organizations tend to be independent of state leadership. This varies from state to state, but there is a tendency even in states with fairly potent state organizations for local party leaders to protect their boundaries from outside invasion. Local organizations fight hard to protect their autonomy because they make the most out of their operations if they have to offer no tribute to any other feudal lord who might want to interfere. It is illustrative that back in the days of rampant bossism the battle cry in Brooklyn was that "The Tiger shall not Cross the Bridge," which meant merely that the local Brooklyn bosses would fight to keep the powerful Tammany machine from Manhattan from interfering in Brooklyn Democratic party affairs. Local leaders usually pass this off (piously) as "home rule," or "local control," but any implication that it is popular control was and is frankly bogus. What is involved is local politician control over nominations and especially patronage, not anyone's popular control over anything.

If this is in sharp contrast with nearly all national parties of the world, why has this pattern developed here? That is not an easy question to answer, although one can provide some factors that undoubtedly contributed to decentralization in this country. One can say, for example, that it is a huge nation with widely divergent views and that therefore such scattered party strength is appropriate. But so are Australia and Canada large nations with scattered population and divergent interests (although nothing quite to match the North-South split of the United States—even in the case of Quebec) and in those countries there is decentralization but not as much as in the United States, partly because they have parliamentary not presidential systems. There is, however, far more decentralization in those countries than there is in England and this may suggest that hugeness and diversity may be a contributing factor to decentralization.

There is a federal system here and that too has undoubtedly encouraged decentralization. The party tends to conform to the patterns of the government itself and therefore to become a congeries of parties rather than a single party with a strong national organization. A decentralized party system may therefore be said to follow from the dispersal of power to the states, which organize their own state party organizations independently of the national organization—while also nominally a part of it. This explanation has some value, but it too must be treated with caution, for West Germany and Australia have federal systems and do not begin to have as strongly decentralized parties as exist here.

A more likely explanation of our decentralization is that from the origins of the nation politicians have seen distinct advantages in maintaining local as against central power and they have therefore been unwilling to permit the development of a strong central party. It is unnecessary to demonstrate the jealousy with which the individual states guarded their independence in the early days of the nation's history, nor is it hard to convince anyone why that independence remained a hard fact of political life in the frontier days that followed. The states were physically separate, were allowed by the constitutional system that developed to retain their independence, and they saw every need to hold that independence for political gain—whether it be for slavery in the Southern and border states, or resentment about the War of 1812 for the Northern states. Once the business elite saw the political advantage to be reaped from preventing the exercise of national power by posing state prerogatives as a barrier, the sublime value of federalism and decentralization of authority became apparent. Or consider the South's use of the so-called two-thirds rule in the Democratic national convention: what was it but an attempt to protect their absolute hegemony over the Negro? The South fought hard to retain the rule that no Democratic presidential candidate could be nominated unless he had won two-thirds of the delegate vote, the intent being to give the South a veto on all nominations not acceptable to them. (This power was broken only in 1936 when Roosevelt was an almost certain victor and could afford to ignore the wrath of Southern Democrats.) [17] Thus most of the localism of American parties can be traced to some advantage expected to be reaped from decentralization of authority, rather than being traced to any plan or "decision" to have decentralization.

What then are the consequences for policy making of decentralization? Without going into the various ways in which decentralization of party affects dispersal of authority in Congress—which have obvious consequences for policy—let us examine some other ways in which decentralization has policy results. The decentralization process has facilitated the utilization of the vetoes—political and institutional—that abound in our system. That is, when political groups are driving toward some particular objective and a minority wants to resist, there are various ways in which localism protects the dissenters. (Again this omits the various ways in which party practices defend members of Congress who use vetoes there.) For example, localism is a common defense for those who exercise vetoes and incur displeasure thereby. Local political leaders cry out against outside interference if there is any national attack on users of veto powers. Another example is the permissiveness built into many statutes by which federal aid is provided to the states. Responding to localism, the laws permit wide variations in benefit levels for the needy, or permit states to decide whether or not to provide the indigent with medical care. Thus local politicians are handed on a platter an easy means of sabotaging the national will—and to do so furthermore by merely failing to pass a statute (e.g., in the Medicaid program). Those who press for action in individual states have to mount new publicity campaigns and a completely independent intrastate initiative to inaugurate the program. In short localism and party decentralization are basic and important sources of power for nonnational politicians.

In the past it has been argued often that the United States needs a more centralized party system and more stringent party discipline in Congress in order not to have government by "fits and starts," as some have put it. There is something appealing about this position, suggesting as it does that we might develop the kind of tight party discipline found in parliamentary systems. This might permit a kind of systematic attack on problems that under the system of decentralized parties and dispersed legislative power we can hardly develop. But the develop-

17. See V. O. Key, Jr., *Politics, Parties, and Pressure Groups* (op. cit.), pp. 427–28.

ment of such discipline is, to say the least, a difficult task. Austin Ranney has argued that the failure to develop disciplined parties here can be readily explained: the people have not desired it, whatever the academic arguments in favor of it. Others have argued that disciplined parties are alien to these shores and would do more harm than good, because as an alien idea without indigenous roots here it would be perverted if it were created. Some contend that decentralization and semiparalysis merely reflect the actual divisions existing in the society and therefore are natural phenomena, and furthermore they see value in the delay and frustration of the majority will, which may after all be in error.[18]

Most of the jousting about the lack of discipline in America is highly unrealistic. Whether parties are subject to discipline or not is not a question of absolutes. It is not like pregnancy, which one either is or isn't, but a matter of degrees. Furthermore, it is ridiculous to discuss party discipline as if it had never been experienced in the United States. In many state legislatures there is even now the tightest kind of party regularity—enough to match parliamentary regimes in many instances. But there is and has been little of it at the Congressional level, reflecting the great decentralization of the national parties. And therefore the question is what kind of results would follow from somewhat more party discipline than we now have? (In any event it is clear that there will not soon be strict central party control in this country—too many historical and practical reasons run counter to it.) That question cannot be answered with certainty, of course, for one cannot guess what will follow from such a power shift if it does take place. (And if it does it will not be by some grand act of reform, but by gradual change.) But insofar as the lack of unity in the parties does facilitate the exercise of vetoes by small minorities it can be assumed that greater discipline might make it somewhat easier to form majorities in behalf of legislation. This certainly does not mean that the problems of the veto system would vanish —far from it. For there are other forces that also restrain the easy for-

18. Stephen Bailey has proposed a much stronger national party discipline in his brief pamphlet *The Condition of Our National Political Parities* (New York: Fund for the Republic, 1959). His case concurs generally with the *Report* of the American Political Science Association, "Toward a More Responsible Two-Party System," 1950. Austin Ranney makes his case against centralization and discipline in his *The Doctrine of Responsible Party Government* (Urbana: University of Illinois Press, 1954). Another dissenting view is that of the late Julius Turner, "Responsible Politics: A Dissent from the Floor," *American Political Science Review*, March, 1951, pp. 143–52. A nicely vulnerable attack on the centralizing position—one which says the party system is one of the wonders of American culture and should not be tampered with—is by Edward Banfield, "In Defense of the American Party System," in *Political Parties, U.S.A.*, Robert A. Goldwin, ed. (Chicago: Rand McNally, 1964), pp. 21–39.

mation of majorities. Fear of action on the part of leaders would continue to restrain them from taking the initiative and putting pressure on legislators to go along, as it does in all parliamentary regimes. The diversity of interests and the power of money in politics would not thereby be terminated. Thus it is easy to overestimate the consequences of a greater degree of discipline, but at the same time there seems to be, on the one hand, litle ground for fearing that disaster would follow it (other nations survive it as do many of our states), and, on the other hand, there is reason to believe that it would facilitate, within limits, the formation of majorities and the achievement of leadership control over agendas and gradually concentrate some presently dispersed powers.

Finally, concerning the organization and operations of the parties, how significant is it that there are two major national parties in competition with each other? For it is true that the two parties are competitive over most of the country. Despite its sagging fortunes in recent decades, the Republican party manages somehow to win presidential elections with some frequency. (If we consider the six presidential elections between 1948 and 1968 the two parties have split them evenly.) This evenness of competition exists despite the well-known fact that more voters consider themselves to be Democrats than Republicans. But the important thing is that neither party can assume the opposition does not represent a significant challenge at election time. Below the national level competition is growing also. The sectionalism that once made the South all-Democratic and part of the North and West all-Republican has declined sharply. Maine and Vermont now occasionally vote Democratic whereas Florida and Virginia go Republican.

But even if competition does exist, what is the significance of it? In hard truth, present-day means of investigating such questions cannot provide us with fully satisfactory answers, but some recent research has raised doubts about some hitherto accepted ideas. At one time it was assumed that competition forced the two parties to act as mutual watchdogs on each other. The idea was simply that each party wants ammunition to turn against the opposition and will therefore be on the lookout for any chance to expose the opposition's iniquity. The idea has some validity both because some misdeeds are thus revealed and also because in anticipation of possible discovery some possible misdeeds go undone. Certainly the complete absence of opposition is an invitation to try to get away with political murder, as the sorry record of many one-party systems indicates. But it surely does not follow that competition automatically leads to clean politics. For politicians see that mutual accommodation pays off at the trough of corruption as well as or better than revelation of wrongdoing. The latter is after all a chancy process; one may reveal skulduggery and still lose the election. In Connecticut for years the two parties agreed to use insurance fees for policies written on state property as patronage for whichever party held the controller's office. The money was wasted by mutual consent of the parties, and very likely it would still be thus wasted had not the Republicans been without the controller's office so long that some "do-good" legislators broke the silence. Thus one-partyism may invite corruption because there is no opposition to blow the whistle even if it sees an infraction of the rules. All one has to do is look at the record of corruption in Illinois and Massachusetts to see that the existence of competing parties does not necessarily mean that under-the-table politics will be rooted out. Both states have competitive parties and rampant corruption.

Furthermore at the national level there are many critical matters on which the two parties are in complete agreement. Mine safety regulations are not likely to become a partisan issue for the simple reason that both parties play the game of the coal operators and the UMW leadership and care little or nothing about mine safety. Nor did the cold war or the deepening crisis in Vietnam invite much partisan conflict. These were issues on which there was so much agreement that they were covered by the umbrella of a bipartisan foreign policy or where criticism came it was at the margins of the policy rather than its fundamental fallacies.

The fact that we have two parties and only two in competition has other consequences. One is that the ideological aspects of the parties are subdued and sometimes obscured completely. The logical behavior of a party in a competitive two-party situation is not to take positions that will cost it heavily in votes, and the simple result of this is that each will move toward a median position in order to hold the voters they have and not lose others.[19] Some have said that this leads the two parties to be so similar as to be nearly indistinguishable, which is demonstrably not so. Any measure of the behavior of Democratic and Republican legislators, for example, will indicate the difference between them. Although some Democrats "should be" Republicans and vice versa, the bulk of the two groups are distinctly different. The Tweedledee, Tweedledum argument will hold only if one considers the parties *outside the realms that the parties themselves consider to be relevant.* If one talks of the cold war, "defense" policy, the Federal Bureau of Investigation, or the Central Intelligence Agency, there has been little difference between the parties. On issues that the partisans themselves see to be vital—poverty programs, medicare, labor leglislation, for example—there are visible differences.

19. For an exposition of the logic of this situation see Anthony Downs, *An Economic Theory of Democracy* (New York: Harper, 1957).

It does remain true, however, that the parties do not try to make the most of these differences when the campaigns begin. On civil rights, foreign policy, agriculture policy, or internal security the two parties write platforms and present tons of propaganda to the electorate that minimize differences between the parties by exaggerating the political virtue and vice to an extent believable only by a rabid partisan. In the season when all the cracks are being plastered over, men like Hubert Humphrey will embrace (literally) Governor Lester Maddox of Georgia as a great Democrat, although the two have not the slightest use for each other. Similarly Nixon manages to exude friendliness, at least for publicity purposes, with the full spectrum of Republicanism from Governor Nelson Rockefeller to Senator Strom Thurmond of South Carolina. One is tempted to say, "Oh well, they don't really mean it all, so why does it matter?" But the fact is that the two-party system is dependent upon the smothering of real as well as superficial differences. The person in politics who does not agree with the Vietnam policy or who believes that sending men to the moon is less vital than feeding the hungry will have to subordinate his convictions if he is to be considered a reliable member of the party. To leave the reservation and speak openly for beliefs contrary to those endorsed by the great compromising process is to become in some degree a pariah. Some pariahs make out, and manage to stay alive politically. But when they get into political difficulties the leadership of the major parties are little concerned about bailing them out. As the late Speaker Sam Rayburn said to young members of the House of Representatives, "If you want to get along, you've got to go along."

Another often cited consequence of party competition, of particular interest in this context, is the greater tendency of competitive parties to respond to the needs of the have-not's of society. V. O. Key articulated this previously vague notion, saying that parties that have no competitors will have less inclination to do anything in behalf of those in need for the simple reason that they can easily obscure the responsibility for all governmental acts. Those in a competitive situation, Professor Key reasoned, will seek potential voters who may respond to acts in their behalf, whereas those in a noncompetitive situation may do the bidding of the wealthy and escape responsibility for it because in the absence of clue-giving party labels no one can determine who did (or didn't do) what.[20] On the face of it there is a plausibility to this argument and there is probably a measure of validity to it in practice. For there are clearly situations in which political leaders plead with their

20. V. O. Key, Jr., *Southern Politics* (New York: Alfred A. Knopf, 1949), pp. 190–91.

subordinates in a legislature to enact a particular law so as not to be held responsible for negligence on the next election day.

Some scholars, having subjected this question to searching analysis by comparing the public policy outputs of the states, doubt the validity of Key's hypothesis. They used several measures of the party competitiveness of the states and tested to see whether the more competitive states turned out to have higher levels of payoff for the have-not's than less competitive states. Most of those who went through this effort arrived at the conclusion that certain factors they call socioeconomic development (such as industrialization, income levels, education, and the like) are more determinative of the responsiveness to the poor (on such policies as unemployment compensation and welfare payments) than the extent of party competition.[21] But there are serious difficulties involved in arriving at any certainty about the answer to this puzzle. And the basic reason is that one can never completely separate the influence of party out from other factors that influence the making of policy. That is, it would stand to reason that a wealthy state would be able to pay out more for aid to dependent children and aid to the blind than a poor state. But how is one to determine whether it was the wealth of the state that induced it to pay more than a poor state if the rich state is competitive and the poor one is noncompetitive (which is almost universally true)? In fact one cannot determine with certainty which is *the* cause because the influence of each runs in the same direction and is indistinguishable from the other.[22]

Suffice it to say that there is probably truth in the proposition that competitiveness induces somewhat greater effort to respond to the have-not's of the society. But the impact of this is not clearly ascertainable in the comparative research thus far done, and there is some doubt that it will soon be demonstrated to be either clearly present or absent. What is more probable is that it will become increasingly clear that party must be considered as an integral part of a much more complicated system of decision making rather than an independent factor to be analyzed alone. Whatever the impact of parties on helping the have-not's it is safe to say, however, that the extent of the response has been much

21. Thomas R. Dye, *Politics, Economics and the Public* (Chicago: Rand McNally, 1966) presents the fullest development of this argument yet tried. For further relevant bibliography on the subject and for a critique on the research in the area see "State Party Systems and Policy Outputs" in Oliver Gardeau (ed.) *Political Research and Political Theory* (Cambridge, Mass.: Harvard University Press, 1968), pp. 190–220.

22. In statistics the problem is called multicollinearity—that is, when factors A and B are highly correlated with each other it is impossible to tell whether A or B is the more influential on factor C, because their interrelationship obscures their independent impact.

more limited than the need, for under the most competitive of conditions there are strong counterpressures and ample opportunity to obscure the situation.

Another attribute of competition, it is often claimed, is that the two parties produce democratic results in competition with each other much as (theoretically) industrial competitors do: they do not serve better from any desire to do so but rather in the hope of nudging out their competitors. Thus some say that the importance of party is its contribution to democracy via interparty competition not by way of intraparty "democracy." This proposition assumes that a political party is an instrumentality of its own leadership—an idea that has by no means been universally accepted in this country. But in order to examine this argument it is necessary to examine first the question of what indeed a party is.

(Clarifying the term *party* has been left to this point in the discussion intentionally, for I did not want to ascribe specific traits to parties —by way of my arbitrary definition—and force the whole discussion to follow that conception of party. If we have sacrificed some logical rigor by using the term *party* in a loose fashion in the preceding pages, we have at least invited thought about the proper interpretation to put on the word and we shall now demonstrate that what one considers a pary to be can fundamentally affect one's analysis of its role and potential. To have ruled this out at an earlier stage by the fiat of definition would have lost more to the argument than the gain in precision would have added.)

As noted, anyone who argues that the democratic contribution of parties comes via competition with the opposition, not through internal democracy, perforce will conceive of the party as primarily an organization dominated by its leadership. They do not believe that parties can be described meaningfully as consisting of all those who are in any sense members of it, for party membership is too vague to use analytically. That is, who is a member of a party? Anyone who signs up formally to be such? Then what is the party in a state that does not have formal party registration? Shall we say then that party does not exist in that state? Hardly. Then shall we fall back on those who last voted in a general election or a primary election for the party? Again this is very weak, for the sense of personal involvement is likely to be so minute as to be meaningless.

Others have called parties collections of interest groups, which again is impossible to defend. Interest groups do ally themselves with parties commonly and for obvious reasons. (Here one has confirmation of the proposition that the parties are not identical, for the National Association of Manufacturers is decidedly less congenial toward the Democratic party than is the United Automobile Workers, and so on.) Parties perform different functions entirely from those of an interest group, for the party to some extent must be a broker among interests rather than take on the singularity of concern that characterizes an interest group. Hence the party is happy to have as much help from an interest group as possible, but even George Meany, President of the AFL-CIO, was forced to say, "I don't buy the idea [that] we have to toady along behind any political party." [23] Far from being "composed" of interest groups, the party and the interest groups are at the margins mutually antagonistic and characteristically after different goals, which are pursued by different strategies.

Does that then settle the matter: is the party rightly conceived as being essentially embodied in its leadership? (For one other possible definition of party can be dismissed as too absurd to be considered: that, as Edmund Burke said of British parties, they are groups of like-minded men.) In some situations the leadership-is-the-party definition seems almost to be inevitable. But not always. In some jurisdictions nonregulars can have considerable influence. That is, rebellious groups, holding a threat over the regular leadership through their following in the voting public, can become significant party forces. James Q. Wilson argues in *The Amateur Democrat* that the efforts of reform groups within the Democratic party have not fundamentally altered the party and that the ideological orientation and the lack of skills that commonly are found in reform groups doom them to defeat, sooner or later. Or if they do not go down to defeat they adopt the hard-headed policies of the regulars with regard to patronage and nonideological politics and become the new regulars and not the idealistic reformers.[24] If one grants that reform groups tend to come and go and that the regulars outlast each successive wave of reform, has one then granted that the party leaders are the key element and the reformers so marginal as to be irrelevant? Probably that is not a logical conclusion, if only because the leadership is often forced to take into account the dissenting views of the reformers. Although the reformers may be restricted to small areas of a state, and may tend to have an unusually highly educated membership (given, alas, to talk-politics), this does not mean that the regulars can ignore them. Or they frequently ignore them at their peril.

A reasonable interpretation of the situation might run something like this. First there are some areas where the party leadership is so powerful that dissident groups are marginal at best, and irrelevant in

23. *The New York Times*, Feb. 24, 1966.

24. James Q. Wilson, *The Amateur Democrat* (Chicago: University of Chicago Press, 1962), pp. 364-70.

practice (some Eastern cities—like Jersey City, New Jersey, for example, or Albany, New York). Second, there are other places where the party leadership is in a very strong position, but is ready and willing to hear the dissenting groups—if only because it concludes that the counsel of caution commands it. (John Bailey, Democratic Chairman of Connecticut, for example, or the New York State Democratic party and the New York City reform movement, or the California Democratic leadership and the club movement in that state.) Third, in scattered situations the rebels may take power. Thus in a presidential primary rebels may win and for a period of time control the party. (For instance, the Wisconsin delegation to the 1968 Democratic National Convention, or the Mississippi delegation that displaced the regulars altogether in that convention. In the latter case the dissidents had undertaken one of the hardest counterorganizing campaigns imaginable, against the threat of death at the ultimate, to achieve their power.) If one doubts the significance of the last category consider the resistance of the regulars at the 1968 Democratic Convention who did not want the unit rule banned or the new methods required for selecting delegates. The unit rule change was resisted because that rule permits the neutralization of a dissent element when it does exist (i.e., in a delegation a vote is taken and the majority determines how the whole delegation vote is cast). The modification of the process for selecting delegates was opposed precisely because it would push the states toward more popular participation in the choice of delegates—with, so far as the regulars were concerned, some dangerous implications.

Now it may be, in the sense in which Robert Michels propounded the so-called Iron Law of Oligarchy, that these reformist changes mean nothing fundamental has changed. Michels argued that all groups tend to be run by small cliques, even when the group intends to give the rank and file a chance to participate; by nature, says Michels, the few tend to make the key decisions and the rest follow along unable or unwilling to do otherwise.[25] Thus Michels denies the radical left notion that it is possible to have a truly "participatory democracy" in a huge society. For there is a tendency for any group to be dominated by the outspoken few, the most energetic, the ones with the personality traits that make for leadership. And that tends to be true in political groups especially. (Michels based his conclusions on his study of European socialist parties.) Some kind of leadership is requisite for the conduct of political contests, and in the end significant politics involves contests and strug-

25. *Political Parties: A Sociological Study of the Oligarchical Tendencies of Modern Democracy* (Glencoe, Ill.: The Free Press, 1949)—originally published in 1915.

gles. The reform group thus has leadership even if not the rigid kind that characterizes the old-style political organization.

So, the regulars may not be able to comprehend the ways of the rebels (and vice versa), but they have come to recognize in many areas that the reformers cannot safely be ignored. Therefore the reform groups have modified the pure "politics of property" by moving into the arena with ideology and with insistence on consideration of policy issues as well as patronage and customary political "property." "Democratization" through the primary has not revolutionized the party, but it has brought into the combat arena certain political actors not previously involved. That is, the reformers and their potential allies in the electorate have modified the "pure" theory that the party is just the leadership in the customary sense. The leadership of the party remains important—if for no other reason than as possessors of the formal place on the ballot, which in itself means millions of votes—but it faces a serious challenge by reformists who win (or threaten to win) significant public support. Therefore, the definition of party as leadership is less than satisfactory.

Having reached this point, the question that remains to be dealt with is whether the democratization drive is truly significant or whether the parties actually serve the interests of democracy in the process of competing with each other? Perhaps the best approach is to quote E. E. Schattschneider, who expresses a clear choice on the side of competition—or did at least when *Party Government* was written in 1942. He says the parties are essentially "private" organizations, and frank recognition of this will not make them any more or any less responsive to the needs of the voters. He goes on:

> The parties do not need laws to make them sensitive to the wishes of the voters any more than we need laws compelling merchants to please their customers. The sovereignty of the voter consists in his freedom of choice just as the sovereignty of the consumer in the economic system consists in his freedom to trade in a competitive market. That is enough; little can be added to it by inventing imaginary membership in a fictitious party association. Democracy is not to be found *in* the parties but between the parties.[26]

There are several things wrong with this argument. In the first place laws may indeed be required to force merchants to please their customers—or at least to force the merchant not to poison, endanger, or otherwise harm their customers. (We got significant action on automobile safety only when legislation passed, and the same can be said of pure foods, properly labeled drugs, safe toys, and the like; that is, to

26. Op. cit., p. 60.

the extent that in fact we have achieved these goals!) The sovereignty of the voter is perhaps all too aptly compared with that of the consumer, for the voter may have a choice that is no choice (as many felt was the case in 1968 as they picked—or refused to pick—between Richard Nixon and Hubert Humphrey) just as the consumer may have no choice but to buy a car equipped with yards of flashy chromium and to finance the expensive annual refitting of automobile production facilities in order to produce annual models that differ enough from last year's to put them out of "style." Likewise the sovereign voter has about as much opportunity to escape the relentless barrage of party propaganda that distorts reality and confuses the situation as has the hapless consumer to avoid commercial advertising, for which, worse still, he has to pay.

In short there may not be as much democracy within the party as some wish there were, but it does not follow that efforts to increase it would be unimportant. And the reason is that the parties do not necessarily respond in the simplified way that the consumer's choice allusion suggests. I do not question that the parties, like producers of automobiles, compete with each other and that some salutary consequences follow therefrom. But the pure maximization of the buyer's needs or desires is not necessarily produced by either the parties or the manufacturers. The desire of the producer and the party is to maximize its own self-interest, bowing to the desires of the consumer-voter only (a) insofar as *they* think it useful to do so, or (b) where the consumer has been "programmed" to want something because the producer-party has propagandized him into "wanting" it. Parties, for example, praise themselves for their contribution to "defense" and do not stress the costs to young men who have to fight what many consider anything but wars of defense. The parties help "create" a desire for balanced budgets, low spending for social needs, anti-Communist vigilance, and the like and then supply what is "wanted." In short as blind competition—and production in service thereto—does not necessarily serve the interests of the consumer and the general public, so the self-definition of "important" goals by the parties does not produce a party program responsive to real needs. Party competition may produce a responsiveness to certain dominant interests—the medical profession, oil companies, certain labor unions, or corporate agriculture—but it does not induce the parties to exert themselves for those whose need may be great but whose power to produce official responses is small.

Conclusion: The Responsiveness of Parties

My argument has been that the parties are not truly responsive to many important needs in the community. To some pressures the party responds; to others it is inattentive. Why? There are, it seems to me, many reasons for this, and at least in a summary way the following presents some of them.

In the first place the party is not a latter-day version of "economic man" as the liberal economists postulated him in the nineteenth century. In order to reach the logic of economic relationships, the economists assumed a completely rational being who responded to market forces in predictable ways and with comprehensible results. There are difficulties with this heuristic device even if it also clarifies some things. The same can be said for the creation of a "pure" political agent—as Anthony Downs has done in his *Economic Theory of Democracy*—it may clarify some relationships but it may obscure a significant slice of reality also. For the political party in operational terms is not a free agent who can take a particular course because the payoff will be, theoretically, high. A party is the victim of its own ideological commitments; it has a group of human beings for leaders who have their own values and ideals; the party operates in a world of deals and pressure situations and cannot afford the untrammeled rationality that the model presupposes.

Thus the conventional wisdom of American politics holds that parties do not have any ideological positions but seek the middle of the road in order to win. For that reason many observers were unable to believe what they saw in 1964 when at the Republican Convention ideology appeared to prevail. Still enamored of the conventional wisdom, however, they wrote off the Goldwater blitz as a mere aberration from the normal. But ideological commitments may not be as rare as the hornbook rules suggest. In fact it is only the "minority party" that is forced to play the nonideology game so completely. By "minority party" I mean the party that has slipped to second position in the preferences of voters. (The Republicans have been in that position for a generation—as the Democrats were prior to the 1930's.) The "majority party" can afford a certain ideological orientation—such as the dominant Republicans had with their conservative business orientation during the first thirty years of this century, and such as the Democratic party has had with its more progressive programmatic stance in the years since. (Note: Republicans won all but two presidential elections between 1896 and 1928—and lost one of those because of internal division in the party and the second by the narrowest of margins: 1912 and 1916. Democrats have lost only three times since 1932, twice to a war hero and once because of internal division: 1952, 1956, and 1968. It may therefore be of more than passing interest that the Republican party in 1968 had as national chairman Ray Bliss, whose fame rested on his ability as a nonideological organization specialist.) The out party under these circumstances has to play "me too," angering its more devout conservatives or progressives, depending on the party. In no case, however, is the ideological anchor of the party irrelevant; a party is a product of a past and its behavior is never wholly free of the influence of its heritage, partly because of the ideas in the minds of some leaders (producing resistance to the need to move toward the opposition enough to win), and partly because there are unswerving believers in the ideology of the party and they must be mollified, if possible.

The party is not free to play the purely rational maximizer role for other reasons. It must, for example, finance its campaigns somehow, and the only way it can do that is to have enough satisfied or expectant donors to contribute the needed cash. It was estimated that in 1968 somewhere between $250 million and $275 million was spent in all political campaigns, nearly doubling the amount spent in less than twenty years. That is an imposing sum of money to have to be *solicited*, in view of the fact that the one who gives may have an ulterior motive for his largesse. This is not to say that all money comes from interests that expect a quid pro quo for their help. Some of it comes from persons who give small amounts and have no intention of "buying" anything. And some of it comes from individuals who are not so much seeking a selfish return as desiring—for personal, ideological, or moral reasons—to have a particular candidate or party win. (For example, money is solicited by the Committee for a More Effective Congress—to aid generally liberal members of Congress—but the donors have little or no direct connection with the candidates and feel themselves recompensed if most of those assisted win.)

There are other, less innocent kinds of campaign giving, however. Funds come from all kinds of interests—business, banking, construction contracting, architecture firms, the underworld, labor unions—the list is endless. Some interest groups "invest" in candidates of both parties, not because they have any concern with politics generally but because they are consciously buying access to politicians for their economic concerns.[27] Because this kind of purchase of influence has aroused suspicions about the probity of government generally, some laws have been passed requiring formal reporting of who gave what amounts to whom. The dubious theory behind this is that the reports will be publicized and if the public knows who gave to whom that will provide some kind of restraint on giving for illicit purposes or to ethically dubious ends. But if the gift is an illegal one or ethically dubious such laws can be

27. The subject of money in elections is a complex one that has given rise to a voluminous literature. The classic work in the field is Alexander Heard's *The Costs of Democracy* (Chapel Hill: University of North Carolina Press, 1960). The Citizens' Research Foundation, directed by Herbert Alexander, has turned out a number of excellent pamphlets assaying various aspects of campaign financing.

easily evaded—and they are. Publicity, in any event, is not a very serious threat for giver or recipient. Partly this is because publicity is hard to generate, and the data are presented in such obscure ways that not even the most astute reporter may discern what is being done. The laws also bar specific kinds of donations—such as from unions and corporations. Unions don't spend directly from their treasuries but send shop stewards to put pressure on workers for contributions to "independent" organizations with labor connotations. Similarly no rule prevents the officers of a corporation from giving, and there are ways in which the corporation can see to it that their officers do not "suffer" for their generosity in behalf of a good cause. For example, in 1968 the top officers of Merrill, Lynch, Pierce, Fenner and Smith, Inc., a brokerage house, gave a campaign contribution to a member of the House of Representatives who did not even have a campaign opponent. The Congressman, a Georgian from a one-party district, claimed that he used the money to pay off debts incurred in the 1966 campaign. The corporate officials gave the money through an organization they created for this purpose—called the Effective Government Association—and they refused to talk to reporters about the contribution, saying, "We never wanted any publicity on this." That is an understandable reaction in view of the fact that the Congressman was a member of the House subcommittee that handles legislation affecting the securities industry.[28] Other corporate executives have formed organizations with unrevealing names to make contributions that the law prevents a corporation from making directly.[29] Reports by parties and candidates are filed with the clerk of the House of Representatives to indicate the volume and sources of finances, but there is a great deal of laxity in reporting and virtually no enforcement of the rules. Neither party wants to blow the whistle on the other. In November, 1968, newspapers reported as a straight news story the fact that the Nixon campaign finance report was filed nine days after it was due, and noted that the Justice Department would pass on to the new Attorney General the question of whether criminal liability was involved. The story was at least comic relief from the usual news.

But I hold that the contribution of hundreds of millions of dollars to campaigns does not necessarily mean that the recipients are thereby bought. Some officials may be purchased by the contributions, but the probability is that most are not. In the majority of cases the donor knows from the record what the recipient will do. The contributor

28. "Merrill Lynch Officers Give Money to a House Candidate Who Has No Rival," *The New York Times*, Nov. 3, 1968.

29. "Corporation Executives Contribute to Political Candidates Through Groups with Unrevealing Names," *The New York Times*, Oct. 25, 1968.

merely backs those whom he has reason to believe will act consistently with the donor's views. Crassly to attempt to buy a legislator today would probably infuriate most (but not all) of them, and even insinuations that a legislator should come across because of a contribution might have an opposite effect to what is intended. A little subtlety can go where crudeness cannot.[30] If personal experience is acceptable as evidence I cite the fact that when I once ran for state senator I was given money by labor unions, and, although the labor lobbyists and I often collaborated in the legislature once I was elected, there was never a single occasion on which they "pressured" me to do anything. More important than purchasing then is that the contributor may win access to an official; few would deny that contributions open doors to the mighty.

Apart from the matter of campaign contributions, there are other forces acting on the party. The party and those elected under its aegis are constantly in communication with agents from all manner of special interest groups. So much has been written about the lobbyist that it hardly seems necessary to repeat much of it here; it is obvious that the interest group representative can do many things that help to influence the official to act as desired. We have mentioned campaign contributions, but the process only begins there. There is also the process of providing information to legislators, a process that can be critically important where factual data or persuasive arguments are needed. (And being knowledgeable on his special interest is a stock in trade for the lobbyist.) Many lobbyists and Congressmen (and also bureaucrats) are allies in a common cause, not antagonists. A legislator from a region that specializes in coal production, steel manufacturing, or corn raising is likely to be in constant communication with the relevant lobbyists and to plan strategy in concert with them.[31]

Moreover the sure knowledge on the part of party leaders and officials that they can evade responsibility for actions is an additional reason not to assume the "rational maximizer" role of the abstract theory. The leaders can rest fairly secure in the virtual certainty that the public will never be able to figure out who is responsible for what in the

30. President Eisenhower vetoed a natural gas bill in 1956 after the late Senator Francis Case of South Dakota announced he would vote against the bill because an oil man had offered him a "campaign contribution" of $2,500 (in cash). Eisenhower called the incident "arrogant." See Congressional Quarterly Service, *Congress and the Nation, 1954–1964* (Washington: Congressional Quarterly, 1965), p. 983, for a summary account.

31. On the innumerable ways in which legislators and interest groups collaborate and on interest group operations generally see David B. Truman, *The Governmental Process* (op. cit.).

way of promoting or killing much legislation or setting many policies. There are annual publications of the voting records of parties and legislators, but few bother to read them. One would have to read *The Congressional Record* with great diligence to discover who is responsible for particular actions, and the vast majority of the public has no interest in such minutiae—understandably.

Research on opinions held by party leaders and by the public does not suggest that parties greatly obscure divergences that exist in the public mind. In fact it was shown that there were wider differences between Republican and Democratic politicians (national convention delegates actually) than exist between Democratic and Republican voters.[32] But this is not surprising—nor does it indicate that the parties are therefore agents for the expression of as much difference as exists in the society. In the first place the comparison is between persons of higher than average education and deep political involvement on the one hand and, on the other, a group of average voters whose political antennae naturally are less well tuned. That voters disagree less is certainly no ground for surprise when one takes a further look at opinion and attitude sampling and discovers that voters have less knowledge of political issues generally—and if less opinion why not less divergence thereof? The parties may therefore be said to be guiltless of suppressing conflicts that are felt in an average sampling of voters, but they are not without guilt where the obscuring of issues of great seriousness are concerned. Can there be any questioning—from the evidence presented here and from direct observation—that the parties fail to search for the questions that might be raised by the starving people in the hollows of Appalachia, the Mexican-Americans of out-of-sight shantytowns in Texas, the ailing migrant farm workers somewhere along their trail of labor where home never exists, the welfare mother in the ghetto, the aged caught in the festering slum? There are vital issues for all these classes of people—for the ten million estimated to have seriously deficient diets in this country, as an example—but the party system, like the rest of the political machinery, has no means for focusing on these priorities. Lacking widespread demands on their behalf, lacking powerful agencies or agents to open the way for them, and facing the implacable forces of the veto system, these groups have no way of forcing an issue to become a public issue. For logical reasons that can be deduced from the operations of the political system *an issue for a political party is something that cannot readily be avoided.*

32. Herbert McClosky, et al., "Issue Conflict and Consensus Among Party Leaders and Followers," 54 *American Political Science Review,* 416–27 (1960).

CHAPTER FOUR

Federalism:
An Assessment

W HAT are the consequences of federalism? Does it matter that government is organized federally rather than as a unitary system? Does federalism facilitate or hinder efforts to cope with the kinds of problems discussed here? Granting that it is difficult to answer such questions with precision, there are some more or less clear results of federal operations that are instructive. For example, so long as the Supreme Court acted as the great nay-sayer of Dual Federalism there can be no denying that their reading of the federal agreement constituted a formidable barrier to public action to meet the issues of an industrializing society. But for thirty years the Court has declined to exercise that kind of veto. Does that permissiveness end the importance of federalism? Some right-radicals apparently so believe, and they cry out that the "Constitution is dead"—meaning that government can now do things they dislike. Others see the post-1937 phase of federalism differently; they call it cooperative federalism, by which they mean the federal system has become more an avenue to progress than a set of barriers because the states and nation find means to cooperate with each other.

Neither of these alternative arguments is very persuasive. Although it does matter that the Supreme Court no longer poses the kinds of legal barriers that it did in the past, it by no means follows that federalism involves no limitations on effective action. Federalism remains a formidable barrier. Nor does the admitted emphasis on cooperative relations among governments herald a new day of simplicity in dealing with the chronic problems of unresponsive government. Cooperation is more extensive now than in the pre-New Deal days, but that does not make cooperation either new or universal. From the beginning there was cooperation among the states and between the states and the National government; indeed such cooperation is a precondition of effective federalism.[1] It should not be supposed, however, that the greater degree of cooperation through, for example, grants-in-aid from the federal to the state government has ended the conflicts, confusion, delay, inequity, and tyranny that continue to characterize the federal system.

For make no mistake about it: federalism is not cost free. It is after all a device that permitted and protected the reign of terror and absolute tyranny over the black population of the South. It has been one avenue through which the most appalling inequities in the distribution of benefits has continued. It is the means by which some governments delay, seemingly forever, the application of rules decreed for the whole society—like school desegregation. However valuable federalism may have been in creating a nation that nearly was not capable of being one, however valuable it may have been in diminishing the crushing weight of an enormous national bureaucracy, there are heavy countercosts of federalism to be placed in the balance. First consider the connections between federalism and racism.

Racism and Federalism

William H. Riker in his analysis of federalism argues that

The main beneficiaries [of federalism] throughout American history have been the southern whites, who have been given the freedom to oppress Negroes, first as slaves and later as a depressed caste. Other minorities have from time to time also managed to obtain some of these benefits: e.g., special business interests have been allowed to regulate themselves, especially from about 1890 to 1936. . . . But the significance of federal benefits to economic interests pales beside the significance of benefits to the southern segregationist whites. The judgment to be passed on federalism in the United States is therefore a judgment on the values of segregation and racial oppression.[2]

This is a sweeping generalization and one that it would be supposed political scientists evaluating federalism would have dealt with at some length, for it is certainly a challenging assertion. However, the writers

1. See Daniel Elazar, *The American Partnership: Intergovernmental Cooperation in the Nineteenth Century United States* (Chicago: University of Chicago Press, 1962). See also his useful commentary on the history and character of federalism in his article "Federalism" in the *International Encyclopedia of the Social Sciences* (New York: Macmillan, 1968).

2. *Federalism: Origin, Operation, Significance* (Boston: Little, Brown, 1964), pp. 152–53.

of textbooks and other professional commentators on federalism have had little to say about Riker's assertion. Among the few who have responded to Riker are James MacGregor Burns and Jack Peltason, who reply he may have attributed to federalism difficulties for which it is only partly responsible. They go on:

> We are a nation of continental proportions with a rich variety of sections and groups. Even if the federal form of government were abolished tomorrow, there would still be a South and a New England. Giant capitalists and trade unionists would remain strong, and white supremacists would still oppose the passage and enforcement of civil rights laws. Even without federalism there would be local units of government, and local majorities would use these units to resist national majorities. True, the ideology of states rights and the general support for federalism permit segregationists and others who dominate state governments to work for their goals in the name of local self-government, but such appeals are not unknown in governments that operate under unitary forms. And as far as the constitutional structure of federalism is concerned, today the *national government has all the constitutional power it needs to deal with virtually every problem of national extent.*[3]

In analyzing these two contradictory positions it is well to begin with a reminder that Southern Negroes have existed under tyranny, using the word in a strict sense. (Webster's calls it "very cruel and unjust use of power or authority.") Indeed the tyranny was so total and so malignant that even restrained description of it sounds like exaggeration. Until recently historians have so faithfully followed the apologists for the South in their treatment of the condition of the slave and the freedman that the average American gained no realistic conception of what life for the black man in most of the South has been. The distortions remind one of the totalitarian rewriting of history. For example, many Americans still believe that for some strange reason the Negro played no significant role in the Civil War; that after all is what their history textbooks said. A biographer of General Ulysses S. Grant, writing in 1928, was capable of saying that the

> American negroes (sic) are the only people in the history of the world, so far as I know, that ever became free without any

---

3. *Government By The People*, 6th ed. (Englewood Cliffs, N.J.: Prentice-Hall, Inc., 1966), p. 124. Italics in the original. I am aware of no other analysis of Riker's argument, nor does Riker himself know of any.

effort of their own. . . . They twanged banjos around the railroad stations, sang melodious spirituals, and believed—that some
Yankee would soon come along and give each of them forty acres
and a mule.[4]

Yet over 200,000 blacks served in uniform, over 37,000 lost their lives
in the service, and many were decorated for heroic service. Another
200,000 served in civilian support roles of various kinds. Yet what
comes through from the biographer is more reinforcement for the Black
Sambo image—the grinning fool, deferential and happy with his lot.

That slavery was tyranny not many would now deny, but generations of white Americans, brought up on Uncle Tom legends, failed completely to see slavery as systematic dehumanization. One analyst has
compared the slave system with Nazi concentration camps with respect
to the impact on the personality of the victim: both faced absolute and
total authority and had to adjust to it in whatever ways were available.[5]
While such total debasement of men was being practiced it was possible
for a President in an Inaugural Address to ask, "On whom has oppression fallen in any quarter of our Union? Who has been deprived of any
right, person or property? . . ."[6]

Nor did the coming of emancipation end the tyranny. In some respects
it became worse. The economic interest that the slave owner had in the
survival and physical fitness of slaves was now at an end. Whereas the
wealthy slave owner would previously protect his slaves in his own self-
interest, the newly freed slaves now became unguarded targets for the
fearing and depraved whites who took it on themselves to replace the
controls of slavery with vigilante suppression. The one thing that could
have saved the nation from the worst consequences of slavery—namely
the removal of the vast proportion of Negroes from their Southern oppressors and their relocation on lands being newly opened up in the
West and provided to all white persons who wished to take them—was
a "solution" that had no attraction for the North or the South. The
North did not want the trouble and cost of dealing with the problem and
the South needed black labor on the plantations. (Brief experiments
with imported white labor soon proved to be economically impossible
for the South.) And so the suppression went its way. The records—inadequate but revealing—show that hundreds per year died at the hands
of mobs. Fatuous statements by men like Theodore Roosevelt that the

4. Quoted by James M. McPherson, *The Negro's Civil War* (New York: Random
House, 1965), p. viii.
5. See Stanley M. Elkins, *Slavery* (Chicago: University of Chicago Press, 1959),
Ch. III.
6. *The Writings of James Monroe* (New York: G. P. Putnam, 1902), Vol. 6, p. 7.

lynchings were occasioned by the rape of white women served to dampen any Northern will toward correction of the problem. In an infamous message to Congress Roosevelt decried lynching, but added that it happened so often because of rape, "especially by black men." He then went on to call on Negroes to inform against suspected rapists, notwithstanding that in the same speech he quoted a Georgia governor who spoke of the rescue of innocent Negroes from the hands of mobs. But long before Roosevelt offered that falsehood to Congress, the North had turned over to the South complete control over the lives of Southern blacks. The infamous compromise of 1876 sealed the fate of the black South: the withdrawal of the Army signified to the Southern lyncher and those intent on denying all rights to Negroes that they were to have ample opportunity to complete the job.[7]

Apart from physical violence, however, the South found other means to deny the Negro equality. The law was chief among those means. By statute the Negro was denied, for example, the right to use facilities like public parks; they were forced to ride in Jim Crow train cars, given separate and unequal educational facilities, and by devious statutes denied the right to vote. The statutes were reinforced by a system of intimidation, and thus even the "rights" that Negroes presumably had as United States citizens were suppressed. When they sought to use the judiciary to secure those rights they were threatened with physical violence or economic reprisals. Although laws such as the "Grandfather Clause" formally kept Negroes from the polling place, if any educated Negro should find his way around the legal barriers, there were other devices to discourage him from voting. The common (and alas casual) saying "sweating like a nigger at election" eloquently expressed the norms that prevailed—and in widespread areas of the South still prevail.[8] Neither the law nor the informal intimidation can be adequately evaluated independently from the other. Both were aimed at keeping the Negro down. The following comments written in 1967 by a Negro psychiatrist indicate that legalized intimidation is not merely history:

> Once last year as I was leaving my office in Jackson, Mississippi
> . . . a white policeman yelled, "Hey, boy! Come here!" Somewhat

7. I have forborne to present evidence to sustain my case here, but that is not for lack of evidence. See, for example, Vernon L. Wharton, *The Negro in Mississippi, 1865–1890* (Chapel Hill: The University of North Carolina Press, 1947), or August Meier, *Negro Thought in America, 1880–1915* (Ann Arbor: University of Michigan Press, 1963). By the way, if any Northern reader feels smug about the conditions in the North in the early years I commend to him Leon F. Litwack's *North of Slavery* (Chicago: University of Chicago Press, 1961). Roosevelt's message is in the *Congressional Record* for December 4, 1906, pp. 24–25.

8. See "Political Participation," U.S. Commission on Civil Rights, 1968.

bothered, I retorted: "I'm no boy!" He then rushed at me, snorting, "What d'ja say, boy?" Frightened, I replied, "Dr. Pouissant, I'm a physician." He angrily chuckled and hissed, "What's your first name, boy?" When I hesitated he assumed a threatening stance and clenched his fists. As my heart palpitated, I muttered in profound humiliation, "Alvin."

"Alvin, the next time I call you, you come right away, hear? You hear?" I hesitated. "You hear, boy?" My voice trembling with helplessness, but following my instincts of self-preservation, I answered, "Yes, sir." Now fully satisfied that I had performed and acquiesced to my "boy status," he dismissed me with, "Now, boy, go on and get out of here or next time we'll take you for a little ride down to the station house." [9]

And what discriminatory laws and intimidation did not achieve, dubious court decisions did. The Fourteenth Amendment, passed in order to protect the ex-slave, called for "equal protection under the law," but the judiciary (North and South) simply ignored the command of the Amendment. In decision after decision the courts averted their eyes from reality and permitted the creation of tyranny just as the politicians had previously done in 1876. And note that when the Supreme Court invalidated the Civil Rights Act of 1875, it did so on the grounds of federalism! The Act had provided equal access to certain places of public accommodation for all persons, but the Court denied that Congress had power to pass such legislation, such being the province of the states. Nor was the Court impressed by the unequivocal language of the last clause of the Fourteenth Amendment, which says that "Congress shall have the power to enforce, by appropriate legislation, the provisions of this article." The Court merely held that the Congress had been authorized to pass legislation that would prevent the states from acting to deny the rights of citizens, not to pass laws to bring the equality to fruition by its own effort.[10]

Or consider the notorious *Plessy* v. *Ferguson* decision.[11] This decision was handed down a dozen years after the *Civil Rights* case, and if the Court was anxious to be consistent and show that the Fourteenth Amendment was meant to apply to the states and not Congress—as they had claimed in the *Civil Rights* case—this was their chance. For the case involved a Louisiana law that provided for Jim Crow cars on

9. Alvin Pouissant, "A Negro Psychiatrist Explains the Negro Psyche," *The New York Times Magazine*, Aug. 20, 1967, p. 53.

10. *Civil Rights Cases*, 109 *U.S.* 3 (1883). See Mr. Justice Harlan's logical defense of the statute in his dissenting opinion, however.

11. *Plessy* v. *Ferguson*, 163 *U.S.* 537 (1896).

railroads operating within the state, and it provided criminal penalties for those who refused to abide by segregation. Plessy, one of whose grandparents had been black, which made him all Negro by American standards, refused to accept this humiliation, and appealed his case to the Supreme Court after his conviction. Predictably he lost. In handing down the decision, the Supreme Court revealed the depravity to which the nation had stooped in dealing with the Negro in the South. The white South wailed of its need to control the dangerous blacks and of its need to maintain a stable social situation, and the North heard its erstwhile enemy more clearly than the cries of the suppressed. In this instance, whatever the intent of the law, the Supreme Court wasted no time in finding it a "reasonable" use of the state's police power. The law was intended to promote the public good, and Plessy's claim that this was in some sense invidiously discriminatory was to no avail. Said the Court:

> We consider the underlying fallacy of the plaintiff's [Plessy's] argument to consist in the assumption that the enforced separation of the two races stamps the colored race with a badge of inferiority. If this be so, it is not by reason of anything found in the act, but solely because the colored race chooses to put that construction upon it.

Although the Court did say that "equal" facilities would have to be provided for Negroes, the Court emphasized how futile it was to use the law to establish equality of the races. The latter was a strange argument to employ in a case involving a state law obviously intended to further inequality of the races, but this never apparently occurred to the majority of the Court.

A single member of the Supreme Court dissented from this specious reasoning. Mr. Justice Harlan (it is interesting that he came from a slave-owning Kentucky family in contrast with most of the other justices, who had Northern backgrounds) spoke out as he had in the *Civil Rights* cases. He invoked the highest ideals of the society when he said that

> Our Constitution is color-blind, and neither knows nor tolerates classes among citizens. In respect of civil rights, all citizens are equal before the law. The humblest is the peer of the most powerful. . . . It is, therefore, to be regretted that this high tribunal, the final expositor of the fundamental law of the land, has reached the conclusion that it is competent for a State to regulate the enjoyment by citizens of their civil rights solely upon the basis of race.
> In my opinion, the judgment this day rendered will, in time,

prove to be quite as pernicious as the decision made by this tribunal in the Dred Scott Case. . . .

The arbitrary separation of citizens, on the basis of race, while they are on a public highway, is a badge of servitude wholly inconsistent with the civil freedom and the equality before the law established by the Constitution. . . . The thin disguise of "equal" accommodations for passengers in railroad coaches will not mislead anyone, nor atone for the wrong this day done.

The "wrong" did indeed prove pernicious. It helped place the stamp of inferiority on black men and labeled them irrelevant. How else could anyone read the words of the majority of the Court? Consider their comments about this being a badge of inferiority only if the Negro insisted upon making it so. Why was the law passed? Was it because the whites thought the blacks were a superior group that deserved special status? Was it because they thought the two groups were essentially alike? Neither proposition is remotely applicable. The law was patently based upon the only remaining alternative ground: Negro inferiority. And everyone knew it, including every single member of the Supreme Court, their rationalizations to the contrary notwithstanding. But even Justice Harlan failed to perceive the grossness of the evil done, for he probably would not have assumed that the requirement of "equal" accommodations would be nearly universally ignored for the next half century—as in some respects it is still being ignored. Thus in a hearing, counsel for the U.S. Commission on Civil Rights questioned the Alabama Superintendent of Education about the disparity of white and black schools in an Alabama county—the former valued at $110,000 and the latter at $750. His reply was

Well, I would assume that the building which is assessed for $110,000 is a more expensive building than the one assessed for $750. . . . The state has nothing to do with either one of those buildings. All the plans were promulgated by the local school system. It is a little something that we call democracy and we think it has worked pretty well.[12]

One could cite countless other illustrations. Regarding education, the Supreme Court found that a Georgia county could legally provide a high school for white children and none for black ones.[13] In another case the Court sustained a state law forbidding a private college to run

12. "Cycle to Nowhere," U.S. Commission on Civil Rights (Clearinghouse Publication #14, 1968), p. 13.

13. *Cumming* v. *County Board of Education*, 175 *U.S.* 528 (1899).

an integrated institution.[14] Negroes were systematically excluded from participation in the Democratic primaries in Southern states for at least fifty years, and rather than meet the issue directly the Supreme Court toyed about with the subterfuges of racist politicians. Indeed at one point in a quarter of a century of litigation on the question the Court threw up its hands and admitted defeat by federalism.[15] There are innumerable other cases in which the Court either rejects the black man's claims or gives them the barest support only. Thus the Supreme Court rejected racial zoning of land to provide segregated housing,[16] but when this resulted in the increasing use of the "restricted covenant" (a private agreement to exclude Negroes written into a deed), the Court would go no further than say the courts could not be used to effectuate the agreements; it would not attack the agreements as Negro counsel argued they should.[17]

In all this legal, judicial, and political maneuvering to sustain the tyranny of white over black, federalism has been an important legal resort. This is not to say that federalism "caused" the tyranny. On the contrary it would be more nearly correct to claim that slavery was a prime cause of federalism. In the Constitutional Convention slaveholders perceived the threat to the slave system by Northern meddlers, and they sought and won concessions in the Constitution that would protect not only slavery but local autonomy. Thus they got the specific protections of slavery (inflated representation based upon the rule that a slave, although not a citizen, represented three fifths of a person, agree-

14. *Berea College* v. *Kentucky*, 211 *U.S.* 45 (1908).

15. *Grovey* v. *Townsend*, 295 *U.S.* 45 (1935). That is, the Court admitted that Texas had found a way around the positions taken in earlier decisions. In earlier white primary cases from Texas the Court had invariably found some state action that put the case within the purview of the Fourteenth Amendment, but when Texas left the matter of Negro-exclusion to the Democratic party, the Court surrendered, and held that the party was a private organization and the primary essentially not an "election" within the meaning of the Constitution. That was altered in *Smith* v. *Allwright*, 321 *U.S.* 69 (1944)—but not until nine years after *Grovey*.

16. *Buchanan* v. *Warley*, 245 *U.S.* 60 (1917).

17. *Shelley* v. *Kramer*, 334 *U.S.* 1 (1948). See also Clement Vose, *Caucasians Only* (Berkeley: University of California Press, 1959). For an excellent analysis of the travail of the Negro in the courts, see Loren Miller, *The Petitioners, The Story of the Supreme Court of the United States and the Negro* (New York: World· Publishing, 1966).

The racism of earlier courts is undeniable, but it came as a shock to many to have the Warren Court accused of being "Nine Men in Black Who Think White" (Lewis M. Steel, *The New York Times Magazine*, Oct. 13, 1968). In fact the author of the article so outraged the elders of the NAACP that he was dismissed from that organization's legal staff. Virtually the whole of the remaining legal staff resigned to protest the unfairness of the dismissal.

ment that no law should prohibit the importation of slaves until 1808, and a specific clause to facilitate the return of fugitive slaves), and they also achieved state independence to further sustain the system. That independence became increasingly important to the South as the Abolitionists grew more numerous and insistent. In retrospect it is clear that the independence of the Southern states helped greatly to assure their complete discretion in handling not only the institution of slavery but also the social and economic conditions of the freedman. And once that discretionary power had stood for at least a century and a half, it was and is exceedingly difficult to terminate it, as the history of desegregation (in education, employment, housing, and public accommodations) and the laborious progress toward enfranchising black Southerners so poignantly demonstrate.

Having thus summarily described the suppression and some of the means used to sustain it, let us turn to the specific points of the rebuttal offered by Burns and Peltason to the Riker claim about racism and federalism. They say, first, that even if federalism were absent there would still be a South—that there would still be a history of Southern race relations with all its implications. And they contend that even in the absence of federalism white supremacists would oppose national action to remedy the situation. Furthermore segregationists under any conditions would dominate some local governments and would use the plea of self-government to shield their actions. And finally Burns and Peltason say that adequate national authority exists to deal with "virtually every problem of national extent."

Consider first the argument that historical forces, regardless of federalism, exist and therefore have a political impact. This may or may not be valid, depending upon the extent to which these historical forces and federalism can be separated from each other. It would be a strong argument perhaps if it could convincingly be shown that federalism had contributed nothing to the virulence of the hatreds, the bitterness of interracial feeling. But such a separation is inconceivable. Federalism has existed and it has contributed to the dominance of white over black by offering a rationale for acts of suppression when challenged on constitutional grounds. Can we deny the importance of federalism's contribution to the sanctification of the idea of state independence upon which the South relied to sustain its system of tyranny?

Burns and Peltason claim that pleas would in any event be made for local self-government by white supremacists, who would inevitably control governments in the South. One must grant that it does not require the existence of federalism for the claim to be made, but it does not therefore follow that such claims have the same impact in all systems of government. And the reason has little to do with structure as such; rather it is a question of the mindset of persons who have been socialized by all their political experience to revere the idea of local self-government as a prime value. And how could anyone deny that a history of federalism tends to implant that set of attitudes? Men who are not especially concerned about the Negro one way or the other tend to hear such pleas for local autonomy in the light of their own political values and their expectations about what they would want from the political system if they were the pleaders. And the history of political contesting in this country certainly leaves no doubt that the plea for self-government can be enormously persuasive.

But the plea is not the whole of the question, for federalism also grants formal means of making demands for recognition of local desires. That is, the institutions of federalism and the norms of behavior associated with it offer all kinds of opportunities to do more than make pleas: the local objector is offered all manner of tools with which to resist. Through legal, constitutional, and administrative devices the resister can long delay and sometimes defeat entirely a national decision he detests. I do not mean that resistance cannot be practiced under other forms of government; it can, of course. The point is, however, that federalism provides a special set of weapons for resistance. For example, although it could be expected that school desegregation would be resisted in any kind of governmental setup if antagonism to blacks were as severe as it is in the United States, federalism provides an unusual array of means to resist. Federalism places control over school systems in the hands of state government. That means that the national effort (such as it has been) to end school segregation involves a series of battles, state by state and school district by school district, to achieve its goals. It is true that a small percentage of Negro students in Southern states is now in integrated schools, but it took over a decade for much progress to be made where resistance was firm, and even now (especially when the pressure of denial of grant funds has been used occasionally) much less than a quarter of the black students in the South are in even tokenly integrated schools. Let me illustrate some ways by which the separateness of state educational systems facilitates these delays.

For one thing no central government authority makes appointments to key positions in the school systems of the country as it would if there were a unitary system. There is no direct supervision at all over the state systems by the national government, and all political loyalty of school officials belongs to state or local politicians (used broadly here to include officials and interest groups that might range from the White Citizens Council to the NAACP or the Parent-Teacher Association). State school officials are therefore in a position to do several things to defy the law. First they can rely on their lawyers to provide delay. (Recall that the school desegregation case was decided in 1954 and that enforcement orders were delayed until 1955 by the Court, and further that operational enforcement, unless a state went ahead voluntarily—as some border states did—depended upon further lawsuits.) General orders to desegregate they merely ignored. Second, when directly ordered to act, they could provide a watered down version of a desegregation plan and leave the initiative to local black parents, depending on that to discourage any action. Third, they could put pressures on local schools that did try to desegregate, making them object lessons for other districts. Fourth, they could dawdle along the administrative path and wait until court action forced them to take each step.

It is true that in each dramatic confrontation between the United States government and a state, the "Feds" always win, at least nominally. Governor Orval Faubus did not keep federal troops out of the streets of Little Rock in 1957, in the desegregation of that city's high schools. Governor George Wallace was perhaps making the first steps toward his campaign for the Presidency when he "stood in the school house door" and read his futile message to a federal official at the University of Alabama, but the Negro students entered nevertheless. And Governor Ross Barnett talked a strong fight but had to relent and permit a Negro to enter the University of Mississippi—even though it cost the lives of several persons in a nightlong battle on the campus. But the dramatic confrontations are normally avoided; they are almost certain to be lost, for the states cannot challenge federal power too strongly and hope to prevail. As the irreverent Earle Long is reputed to have asked the arch segregationist Leander Perez, "What are we going to do now that the Feds have got the A-bomb?"

Consider another area of public policy where the Negro is subjected to inequitable treatment: the criminal law. I suppose not many Americans would deny that the Negro did not have anything like equal treatment before the courts of the South in the past; probably some would claim, however, that this has fundamentally changed today. There have been improvements in criminal law process for the Southern Negro (just as there have been in the courts of the North). Some of this unequal treatment is undoubtedly due to white racism and probably would take place whether federalism prevailed or not, but where the courts are self-consciously used as a device to keep the Negro "in his place," federalism does certainly enhance the state's opportunities.[18]

The criminal law is in the first place a highly discretionary phase of the law. That is, the policeman has discretion when he decides whether

18. See Claude Sitton, "When the Southern Negro Goes to Court," *The New York Times Magazine*, Jan. 7, 1962.

to arrest. The prosecutor is free to decide to prosecute or to drop the charges. The judge is more or less lenient in his rulings as his predilections dictate. And of course juries are free to decide as their inclinations determine. (It is significant that a great number of reversals of convictions have now put many Negroes on Southern juries; as a direct result there are fewer convictions of Negroes on doubtful evidence and more convictions of whites for crimes against blacks. Such actions are, however, rare enough still to deserve newspaper headlines.) Although there are possibilities for the reversal of state trials on appeal to the Supreme Court and a means thereby to hold state courts to more exacting standards of justice, this by no means achieves completely equitable application of the criminal law in areas where Negroes are the categoric undercaste. For it is difficult and expensive to appeal cases. And if a white jury finds a white murderer of a black man innocent there is nothing directly the federal courts can do about it, for no appeal is possible. An indictment can be won in federal court on grounds of willful denial of the civil rights of the deceased, but that will require another trial, and if a prejudiced jury again returns an innocent verdict there is again not much that can be done to get justice. It might be said on behalf of federalism that the prejudice is (in these latter examples) a local phenomenon and not directly attributable to federalism. That is true, except that local court systems have independence and encourage that kind of prejudice in juries because prosecutors, judges, and police officials constantly get away with prejudicial behavior as an example for the juror to follow. And there is nothing—except in the most flagrant cases—that the national government can do to affect these independent judicial systems. If there were one judicial system with appointments reflecting a broader orientation than just Mississippi or Alabama, there might be possibilities for affecting the behavior of court officials. (Evidence of this is apparent in the changing behavior of Southern federal judges—a behavior that has altered only when the appointing presidents found it politically wiser not to appoint ardent and irresponsible segregationists to the federal bench.)

Consider one further illustrative case: that of discriminatory welfare systems. The welfare system is a relatively modern device for keeping the Negro in his place. Prejudiced local officials harass families on relief and deny welfare grants to those who are legally entitled, and local agencies have simply not inaugurated federally financed but locally administered programs to aid the starving. These may seem to be extreme statements, but it nevertheless is true that the behavior and the attitude of a welfare recipient can determine whether children will have food to eat. Many a welfare client has had his aid terminated because he dared to vote, to join a civil rights organization, or merely to express his convictions.[19] For example, before the Supreme Court overruled the practice, it was a rule to exclude from aid to dependent children all those families where there was a "substitute father" in the home.[20] That is to say if no father resided with the family and the mother established what was called in the niceties of welfarese a "relationship" with a man, then the assistance could be terminated. Or as the proposition was more vulgarly put by some welfare officials, "If a man wants to play, then let him pay." Ostensibly this was intended to discourage women from having children while on relief, and indeed some welfare officials and legislators seem to be under the illusion that mothers had children *in order to draw the starvation pittance* that is paid for a dependent and needy child. (That suggests a poor knowledge of biology and a worse one of economic motivation.) In any event in Alabama the "substitute father" rule resulted in the removal of some 15,000 children from the rolls between 1964 and 1966, and furthermore applications for aid on behalf of 6,400 more were rejected. Those affected, in one survey of seven representative Alabama counties, were 97 per cent black.[21]

But are these "control" features of the welfare system attributable to federalism? Not all of them, of course. But in a significant number of ways the impact of federalism can be seen. For instance it is partly because the federal system exists that state and local agencies are made the administrative agencies for carrying out national programs. The national government could conduct such programs, but state and local governments are there and have traditionally been the providers of relief—if any. The same deficiencies might appear under any form of government, of course, but the problem is that under a federal system there is a barrier of intergovernmental confusion between the national governmental agency that finances and the local government that carries out the program. If the local agency is prejudiced and is out to conduct a discriminatory program, the capacity of the national officials to prevent it is limited. Even granting that the possibilities for evasion of central office directives are enormous in any bureaucracy, it can hardly be irrelevant that the local officials under the federal system owe

19. The evidence to support these assertions is bountiful, but three sources may be cited: the publication cited above of the Civil Rights Commission: "Cycle to Nowhere," pp. 39–43, and "The Case of Mrs. Sylvester Smith," by Walter Goodman, *The New York Times Magazine*, Aug. 25, 1968, pp. 29ff., and Richard M. Elman, *The Poorhouse State* (New York: Random House, 1966).

20. Twenty-nine states, as of the end of 1968, refused ADC if there was a father at home—even an unemployed one unable to find work. This provides an incentive for a father to desert his children so they can eat. The "substitute" father rule, used by nineteen states, mostly Southern and border states, went further and denied aid if a mother had a too frequent male visitor.

21. See Goodman, op. cit., p. 62.

no allegiance whatever to their "superiors" in the federal office. More-over state options to set welfare levels according to their own value judgments result in wide variations in welfare benefits from one state to another. If the welfare system is bad under the best of circumstances, it is at its worst when further complicated by racial antagonisms pro-tected by federal isolation.

On balance then the Burns-Peltason argument concerning "pleas" for self-government is not very convincing. The federal system en-hances the plea, provides reinforcement for it, offers tools for making local demands effective, and allows myriad ways of avoiding central directives. In short the federal system distributes power in ways ad-vantageous to white supremacists, who apply the yoke of oppres-sion.

What about the next point of the rebuttal—namely that there are always whites who would oppose national corrective legislation, fed-eralism or no. This undoubtedly is true, but Riker was not asking whether it will be difficult under any conditions to rectify the situation —it obviously will—but whether the states have been able to use their independence to assert control. We are concerned, that is to say, pri-marily with what the states do with their independence, not whether national policies of alleviation are readily developed. One may grant that a unitary form of government will not necessarily provide a po-litical atmosphere conducive to action in behalf of the denied. The case of Great Britain is assuredly a relevant example. There, although the black population is small, antagonism toward immigrants from Asia, Africa, and the West Indies has mounted. The British Parliament has full legal authority to pass laws to protect the minority population and, hesitantly, it has to a degree, but more importantly it enacted a policy that eliminated free immigration and imposed a strict quota system. Political pressure in the parliamentary system is potent, as it is in the American government. But it remains true that municipalities and re-gional governments of England have nothing like the opportunities to suppress nonwhites that American states and localities have. And that is the key point concerning federalism; i.e., the question is not whether the absence of federalism would cause racism to vanish, but whether federalism makes it worse.

Finally it is claimed that national authority now exists "to deal with virtually every problem of national extent." It is not entirely clear what Burns and Peltason mean, but presumably they refer to the rela-tive absence of constitutional barriers to the enactment of legislation to deal with broadly national problems concerning the Negro. Again the point may be granted, but it does not reach the substance of the issue. Opportunity to enact legislation does not deal with discriminatory enforcement of the law by states and localities. How does it help the problems of discriminatory application of the criminal law to pass a national law? The state judiciary is independent—by law and by tradition—and although the Supreme Court possesses and has exercised the power to reverse lower court convictions won on unfair grounds, this does not solve the problem. In fact it should be observed that this is one matter of concern to Negroes in which the Supreme Court has long been active. As far back as 1923 the Court had invalidated a conviction that only outwardly provided due process of law for Negroes in an Arkansas trial.[22] There have been numerous subsequent cases of reversal, but the problem persists.

There is one important point concerning racism and federalism that Burns and Peltason do not mention and it is perhaps one of the most significant of them all. It is that federalism does permit action on behalf of Negroes in states where there is a will to do so. Many such laws have been enacted by the states although it would be impossible to attain national majorities for such corrective laws. I am ready to grant that laws against discrimination are not the earthshaking events that their promoters promise and their opponents fear. Laws against discriminatory employment and especially against unfair housing practices are so easily evaded and difficult to apply effectively that their impact has not been revolutionary. Laws against discrimination in places of public accommodation are more difficult to evade, but even in that case a proprietor anxious to exclude the unwanted finds ways of doing so. It is impossible to present an adequate assessment of the significance of these laws in brief compass, partly because so much depends upon how they are administered and because the methods of giving them effect vary enormously across the nation.[23] Suffice it to say that it can hardly be of no significance that dozens of Northern states and cities have enacted laws or ordinances against various forms of discrimination and with varying degrees of success have sought to enforce them. Whatever their shortcomings, these laws have been a resort for many individuals subjected to discrimination; they have served organizations setting out on campaigns to provide open housing or better employment opportunities for minorities; and they have eliminated a great deal of discrimination in public places that until only yesterday was common. As a consequence many thousands have access to housing that otherwise would have been blocked to nonwhites.

One fatuous argument against such laws has been that "you can't

22. *Moore v. Dempsey,* 261 *U.S.* 85, 1923.
23. Elsewhere I have devoted considerable attention to this question; see *Toward Equal Opportunity* (New York: Macmillan, 1968).

legislate morals"—that it is impractical to fight discrimination in this way because discrimination arises in the mind and laws will never change opinions and prejudices. More importantly, however, laws do change behavior. That is, when it becomes contrary to law for a person to deny a Negro a job because of his race, some men will comply with the law even though they do not necessarily agree with it. In other cases landlords are required to accept Negro tenants against their will, and although the law may not change their minds directly it may prove to the landlord that the fears he harbored about integrated housing are false. In short, if behavior tends to follow opinion, so can opinion follow the law, for clearly laws can induce certain behavior and behavior in turn affects opinion.

Politically it has been possible to enact these laws at the state level decades before it was possible to get national majorities for them. During World War II Franklin Roosevelt was pressured into creating a Fair Employment Practices Commission through an executive order, but at the end of the war no amount of presidential push or liberal maneuvering could get Congress to give FEPC statutory status—nor indeed could they keep the Southerners from quashing the whole FEPC operation through an appropriations rider. But Negro political strength, weak though it was, was still sufficient to combine with other allied interests and get fair employment legislation through many state legislatures. By 1955 eleven states in the North and the West had enacted enforceable laws against discrimination in private employment, and many others were to follow in the next decade, so that now a majority of states have such requirements. Most people are unaware that many of these state laws are much more stringent than the federal law finally passed in 1964. For example, the enforcement of the federal law is unusually clumsy; the administrators after finding discrimination in employment cannot order that the practice cease as can be done under most state laws, but must institute a court proceeding. This much then can be said for federalism's positive effect on racism: where some states are ready to act in a nonracist way federalism permits it where a unitary system might not.

On balance, then, federalism appears to have done far more to advance than to retard racist policies in the United States. Does that observation give validity to this concluding comment of William Riker on the subject:

> Thus, if in the United States one approves of Southern white racists, then one should approve of American federalism. If, on the other hand, one disapproves of the values of that privileged minority, one should disapprove of federalism. Thus, if in the

United States one disapproves of racism, one should disapprove of federalism.[24]

If there were nothing more to federalism than its implications for racism, one would have to embrace the conclusion, assuming one agreed with the oppressed more than with the oppressors. But is that all there is to federalism? Obviously not. Therefore I turn to other facets of federalism and defer judgment for the moment.

Is Federalism Worth Saving?

In recent years few have posed the simple question whether federalism is worth saving. There was a time, particularly during the Depression, when the question was asked, but with the worst of that crisis over most Americans ignored the question. Federalism had either become so accepted as to be considered a "given" or so seemingly impregnable as to be beyond attack. Still, it may be worth considering the implications of federalism, whether it is possible to replace it or not. In cold truth it probably cannot be terminated short of a complete revolution, but that should not obscure the fact that it constantly is changing, gradually and inevitably. And therefore it may be worthwhile to raise the question of its ultimate value, because inevitably the nation must make innumerable decisions that go in the direction of fortifying or alternatively undercutting federalism.

One person who posed the hard question and gave a characteristically assured answer was Harold J. Laski. Laski, a British political scientist who was a confidante of many American political figures, had no use for federalism. Just before World War II when the United States was still struggling to find answers to the Depression, he dismissed federalism as

> insufficiently positive in character; it does not provide for sufficient rapidity of action; it inhibits the emergence of necessary standards of uniformity; it relies upon compacts and compromises which take insufficient account of the urgent category of time; it leaves the backward areas a restraint, at once parasitic and poisonous, on those which seek to move forward. . . .[25]

In Laski's view the states were no match for giant corporations whose economic power could not be matched by the scattered authority of the divided states, whereas the united power of the nation might at least offer a chance.

24. Op. cit., p. 155.
25. "The Obsolescence of Federalism," *The New Republic*, May 3, 1939, p. 367.

The indictment does not end there. Other criticisms of federalism, implicitly (or occasionally explicitly) raised by reformers, include the following.

1. That the states are inept, corrupt, and ill-organized to cope with contemporary problems that know no state boundaries.
2. That the states are naturally in conflict with each other and therefore unable to mount attacks on problems.
3. That the economic inequalities of the states imposes unjust variations in benefits to the people.

In all these attacks, it is assumed that the independence afforded the states by federalism invites the evils cited, and it appears to be the assumption that if the states lacked that independence it would be feasible to end the problems by unified government. These assumptions are not entirely well founded, but we shall not let doubts about the assumptions forestall assessment of the validity of the evil, for assuredly our capacity to arrive at certainty in this area demands an inclusive approach.

Consider first the charge of ineptitude, corruption, and poor organization. In the beginning one has the lingering history of utter corruption that has characterized state government frequently in the past, and evidence keeps cropping up to suggest that this is not just a matter of history. Although there is little of the flamboyant style of wholesale bribery that once was common in state capitals, there is enough criminal influence, enough conflict of interest, and occasionally enough outright bribery to tarnish the image of state government. Now and then an official goes to jail for boodling, but prosecutions are widely believed to be much less frequent than warranted. Thus, much of the literature condemning these malpractices is more suggestive than specific: it is accusatory in tone but often unable to provide conclusive evidence. There are innumerable reasons why the evidence is elusive. Men whose livelihoods are tied up in politics often go to great lengths either not to see what is going on or, if they see it, find ways of rationalizing it even if they themselves are not profiting from it. A clublike camaraderie develops among legislators, for example, that induces them to close ranks when under attack. They will say that anything unsavory going on in the legislature is peanuts compared to what goes on in business offices, that conflicts of interest are difficult to define and usually involve no more than the accused's having special knowledge and competence in the subject matter in question, which he uses for the public benefit as well as (perhaps) private gain, and that anyhow newspapermen exaggerate.

The case of the Mafia's influence in New Jersey will perhaps be illustrative. (New Jersey is far from being the worst example, however; the legislatures of Illinois, Texas, and Rhode Island—among others—have sadder reputations than New Jersey's: the example is chosen partly because it perfectly illustrates the difficulty of dealing with the problem.[26] Late in 1968 a young New Jersey assistant attorney general, William J. Brennan, assigned to probe the influence of organized crime in the state, made the frank assertion to a gathering of newspapermen (of all people!) that there were some state legislators who were "too comfortable with members of organized crime." Ultimately he named six members of the legislature, and a seventh was cited otherwise who reputedly had some association with a Mafia leader. In some instances the association was a lawyer-client relationship, in others closer connections were alleged. Members of the legislature immediately cried "foul" and said that all their reputations had been tainted by the charges, and for about a week there were three-sided maneuvers among leaders of the Republican-dominated legislature, the Democratic governor and attorney general, and the press, who kept the pressure on by digging out parts of the story and forcing revelation of more than the other participants liked.

Brennan, called before a specially selected legislative investigative committee, was castigated for making charges on the basis of "flimsy" evidence—a charge that the New Jersey American Civil Liberties Union in effect amplified in a collateral attack on Brennan (himself an ardent civil libertarian). The ACLU berated Brennan particularly for making accusations on the basis of guilt by association and on grounds of lawyer-client relationships between legislators and racketeers. Brennan was, of course, facing the standard difficulty in such situations. The influence of the criminal world is exceedingly hard to pinpoint: the gangsters have friends in the right places, they have power and money to protect their position, and therefore convincing evidence on them is hard to produce. All this leads some to say: sure, the reason it is hard to prove is that it isn't there, but that isn't very convincing either in the face of the fact that racketeers are not only present but numerous in New Jersey. Some say their numbers are due in part to Prohibition, claiming that New Jersey's indented seashore adjacent to densely populated areas invited the gangs as a "service" industry. Others add that the state has also been a haven for New York City's mobsters—when the

26. See, for example, Paul Simon, "The Illinois Legislature: A Study in Corruption," *Harpers Magazine*, Sept. 1965, pp. 125ff.; Duane Lockard, *New England State Politics* (Princeton: Princeton University Press, 1959), Ch. 8. The New Jersey Story can be found in *The New York Times* with nearly daily stories during December, 1968, and January, 1969.

heat is on they merely retreat across the river. But however they got there, the evidence of their existence is too strong to ignore. That they have had considerable influence in many city halls and with many police forces can hardly be denied—but proving it remains difficult. A reporter for *The New York Times,* Martin Arnold, wrote the following from Trenton, the state capital, during the flurry of investigation, charge, and countercharge, about the Mafia:

> New Jersey officials generally concede that every major racket in the state—gambling, loan-sharking, narcotics—is run by the Mafia. But speaking to the officials about the situation is like talking to a man who cheats on his income tax. The cheater's response is, everyone cheats—so why can't I? Here the immediate response is, the Mafia is all over—so why single out New Jersey?
>
> The other afternoon . . . in a room off the Assembly chamber, one state law enforcement officer summed up the situation this way: "I've got a mortgage to pay off, so I've stopped fighting. Look, I'm a good guy. I'm for the good guys. I want to see the bad guys put in jail, like everyone else does. We don't want to rock the boat. There are too many good guys in it. We'd all go down together. I guess you could say we're all part of the same establishment, the criminals and law enforcement."
>
> What he was saying, he conceded, was that many perfectly honest law enforcement officials find it easier—or more "comfortable" to use Mr. Brennan's phrase—to seek an entente with organized crime; not a way but peaceful co-existence. Don't be too blatant and we won't be too tough.[27]

Confirmation of the deep involvement of the Mafia in New Jersey public affairs came in less than six months when the U.S. Attorney for the State released a thirteen-volume record of bugged conversations in the office of the Mafia's reputed leader in New Jersey. The FBI had placed a secret microphone in the office of the suspect and taped every word said for three years; the record was filled with discussion of murder, bribery, and other crimes.[28] The reactions of the Brennan charges were probably typical. Some thought this demonstrated well the prevalence of the Mafia in politics and the tentativeness of the proof was no deterrent to that conclusion.

27. "A Racketeer-Infested Garden State," *The New York Times,* Jan. 8, 1969.

28. The story unfolded in two long series of articles in *The New York Times* and the Newark *Evening News* beginning June 11, 1969. Later a large number of Newark officials were indicted for corruption—including the mayor and most of the city councilmen.

Some paid little attention to the affair and very likely that would be true of most residents of the state—one reason why some politicians merely shrug off such disclosures. Still others take the position that, even assuming no law was broken, at least a major threat to the integrity of the state's politics is involved when officials associate with gangland leaders. That is, the person in public life is expected not only to remain "pure" in his public and private life but also to preclude suspicion that he failed to do so.

Such is the objective of those who press for rules against conflict of interest by public officials, but the difficulty of achieving their goal is to be found partly in the fact that officials do not like to live by higher standards than would apply to others. Most state legislators are hesitant about enacting stringent conflict-of-interest rules, partly because one of the most difficult aspects of the rules concerns lawyer-legislators who want to represent all clients but might be barred from it by a strict conflict-of-interest rule. Thus the *Newark News* editorialized about the Brennan affair:

> A lawyer's door, we are assured, is always open to all comers. Of course, this is accepted where the lawyer is engaged in private practice; it does not go down when the lawyer forsakes privacy for public life as a legislative-lawyer. Here the public is entitled to know the facts and circumstances of such relationships.[29]

To summarize: the charge that state government is corrupt is difficult to deny but also difficult to prove. Proof comes only in the flagrant instances, but the uneasy feeling that there is improper influence persists partly because of the lack of rules on conflict of interest, although the reasons for the lack of such rules only reflect the political climate that prevails in state government. Suffice it to say that certainly not all states are alike with respect to corruption and not all legislators are corrupt (nor perhaps even most of them) in states where corruption has been found. There is enough of it in enough places, however, to lend credence to the charge.

But how much of the evil is attributable to federalism? In the first place, there are also flagrant conflicts of interest in national government —in Congress and in national administration. It may be true that federal officials commit proportionately fewer law violations than do state officials, but even this (though widely believed, apparently) would be hard to demonstrate in view of the lack of hard evidence. But assuming it to be true, does federalism contribute to state and local corruption? The isolation of state politics and the absence of adequate administrative checks on behavior have no doubt encouraged state corruption.

29. "Elastic Ethics," *Newark Sunday News, Jan. 12, 1969.*

That is, the state is relatively autonomous, and if there is not much political opposition in a given state—and in many there is little—the opportunities for boodling are considerable. And, be it noted, if politicians of opposite parties decide there is more profit in mutual malfeasance than in "telling," then the boodle game will go on whether a state has competitive parties or not. Still the fact that so many state programs receive grants-in-aid from the United States government has opened their books to federal auditors. In the opinion of some observers this may be the most significant effect of the widespread use of grant programs, for in the not too remote past state and local programs were often almost without audit and the opportunities for graft were rampant. Not that the federal audit eliminates all dubious business; it may, however, make it more difficult to conceal and therefore make it a little less prevalent.

In short, there is corruption at the state and local level, and it does seem on the whole to be at least not impeded by the existence of state independence. However, an indeterminable amount of skullduggery probably would take place if federalism did not exist. That is, corruption is more likely to be the product of moral and social conditions in a community rather than of political structure. Whether unitary governmental structure would result in less corrupt government is at best an unproved case. And probably it is an unprovable case, because if unitary government were to supplant federalism it would be impossible to say whether the structural change was the cause of the reduction of corruption (assuming it could be measured) because so many other changes would have taken place simultaneously. Hence: case not proved.

Is state government inept in handling its problems? (Given the wide range of variation among state governments—from quite good to terrible—this is not exactly an easy question to deal with. But let us assume that some kind of state averaging out can be achieved for the sake of analysis.) For one thing, the states are accused of failing in the one thing that their defenders have long touted them for: being experimental laboratories for each other and for the national government. It is usually pointed out that in Wisconsin there was early experimenting with social security programs, but that in more recent years it has been the national government that has taken the lead in innovation, often by providing the states with cash to take on new projects that Washington has proposed. A more precise accounting of actual state innovation than has ever been undertaken would be helpful in assessing this question, but it does not seem that the states on the whole have been very active experiment stations. But some innovation has come from that quarter, contrary to some arguments. In civil rights legislation, as observed before, the states of the North and the West have done more pioneering than the United States government. Indeed all the civil rights laws enacted by the United States in the mid 1960's was first experimented with in the states.

Nevertheless it has been the Federal Government that provided recent innovations in such areas as health care, water pollution programs, highway safety, law enforcement, educational integration, antipoverty programs, and urban renewal. More modest recent state innovations have concerned housing, urban and regional planning, transportation, and water resources development.

But on the whole the Federal Government has been more innovative than the states in recent decades. What does that imply? That the states are politically moribund and incapable of innovating? That state political leaders are unable to fight off the forces of inaction? Not necessarily, although it does mean just that in some states and in all to some degree. More of the difference is to be accounted for by the differences in federal and state fiscal positions. Whereas the United States is a self-sufficient economic system that can borrow from itself when it needs development funds, the states are in no such position. They, like a debtor nation, are in the position of having to borrow from outside. The United States is in the position of being able to *reduce its tax rate* and thereby stimulate economic activity to such an extent that its revenue intake goes up instead of down. The states, despite overall economic growth, have been forced to resort to higher rates and new taxes to provide demanded services and governmental functions. (Granted, the competition of the states with each other has also forestalled new taxes to meet needs or to innovate, but that issue may be held aside for a moment for later consideration.) How much fiscal problems in the states reduce the capacity to innovate it is difficult to know, but it must be a factor of some significance.

The states are also claimed to be ill-organized to deliver public policies appropriate to needs. This usually refers to the overall administrative organization of state government. (It used to refer also to the malapportionment of the legislature, but since the Supreme Court mandated equitable representation in the state legislature and the states, either by constitutional conventions or other amendment procedures, have reapportioned, that is not a serious problem.)[30] Numerous study commissions, reporting to the states during the years since World War II, have called for rationalizing or "modernizing" state administration, stressing the need for greater efficiency and a saving of money. The standard reform plan gives the governor better control over state gov-

---

30. See *Baker* v. *Carr*, 364 *U.S.* 339 (1960), which opened this issue, and *Reynolds* v. *Sims*, 337 *U.S.* 533 (1964), which said that both houses of a state's legislature must be fairly apportioned.

ernment by placing all agencies within departments whose heads are appointed and removable by the governor. There have been other streamlining proposals, but executive control has been the heart of the issue. Invariably these proposals face trouble in the legislature when the proponents try to demonstrate that their ideas will save money. Also legislators have been jealous of the governor and often unwilling to grant him such authority. Thus in most states the "modernization" has not taken place—or on only a limited basis. Hence the charges about ill-organized states.

But the issue is not that simple. It is exceedingly difficult to pinpoint the reasons why a political system is or is not responsive and effective in its operations, and attributing ineffectiveness primarily to governmental structure is dubious. Some states with apparently "weak" governors appear to have fairly effective executive branches; others with model arangements grind out pitifully small results. The matter is too involved to discuss fully here, but suffice it to say there would seem to be reason to believe that the political climate of the state is as important for determining its policy output as its structure—if indeed not much more so.[31]

Reformers often call for other nonstructural changes that they think would further strengthen the governor. The Commission on Intergovernmental Relations, for example, has urged the elimination of restraints on the policy-making authority of the state legislature, the reduction of the clutter of detail in state constitutions, the improvement of legislative operations (through longer sessions, the provision of professional staff, higher legislative salaries), and similar rationalizations of the governmental process. No doubt all these changes would be of some importance for improving the operations of state government, but it would be a serious error to assume that they would revolutionize the responsiveness of state government. Such changes would be of only marginal importance if the political climate were such as to stifle initiative or so long as the financial resources are inadequate. Thus my argument is not that the reforms are irrelevant, but that they probably would aid the states less than is often believed.[32]

31. The insatiably curious may want to read my further comments on this question in *The Politics of State and Local Government*, 2nd ed. (New York: Macmillan, 1969), Ch. 12–14. For an interesting assessment of the variations in state organization see Joseph Schlesinger, "The Politics of the Executive," in *Politics 'in the American States*, Herbert Jacob and Kenneth Vines, eds. (Boston: Little Brown, 1965), pp. 207–38.

32. See, for example, *The Report* of the Commission on Intergovernmental Relations (Washington; U.S. Government Printing Office, 1955) and an even more naïve argument for reform presented by the Committee for Economic Development in its *Modernizing State Government* (New York: Committee for Economic Development, 1967).

In a more significant sense the states are ill-organized to do their job: namely their boundaries often make no sense. Metropolitan areas around the nation are often split by state boundaries, and it becomes difficult, to say the least, for the legislatures of the states to act in concert on the complex problems of their common metropolitan areas. Rivalry between parts of metropolitan areas is standard, and the resulting sand in the gears *within* a state when a metropolitan area lies in one state is serious enough; when two or three states are involved, collective action may be piecemeal, halting, or impossible. In matters of taxation, transportation, water supply, and air pollution there are some interstate compacts, but often the compacts arrive only after the states involved have faced a crisis of some kind. (The Delaware River Compact, for example, came into being when a drought frightened the parched states of New York, New Jersey, Pennsylvania, and Delaware into the creation of an agency to develop rational water resource policies for the threatened Philadelphia and New York metropolitan regions.)

In matters of transportation planning, however, the states have great difficulty in collaborating because of the economic and social importance of transportation. That is, a transportation decision (the location of arterial highways, for example) determines much more than highway location: it affects industrial location, other transportation networks, housing policy, taxation, zoning, and more. Accordingly, transportation planning and development become infinitely complicated—especially so if more than one state is involved. Thus the Port of New York Authority was created in 1921 in part to provide transportation planning for the New York Metropolitan region. The Authority has played a very small role in planning and a very large one in the development of airports and of major bridges to serve rubber-tired traffic. The states of New York and New Jersey have nominal control over the Authority because they created it and because its minutes are subject to review by the respective governors of the states. But the Authority has carved out an area of independence within which it operates pretty much at will. But what it cannot—or at least does not—do is to provide any kind of overall planning for metropolitan regional transportation. It is one of the giant powers in the region (it has an annual budget over half a billion dollars) and therefore battles for interests it has acquired over the years. It is revealing that the states have not been able to use the PNYA for planning and that it has become a quasi-independent transportation giant in the region.

Apart from metropolitan areas, boundaries of states may also make no sense. Boundaries are lines drawn arbitrarily by surveyors in many instances, or they may follow rivers. But a river is usually not the natural divider it was in an earlier age, and arbitrary lines on a map may not reflect mountain ranges, transportation systems, agricultural areas, or other natural or man-made areal patterns. Redrawing the lines would provide no answer, for most alternative ways of dividing the states would produce equally complex and unsatisfactory patterns. One may grant that the drawing of boundaries between administrative areas in a national governmental system will face the same kinds of problems—some kinds of overlap and non-fit will inevitably occur. But in the latter case there need not be uniformity of areas for numerous purposes. If water, recreation, or health problems require different district lines, they can be constructed by mere fiat—or at worst by legislation. State boundaries are not only inflexible but uniform for all matters. One cannot say with much certainty how much cumbersomeness and inefficiency is involved in these arbitrary boundaries, but at least some must be.

So to the charge of poor organization there is a mixed conclusion. In overall administrative organization and in some broad constitutional respects there are shortcomings in state government, but they probably are not as important as the political climate of a state in determining its capacity to govern. Where state boundary lines artificially divide metropolitan areas or other functional areas and result in confusion and working at cross-purposes, there is no doubt some validity to the charge. A simpler national administrative system would no doubt be more adaptable to socioeconomic factors as they exist or change over time—at least as compared to the inflexible and arbitrary state boundaries.

Another charge against the states is that they are so much in competition with each other that they cannot cooperate to achieve their common goals, resolve their conflicts sensibly, or even achieve reasonable uniformity where needed. The states do compete in innumerable ways, and one major point of competition is taxation. Every state's officials are anxious to attract and hold industry for the employment of the population and the wealth of the whole state, and business taxes are often cited as a factor in determining the location or relocation of industry. To some degree the importance of taxes tends to be exaggerated in the rhetoric of business spokesmen, who naturally wish to maximize return on investment by holding tax payments to the minimum. Politicians who wish to raise taxes to provide services in a state therefore face a hazard beyond the normal expectations of voter reaction: they must face a hazard beyond the normal expectations of voter reaction: they must face the possibility that the next time a plant moves away it will be claimed it was because of the tax load. Because some states with high taxes also are attractive to industry, and because many of the industries attracted to states with special tax incentives are often businesses of a marginal character, it would appear that this argument would have little effect on those who have to make tax decisions. Nevertheless the argument does have appeal. Part of the appeal may be to legislators who would not have voted for tax raises on any ground, but when the issue is given great fanfare—especially in view of the political dangers that surround taxation—it can have considerable impact.

But taxation is not the only basis of interstate competition. States also vie with each other to attract business with other concessions—such as antilabor laws, the provision of subsidized buildings, severe restraints on public spending so as to hold taxes down, and limitations on regulatory activity. All these are advertised widely as evidence of a "friendly" attitude toward business. Competition between states can also arise over such matters as highway location, water resources, and liquor and cigarette tax evasion. Thus it took years before the southern New England states could reach agreement in order to collaborate in shoring up the sagging New Haven Railroad. States disagree about the location of highways, each preferring separate routes, with the result that in more than one case multilane highways debouch at the border of a state into a narrow road, whereas the reverse is true some miles away.[33]

In sum it must be said that this competition has served favored economic interests well. It has served to keep regulatory actions at a minimum and helped reduce expenditures for public purposes. Thus industry's advantages from federalism did not end with the change of heart of the Supreme Court in 1937 (as Riker seems to say implicitly). Moreover the states in their petty (or serious) competition with each other may make a bad situation worse. That is, one might expect even in the absence of federalism that there would be conflict between center city and suburbs, between agricultural areas and cities over water supplies (as there has been in the West), but these differences might be more manageable in the absence of state independence.

It is true that the states have adopted many interstate compacts intended to promote cooperation. More than one hundred compacts have been ratified and they deal with subjects ranging from the interstate rendition of fugitives to water supply and water pollution, and even problems of education. It is possible to overstress these compacts, however, for at best they are but minor palliatives when the real battles begin between competing states. Their imporance has been greater where economic competition has been unimportant. They have pro-

33. This silly game was played between Rhode Island and Connecticut a few few years ago and as a consequence the Federal Government refused to contribute to Connecticut's part of the highway until it agreed to extend the Connecticut Turnpike to the southern part of Rhode Island.

vided means for cooperation on programs such as the provision of higher education among the southwestern and the New England states and for education generally through the Compact for Education of 1966, which had thirty-eight member states as of 1968. It is true that the Education Commission of the States (established under the Compact) has no operational power, but as a forum for exchange of ideas, as a place for interstate cooperation on technical matters, and a forum for political promotion of education, the Commission has some importance.

Is it important that the states have been incapable of enacting uniform laws in areas where such might be useful? That depends upon the importance one attaches to uniformity in various areas. For uniform laws to prevail in all matters of commercial law—which they do not—may be of considerable importance to business. This is no doubt shown by the fact that some of the leading successes of the National Conference of the Commissioners on Uniform Law have been in the commercial law field. But the Commissioners have in the years of their existence since 1892 proposed some one hundred uniform statutes, and in a great many areas their efforts have been barren. There remain vexing differences in many state laws—for example, concerning inheritances, motor vehicle and trucking regulations, and divorce law. How much of a problem these differences create for businesses and individuals is hard to say, but they certainly do not facilitate matters and they do lead to some handsome legal fees.

Exchanges of information among officials of states is widespread and is highly organized through associations of various kinds. Conferences are regularly held for governors, attorneys general, legislators, and many others, including parole officers, welfare officials, and even a conference of officials associated with interstate agencies. Many of these organizations are associated with the Council on State Governments, which provides not only an umbrella organization for them all but publishes information on state government problems generally.[34] Because the states tend to imitate each other, there is no doubt that these conferences of officials facilitate the exchange of information and ideas. But it seems to me that this is a small palliative for the problems of disuniformity that federalism invites.

A final charge leveled against the states is that their artificial boundaries and great inequities in wealth result in wide variations in benefits paid to persons, thus increasing the differences that otherwise are serious enough among the states. As Table IV-1 indicates, there are enormous variations in the average per capita income among the states,

34. See the biennial publication, *The Book of the States* (Chicago: The Council of State Governments).

TABLE IV-1.
PER CAPITA PERSONAL INCOME BY STATES, 1967

Connecticut	$3,865	Missouri	2,993
New York	3,726	Nebraska	2,938
Illinois	3,725	Florida	2,796
Delaware	3,700	Virginia	2,776
California	3,660	Vermont	2,775
Maryland	3,434	Montana	2,759
Michigan	3,393	Texas	2,704
Hawaii	3,326	Arizona	2,681
Indiana	3,241	Oklahoma	2,623
Rhode Island	3,238	Maine	2,620
Alaska	$3,629	Utah	$2,617
Nevada	3,626	Idaho	2,608
New Jersey	3,624	South Dakota	2,550
Massachusetts	3,488	Georgia	2,513
Washington	3,481	North Dakota	2,485
Ohio	3,212	New Mexico	2,462
Wisconsin	3,153	Louisiana	2,445
Pennsylvania	3,149	North Carolina	2,396
Minnesota	3,111	Kentucky	2,387
Iowa	3,093	Tennessee	2,369
Colorado	$3,086	West Virginia	2,341
Oregon	3,055	South Carolina	2,167
New Hampshire	3,019	Alabama	2,166
Kansas	3,009	Arkansas	2,090
Wyoming	2,997	Mississippi	1,895

SOURCE: Bureau of the Census, *Statistical Abstract of the U.S., 1968* (Washington: U.S. Government Printing Office, 1968), p. 322.

amounting to a two-to-one disparity at the extremes. Although the Federal Government helps to finance many programs that help the impoverished—such as welfare, housing, and education—the amounts expended by the states still vary enormously. This is partly because of the incapacity of the less wealthy states to provide supplementary funds to add to the federal grants and make the payments and expenditures more nearly uniform across the country. But it is also because some states that could provide supplemental funds simply do not choose to do so; some less well-off states surpass their wealthier sister state—as Tables IV-2 and IV-3 show. Note that two states paying higher amounts for welfare are not among the wealthiest fifteen states. Note also the wide range variations in welfare expenditures and in expenditures for education. The incongruous result is that where need is greatest the least is done to assist.

This is a matter of concern because it means that families are pressed to the edge of starvation because states provide too little to live on. It is a matter of concern that families can afford no medical attention because of inadequate welfare payments. It is a matter of concern when some states spend so little for education, resulting in the waste of countless lives because they will not be even remotely prepared to compete for employment in the technological world of the present, not to say the future. Nor are these merely local matters of no particular national concern. They are of national interest because those who are pushed off the cotton land by the cottonpicking machine or by other conditions in the South migrate to Los Angeles, Chicago, or Newark, bringing all their problems with them. If they are incapable of reading, they are unemployable in today's economy, and that becomes not only their per-

TABLE IV-2.

AVERAGE MONTHLY PAYMENTS FOR PUBLIC ASSISTANCE
FOR SELECTED STATES, 1967

| | *Average Monthly Payment* | | |
States	*Old Age*	*Aid to Dependent Children* *	*General Assistance*
California	105	181	74
Iowa	104	193	NA†
New Hampshire	121	174	78
New York	92	243	124
Arkansas	60	81	14
Maine	53	111	46
Mississippi	38	35	18
South Carolina	45	73	39

* **Payment per family.**
† **N.A.—not available.**
SOURCE: *Statistical Abstract*, 1968, op. cit., p. 301.

TABLE IV-3.

EXPENDITURE PER PUPIL IN PUBLIC SCHOOLS, SELECTED STATES, 1968

New York	$982	Arkansas	$441
New Jersey	807	South Carolina	427
Massachusetts	728	Alabama	403
Minnesota	725	Mississippi	346

SOURCE: *Statistical Abstract*, 1968, op. cit., p. 102.

sonal problem, but a problem for the city to which they go. They often become public charges; families are broken; crime and despair multiply. Welfare costs go up, the tensions rise in cities as conflict deepens; riots follow and public and private losses run in the millions. All these costs are directly traceable back to neglects that exist in the areas from which the deprived ones come.

It would be fatuous to say that all the difficulties of the modern city center are attributable to variations in state expenditures. It is reasonable to claim, however, that the problems of the state of origin do not know state boundaries, and part of the crisis of the ghetto of the North originated elsewhere. Whatever the contribution of unequal state expenditures may be to the urban crisis, it remains true that the inequalities are an essential part of federalism as its exists today. Partly that is because welfare and education expenditures are in good measure financed by grants from the Federal Government to states and localities. Is it because of federalism that the inequalities exist? Within the federal framework the national government *could legally* bring all such state expenditures to a much higher if not uniform level. But such reasoning is the kind of fallacy I have been attacking: federalism is not just a matter of *structure*; it is also *politics*. The federal idea endorses state autonomy, and therefore national efforts to provide a uniform—or even a high minimum—level of payment arouse the cry of centralization, of dictatorship from Washington. That rallying cry was part of the reason why federal aid to education was so long delayed. Federal aid frightened those who accepted the conventional wisdom of American dispersionist politics.

Grants are now a major factor in state-local finance and a brief analysis of their impact on federalism is necessary. Grants from the Federal Government are by no means new; they have been used in one form or another from our early history. But as a significant fiscal and political force they came into prominence during the New Deal, when they were used to bail out the states and localities unable to meet the crises of the Depression. Even so, at the end of the 1930's federal grants to states and localities were well under $1 billion and by the end of the 1950's reached only $6 billion. As the data plotted in Figure IV-1 show, the rise of grants has been steady and dramatic during the 1960's, and in 1970 they will almost reach $25 billion. At present levels grants constitute 20 per cent of all federal expenditures for domestic purposes, and represent 18 per cent of state and local revenues.

Watching the ballooning of grant programs the radical right has concluded that these programs have transferred all power from the state capital and the city hall to Washington. Their argument is that if the Federal Government pays a considerable share of the cost of a program

it will naturally determine what is to be done and how. The grant programs are conditional—that is, strings are attached, and at times the
"Feds," as the staff men of state and local agencies are wont to call
their counterparts from the national government, do exercise some control over what a receiving government can do. But an interpretation of
grant administration as a transfer of authority to Washington, leaving
the states and localities with no significant power, is nonsense. The operational reality sustains no such conclusion.

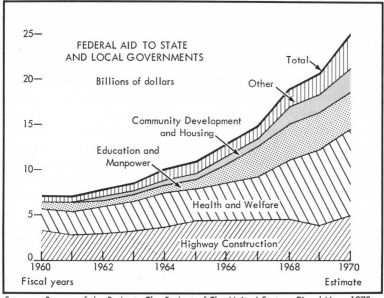

Source: Bureau of the Budget, The Budget of The United States, Fiscal Year 1970
(Washington: U.S. Government Printing Office, 1968), p. 51.

THE GROWTH OF FEDERAL AID
TO STATE AND LOCAL GOVERNMENTS

For there is much reciprocal power in the hands of the lower governments. In the first place national bureaucrats need to have the local
programs alive and working well in order for their own programs to be
deemed successful. If urban renewal programs do not get under way,
if highway programs cannot be initiated, or health programs do not
materialize, then the federal agency in charge of the respective grant
will have no persuasive case to make for the continuance—not to say
the expansion—of its program. If the Urban Renewal Administration,
to take a more specific example, were to insist adamantly that urban
renewal operations in each city be halted until it is definitely shown

that the victims of renewal will be relocated in safe and sanitary housing, there would be much more delay and controversy in the program than there has been in the past. The law not only permits but mandates that the city be required to show that relocation provisions are made, and were the national agents to be serious about this critical phase of the program, many projects—perhaps nearly all—would have been either stopped completely or at least slowed down. The reasons are not hard to find. The authority has not been used. Negroes and the poor, who are normally the victims of the urban renewal bulldozer, are not powerful people, but the economic and political interests that raise objections if the Urban Renewal administrators stopped projects are powerful and the national bureaucrats are appreciative of that fact.

To be sure federal bureaucrats have at times said no to local and state agencies. They have insisted that states not publish the names of welfare recipients in local newspapers. They have rejected road alignments when they seemed politically motivated. They have called for audits when corruption was suspected. And they have demanded that agencies complete in quintuplicate an infinite number of forms before they receive federal cash. They are particularly rigid about the last provision, for it is simpler to enforce an arbitrary but objective demand than it is to act subjectively and say that the local government has not done regional planning as required by law or has not provided for replacement housing for the victim when his house falls before a new highway. The bureaucrat always wants to cover his actions with evidence that he complied with the rules and that he insisted others do likewise. That way the chances of his being reprimanded for deviation are reduced even if the chances of his achieving anything are also sacrificed. Thus there is a tendency to burden agencies with mountains of trivia to conform to, and although there is a willingness to blow the whistle when a flagrant abuse is involved, the politically difficult cases tend to produce less federal pressure. The reason is that state and local agencies have some weapons in their hands too. If they rebel the program bogs down; if they go to their Congressman or their governor and get help they may produce a controversial public hearing and criticism, which the administering agency wants to avoid like a plague.

States and local governments have not become mere extensions of the national government—carrying out federal programs paid for by federal revenues. Indeed in recent years states and localities have administered two thirds of the money spent for domestic purposes in this country. Nevertheless the percentage of the federal contribution to these state and local finances has rarely gone beyond 20 per cent. These governments had to find 80 per cent of the cost of domestic government at home. Slothful and negligent states and localities may be, but they have been more willing to make difficult taxation decisions than has Congress. It remains true, however, that much of this tax effort is dictated by the carrots offered by Congress, and that leads critics to say the Federal Government really decides how state and local money shall be spent because they, in effect, force legislative bodies to go along so as not "lose" their share. This criticism has a degree of truth in it, particularly with respect to those programs that are financed on a 90 per cent federal and a 10 per cent state or local basis—as is the interstate highway system. That much of an inducement becomes impossible to refuse.

But do such grants mean a transfer of power to Washington? On the contrary, it is likely that one of the significant effects of the grant programs has been to strengthen state and local governments in their operations and to further decentralize political power. This paradoxical statement is not the enigma it appears to be. For the receiving governments do not lose all their autonomy when they enter such programs. They distribute money, hire personnel, and make key decisions that affect the public and doubtless tend to give these governments much greater visibility than they would otherwise have. They are at least much more visible than they would be if there were no grant programs and the United States government attempted to do these things on its own. And the distribution of cash from city hall or the state capital should not be considered politically unimportant. All public money spent has a potential for political support, patronage, and party contributions. Architects want to do design work for the state and therefore contribute to the coffers of Democrats and Republicans alike, gambling on nothing. Contractors want to work on urban renewal projects and see fit therefore to help the mayor in his campaign. Manufacturers of building supplies or highway materials are targets for political promoters who dangle the possibility of future orders. There may never be enough cash in the local party till, to hear the party leaders tell the story, but it is certain there would be much less if federal agencies carried out all projects that are now funded through local agencies. And political money goes where political power is; hence the tendency for the grant programs to subsidize the decentralization of American political power.

Another bit of evidence may be drawn on to illustrate the range of activity of the state and local as opposed to the national government— namely the public personnel employed by each. Whereas federal employment has remained about steady in the last twenty-five years (or decreasing proportionally if one thinks of population growth), state and local employment has zoomed upward, growing by nearly three times. Much the same thing is true of public indebtedness.

The question is sometimes asked, however, whether this is not a matter of the public employees' merely being nominal state-local employees because their salary comes in part from the national government and their programs exist because of those grants. The argument will not hold—precisely on the grounds cited for the previous contentions. Their loyalties are not to Washington but to their direct superiors.

TABLE IV-4
PUBLIC EMPLOYEES
(in thousands)

Year	Federal	State-Local
1942	2664	3251
1944	3365	3171
1952	2583	4522
1957	2439	5608
1959	2234	6387
1966	2634	8168

SOURCE: *Historical Statistics of the United States, Colonial Times to 1957* (op. cit.); *Statistical Abstract*, 1960, 1961, 1968.

Moreover the grant programs, as suggested earlier, probably have made a contribution of some significance in that they have reduced corruption. Federal auditors at least, as we have said, have made corruption harder to get away with. Nor should it be ignored that some of the conditional aspects of grants have demanded that the states and localities improve their administrative systems and hold down needless administrative expense. How much these factors have improved state and local operations it would be difficult or impossible to say, but it is true that in some states the only public employees covered by merit systems are those whose salaries are financed in part by federal funds.

If on the one hand conditional grants "interfere" with state prerogatives, on the other these conditions also can be used to persuade non-national governments to meet nationally decided norms—such as on racial matters. There are certainly limitations in the capacity of the grant system to achieve such objectives, but it does have some effect. For example, the most effective tool for forcing school integration has been the authority to withhold federal funds. The power has been sparingly used, but the threat of its use has had some effect. Many defenders of the categoric grant (meaning a grant designated for a specific purpose as opposed to block grants to be used as the local government chooses) stress the importance of these goals. The Civil Rights Act of 1964 in its Title VI specifically authorized the withdrawal of funds from any government using grants in segregated programs. In isolated cases the power has been used or threatened to achieve greater opportunities for black persons.

Because they distrust such controls as Title VI some critics strongly object to the kind of block grants proposed by Walter W. Heller, former Chairman of the Council of Economic Advisers, and Joseph Pechman of the Brookings Institution.[35] Sometimes called the Heller Plan, this proposal was first widely discussed during the 1964 presidential campaign, but after the election President Johnson became preoccupied with the Vietnam war and that in turn absorbed so much federal revenue that the Heller Plan was quietly tabled. The surplus federal income that Heller would have distributed to the states was absorbed by the war. The idea behind the Heller Plan was that Congress would probably never be capable of diverting surplus funds to public purposes but would succumb to the inevitable political pressure to return it to the private sector by cutting taxes. Because there were pressing problems to be dealt with, the argument was that a certain proportion of the annual federal income should be allocated to the states for them to spend as they desired.

The plan has gained a peculiarly broad spectrum of supporters—from conservative to liberal—but it has also evoked sharp criticism. One objection is that the states would merely substitute these funds for other money that they have to raise by taxation, thus adding nothing to the attack on critical problems. If the states had been the laggard ones in raising funds to meet needs, this would be a more valid objection. For the evidence clearly shows that states and localities have taxed themselves heavily on the whole and clearly also the catalogue of needs will not become briefer but fuller in the decades ahead. Therefore the insatiable demand for revenue will likely prevent mere substitution. Even if substitution were a serious problem, it would not be a fatal flaw, for it would be simple to include in the legislation a provision requiring a certain level of "tax effort" as a prerequisite for the grant. This is simple to decide and would impose no hardship on the states.

More serious, but again not beyond remedy, is the problem of the failure to provide money for the cities. Many mayors criticize the Heller Plan on the ground that it aids the states but provides no assurance that a proportionate share of it will reach the hard-pressed cities. Again, it would be feasible to provide in the legislation for a specified percentage of the grant's being allocated to cities over a certain size. Admittedly these are restraints on the block grant, leaving it less than completely

35. See Walter W. Heller, *New Dimensions of Political Economy* (Cambridge, Mass.: Harvard University Press, 1966), Ch. 3. A modified version of this was proposed by President Nixon in August, 1969.

free for the states to use; nevertheless they are minor restraints and in most states would amount to no limitation at all.

An extension of the Heller Plan principle might also achieve a reduction of the complex maze of categoric grants now in use. The grant programs are now so numerous, overlapping, and confusing that states and localities find it difficult to keep abreast of what the federal cafeteria offers. Partly to accommodate these needs (while doing no damage to his presidential campaign), Vice President Hubert Humphrey issued *The Vice President's Handbook for Local Officials*, a 297-page compendium of data on local grant programs alone. This supplemented a publication of the Office of Economic Opportunity called a *Catalog of Federal Assistance Programs*, containing 700 pages of data on all manner of grant programs.[36] How many grant programs there are is difficult to say precisely, for it depends upon the way one counts them. In the OEO volume there are over four hundred grant programs. Some of those listed are minor subdivisions of broader programs—such as the many subcategories of educational aid: vocational, handicapped, college, adult, secondary, and many more. Inevitably much bureaucratic wheel-spinning occurs in making and processing thousands of applications, and in supervising program operation. In fact, so complicated has the whole process become that many states have created special agencies whose purpose is to serve the state's local governments in helping them get the grants that are legally available.

Although this profusion of grant programs may incite localities and states to undertake projects they might otherwise ignore and although it may also provide an avenue for cajoling lesser governments into ceasing to discriminate, or to goad them into regional planning efforts, it may still be questioned whether the optimum use of time and resources is best spent in the bureaucratic red tape that these hundreds of programs inevitably involve. There are enough serious problems to be dealt with so that it does not seem very likely that block grants would be spent frivolously even in the absence of the incentives that come with categoric grants. And where Congress places a very high priority on a given problem, a categoric grant could be retained.

This still leaves the problem of inequitable expenditures for vital programs among the states. This is a simple enough matter to remedy legally. Because the financing for a wide range of programs of vital concern to the poor is in good measure provided by Washington, the remedy is simply to increase the federal proportion and to use state contributions to bring payments to equitable levels. The problem is a political one, as noted previously. Besides the local autonomy factor, there

36. The Vice President's book came out in November, 1967, and the OEO compendium six months earlier. (Washington: U.S. Government Printing Office, 1967).

is a matter of plain selfishness. Although one of the ideas behind the grant program is that the wealthier states help pay the way of the poorer ones, this is a hard proposition to sell in the wealthy states. There is a small amount of redistribution of wealth through the grant programs, but the needs of all the states have become so demanding that grant programs are written so as to minimize redistribution. On welfare, for example, the statute often states a specified sum with a small incentive for the receiving government to supplement it in order to bring the payments to individuals to a minimally satisfactory level. That defeats the purpose of providing a floor payment. For the less wealthy or more negligent states merely take the federal grant as the base and add only a minimum supplement. Some genuine redistributing would be achieved if the federal share were greatly increased, or in some cases if the whole amount were provided from federal funds. But politically this is difficult if not impossible to achieve.

A Balance Sheet on Federalism

Having weighed federalism and found it wanting in many respects and advantageous in some others, the time has come to reach some kind of balanced judgment about it. In reaching that conclusion we need to take into account more than the specific feature of federalism already discussed. That is, if there are on the whole more reasons to suspect that federalism contributes to governmental inefficiency, if it tends on the whole to be helpful to the white minority who oppress blacks, if it results in certain serious inequities of treatment of the poor, then one is inclined to come down against it. But to do so is to take some serious risks, which should at least be recognized. To adopt a unitary government for a nation as large and complex as this one we would be taking a step of sweeping potentiality.[37] It is a step of grave importance because centralization of authority in a huge society has great implications for the individual and his control over his own destiny.

Consider the gains in efficiency from centralizing power and eliminating federalism. That is, by eliminating federalism one might improve the administration of welfare and eliminate some of the discrimination and some of the inequities that now prevail. And one might get rid of some biased judicial systems and place restraints on some irresponsible police departments. But by the creation of a national welfare system, a

37. I am well aware, as I have stated earlier, that the "real" question here is not federalism *versus* unitary government for the simple reason that federalism does not wither away when there are strong political forces supporting it; on the contrary the question is whether federalism should be shored up or undermined when critical occasions arise. But in order to put the argument in its sharpest terms I have argued as though the question were retention or abolition.

national judiciary, and a national police system one might also bring in other complications as severe as the ones to be corrected.

A national government would have difficulty at best in setting policy on complex and controversial matters and would tend to have a dangerous kind of immobilisme on critical issues. Second, one cannot be assured that a national government would not turn racist and suppress on a national basis rather than in a limited territorial area. A national police force that resembled the Federal Bureau of Investigation at its anti-Communist worst and not at its best (as for example, in its general treatment of arrested persons) would be ominous—at least to me. Moreover a movement toward genuine unitary government would nationalize many other aspects of government—education, housing, planning, land-use control, resources development, water policy. In some instances these changes might have salutary results but not necessarily in all cases; local variation also has utility. In addition the sheer size and scope of the resulting bureaucracy would not only invite a different kind of inefficiency but would also tend to become more dehumanized, more routinized, than bureaucracy now is.

At this point it is appropriate to quote Robert A. Dahl on the issue of the appropriate size of a democratic government. Dahl is not talking about federalism, and he has no particular faith in the capacity of the states, but the general principle he enunciates is applicable to our discussion. In his presidential address to the American Political Science Association in 1967 Dahl said:

> The larger and more inclusive a unit, the more its government can regulate aspects of the environment that its citizens want to regulate, from air and water pollution and racial justice to the dissemination of nuclear weapons.
>
> Yet, the larger and more inclusive unit with a representative government, and the more complex its tasks, the more participation must be reduced for most people to the single act of voting in an election.
>
> Conversely, the smaller the unit, the greater the opportunity for citizens to participate in the decisions of their government, yet the less of the environment they can control.
>
> Thus for most citizens, participation in very large units becomes minimal and in very small units it becomes trivial.[38]

Dahl places great emphasis upon the importance of citizen participation in government—and in meaningful terms to the citizen's own life. He grants that we have no answer to the riddle of how large (or small)

38. "The City in the Future of Democracy," 61 *American Political Science Review* 953–70, at p. 960 (1967).

government should be to avoid the problem of too-encompassing scope or small town triviality, but he stresses that a government of huge size in which the citizen has no more than an opportunity to participate in periodic elections is not a very satisfactory resolution of the problem.

This argument seems to me profoundly important. If one wants further evidence of its impact, he should consider the complaint of the black American who is now fighting for a small amount of self-government in the drive for school decentralization in the large cities.[39] If too little democracy exists for the white man in a huge and impersonal society, how much less of it exists for a black man. He has no sense of economic control for he owns few businesses and no one he considers close to him has much control over any economic decisions. He usually does not even belong to a labor union with which he might assert at least some economic pressure. He doesn't own a house and cannot make demands as a taxpayer. He is automatically suspect to the police and he finds it difficult to get legal aid for any criminal or civil matter he faces—assuming he knows the importance of counsel. The white man in metropolitan America may have much less sense of control over his destiny than he would like, but he has infinitely more than his black counterpart. The white man tends to live in suburbia, where he has at least some opportunities for self-assertion. He can vote down a school budget if he objects; he can call the city councilman and get potholes filled in the streets or the garbage collected. He expects to get a response —and by and large he does. In short the decentralization of power that the suburbanite has, the black slum dweller wants also and wants it for essentially the same reason: to get a greater sense of control over his destiny than existence in the sea of mankind in the center city permits.

It should be remembered in short that federalism serves more than the purposes of racists. The Czechs and Slovaks, even under the pressure of Moscow's 1968 invasion, continued to work out their modified version of a federal system with the objective of granting to the ethnic components of the nation a degree of identity and self-control. The French-Canadians struggle for their interpretation of Canadian federalism so as to assume the continuance and respect for French culture in Canada.[40] Federalism may indeed offer little in the way of direct control to the people who inhabit California or New York, but it may offer

39. The rationale for school decentralization is forcefully put by the Mayor's Advisory Panel on Decentralization of the New York City Schools, *Reconnection for Learning* (New York: Mayor's Advisory Panel, 1967).

40. See the remarkable volume *Federalism and the French Canadians* by Pierre Elliott Trudeau (Toronto: Macmillan of Canada, 1968). It is a remarkable book to have been written by a French Canadian, an astounding book to have been written by a prime minister. Not many politicians achieve such candor and insight into the problems of federalism—or anything else.

them more than would be afforded them in a unitary nation. The state may play only a marginal role for the protection of regional or state identity—in the French-Canadian sense—but to those to whom this matters it is important. More importantly the state can play an intermediary role between the national government and the locality. By urging or demanding something more than the narrowest provincial interests of localities and narrower ones than those of national sweep, the state may play a role of some significance in the resolution of the conundrum posed by Dahl.

My final judgment on federalism is this. Flawed though it may be by giving power to those who may use it irresponsibly and by inefficiencies that are galling and costly, federalism may nevertheless have benefits of sufficient value to merit its retention, especially in this age of technological complexity and incredible size that invites dehumanization. This is not to say I would at every occasion take the federal route when alternatives appear. On the contrary, there are sufficiently heavy costs associated with federalism so that at times only a nationalizing tendency will make much sense. But embracing unitary government for a society as large and complex as this is seems to me equally ridiculous. Only pragmatic answers that embrace neither dogma seem appropriate to me.

CHAPTER FIVE

Congress:
Prometheus Self-bound

Power in American politics is not hierarchical but dispersed. Congress fully reflects and well illustrates that distribution of power, its uses and abuses. For the key to comprehension of Congress is recognition of its scattered authority. And this has long been true. Woodrow Wilson, writing in the 1880's, called Congress a "disintegrate ministry." But power is not distributed evenly in Congress by any means. Most members of Congress, especially of the House of Representatives, have relatively little power personally, but there are about fifty to seventy-five members of Congress who possess considerable power—especially negative power —although these Congressmen rarely work in concert. Nor is power distributed in a neutral way; it favors the status quo. Congress is like the rest of American government: it is geared to grind slowly. Congress, through its formal rules and its informal practices, is an institution devoted inordinately to the prevention of action. Indeed it is so well equipped to stop legislation that even conservative interests at times have difficulty when they seek changes in the law. Usually conservatives need only to stop action to achieve at least their more limited goals, but liberal legislators, because they seek innovation more frequently, encounter obstruction from well-entrenched conservative opponents in addition to the usual difficulties in putting together majorities for their proposals.

For many reasons, including this willful decision not to act as a collective entity but as an assembly of feudal lords, Congress fails to address itself to the critical issues of our time. Bogged down by its own venality, it cannot affect the inequitable distribution of income. Bound down in racism, which is sustained by the seniority system, it has little capacity for correcting racial injustice. Distorted by a warped system of representation, it responds to wealth and power, not desperate need. Congress, powerful as it is in some respects, is, alas, nearly irrelevant where the burning issues of our time are concerned.

In part Congress does not deal with these important questions because a good portion of the nation and of the Congress does not accept as real problems the issues of racism, of social and political inequality, or of economic manipulation. But even members of Congress who do perceive injustice in the tax laws, in racist practices, or in the Vietnam war do not find it easy, or possible, to make Congress act on these issues. It is difficult to focus Congressional attention on these issues for reasons that involve more than national division on the issues themselves or the relative ease with which opponents can stifle initiative. Some of those reasons are beyond the capacity of Congress to correct if it were inclined to do so; others it could theoretically deal with but would certainly have difficulty with even if it tried. For example, Congress can do little about its loss of initiative in many matters. The bureaucracy has been given wide discretionary power for reasons that are inescapable. That is, if a matter is technologically complex there is not a great deal that Congress can do to legislate in detail on it—discretion in handling details must pass to the bureaucracy. If matters are secret—as much of foreign and military policy is—then Congress may or may not really be able to find out what is going on. And if its supply of information is limited, its capacity to control is bound to be limited accordingly. Similarly the President has gained enormously in popular prestige and political power, and it is difficult for Congress to compete with him. The discordant chorus of Congress is no match for a presidential press conference in focusing public attention.

Similarly the Congress has lost ground to the judiciary—both in specific powers and in prestige. On matters of race, for example, Congress was utterly incapable of acting, and the task fell to the judiciary. The courts garnered some enemies but probably far more friends by attacking segregation. While Congress was suppressing probable legislative majorities seeking civil rights legislation, the Court decided numerous segregation cases. All this has even led some commentators to say that the judiciary is indeed the more representative branch of government—which must have shocked the ghosts of Henry Clay and Daniel Webster.

Congress has also lost prestige on other grounds. In part this is due to the venality of some members of Congress and the complacency with which their colleagues receive evidence of corruption. Conflicts of interest and dubious maneuvers on behalf of special interests in addition to implicit bribery have brought the prestige of Congress to a low position. In addition, the overdevelopment of the capacity to say no has gained Congress the animosity of innumerable large minorities because legislative roadblocks can be erected easily by members in key positions. A minority in Congress that feels intensely about an issue can almost always defeat legislation desired by larger minorities, and the resulting frustration has been spread to many groups. And the antic behavior of any member of Congress does damage to the prestige of the whole body. The more ridiculous the behavior of a legislator the more likely it will be reported. A member of Congress is newsworthy by reason of his position and he is therefore news when he gets drunk in public, calls someone a "Communist," a "Dago," or a "Nigger," cheats on an expense account, hides behind Congressional immunity to malign an opponent, or makes an ass of himself in a filibuster.

Thus Congress faces a challenge to its position and has suffered a relative decline in authority. Debate about whether its power has absolutely declined is futile, because it involves comparison of a time when laissez-faire prevailed and Congress was doing little but was the major source of such innovation as occurred, and a later time when the total area of Congressional involvement has expanded but the initiative has passed to others. Congress has, however, retained its capacity to say no. And because it may say no—and often does—it therefore has real authority to affect legislation. The power to deny or delay is the power to exact a price for complying—not a price in the sense of a bribe, but in terms of conditions that must be met to get legislation moving. It may mean the gutting of a proposed program or some other, perhaps hidden, quid pro quo. In any event the use of power in Congress is a subtle process and not one easily measured by the general statistics on the number of bills introduced, considered, passed, stalled, or defeated. Power in Congress is subtle, not obvious, often confusing, and commonly misconstrued.

Whatever else may be said of Congressional power, this much is true: it is exercised so as to render difficult or impossible the task of developing policies addressed to the needs of those in the most desperate straits. It is not especially difficult to get a huge defense budget through Congress with relatively little examination and not much dissent. Defense budgets have formidable support: they are endorsed by the President, they have the awesome backing of the military-industrial complex, they are difficult to oppose for to do so may appear to be failing the troops in battle or "endangering" the safety of the society, and they are, after all, a test of the national power, which arouses nationalistic feelings in the patriot. It may well be—as with many aspects of the arms race—that the appropriations will do more to endanger the whole world than to provide for the "safety" of anyone, but that is an argument only a radical would offer and such is rarely heard in the chambers of Congress.

To get through the needle's eye of Congress a law to protect farm workers attempting to form unions or to feed the starving is another matter. For there are almost limitless ways in which an intensely interested minority can block such laws. In this respect Congress perverts the priorities of the nation; it responds to money, to organized power, to vested interests of various kinds, but it has little sympathy for migrant farm workers, the poor, or the prisoner. An illustration of this is found in the spectacular show Congress stages annually in denunciation of the administrative shortcomings of the poverty program. By contrast it practically ignores messes in the military that outdistance the waste in poverty programs by a hundred or a thousand to one. But poverty alleviation is unpopular, and shoddy management there arouses an almost unanimous denunciation. Even the friends of such legislation must condemn vehemently; they are annoyed that it happened in "their" bailiwick, which means trouble. Critics little note the exceedingly difficult problems encountered in reaching the long-term poor and dealing with their complex problems. Somehow it never occurs to the critics that the routines of bureaucracy had failed to make a dent in the problem despite growing welfare expenditures, and that experimenting with alleviation of poverty at least posed risks of failure.[1] Nor are there many comparisons between the relatively small losses in the administration of the poverty programs and the monstrous losses—in the billions— from military stupidity or theft. When in 1968–69 the New York City antipoverty program was being wrung out for peculations that may have amounted to $3 million, the Pentagon was shown at that same time to have wasted billions in the development of an aircraft—the C5A. A gross miscalculation (or perhaps a deception of Congress) on the costs of the C5A resulted in the expenditure of $2 billions more than anticipated. Or consider the revelation that some 5.5 million gallons of gasoline had been stolen in Thailand in 1967. Bribery, forgery, and theft in this case resulted in little publicity. In fact there was very little interest shown even when the man who blew the whistle was transferred to a clerical job and told that he lacked civil service status and that he was being dismissed. Newspapers and Congressmen were in full cry about the antipoverty case, but little was said about the two Pentagon messes.

Or consider another example: the tax laws. It is commonly believed that the federal income tax is steeply progressive with the little or nothing paid by those who earn little and with as much as 91 per cent being levied on incomes over a million dollars. In actuality the person earning between $20,000 and $50,000 pays about the same proportion of his income for federal taxation as does a person earning over $5 million and nearly the same proportions of total income are paid in taxes by those earning between $50,000 and $1 million. The reason for this is

1. See Daniel Moynihan's *Maximum Feasible Misunderstanding* (New York: Macmillan, 1969) for a denunciation of the attempt to engage the participation of the people involved through the requirement of "maximum feasible participation" of the poor in the programs.

that tax laws are so full of legal means of evasion that the rich can escape levies that ordinary taxpayers, lacking special exemptions, must pay. At the extremes are cases where those earning millions pay not one cent of federal income tax. Indeed the Secretary of the Treasury in 1969 told Congress that no fewer than 155 persons earned in excess of $200,000 in 1967 and paid no federal income tax at all. Of these 21 had incomes in excess of $1 million.[2]

The loopholes through which millionaires escape are numerous and often ingenious. For example, earnings from state and local bonds are not subject to taxation—in theory because this aids government to borrow more cheaply. It also permits really wealthy persons to invest heavily in such bonds and be free of any tax obligation. For instance an automobile heiress put a $56-million legacy entirely into state and local bonds and could earn, even at 3 per cent, over one and a half million a year on which she owed not a penny in taxes.[3] Proposals to provide alternative means for holding down the cost of municipal bonds have got nowhere, demonstrating that the true objective of this gimmick is not assistance for the borrowing governments but for the coupon clippers.[4] The oil depletion allowance is a well-known route by which millionaires become multimillionaires; less well known are the resource depletion allowances now granted for some eighty-five other minerals. (See the discussion of oil depletion allowances in the assessment of lobbies.) Rapid depreciation allowances for real estate are another public subsidy to the greedy. Individuals build or buy buildings in order to depreciate them rapidly, thereby allowing the owner to write off taxes from other sources while, in the course of a decade, the property is depreciated. Then another speculator buys the building and the depreciation process begins all over![5] Mortgage interest payments and state

2. "Treasury Secretary Warns of a Taxpayers' Revolt," *The New York Times*, Jan. 18, 1969.

3. See Phillip M. Stern, *The Great Treasury Raid* (New York: New American Library, Signet Paperback edition, 1964), p. 168, for this and many other lurid examples. The book is flashily journalistic in style but it is based on hard evidence and reveals the shoddiness of the situation. A more erudite treatment of the problem is Joseph Pechman's *Federal Tax Policy* (Washington: Brookings Institution, 1966).

4. Congressman Reuss of Wisconsin, for example, has proposed that a Municipal Bond Guarantee Corporation be established to reduce interest rates on such bonds by giving them a federal guarantee. See his H.R. 5250, Title VIII, 91st Congress, First Session.

5. What this has done to center-city office-building construction and to the degradation of architectural style is beyond imagination. What it has done for the get-rich-quick types is well put by Stern, *op. cit.*, pp. 139–53. His chapter title: "How To Get Rich in Real Estate—With Uncle Sam's Help."

and local tax payments are exempt from federal taxes—a boon to the homeowner not afforded the renter, and fantastic indirect subsidy to banks, who are in the money-lending business. Congress thus has provided endless billions for middle- and upper-class homeownership but almost defeated a bill providing a hopelessly inadequate $30 million for rent subsidies for the poor.

A business can get an exemption from taxation not only for its expenditures on advertising, with which it attempts to stultify us all with revolting television commercials, but it can also, if it is clever, get a write off for lobbying, huge expense accounts for entertaining, and other self-promotional operations. It is true that some of the worst aspects of expense account boondoggling were restrained by Congress in 1962, but what still can be done at the expense of other taxpayers is indefensible—except by those powerful enough to fend for themselves: the expense account boodlers, the hotels, restaurants, and transportation interests that get rich off the expense account privilege. Thus lawyers schedule their conventions (for educational purposes, of course) in the Bahamas in January; then the cost of a winter's vacation is written off as a business expense. Using data for 1963, Philip Stern estimates that the treasury did not get the following amounts that it might have except for the respective loopholes: [6]

Loophole	*Billions lost*
Municipal bonds	$1.0
Depletion deductions	1.5
Other oil (drilling)	.5
Travel and entertainment (excess, not total)	.3
Real estate depreciation	.2
Dividend credit	.5
Capital gains	2.4
	$6.4

By 1970 these tax gimmicks alone probably amount to some $10 billion in lost revenue. And this does not even touch the phony foundations created to provide nontaxable income for their creators, the spurious charitable contribution dodges, stock option deals, or many other schemes that tax lawyers get rich in exploiting for wealthy clients.

The injustice of this is multiplied by the fact that the poor pay the full amount demanded by the law, and especially the unmarried person pays a high proportion of his income in taxes, even when his earnings are meager. If tax dodges could be eliminated, the rates for all could be

6. Op. cit., pp. 31–32.

reduced drastically, resulting in a genuinely progressive tax, but with the burden much more equitably distributed. It would be possible to require that no one would ever have to pay more than half his income in taxes and still bring in more revenue than is now received. The steep rates for the millionaire are therefore *a protection* of his income rather than its deprivation, for the high rate gives the appearance of progressivity and inhibits reform of the loopholes. If there were many who really paid 90 per cent of income in taxes, the system would have been changed presumably, for nothing is more obvious about our tax system than that the rich have been able to persuade Congress to give back in tax gimmicks what it appears to be taking away with the steeply progressive rates.[7]

What must be realized is that tax laws do more than establish tax rates and exemptions. They also determine housing policy, affect land use decisions, influence investment and capital formation—in short, establish national priorities in innumerable ways. It is no accident that, for example, suburbia has grown like a weed since World War II; suburbia grew so readily in part because it was financed by tax gimmicks that grant the middle and upper class very valuable exemptions on their mortgage costs. And with each decision of that kind (such as oil depletion allowances, municipal bond exemptions, accelerated depletion of the value of office buildings and machinery, the expense account boondoggle), a series of interrelated interests are granted something worth fighting to protect. The banks that finance suburbia, the contractors and construction trade unions that build it, the lumber and supply industries that fatten on it, the public utilities that grow with it, all shed crocodile tears on behalf of the hard-pressed homeowner who greatly needs tax relief on his housing. A straight, outright payment of, say, a thousand dollars a year to families owning fifty-thousand-dollar homes, taken from the treasury in open transactions, would be next to impossible to get approved, but doing the same thing under cover of the tax laws is just fine.

So the concatenations of interests press for their subsidies, ostensibly in behalf of someone else. If it were possible to examine the wisdom of subsidizing these interests directly by outright subventions, the out-

7. At the time I write Congress is considering revision of the tax code, and probably will at least relieve the lowest earners from tax liability, but I doubt that such loopholes as the oil depletion allowance and the special rate for capital gains will be deleted. If a lower tax rate is established based upon general elimination of loopholes and gimmicks then my argument will have been undercut. I doubt that Congress will do more than tinker, leaving both my argument and the loopholes intact. [Later: Congress acted: it tinkered, leaving the worst tax inequities intact, as predicted.]

come might be different. Or if the desirability of such subsidies were compared with outlays for controlling pollution, the policies might be different. But it is the genius of American politics—which Congress mirrors in practice and in spirit—to obscure such decisions and prevent them from ever being subjected to comparative scrutiny. Not only, that is to say, are the outsiders in American society left out of the decision-making process because of their lack of power and organization, but also to the maximum extent possible the decision is made by mirrors where the actual objectives are obscured from view. If ever subjected to the full glare of public view with some kind of national referendum possible, is there any doubt what the decision would be on whether to subsidize the hotel-restaurant-vacation interests through the expense account dodge?

Tax policy is only an example; similar situations are numerous. For example, Congress refused to legislate against lynching, despite a campaign for action that continued from about 1920 to the 1950's. Each session brought antilynching bills, but either in the catacombs of the House committee system or by way of the filibuster they always died. More recently civil rights legislation has passed, but only after long disruptive battles and after the legislation had been shorn of much of its effectiveness. The 1964 Voting Rights Act, for example, contains an important clause barring the use of literacy tests, in effect, in areas where such tests were a means of disenfranchising Negroes. But a provision was slipped in to terminate that clause in five years. To continue protection of the franchise therefore will require running the legislative gauntlet once again. Often at the close of a long legislative battle—literally stretching into years—the proponents of civil rights legislation "win" but openly wonder if the shredded remains that survived was worth the parchment it was issued on. One could go on—with coal miners dying of black lung and fire, with families starving when the nation owns vast stores of "surplus" food, with an infant death rate that places this prosperous and technologically advanced nation fifteenth among the nations of the world in infant mortality. Let us examine how Congress disregards questions like these as we consider the exercise of power in Congress.

Power in Congress

A key to the comprehension of power in Congress is the recognition of the prevalent and paranoic fear of majority rule—everything, almost, is sacrificed to see to it that majorities are not easily mustered and registered. The rules of Congress—both the codified, formal rules and the informal, traditional rules—distribute power to small groups and even to individuals so as to restrain activists. Control over the schedules of the two houses is rigged so that a determined minority can at the least delay and sometimes kill legislation without its ever being considered on its merits. Power is parceled out to committees and subcommittees and especially (informally) to the chairmen of these committees. With each parcel of power for a subgroup or individual there goes an understood guarantee that only on the most extraordinary occasions will the granted prerogatives be withdrawn or overruled. Because each member expects reciprocity in the all-important matter of his trying to stop something tomorrow, and because the ethos of the institution is so unstintingly dedicated to the protection of these prerogatives, the system is ironbound and durable. Newcomers lack the numbers or the status to change the system and old-timers have either made their peace with or benefit from it. In short *Congress will go to all lengths to avoid making a divisive decision if it can.* The rule is that if something can be resolved by resort to tradition, rules, or personal prerogatives, then let that decide the issue rather than ever taking a chance on a divisive vote on the one hand or allowing someone in the elective leadership to acquire formal authority to decide anything.

It was not always so. From about 1890 to 1910 the Speaker of the House, for example, was a powerful figure who could and did tend to lead the House according to his partisan desires—usually in collaboration with the President but always on terms that the powerful Speaker found acceptable. But a progressive minority of Republicans, smarting under the control of "Czar" Joe Cannon, long time autocrat of the House and an ardent economic conservative, and a large contingent of dissident Democrats trimmed the power of the Speaker, and from that day forward the dispersal of power in the House has persisted. Although it is true that the progressive Republicans may have objected more to the policy orientation of Cannon than they did to the rules he administered, the important result of the revolt was a dispersal of power that has proved itself highly resistant to recall.[8]

Look at some ways in which power is dispersed and some of the roadblocks that result. First consider the committee system. Congress is highly specialized and its most important work takes place in committee. In the sixteen Senate and twenty House committees little by way

8. See Kenneth Heckler, *Insurgency: Personalities and Politics of the Taft Era* (New York: Columbia University Press, 1940). For a brief account of the overthrow and its implications see James A. Robinson, *The House Rules Committee* (Indianapolis: Bobbs-Merrill, 1963), pp. 60–62. See also the excellent analysis of the Seniority System and the power of the Speaker: Nelson Polsby, Miriam Gallaher, and Barry Rundquist, "The Growth of the Seniority System in the House of Representatives," 63 *American Political Science Review* 787–807 (1969).

of initiation of legislation takes place, but about 90 per cent of all proposed bills die there—usually without even being considered. (That is
not necessarily the tragedy it appears, for many bills are offered only
to appease some group that thinks "there oughta be a law" and urges
a member to introduce it—or else it is dumped into the hopper, often
as a duplicate of other bills, by a member who wants publicity but never
even remotely expects it to become legislation.) More importantly the
committee scrutinizes all important legislation, and it has the opportunity to revise it substantially, to delay it indefinitely, or to vote negatively on it. A negative vote is fatal because there is no practical way to
get a bill to the floor when a committee rejects it.

There are numerous booby traps in the committee system and they
go off under many a well-conceived piece of legislation. One is the subcommittee system. The chairman of a committee can decide the fate of
a bill, at times, by his choice of the subcommittee to which he sends a
bill—either because he selects an ad hoc committee to consider it or
because of his choice among standing subcommittees.

A good illustration of the use of these prerogatives is the case of the
Depressed Areas Bill in the Senate Banking and Currency Committee.
This piece of ill-starred legislation, which languished in the Congressional labyrinth for six years, was intended to provide assistance for
"pockets of poverty" that persisted in widespread areas around the
nation. Former Senator Paul Douglas of Illinois introduced the original
version of the law in 1956. It provided an authorization of $390 million
and gave depressed areas preferential treatment in the allocation of
government contracts, and provided loans and grants to attract industry, along with technical assistance and training programs for employees.[9] The Eisenhower administration produced a milder version with a
$50 million authorization. To illustrate the troubles Douglas faced in
the long struggle for his idea, consider the travail of the 1957–58 session of Congress. The bill went to the Senate Banking and Currency
Committee. Senator William Fulbright, Chairman of the Committee,
was not friendly to the bill, partly because he feared that emphasis on
previously industrialized but now depressed areas would hamper efforts
of rural areas (like Arkansas) to attract industry. Senator Douglas was
chairman of the subcommittee of Banking and Currency to which Fulbright sent the bill, but as long as it was before that subcommittee it
stood little chance because only two Democrats on the subcommittee
favored it, whereas the subcommittee's other two Democrats and three
Republicans opposed the bill. Douglas complained that the subcommit-

9. This brief account of the law owes much to the fuller and excellent analysis
by John Bibby and Roger Davidson, *On Capitol Hill* (New York: Holt, Rinehart
and Winston, 1967), Ch. 5–6.

tee was "stacked" against him but Fulbright denied any such intent. Through a ruse Douglas got the bill before the whole committee, resulting in an angry argument between Douglas and Fulbright. Two scholars have observed, concerning this contest, that

> The unhappy incident in the committee illustrated that a chairman's prerogatives may border on the arbitrary, and that to control the exercise of these prerogatives may require a determined majority willing to risk the costs of forcing a confrontation. Fulbright could not have been expected to make concessions until Douglas had enough votes in full committee to pass the bill. Once his bipartisan coalition had been fashioned, Douglas could force Fulbright to back down, either through informal agreement or a committee showdown.[10]

Once Senator Douglas and his Republican allies had maneuvered the bill out of the committee it easily passed the Senate by a vote of 46 to 36. Nor was there difficulty with the House Banking and Currency Committee. The Rules Committee was another matter, however. Then presided over by "Judge" Howard W. Smith, the Rules Committee is the graveyard of much important legislation. In effect the Rules Committee sets the schedule for important legislation in the House, instead of that function's being in the hands of the leadership, as is common in most legislative bodies and as it is, by and large, in the U.S. Senate. But in the House all legislation is placed on calendars strictly in the order of being reported out of committee, and that inevitably results in many significant pieces of legislation's being very low in priority, making it necessary for some exception to be made to bring up a bill "from the foot of the calendar." In the average session the Rules Committee receives about 150 bills that need "special rules." (The special rule states the conditions of the debate—length of time, permissibility of amendments, and the like.) Of these 150 bills the Rules Committee usually kills about two dozen, either by refusing to hold a hearing on the bill or by rejecting a special rule request after a hearing.[11]

Two dozen bills killed may not sound very impressive when one considers the hundreds of bills passed by the House and the thousands proposed. But it is important because only the most critical and controversial bills ever are brought to the Committee. It is a serious mistake,

10. Ibid., p. 206. On subcommittee operations see Lewis A. Froman, Jr., *The Congressional Process* (Boston: Little, Brown, 1967), pp. 37–43.

11. The definitive work on the Committee is by James A. Robinson; see his *The House Rules Committee* (Indianapolis: Bobbs-Merrill, 1963). Concerning the Committee's disposition of bills see Robinson, pp. 23–30.

however, to assume that the Committee's power can be judged by either the kind or number of bills it buries. For it also modifies legislation as a condition of freeing it for floor action. Although it possesses no direct power to amend a bill, the committee can bargain for changes as one stage of the Depressed Areas Bill fight demonstrates. As is often the case the pressure of time began to become a major factor in the probability of passing the bill; 1958 was a campaign year and as the summer wore on access to the floor for action on bills became a major concern. All the opposition has to do under these circumstances is to delay consideration for a few strategic days or weeks and the issue is decided, for the bill will have to be reintroduced and the process begun anew in the legislative session following an election.

Thus, although the House Banking and Currency Committee had reported out the bill on July 1, 1958, the Rules Committee did not act on it for six weeks—and then only after it won concessions to modify the method of financing the project. Judge Smith then had three legislative days in which to file a report and then seven more days could lapse before it came to a vote. If the Judge met these deadlines it might be possible to get action before adjournment, but if he did not the bill would fail for lack of time even though the concessions had been made. A delegation of Congressmen favoring the bill traveled to Judge Smith's home in Alexandria, Virginia, to plead with him to permit the bill to be reported out in time. He complied, but only after the delegation agreed "to delete a section of the bill providing subsistence allowances for unemployed workers while they were being retrained." [12] With that enlightened gesture Smith permitted the sizeable House majority in favor of the bill to enact it.

But President Eisenhower vetoed the bill and the whole process began again in 1959. In the spring of 1960 the bill reached the Rules Committee again and by a vote of 6 to 6 it refused to give a rule for the bill. House managers found it necessary to resort to a risky device called Calendar Wednesday to get it on the floor. (More on the Calendar Wednesday gambit later.) The formidable power of the Rules Committee is self-evident, but it remains a good question why it is allowed to function as it does. Why does the House permit this small group to stymie legislation? Why not leave such questions to the leadership or to the membership? The answers are consistent with the general point made earlier; the fear of vesting power in an elective leadership or a majority. In Speaker Cannon's day the Rules Committee was chosen by the Speaker and the Speaker himself sat as a member of it. Today the Rules Committee is chosen by the Democratic and Republican

12. Bibby and Davidson, op. cit., p. 208.

caucuses—at least nominally. In reality the leadership of the House has considerable influence in the selection of members of the Committee— in the beginning. But once on the Committee a member will normally be removed only at his own request, and the inexorable working of the seniority system moves the member toward the chairmanship and all its power—if he lives so long and does not get defeated. It just happens, however, that the membership of the Committee is normally loaded with conservatives. James A. Robinson did an analysis of the background of fifty-three members of the Committee who served between 1937 and 1962 and the following are some of his findings. First the median term of service during which members were appointed to the Committee was four terms—eight years in the House, that is, or ample time to accommodate to its traditions. Of the fifty-three members who served during that period ten were Southern Democrats and nine were Midwestern Republicans. And thirty-two of the total were from rural districts. Thirty-seven represented safe seats, and in terms of man-years of service the members from safe seats had served 270 years and those from competitive seats 64 years.[13] The Rules Committee, that is to say, is a conservative body.

Its essential conservatism is another reason for the Committee's invulnerability to attack. The House is a conservative institution fundamentally and it is not often offended by the actions of the Committee. In many instances failure of the Committee to grant a rule will please most members of the House because they do not wish to vote on a bill—say for veterans' pensions—because they don't want to vote yes, but feel they cannot vote no. Also many of the bills bottled up by the Committee are ones the leadership wants stored away without controversy. But there are other bills that the leadership and perhaps a majority (or near it) of the membership want and the Committee will not consent to give a rule. Or the Chairman will resist on the basis of his prerogatives and be unreachable by the leadership or anyone else. On one occasion, for example, Judge Smith just took off for home, supposedly to check on a "burned barn," in order to prevent the Committee from meeting and acting favorably on a civil rights bill he was determined to defeat. (Speaker Sam Rayburn is said to have commented that he knew Howard Smith would do nearly anything to stop civil rights legislation but he hadn't suspected him of arson.) But usually the committee is not resisting but complying with the will of the membership, however much it is in conflict with the progressive members of the House. This is demonstrated by the restraint placed on the Committee during a brief period when the conservatism of the House was

13. James A. Robinson, op. cit., pp. 92–109.

submerged somewhat. In 1965, when the House was lopsidedly Democratic and there was a cushion of liberal Democratic strength to depend upon, the Committee was put under the "twenty-one-day" rule. This provided that after the Committee had held a bill for twenty-one days the Speaker could recognize the chairman of the committee from whence the bill came originally and have it acted upon on the floor. But as soon as the Goldwater gift to the national interest (namely his overwhelming defeat, which helped elect one of the most liberal Congresses in the history of the nation) vanished in the 1966 election, the twenty-one-day rule immediately was rescinded and the Rules Committee began business at the same old stand in the same old fashion. It is true that the defeat of Smith in 1966 and the subsequent replacement of him and some other conservatives with relatively liberal members has reduced the threat of the Committee. Smith's successor as chairman, the seventy-eight-year-old William Colmer of Mississippi, is no less conservative, but he is inept politically where Smith was clever. Moreover, Colmer's potential power is obviously restrained by the new, more liberal majority on the Committee. Characteristically these superficial changes have cooled the ardor of the progressive Democrats for reform of the Committee's powers, which are as subject to abuse now as ever.[14]

What the Rules Committee is to the House the filibuster is to the Senate. Whereas House debate is limited and formal, debate in the Senate is informal, often not germane to the subject at hand, and sometimes interminable. Senate rules do not provide for the familiar "previous question" motion by which debate can be terminated and a vote taken. In the pre-Civil War era, when the slavery issue was fought politically, the filibuster became common. (The term *filibuster* means "pirate.") Although the Senate rules stated (then as now) that "No one is to speak impertinently, or beside the question, superfluously or tediously," the admonition could hardly be more descriptive of what actually took place when a determined minority set out to prevent action on a measure they lacked the votes to defeat. Not until 1917 was even the most tentative limitation placed on Senate debate, and that happened as a result of war fever. President Wilson proposed and the House readily accepted a bill to arm merchant vessels. But what Wilson called a "band of willful men, representing no opinion but their own" filibustered the bill to a standstill in the Senate. After Wilson's angry blast at the filibusterers and with public sentiment apparently strongly in favor of

14. It might be added that the new Rules Committee majority established a specific meeting day once a week, thereby making it a bit more difficult for a chairman to defy a committee majority. This too is a bandaid where surgery is indicated.

the bill, the Senate adopted a "cloture" rule. This rule, called Rule XXII, provided that on the petition of sixteen senators and after the lapse of two days, by vote of two thirds of the Senators voting on the issue, debate could be concluded and a vote taken *after each Senator had had one further hour to speak.*

Such a cumbersome restraint is the rough equivalent of no restraint at all. Although on seven of forty-three attempts cloture has been applied, there are innumerable instances when filibusters have achieved their ends without a cloture petition's even being filed. And when modification of the rule is sought, that too faces a filibuster and moreover *one on which the cloture rule does not apply.* The latter provision along with a modification of the number required for cloture (making it *two thirds of the membership,* not of those voting on the issue, resulting in a tougher requirement) was the strange product of an attack on the filibuster in 1949. Biennially with the opening of a new session of Congress there is a battle on Rule XXII, but there are never sufficient votes actually to curb filibustering. (In 1959, however, the number required for cloture reverted to two thirds of those voting and not of the total membership.)

Breaking a determined filibuster is no simple matter. The minority sees to it that repeated quorum calls force the majority to remain in the chamber or near it for days on end, while the filibusterers spell each other with regular hours of duty and relief so as to remain fresh for the battle. Not only does this take a dangerous physical toll on some of the older members of the Senate, but it also completely stops all legislative activity. If the filibuster begins late in the session, which is common except for the rules change debates, all the other pending legislation becomes a hostage. And the pressure grows for giving up the cause because there are few subjects that vast majorities of the Senate will agree on enough to suffer torment for. Even where a majority can be mustered for a bill once it has been watered down sufficiently, it may not be possible to persuade Senators with only a marginal interest to sacrifice much in behalf of it. The risk to other legislation, sheer physical exhaustion, and respect for the intense feelings of the objecting minority are usually enough to persuade the only marginally concerned that the price is not worth the paying, and the filibusterers prevail.

The important filibusters are not dramatic (and futile) one-man stands, but those that involve a dozen or more Senators pitted against much larger contingents. Although Senator Strom Thurmond once put on a circus performance, holding the floor for twenty-four hours and eighteen minutes, opposing the civil rights bill of 1957, such performances do little except further tarnish the reputation of Congress. Filibusters that have provoked attempts at cloture have most commonly

been on civil rights issues (eight successful filibusters killed a series of
bills concerned with lynching, the poll tax, and fair employment practices). In 1962 cloture was adopted (for the first time in thirty-five
years) on a bill that liberal senators were filibustering—a bill concerning the "Telestar" Corporation, which they saw as a government give-
away to corporations.[15] In 1964 for the first time a civil rights filibuster
was broken, and this led some observers to believe the filibuster is waning in importance. This is hardly the case; it still remains a threat with
which concessions can be won. Although infrequent, filibusters are
usually successful, but one cannot judge the impact of the filibuster by
the number of bills thus dramatically defeated. For the importance of
the filibuster lies in the *threat* of its use more than in its actual imple-
mentation. That is, a subtle hint that a group will adamantly oppose
a bill on the floor late in the session is enough to win concessions that
would otherwise be impossible to achieve.

How the filibuster-as-threat shapes policy can be demonstrated by
the impact on civil rights legislation of the late Everett McKinley
Dirksen, Republican leader in the Senate. In 1969, when the Senate was
staging its biennial attempt to revise Rule XXII, Dirksen pleaded with
his Republican colleagues not to vote for an easing of cloture. He conjured up horrible bills that might be passed but for the filibuster, and
he urged resistance to the "tyranny of the majority." Thanks to the
filibuster, he said, reformers had to get traffic clearance from him personally to go on with their bills. Then he boasted, "Virtually every
major civil rights bill since 1959 was written in my office down the
corridor." Senator Jacob Javits conceded the truth of this, but doubted
there was constitutional authorization for the minority leader's intermediary role. Javits said the Dirksen screening system has exacted a
price that "we are paying now in the dreadful situation which we find
in our cities." [16]

Other facets of the rules empower minorities, even single individuals, with considerable power to delay and sometimes to defeat legislation. In the Senate a considerable portion of its floor action requires
unanimous consent, giving a single individual the power to stop proceedings. In the House greater formality, required by its larger size,

15. On the recent attempts at cloture see William J. Keefe and Morris S. Ogul,
The American Legislative Process, 2nd ed. (Englewood Cliffs, N.J.: Prentice-Hall,
Inc., 1968), pp. 258–60. Ray Wolfinger reviews the use of filibusters in an as yet
unpublished paper, "Filibusters" (Mimeo), Aug., 1969. He concludes that a clear
majority of the senate favors the retention of the filibuster, that it is rarely used,
and usually on civil rights issues. However, he takes little note of it as threat or in
terms of end of session time limitations.

16. See the brief account of this debate in "TRB," *The New Republic*, Feb. 1,
1969, p. 6.

prevents individual stalling to the extent it exists in the Senate, but even so individual sandbagging is possible. Consider the Depressed Areas Bill in its 1960 phase. Having failed to get a special rule from the Rules Committee, there was but one alternative to get action, namely the Calendar Wednesday rule. Because the Democratic leadership was in favor of the bill (partly for partisan reasons, hoping that President Eisenhower would give them a campaign issue by vetoing it, which he did), Speaker Rayburn fully cooperated in resorting to the Calendar Wednesday routine. The rules provide that on Wednesdays the Speaker may recognize the chairmen of committees as they are read off in alphabetical order, at which time they may bring to the floor legislation that is at the foot of the calendar. Banking and Currency is high on the list, so it was not possible to forestall the drive for the Depressed Areas Bill by taking up all the time with bills from other committees higher up the alphabetical list. There were other delaying tactics, however, and opponents of the bill proceeded to use them. One aspect of Calendar Wednesday is that all action on a bill must be completed on the same calendar day, making delay an obvious stratagem. As soon as the chaplain's invocation ended on that particular Wednesday, the conservative Republican campaign of delay began. First they forced a roll call to test the presence of a quorum, and by the time the motions, countermotions, and roll calls had been made, an hour and a half had been consumed. Then came the question of the journal of the previous day, the actual reading of which is normally dispensed with by unanimous consent. Because of the refusal of unanimous consent the complete journal had to be read. There followed more quorum calls and further delays involving a total of five hours between the time the House had been ready to consider the bill and the time it got to it in fact. That did not exhaust the dilatory ploys, however, for it was still possible to demand that lengthy amendments be read in full—which happened twice. Had the margin in favor of the bill been thinner, the opponents could undoubtedly have raised still more blocks and defeated it. Partisan pressure on behalf of the bill and the large majority in favor (in the end 223 to 162) persuaded the delayers to relent, because in all likelihood, one way or another the bill was going to be rammed through. To arouse wrath unnecessarily is never the way to play the game in Congress.

Another device in the rules that permits the House to evade an obstreperous committee is the discharge petition. But to use it requires 218 signatures, or a majority of all the members of the House. Evidence of the difficulty of using that weapon is illustrated by the fact that only two bills in modern times have been enacted through this device.[17] For

17. The Fair Labor Standards Act of 1938 and a 1960 bill providing a pay raise for federal employees.

many reasons it is difficult to get 218 signatures on a petition, even if ultimately it might be possible to get that many votes for the bill on the floor. For signing a petition is far more than casting a vote. It is an expression of rebuke to the committee in question and especially to its chairman, and, if the committee is an important one, antagonizing it and its chairman is an act taken only in extreme circumstances. Moreover, not signing a petition is so easy to get away with, because it is not circulated by individual members but kept at the Speaker's desk, where members sign it. As an illustration of how the secrecy of the petition prevents members from risking offending a committee—or merely invites the easier course of noninvolvement—consider this episode in the fight for a civil rights law in 1960. As usual the Rules Committee was holding up the bill, and a liberal group in the House (calling themselves the Democratic Study Group) tried speeches on the floor to embarrass the Republican leadership into dropping its opposition to signatures on a discharge petition. Because the petition had 175 signers, only a few converts were needed, but the oratory of the DSG liberals did not affect the Republican leaders. Accordingly the liberals resorted to a ruse to find out who had signed the petition. Members of the DSG went to the Speaker's desk, ostensibly to check their memories as to whether they had in fact signed, but in reality each was assigned a number of names to memorize and they thereby got the full list and leaked it to *The New York Times*. The *Times* gave full coverage to the fact that of the 175 names, only 30 belonged to Republicans. That did it; with publicity focused on the issue signers began coming to the rostrum, and soon only 29 more names were needed. At that point, in order not to appear to be forced to act and also not to lose control over the conditions of floor consideration of the bill, Judge Smith announced that the Rules Committee would soon hold hearings and report out the bill.[18]

Individual members of Congress who have an intimate and detailed knowledge of the rules and who have won the respect (and/or fear) of the membership can pyramid their power to amazing heights. And the prices they charge for relenting in their opposition to legislation can be high indeed. The following brief tale will illustrate what one man can do to tie up a piece of legislation, more or less single-handedly. It is the story of the Displaced Persons Act, intended to permit entry to the country of persons who had been uprooted by World War II. An implacable enemy of the idea of such immigration was the late Senator Patrick McCarran. McCarran had been born of immigrant parents, but he was no friend of further immigration, for he was apprehensive that

18. The story is told in more detail in the late Daniel M. Berman's *A Bill Becomes a Law*, 2nd ed. (New York: Macmillan, 1966), pp. 88–91.

these new migrants were going to be radicals, Communists, or otherwise undesirable. The king of Nevada politics, McCarran ruled over the Senate Judiciary Committee, which conferred on him the power to reward or punish any Senator because judicial patronage and most private legislation goes to the Judiciary Committee.

In the House there was a safe majority for the legislation when it was introduced in the 1949 session and by June the House had sent the bill to the Senate. Then began the long series of dilatory tactics that held up passage of the law for fifteen months. First McCarran assigned the bill to a carefully selected subcommittee of five, four of whom opposed the DP Bill, as it was called. For four months in the summer and fall of 1949 the Senate subcommittee held intermittent hearings on the bill, although an increasingly insistent group of Senators, both Democrats and Republicans, kept demanding that the bill be brought to the floor. Pushed by Democratic leaders and needled by Republican speeches to release the bill, McCarran instead announced he was going to Europe to study the operation of the Displaced Persons camps and the clearance procedures used for selecting potential immigrants. In October a group of Senators cabled McCarran asking when he would return so the bill could be taken up. He did not reply. On October 11 in McCarran's continued absence, a majority of the Judiciary Committee members voted to bring the bill to the floor. A filibuster was immediately threatened and there were crocodile tears shed over the disrespect being shown McCarran by the bringing of a bill to the floor in the absence of the committee chairman in charge of it. In the face of bitter opposition the Senate then voted to return the bill to committee with the stipulation that it would be returned to the floor by January 25, 1950.

When Congress reconvened, the Judiciary Committee once again took up the DP Bill and on January 25 did report out a much revised bill. In an unusual step the subcommittee resumed hearings on the bill, despite the fact that it had been reported out. On March 7 the bill came up for debate on the floor, and after a long list of time-consuming amendments was disposed of, the Senate passed the bill on April 5 by one vote short of a two-to-one majority (49 to 25). But the battle was still not over, for there were differences between the Senate and the House versions and these had to be settled in a conference committee, a group of Senate and House members who compromise to reach a single version of a bill. By tradition the conference committee leader from the last house to act on a bill calls the first meeting. Accordingly McCarran refused to call a meeting of the conference committee, and after several weeks had passed, the House Chairman threatened to call it himself unless McCarran did soon. His last means of obstruction removed, McCarran capitulated and on June 6, 1950, the final version of the law won approval in both houses. Thus, despite large majorities in both houses in favor of the principle of permitting the victims of Nazi aggression to enter the United States, McCarran and a small band of dissenters held up the works for fifteen months. A tradition of deference to committee chairmen, a threatening position as Chairman of the Judiciary Committee, an adroit use of the rules, combined with skill and determination to use every resource of a system of dispersed power, resulted in an unconscionable delay in making a policy.[19]

Let it be repeated that unless one gets behind the scenes to observe how the dispersed power is deployed, one may fail to recognize the character of that power. If one does not realize the backroom clout of a Smith or a McCarran and looks primarily to the number of instances of overt obstruction and not to the subtle and indirect methods by which leverage is applied, then one will not appreciate much about the nature of power in Congress.

Some observers contend that Congress has undergone so sweeping a change in its operations as to merit the word *revolution*—a sweeping set of developments that have produced a "New Congress." [20] Noting that greater equity in representation had come from Supreme Court decisions, that the Rules Committee was curbed somewhat in 1961 and again in 1965, that cloture had been applied on a civil rights bill, Stephen K. Bailey, a long-time student of Congress, concluded that Congress had undergone a genuine transformation. But Congress following the 1966 and 1968 elections has not appeared so strikingly different from its old self. In the 1965–66 period (the Goldwater gift era), at which time Professor Bailey published, Congress was different. But the changes were less noticeable once the large liberal majorities disappeared. President Johnson's legislative successes in the period 1965–66 were not repeated in the next two years. After the 1966 election Congress began trimming and hedging on the programs it had previously inaugurated—such as the poverty program. The celebrated twenty-one-day rule for the House Rules Committee was rescinded. The coalition of Southern Democrats and conservative Republicans prevailed more frequently in the 1967 session than in any time in the last ten years. According to the reporting service, *Congressional Quarterly,* the coali-

---

19. This sketchy account is based upon the detailed case study presented by Stephen Bailey and Howard D. Samuel in *Congress At Work* (New York: Henry Holt, 1952), Ch. 9. The case studies presented in that volume provide an excellent basis for analysis of Congressional operations; that the book is nearly twenty years old does not greatly detract from its validity. Congressional behavior keeps it relevant.

20. Stephen K. Bailey, *The New Congress* (New York: St. Martin's Press, 1966), p. ix.

tion prevailed on thirty-seven roll calls in 1967, even surpassing its performance of 1961.[21] The cloture rule, challenged again in 1967 and in 1969, still survives unchanged. True, some of the roadblock committee chairmen are gone, one actually by defeat (Judge Smith), the others by retirement or death. But their successors are for the most part not astoundingly different in behavior. Granted, too, there have been improvements in the representativeness of the House due to the Supreme Court's holding that house districts must reflect the one-man—one-vote rule, but as I shall argue a little later the representativeness of the House remains circumscribed by other practices such as the gerrymander. It is true that Congress after decades of resistance has enacted a medical insurance plan, but medicare came in the minimum specifications, applying only to the elderly, and the law was rigged so that the medical men who had fought it so long could now enrich themselves on the new program. One must concede that there have been some changes in Congress, but one may still question whether anything like a "revolution" has taken place.

For one fundamental truth about power in Congress remains: innumerable catch points still can kill, delay, or force modification of legislation. The changes have not broken the filibuster threat, the capacity of the Rules Committee to demand concessions, the authority of committee chairmen to pigeonhole bills. There are still opportunities to use unanimous concent, and the general pressure for control over time on the floor during the last months and weeks of a session still confers power. What is one to conclude if it is shown that ways around these roadblocks have sometimes been found? First the unusual majorities of a brief period made the roadblocks seem less significant, for with sizeable majorities they can be overrun. Some deduce from this that if there were *real national majorities in favor of innovative legislation it never would have significant trouble.* This is a deceptive observation, for it does not consider what is involved in creating large national majorities for any policy.

In the first place there are few policies that really arouse wide national support. As pollsters never tire of telling us, the public, when asked about specific policies, often reveals the most appalling ignorance of details, and it can hardly be said that people who know little or nothing about a subject can constitute part of a passionate majority in favor of or against it. Members of Congress are to a lesser degree in the same situation—they don't know the details on all legislation or even most legislation on which they have to decide when they are confronted with

21. John Herbers, "G.O.P.—Southern Coalition," *The New York Times,* Dec. 19, 1967.

a yea-nay vote. To achieve that would be superhuman, for the range of issues is too broad. Specialization has been a means of maintaining Congressional authority vis-à-vis the executive, but it has necessarily cost much in the way of opportunities of members to become conversant with a wide range of issues. They emphasize issues of concern to their constituencies or ones in which they are particularly interested: foreign policy, cutting government costs, civil rights. But the average Congressman has no passionate concern with most of the issues that come up in a session. If he is from a Midwestern agricultural area he will be interested in farm price supports, but he may have few or no Negroes in his district and he may have no concern with civil rights legislation except perhaps as it becomes a partisan issue. He may be willing to vote for improvements but he will not be willing to squander any of his political capital to promote such laws. There simply is no return in it for him.

And out of the ordinary political actions, the true innovations, never come without the expenditure of political capital. To have the courage to sign a discharge petition against a committee from which you will certainly want help tomorrow is to take a political risk. To vote against the chairman of one's own committee in order to get a bill moving is to risk retribution. To vote for cloture—or a change in cloture rules—may offend powerful figures on questions about which they feel so deeply that lasting resentments and reactions may follow.

The normal distribution of opinion on most matters before Congress is by no means a simple majority for or against a minority of the opposite persuasion—that is only the artificial appearance created by the ultimate necessity to have divisions in both houses to decide. On the contrary the standard distribution is more like a group passionately in favor, a group passionately against, and usually a still larger group that doesn't care one way or the other. Richard Bolling, a leader in the liberal wing of the Democratic party in the House, says that in 1963–64 a group of 175 House liberals faced about 185 "hard core" conservatives, while the remaining 75 voted with first one side than another.[22] But few issues divide members in such neat segments; sectional interests, constituency problems, the personal inclinations of a member, and other factors reduce the genuinely concerned, hard-laboring proponents and opponents to groups far smaller than 175 members.

Therefore it makes little sense to talk about the absence of clear national or legislative majorities for or against legislation. When there

22. Richard Bolling, *House Out of Order* (New York: Dutton, 1966), p. 50. Bolling's book along with the late Clem Miller's *Member of the House* (New York: Scribner's, 1962) are both highly informative volumes on the House. See also Bolling's more recent *Power in the House* (New York: Dutton, 1968).

have been large national majorities for propositions (such as a declaration of war) there is unlikely to be sufficient opposition to prevent action and the problems we have been discussing do not arise. Otherwise, judging at least from opinion polls, public opinion is likely to be an expression of broad attitudes rather than approval of specific legislation. Therefore the normal situation is the three-minority case described here—those for, those against, and those undecided.

No doubt this is nearly universal among any group of policy makers. What makes the case of Congress different, although not really unique, is that there are so many ways to waylay legislation and such an extensive dispersal of power that the problems of the promoter become unusually difficult. That is, the promoting group and the opposing groups are by no means on equal standing; the opponents obviously have the advantage. When opponents can readily prevent legislation from getting to the floor for consideration their advantage is enormous, for, as we have noted, once the issue is out in the open and choices have to be made (or more or less conspicuously avoided), the battle changes. The once neutral and uninvolved element now must make a choice. Making a yes-no choice may not be simple, involving as it does repeated half-loaf-or-nothing situations, but it remains far simpler than entering the struggle to convoy a piece of contested legislation through the dangerous shoals.

Thus the out-of-sight poor, the underrepresented, and otherwise inconspicuous elements face great odds in Congress. For publicity is vitally important in Congressional operations. And wide publicity is hard to generate on most issues of the have-not people. The case of the discharge petition signatures for the civil rights bill is indicative; when the publicity highlighted the issue, the member who found it easy to duck the matter in secrecy now decided to take a stand. Or consider the long efforts of the late Senator Estes Kefauver to get legislation to control dangerous drugs. For years Senator Kefauver and several collegues had been seeking federal legislation to curb the malpractices of the drug industry. The Senators had discovered excessive profits—in some cases charging fifty or more times than cost for drugs and claiming that was necessary to support research activities. They had numerous reports of useless and of dangerous drugs, and of inadequate testing of drugs before their distribution. Kefauver began hearings on this subject in 1959, and introduced legislation in 1960 and again in 1961, but neither bill got anywhere. Then two things happened in the legislative session of 1962. First President Kennedy warmly endorsed the Senator's proposed regulations and, more importantly, during the summer there was wide publicity concerning the tranquilizer Thalidomide. This drug had been widely used in Europe by women in pregnancy, and it had caused gross deformities in the fetus. Horrifying stories with accompanying pictures of children born without arms and legs brought an enormous amount of public interest in the matter of drug regulation. Before the publicity worked to his advantage Kefauver had decided his bill had been so mutilated in committee that he preferred to have it remain there so he could use it as a campaign issue in the 1962 election. But the publicity and the forthcoming election made supporters out of former opponents. In mid-July the drug industry in a secret meeting with its friends on the Senate Judiciary Committee won acceptance of severe amendments to Kefauver's bill. Kefauver talked of a "haymaker" from the drug interests that "just about knocked the bill right out of the ring." Then the Thalidomide story broke, beginning with a Washington *Post* news story. President Kennedy at an August 1 press conference referred to the Thalidomide scare as grounds for action on the drug bill. Accordingly the Judiciary Committee recalled the bill, removed the weakening amendments, and returned the bill to the Senate, where it passed two days later by a vote of 53 to 28.[23] The law required substantial testing of drugs prior to their distribution, inspection of drug production, and authority for the Food and Drug Administration to remove any dangerous drug from the market on the ground of suspicion of danger. What had been an impossibility suddenly became feasible, for previously uninvolved legislators became anxious to be recorded in favor of drug regulations.

One could cite other examples. Ralph Nader with his book, *Unsafe at Any Speed,* and his campaign on automobile safety aroused the public to great consciousness of the dangers of driving and the irresponsibility of the automobile industry.[24] Nader is a quiet, determined, and relentless crusader for the interests of the consumer—the unknowing ones who eat filthy meat, consume dangerous drugs, drive lethal cars, and reside in houses near dangerous gas lines. Early in the Kennedy Administration Nader, a Harvard Law School graduate, went into the Labor Department, where he did some research on auto safety. From that position he came to the attention of Senator Abraham Ribicoff, who asked Nader to come to his Senate Subcommittee on Executive Reorganization and serve as an unpaid consultant on auto safety. Nader gave up his salary and went to work preparing for hearings on the safety issue. Those hearings began in 1965, the same year as the publication of Nader's book. The book sold nearly half a million copies and it got publicity in all major news media. At this point the General Motors Corporation hired a band of detectives to search out Nader's private

23. See Congressional Quarterly, *Congress and the Nation, 1945–1964* (Washington: Congressional Quarterly, Inc., 1965), pp. 1181–82.
24. Ralph Nader, *Unsafe at Any Speed* (New York: Grossman, 1965).

life and see whether something discrediting could be found on him. The secret investigation turned up nothing on Nader, but it did discredit GM. When two private eyes were found tracking down Nader in the Senate Office Building (and were thrown out by the guards) and when it was learned that the investigators had been posing as preemployment investigators asking personal questions about Nader, the fat of publicity was in the fire. Ultimately the president of GM found it necessary to apologize to Nader before the investigating subcommittee and to further state that "It will not be our policy in the future to undertake investigation of those who speak or write critically of our products." [25]

The denouement of all this was a whirlwind of publicity and the passage of the first law of any significance on auto safety. The law is less than satisfactory—the price of passage being crippling amendment —but it is clear that lacking the flamboyant publicity there would have been no law at all.

One final illustration. In August of 1963 an absolutely unprecedented mass of human beings appeared in Washington to plead for action on behalf of the black American. A crowd estimated to have been as large as 125,000 persons massed in an orderly but insistent assembly in the area around the Lincoln Memorial. Political pundits immediately said what they always say in such situations: it probably will not change any votes in Congress. That is a correct statement but also an utterly fatuous one that reveals no comprehension of power in Congress. For that outpouring of citizens meant to the theretofore uninvolved legislator that genuine public concern for black rights existed. Huge numbers not having before assembled in this way for a political purpose, legislators were impressed, for they view all unprecedented political phenomena with the deepest interest. The politician plays the game according to public reactions, at least in part, and when the public seems really aroused he takes note. Thus it may well be that no all-out racists and no civil rights advocates were affected by the march, except perhaps to reinforce their previous convictions. But the real impact of this gathering was on the noninvolved Congressmen. If it helped persuade the noninvolved to bear the rigors of a filibuster for civil rights legislation (which they did within a few months), then the true significance of the march might be seen.

But dramatic publicity is hard to muster. It comes by fortuitous accident at times—like the Thalidomide tragedy or a mine disaster. The obscure ones rarely gain such publicity. The starving poor in the back hills or on the remote farms of Mississippi have not yet received any-

25. Oddly enough the best article I have seen on Nader's untiring campaigns is in an unexpected place: an interview in *Playboy*, Oct., 1968, pp. 73ff. It is lengthy and informative.

thing like the publicity they will have to have if their problems are to be met. The migrant farm workers, the coal miner, the victim of penal sadism—all get a certain amount of intermittent attention, but given the character of power in Congress, infinitely more public concern would have to be generated to provide the momentum to ride over the roadblocks of Congress.

I am not contending that publicity alone can overcome the obstructions. If publicity widens the theater of involvement—as E. E. Schattschneider has aptly pointed out—the opportunities for small minorities to kill off legislation will be reduced.[26] Lacking money, organization, status, and representation, the have-not's therefore have little pressure to bring to bear directly. Under these conditions publicity can be marginally helpful—even decisive at times—but publicity, as noted before, is often fortuitous and usually very hard to generate, especially on behalf of those whom the majority of the public are unaware of or antagonistic toward.[27]

Thus any group trying to persuade Congress must not only muster a legislative majority for the issue but also must generate enough support inside and outside Congress to get around the obstructions, at least some of which will certainly be manned by enemies. Some groups have little difficulty in mustering this kind of support. A new military program, for example, has an obvious advantage. It comes out of the Pentagon, whose friends in Congress are numerous, to say the least, and it has the support of the President or it would be unlikely to be proposed.[28] The military-industrial complex has an obvious stake. In addition to jingoistic legislators who will push for any militaristic pro-

26. *The Semi-Sovereign People* (New York: Holt, Rinehart and Winston, 1960), Ch. 2.

27. For example, a certain amount of awareness of the problems of migrant farm workers has been generated in the last few years, but the extent of awareness by no means is far reaching. These workers, being migrants, are unrepresented, out of sight and therefore out of mind. In a recent legislative session in New Jersey, the Governor, his Task Force on Farm Labor, and their legislative allies had been trying to get some protective legislation through the state legislature on behalf of the thousands who labor in the fields of the "Garden State." It looked as though their mountain of effort would come to naught, for there were no major forces that could be rallied in behalf of the bill. And then a dawn fire in a tarpaper shack took the lives of five small children of a migrant worker. The newspapers gave the tragedy front-page coverage, awareness of the housing problems of the migrant grew, and within days the heretofore reluctant legislators voted for the bill.

28. Presidential support is a key factor and lacking that most projects falter. Presidents Eisenhower, Kennedy, and Johnson all disapproved of the RB70 bomber project, and, despite the Congressional majorities in favor, the project died.

posal, many Congressmen are eager to have military installations or defense contracts for their constituencies. There are, after all, at least four million defense-related jobs involved. Furthermore Congressmen who specialize in military matters do not consider the broad implications of weapons policies or resource allocations but tend instead to be concerned with expenditures as they affect constituencies—as pork barrel, that is.[29] The technological complexities and secrecy of military policy also inhibit Congressional assessment of policy, and alternative technical information may be hard to generate. Finally the military can play the corruptor by giving free transportation, red carpet treatment, and royal deference to important legislators.[30] Theoretically the Defense Department is bound by law from lobbying for its programs, but a force of 339 persons serve the Pentagon on Capitol Hill.[31]

Similarly the housing industry had little difficulty in collaborating with banking, construction, and manufacturing interests to persuade Congress to back an expensive program for middle-class homeownership in the post-World War II era. Housing for the poor, being less profitable, is another matter. The automobile-highway-oil combine convinced the conservative Eisenhower Administration to venture into the most expensive peacetime spending spree in the nation's history: the $75 billion Federal Aid Highway Act of 1956.

Indeed some strategically placed and powerful interests even manage to convert their disasters into partial victories. The cigaret industry seemed to face possible disaster in 1956 when the evidence of a causal connection between cigarette smoking and cancer became so overwhelming that Congress finally began to respond to demands for action. On one level the industry lost: the familiar warning on the package. But this was not the loss it appeared, for it gave the industry a future insurance policy against damage suits that were being filed by the heirs of cancer victims. The power of the tobacco interests was more aptly indicated by their salvage job on the issue of advertising. The industry is convinced, no doubt validly, that their business is built on advertising: at least they spend some $300 million a year for the purpose. They therefore feared prohibition of cigaret advertising. When the legislative skirmish ended, the tobacco men not only achieved the exclusion of

29. See Lewis Anthony Dexter, "Congressmen and the Making of Military Policy" in Robert Peabody and Nelson Polsby, eds., *New Perspectives on the House of Representatives* (Chicago: Rand McNally, 1963), pp. 305–24.

30. Drew Pearson and Jack Anderson report that Mendel Rivers, Chairman of the House Armed Services Committee, regularly flies home to Charleston, South Carolina, in an Air Force jet, arriving at L. Mendel Rivers Field, which he leaves along Rivers Avenue. Ibid., p. 264.

31. United Press International newstory in Newark *Evening News*, Feb. 20, 1969.

such a prohibition, but they also got a provision into the law that *no agency or state, local, or federal government would be permitted to ban cigaret advertising for the next five years.*[32]

How did the tobacco interests achieve this? First, of course, they depend heavily on members of Congress from the tobacco growing and processing regions. These are men who need no pressure from the lobbyists for tobacco; rather they and the lobbyists plot a common strategy. Tobacco men spend enormous sums in lobbying, and to that they add judicious contributions to Congressional political campaigns. They choose their lobbyists with the greatest care. Their chief representative at present is former Kentucky Senator Earle C. Clements, who was once assistant Democratic leader in the Senate. Clements is officially president of the "Tobacco Institute" and has the reputation of being one of the most effective lobbyists in Washington. (The Tobacco Institute is financed by four of the six largest cigaret producers.) The vice president of the Institute is Horace Kornegay, an erstwhile member of the House from tobacco-dependent North Carolina.

But the tobacco men did not stop at that. They made what appeared to be a deal with the American Medical Association: opposition to medicare in exchange for help on cigaret advertising. The prime basis for legislation against cigarets was the Surgeon General's extensive investigation of the medical implications of smoking, and earlier the AMA had refused to undertake an analysis of smoking on the ground that it would only duplicate the Surgeon General's study. But on the eve of the battle over medicare and cigaret legislation the AMA reconsidered. It announced acceptance of $10 million from six tobacco companies to finance a study that previously they had held to be superfluous. Moreover, within a few weeks the AMA came out in opposition to even the health warning on packages. The AMA wrote to the Federal Trade Commission, opposing the warning notices, saying, "More than 90 million persons in the United States use tobacco in some form, and of these, 72 million use cigarets. . . . The economic lives of tobacco growers, processors, and merchants are entwined in the in-

32. The time limitation came home to haunt them with its expiration in 1969. In February, 1969, the Federal Communications Commission voted to bar cigaret advertising from television and radio, setting the effective date of the regulation for a week following the expiration of the five-year period. This placed the tobacco lobby in the uncomfortable position of having to push legislation to extend the rule against prohibition through the Congress rather than being able to achieve their goals by delay and minority sabotage. As of the time of writing this book the tobacco lobbyists appear to be defeated. Although they persuaded the House to pass an extension of the prohibition, the Senate did not act before the deadline permitting a lapse of the prohibition. The House vote was 252 to 152. See *The New York Times*, June 19, 1969.

dustry; and local, state, and federal governments are the recipients of and dependent upon many millions of dollars of tax revenue."[33] When Congressman Frank Thompson charged that the AMA and the tobacco men had joined in unholy alliance, the AMA issued a denial, but their solicitude about the economics of the tobacco industry remains strong circumstantial evidence against them, because their appropriate concern, lacking some strong incentive to the contrary, would seem to be with the health rather than the economic aspects of the problem.

Which leads to the whole question of the power of the lobbyist in Congress.[34] The lobbyist is often presented as an evil corrupter whose "pressure" on Congress determines policy in some devious manner. The truth is far more complex than the journalists' simplification. There are about seven hundred lobbyists in Washington,[35] most of them registered with Congress as the law requires, and they spend far more than the $4 million annually reported to Congress as their outlay for legislative efforts. They do at times put great pressure on members of Congress, but the pressure is normally applied very selectively, to those who are already allies. In the battle over revision of the Taft-Hartley Law in 1958 labor lobbyists applied incredible pressure on labor-oriented Congressmen not to accept the Landrum-Griffin Bill, but the publicity resulting from the Senate investigations of labor racketeering, combined with the fact that 1958 was an election year, forced many otherwise reliable friends of labor to desert the cause. Indeed one liberal House leader observed that the pressure became so heavy that it was counterproductive. Says Richard Bolling,

> The Teamsters were using methods that may be effective in state and local legislative bodies but not in Congress. Few Members of Congress permit themselves to be treated as if they were either for sale or could be intimated by loud-mouthed bullying. The Team-

33. Quoted by Drew Pearson and Jack Anderson, *The Case Against Congress* (New York: Simon and Schuster, 1968), p. 330. Pearson and Anderson, despite their inside-dopester manner and their muckraking style, provide useful and current information on lobbying and Congressional venality. Their journalistic attack is a new counterpart for the more scholarly charting of Congressional self-indulgence provided by H. H. Wilson in *Congress: Corruption and Compromise* (New York: Rinehart, 1951). See also re the tobacco issue, Elizabeth Drew, "The Tobacco Companies Would Rather Fight Than Switch," *The New York Times Magazine*, May 4, 1969, pp. 36ff.

34. See Lester Millbrath, *The Washington Lobbyist* (Chicago: Rand McNally, 1963), and Raymond Bauer, Ithiel Pool, and Lewis Dexter, *American Business and Public Policy: The Politics of Foreign Trade* (New York: Atherton, 1963).

35. The estimate is that of Malcolm Jewell and Samuel Patterson in *The Legislative Process in the United States* (New York: Random House, 1966), p. 279.

sters techniques became a major unearned asset to management forces.[36]

Such pressure tactics are unusual. In the normal course of legislative operations lobbyists are more subtle. They are, for example, a source of cooperative assistance to Congressmen who are in common cause with them. They provide needed arguments and information on issues, and they aid in drumming up "grass roots support" for issues. The support may be bogus, but an apparent ground swell of public interest may provide a rationalization, an excuse to act, for a hesitant legislator. Thus it is that members of Congress will urge lobbyists to produce some public pressure on themselves in order to get a bill moving. The lobbyist is usually acknowledged to be an expert in his particular field as well as one who is adept in getting along with people in power. As a provider of information, as a pleader for special consideration for a particular group, and as an ally of those in Congress seeking similar objectives, the lobbyist adds a dimension to the representative function. He does represent his interest and promote it, whether it be that of bankers, Negroes, aircraft manufacturers, teachers, or the poor.

One problem with this "representation," however, is that not all lobbyists are equal. Some lobbyists have resources not even remotely available to others—like huge sums of money to spend. Some represent organizations that impress legislators. Consider the role of the banking fraternity, for example. Because banking matters are and have been a matter of public policy since the origins of the nation, banking men make certain that Congress not only gets information about banking matters but that individual Congressmen in key positions get more than the normal amount of attention, deference, and persuasion. At worst this involves bribery. The erstwhile Senate Majority Secretary Bobby Baker was unable to convince a jury that he had delivered to the late Senator Robert Kerr $90,000 in hundred-dollar bills, which had been given to him by executives of California savings and loan banks at a time when savings and loans institutions were fighting an increase in their taxes. The jury convicted Baker of stealing the money, but the more interesting question is what it was intended for in the first place. There are other ways of reaching Congressmen than bribery, however. They can be paid fat fees for making speeches at bank conventions, or their law firms can receive annual retainer fees, or key Congressmen can be permitted to buy in cheaply on real estate deals or in banking opera-

36. Richard Bolling, *House Out of Order* (New York: Dutton, 1966), p. 163. See also Alan McAdams, *Power and Politics in Labor Legislation* (New York: Columbia University Press, 1964).

tions. And all Congressmen need campaign financing. Take the case of
the Chairman of the Senate Banking and Currency Committee, Willis
A. Robertson of Virginia. The banking fraternity became unusually interested in his political welfare in 1966 when the Senator faced a tough
primary. The New York Manufacturers Hanover Trust Company sent
to its forty thousand stockholders a plea for funds, noting that the
Senator had been unusually reliable and that "We believe that Senator
Robertson, Senate Office Building, Washington, D.C., would like to
know you appreciated his attitude and efforts." [37] They got the point:
the Senator got $30,000 in campaign funds. Is it any wonder that getting
a "truth in lending" law through Congress is no simple matter? Is it
surprising that banks are permitted to take a tax write-off of 2.4 per
cent for bad loans when the actual percentage of defaulting loans is
under one per cent?

To focus narrowly on the lobbyist is to misconceive the problem,
however, for the lobbyist is merely the agent for the powers that corrupt
Congressmen. How does it happen that the oil industry is permitted
to write off 27.5 per cent of its earnings on the basis of a depletion
allowance? The claimed reason is that the depletion of a resource requires a favorable tax rate in order to persuade men to invest and
because there is great risk in drilling wells that are not productive. But
a great part of the risk is not undertaken by the large oil companies but
by speculative drillers—the wildcatters—who drill and then sell to
the big producers. In any event the lucrativeness of the oil industry's tax
gimmick, which it has enjoyed since 1926, is such as to breed millionaires. Indeed some oil companies earn millions and pay no taxes at all.
The largest refiners of oil pay well under 10 per cent, and the average
corporation nearly 50 per cent. This bonanza is hardly the work of a
few lobbyists. It is helped along by millionaires, lobbyists, and insiders
—men like Lyndon Johnson, Sam Rayburn, and Robert Kerr, when that
triumvirate protected the interests of the oil barons. The role of the
lobbyist pales beside the efforts of key legislators working from inside
to protect the precious tax loophole.[38] It is said that Rayburn admitted

37. Pearson and Anderson, op. cit., p. 193. See their chapter, "Added Dividends:
Bankers in the Cloakroom," pp. 184–205. In 1969 after the *Wall Street Journal*
reported that Representative Seymour Halpern, a member of the House Banking
and Currency Committee, was deeply in debt to several banks on loans arranged
at unusually favorable rates, Representative Wright Patman, a frequent critic of
the banking industry and Chairman of the Banking and Currency Committee, called .
for an investigation of bank lobbying. He reported on offers to Congressmen of
bank stocks, extensive loan services, and special assistance in raising campaign
funds. See *The New York Times*, Aug. 1, 1969.

38. On the far-reaching strategy of the oilmen see Robert Engler, *The Politics
of Oil* (New York: Macmillan, 1961), especially Ch. 13–16.

no one to the tax-writing Ways and Means Committee without first making sure if he was "right" on the oil depletion allowance. Lyndon Johnson as leader in the Senate was equally zealous. Johnson came to the rescue in the incident previously mentioned involving an attempted bribe of Senator Case in furtherance of an oil bill. When Case denounced this and a full-scale investigation was promised by Senator Gore of Tennessee, Johnson persuaded Gore to turn over the investigation to the friendlier hands of Senator John McClellan of Arkansas. The investigation was not spectacular. "The public did not know, however, that McClellan's law firm in Little Rock, according to its listing of clients in the Martindale-Hubbel directory, at that time represented Standard Oil of New Jersey, Seaboard Oil, Tidewater Oil, and Carter Oil." [39] And Robert Kerr, oil millionaire and Senator from Oklahoma, was the uncrowned champion of all conflict-of-interest dealers. He was, he said "in everything" from oil, uranium, and real estate to banking, cattle, potash and coal—among other things. To him the oil depletion allowance was holy, and he held a place on the Senate Finance Committee to protect it. Indeed the power of oil is so pervasive it is difficult to determine where a clear conflict of interest exists. It probably did not greatly affect Dwight Eisenhower's position on oil questions that his Pennsylvania farm was maintained with funds contributed periodically by three oil barons.[40] He was conservative enough to do what oilmen wanted anyhow, but it certainly illustrates the lack of sensitivity to any appearance of conflict of interest.

The conflicts of interest that sully official reputations and help the chances of the rich to prevail are so numerous that one cannot begin to cite the cases. Farm support programs were instituted to protect the farmers generally, but it is the corporate and the rich farmers who really benefit. An influential member of the Senate Agriculture Committee, James O. Eastland of Mississippi, collected $150,000 from the United States in 1967 for not raising cotton on his plantation. How much sympathy would one expect from Eastland if one were to appear before the Agriculture Committee to plead against a system that pays each of some ten thousand farmers in excess of $20,000 a year not to produce? That, at least, is in the public record, but most conflict of interest is not. For the Congressmen adamantly refuse to enact a rule demanding that

39. Pearson and Anderson, op. cit., p. 142.
40. The oilmen signed a contract to operate the farm and to take such profits as it might produce, but apparently there was no intention of making it pay. The Internal Revenue Service ruled this was not an investment but a gift of half a million dollars. See Pearson and Anderson, op. cit., p. 432. They rightly make the point that the news media gave scant notice to this charity. Abe Fortas was hounded off the Supreme Court for far less.

members of Congress disclose their financial interests. They require this of high members of the executive, but will not apply it to themselves. After some particularly revolting scandals Congress finally required the disclosure of their political contributions and their "honorariums," but not the full revelations required of officials in the executive branch.[41] They scream in anguish at the thought of being forced to become "Class B citizens," as the late Everett Dirksen complained when the Senate was discussing disclosure. But it is a matter of more than passing interest that the Nationwide Food Services Inc. paid the bill for Dirksen's gala birthday parties. Nationwide operates the Senate restaurants for a fee of more than a third of a million a year. It is also interesting that the Peoria, Illinois, law firm of Davis, Morgan, and Witherell (of which Dirksen was a partner) is retained by such corporations as Panhandle Eastern Pipe Line, International Harvester, International Paper, Pabst Brewing, State Farm Insurance, Mid-States Wire and Steel, and many others in banking, mining, insurance, and the like.[42] It may be that these corporations merely find this out-of-the way law firm unusually competent, but as in the cases of dozens of other members whose obscure law offices are retained by key corporations, it looks like a conflict of interest whether it is or not. Drew Pearson and his colleague Jack Anderson in their *Case Against Congress* say they studied fifty "typical" law firms with partners serving in Congress, and they found that forty of them represent banks; thirty-one represent insurance companies, and that some of the biggest corporations in the country have engaged firms in obscure towns to represent them—and these happen to be firms with Congressional partners.[43]

This is not to say that all or even most members of Congress are venal. There are cases where individual members refuse to vote on questions because of potential conflict, and there are a few members who voluntarily reveal their financial holdings. The point is, however, that there are numerous cases of conflict that undoubtedly affect decisions. Both the reputation and the responsiveness of the Congress are inevitably affected—negatively.

The Problem of Representativeness

One of the classic difficulties in the theory of democratic institutions is what representation is or should be. Should it be a mirror image of

41. See the report on the limited disclosures of House and Senate members in *The New York Times* of May 11 and May 16, 1969. Even these limited revelations show many potential conflicts.

42. These facts are gleaned from Pearson and Anderson, ibid., p. 112.

43. Ibid., pp. 101–03.

the public? If so, how can that be achieved? For the public at large is not as intelligent, as educated, as wealthy, as political (and several other things) as are those who inevitably rise to sufficient visibility to win election to office. How can one prevent the distortion of the mirror image by the omnipresence of the political process? Or, even more elementary, how can one draw lines of legislative districts that are literally equal? (On the surface this may seem simple, but anyone who has ever attempted to draw districts knows better: even the most diligent effort will leave technical and value problems that are nearly insoluble except by arbitrary decisions.)

And what is the function of a representative? Is it to reflect precisely the will of his constituents? And how is he to ascertain that will? What if the will, so far as it can be comprehended—and that is not very far on most questions—is deeply divided? Or what if the representative finds untenable his constituents' more or less clearly expressed desire not to spend their money to feed the starving? Does he choose what his conscience says is right or what his constituents appear to desire? If he is to follow the dictates of his conscience what then is his role as a representative? Is he to act as he sees fit, then await the judgment of his voters on his behavior? But if that is the case—and to a degree it must be—how can one accommodate the great difficulty in providing relevant information for voters (not to mention their will to learn and decide)?

It appears that in any but the simplest situation the practice of representation leads to impossible difficulties. Perhaps this was the reason that democrat Jean Jacques Rousseau could not abide the idea of representation, for distortion is inevitable when one person undertakes to reflect the views of many. Under very limited circumstances it may be possible. Apparently in the early New England towns something approaching accurate representation existed when representatives went to the colonial legislatures with strictly specified instructions from their town meetings, but the effective goverance of even a territory no larger than the Massachusetts Bay Colony soon outgrew such limitations and legislators became freer agents, although still subject to instructions from their town meetings.

Thus the assertion that the American people are accurately represented in the Congress of the United States is a dubious proposition. There are formidable distortions between the people and their legislative agents. The foremost of these is the equality of representation in the Senate, which has huge states like New York and California represented equally with states that contain but a small fraction of the population of the largest states. Robert Dahl has calculated that the voters of Alaska, Nevada, Arkansas, Wyoming, and Vermont together constitute less than one per cent of the nation's electorate, whereas the five largest states contain 30 per cent of the average electorate.[44] Each group of states is represented by ten Senators, of course. That thirty-to-one differential is not calculated to make the Senate especially responsive to the problems of urban America, where two thirds of the nation resides. Yet oddly there is probably more responsiveness to metropolitan needs and interests in the Senate than there is in the House, despite the intent that the lower house represent population directly. This is explained by several aspects of the representation problem. One is that a Senator, even from the smaller states, represents some urban population and cannot afford to overlook the issues of urbanization entirely. But the carving up of House districts within states permits the creation of wholly rural enclaves, so that there are more "purely" rural members of the House than of the Senate. In the past the state legislatures, which were heavily overrepresentative of rural population, naturally drew the district lines for Congress in a similar manner, resulting in a disparity of as much as ten to one in population among districts in a single state. But the Supreme Court in 1964 held that the Fourteenth Amendment (specifically the equal-protection-of-the-law clause) required equality in Congressional districts as well as state legislatures, ending the gross disparities that once were common.[45] Since the reapportionment that followed that decision the disparity in size of districts has disappeared, but legislatures that redraw district lines still can gerrymander districts and distort representation in other ways. Incumbents can be protected with safe districts. Democrats and Republicans make deals for mutually safe districts, and some areas are denied the representation they might appear to be due by the canceling out of their votes with other regions. Suppose, for instance, you were a legislator in a Southern state and wanted to see to it that Negroes did not represent your state in Congress —assuming that enough of them could get registered and overcome all other obstacles. By carefully allocating heavy concentrations of Negroes to areas with counterbalancing white majorities, Negroes' chances of election are reduced to zero. And the same can be and has been done in Northern cities, where Negroes are ideally situated for the capture of Congressional seats as a consequence of ghetto concentration. Judicious manipulation minimizes the number of black legislators.[46]

Congress is unrepresentative in another important respect: it is senility oriented, to be blunt about it. The population became "younger" because of heavy birth rates after World War II, but Congress continues

44. Robert A. Dahl, *Pluralist Democracy in the United States* (Chicago: Rand McNally, 1967), pp. 120–21.

45. *Wesberry* v. *Sanders*, 376 U.S. 1, (1964).

46. For illustration see the U.S. Civil Rights Commission, *Political Participation* (Washington: U.S. Government Printing Office, 1968), pp. 26–35.

to be, in membership and particularly in its committee leadership, a gerontocracy. In 1968 the *average age of Senate committee chairmen was sixty-eight and in the House it was sixty-seven*. In short the average was two to three years beyond normal retirement age for ordinary mortals. This is not to say that all men beyond, say, seventy (as were fourteen of the thirty-six chairmen) are incompetent or unduly conservative, but the odds demonstrably favor that more than the reverse.

In addition to these conscious acts of distortion of equitable representation, one has other "normal" inhibitions on the representation of some people as compared to others. The poor are in the main badly educated, fear literacy tests even if they are minimally literate, and participate less than others in social organizations that stress the importance or the saliency of political participation. The black man, penned into his city ghetto or isolated on the Southern farm, is additionally inhibited by traditional fear, apathy, and lack of political experience. The following table, which excerpts from an analysis of political participation by Julian Woodward and Elmo Roper, serves to illustrate the point that there is a remarkable difference between the upper and lower echelons of society in their tendency to be politically active.

TABLE V-1.
POLITICAL PARTICIPATION

Population Groups	Combined Answers of "Very Active" and "Fairly Active"	"Very Inactive"
Top Economic Level	69 per cent	8 per cent
Executives	63	12
Second Economic Level	60	16
Republicans	36	25
Third Economic Level	30	32
White Persons	28	36
Democrats	24	39
Laboring Persons	20	43
Negroes	15	60
Lowest Economic Level	12	57

SOURCE: Julian L. Woodward and Elmo Roper, "Political Activity of American Citizens," 44 *American Political Science Review* 827–85 (1950).

There is little justification for believing that legislators are sensitive antennae for picking up signals from constituents. They know they have a wide range of discretion within which to operate. Furthermore they tend to form a conception of what their constituencies want that is largely shaped by what they themselves believe is right. They are confirmed in this partly because those who communicate with them are predominantly those who agree with their position.[47] But this wide discretion to hear what he wants to and to tune out what he dislikes should not be interpreted as an absolute liberty to do as he pleases. Any time a member feels that his constituency is up in arms (which is to say that a very vocal and perhaps sizable minority is excited about some issue), he will at the very least take cognizance of it. There is no other way to explain many of the actions of legislators. They often vote, for example, in favor of the continuance of the House Un-American Activities Committee despite personal opposition to it, because they can never be sure that the issue will not become a source of contention in the next campaign. As I observed earlier, most Congressional seats are reasonably safe from attack from the opposition, and most members amass longevity without much serious opposition. But defeats do happen, and it does not take many of them to impress on the survivors the *potential* impact of the electorate.

If one can reasonably conclude that the influence of the election is of at least marginal importance where most members are concerned, it follows that very low levels of political participation will adversely affect the political power of a group. The poor and the black, as the data show, are in precisely that situation. Congressmen hear better the voice of the middle class because the middle class is more apt to raise its voice in the first place, is more likely to be a source of trouble if dissatisfied, and will more likely be involved in social organizations that are conscious of social issues but also have means of bringing influence to bear. A minor illustration of this point was demonstrated early in the Nixon administration when the surbanites around numerous cities became aware that antiballistic missiles with nuclear-armed warheads were to be placed in their backyards, theoretically for the protection of major cities. (For some unexplained reason, just possibly related to the residences of Congressmen, Washington, D.C., was not included in the list of "important" cities to be "protected" by ABM sites.) Previous campaigns against the "Sentinel" ABM system had failed to induce any retreat on the part of the military, but outcries from suburbia forced a suspension of all ABM activities pending investigation. Soon the Pentagon hinted it might be possible to locate the ABM sites farther from cities and still achieve their military objective.[48] It is an inescapable inference that the new Administration made its decision because sub-

47. See Lewis Anthony Dexter, "The Representative and his District," in Robert Peabody and Nelson Polsby, eds., *New Perspectives on the House of Representatives* (Chicago: Rand-McNally, 1963), pp. 3–29.

48. See William Beecher, "Sentinel Project Halted by Laird Pending Review," *The New York Times*, Feb. 7, 1969.

urbanites near Boston, for example, became outraged at impending construction in their neighborhood, and mustered some of the nation's leading scientists and erstwhile federal officials to voice their objections. Immediately the Congressman from the district where the ABM site would be located and both Massachusetts Senators loudly denounced the plan. Senator Dirksen of Illinois, theretofore a supporter of ABM, felt the heat from suburban Chicago and told the press that perhaps "the time has come to take a cooler and more deliberate look at this proposal." [49]

But raising similar protest against the demolition of the homes of perhaps tens of thousands of slum dwellers in order to build a highway is another matter. To organize the poor to make the protest is not easy and to make their objections felt is far more difficult.[50] For they are people of low status, not organized, and not politically dangerous. To a degree the ghetto riots provided some of the political clout the slums had not had before, because an implicit threat of destruction made some unconcerned legislators take note. But memory dims rapidly, and a riot remote in time is not much threat; a potential riot is too vague, too imponderable to be a force even nearly equivalent to the power of the middle class aroused.

Consider another illustration of the nonrepresentativeness of Congress. The problem is hunger. This nation possesses half the world's wealth and it is difficult to believe that people here suffer from chronic malnutrition. But gradually in the 1960's awareness did grow, and eventually Congress was presented with demands that something be done about it. A brief tracing of the responses of Congress to this human tragedy will perhaps illustrate how some people in America are unrepresented.

President Kennedy, three days after taking office, expanded the federal distribution of surplus foods to the poor, but because of Congressional reluctance to act, bureaucratic confusion, and greater concern with the farmers' problems than those of the starving, federal programs in the ensuing years failed to reach many of those in need. No one knows how extensive the hunger is but one common estimate is that over twenty million persons are affected. The Surgeon General told a Senate inquiry it was impossible to estimate accurately the extent of malnutrition. When Senator Clark of Pennsylvania pressed him as to

49. Quoted by John W. Finney, "Halt of Sentinel Is Traced to a 10-Month-Old Memo," *The New York Times*, Feb. 9, 1969. This is a detailed study of anti-ABM politics.

50. See Michael Lipsky, "Protest as a Political Resource," 62 *American Political Science Review* 1144–58 (1968) for an excellent analysis of the problems of mounting the protests of the poor.

why no one knew, the Surgeon General, Dr. William H. Stewart, replied, "That has been part of the problem. It hasn't been anybody's job. . . . We can do it all over the world, but not in the United States."[51]

Adequate documentation based upon scientific inquiry has come slowly. At first nonprofessional observers reported their findings, but defenders of the status quo dismissed this as biased and unscientific. After two years of intermittent effort to get better data the group of senators who led the battle for action got some systematic data from the U.S. Public Health Service. Dr. Arnold E. Schaefer of the Health Service told the select Senate Committee on Nutrition and Human Needs that the PHS investigation of twelve thousand persons selected at random in low-income areas of four states (Louisiana, Kentucky, Texas, and New York) had shown nutritional levels as low as those found in similar studies in Central America. He went on

> We did not expect to find such cases in the United States. In many of the developing areas where we have worked—Africa, Latin America and Asia—these severe cases of malnutrition only rarely are found. They either are hospitalized or have died.[52]

The survey turned up cases of rickets, goiter, kwashiorkor (a disease attributed to an extreme protein deficiency), mental retardation, and many other physical-health problems associated with insufficient food. This gave official sanction to what an unofficial medical group had found in an earlier survey. In May, 1967, a team of physicians sent by the Field Foundation investigated the health conditions of children in Mississippi. Among other findings were these:

> We saw children affected with chronic diarrhea, chronic sores, chronic leg and arm (untreated) injuries and deformities. . . . We saw homes with children who are lucky to eat one meal a day—and that one inadequate so far as vitamins, minerals, or protein is concerned. We saw children who don't get to eat fruit, green vegetables, or meat. They live on starches—grits, bread, Kool Aid. Their parents may be declared ineligible for commodities, ineli-

51. Cited in an extensive collection of materials on the problem: "Hunger in America: Chronology and Selected Background Materials," prepared by the Subcommittee on Employment, Manpower and Poverty of the Committee on Labor and Public Welfare of the U.S. Senate, 90th Congress, 2nd Session (Washington: U.S. Government Printing Office, Oct., 1968), p. 49.

52. Quoted by Homer Bigart, "Senate Unit Told of Hunger in U.S.," *The New York Times*, Jan. 23, 1969.

gible for the food stamp program, even though they have literally nothing. We saw children fed communally—that is by neighbors who give scraps of food to children whose own parents have nothing to give them.[53]

Children are most vulnerable to hunger and the youngest ones especially so. The impact of poverty and malnutrition in babies is graphically shown when one compares the "postneonatal death rates" (i.e., deaths between one month and one year of age) of the poor and the national average. The babies of the poor die at three times the average rate, and "In the poorest counties, the disparity shoots up to five to ten times the national average."[54] In affluent Bergen County, New Jersey, the postneonatal death rate for whites is 3.7 per thousand and for non-whites 11.2, but in Navajo County, Arizona, the nonwhite rate is 58.5; in Clinch County, Georgia, the white rate is 11.5 and for nonwhites 45.6.

Despite the growing evidence of widespread hunger, the farm establishment in Congress continued to resist the expansion of federal assistance to the starving. The Agriculture Department gradually gave way to some of the demands of the Senate group making demands for action, but only slowly and hesitantly. The Department moves slowly because it is farmer, not consumer, oriented. Former Agriculture Secretary Orville Freeman became incensed at attacks on the inadequacy of his efforts to feed the poor, and defended his Department by showing that six million persons were assisted and that the program was improving. But he never provided any satisfactory explanation of why the Department annually turned back to the treasury hundreds of millions of dollars that legally could have been devoted to feeding the hungry. Freeman wrote a letter of denunciation to the president of the Columbia Broadcasting Company concerning its program "Hunger in America," calling it irresponsible journalism that would tend to "increase the bitterness and unrest that so disturbs American society today." He did

53. Quoted by the Citizens Board of Inquiry into Hunger and Malnutrition in the United States, *Hunger USA* (Boston: Beacon Press, 1963), p. 13. The authors of *Hunger USA*, not a medical group, were assailed in a report, prepared under the auspices of the Institute of Defense Analysis (of all places) by Dr. Herbert Pollack, that is reproduced in the Senate Document cited in footnote 51, above. Pollack attacked the Citizens Board for being nonscientific and generally took the line that whatever malnutrition existed was not caused by poverty but by ignorance and wrong use of food budgets. This led in turn to two rebutting papers, prepared by professors of nutrition at Cornell and Harvard: Jean Mayer of Harvard and Michael C. Latham of Cornell; both papers are mimeographed and not formally published, but their refutation of the Pollack paper is devastating.

54. *Hunger, U.S.A.*, p. 34.

not, however, provide an explanation for the charge leveled by the CBS reporters:

> The Department of Agriculture has emergency power to bring food to hungry people in any county in the United States. So far, it has been reluctant to exercise this power. In the last two years, the Department of Agriculture has quietly turned back to the Treasury $408 million that could have been used to feed hungry Americans. CBS News has learned that this year the Department plans to turn back to the Treasury another $227 million. . . .
>
> Meanwhile, American farmers, in recent weeks, have slaughtered 14,000 hogs because, they say, there is no market for them. The Department of Agriculture protects farmers, not consumers, especially not destitute consumers.[55]

The Agriculture Department did put pressure on counties not participating under either food program, and even threatened to go into certain of them with its own independent distribution system. But what is one to conclude about the Department when it took enormous pressure to get it to *threaten* to do what it had had formal authority to do for over thirty years? [56] And what must one infer when the *revised* rules require a *family earning $30 to $40 a month to pay $10 for food stamps!*

The campaign for action against hunger became intense in the spring of 1967 when the late Senator Robert Kennedy and Senator Joseph Clark took testimony and made personal observations of conditions in Mississippi. Publicity, legislative resolutions, bureaucratic moves did ease the plight of some, but in the spring of 1969, two years after intensive efforts began, millions were still hungry and dying. Resistance to action came at every stage of the campaign. For example, in February, 1969, the Senate Rules Committee cut the funds of the Senate Select Committee on Nutrition and Human Needs. The Rules Committee reduced by $100,000 a request for $250,000 to continue and expand an investigation of hunger. Senator McGovern, chairman of the special committee, had fifty-three cosponsors for the resolution to continue and expand the investigation, but ironically the chief opponents of McGovern's committee were from the very states where the problem was most chronic. Senator Allen Ellender, Chairman of the Senate Agriculture Committee, is from Louisiana, where the Public Health Service had found hunger in its systematic investigation. More than a third of

---

55. From the transcript of "Hunger in America" presented in the Senate Document cited in footnote 50 above, pp. 120–33; the quotation is at p. 133.

56. Public Law 320, Section 32 (74th Congress).

Louisiana's population lives in poverty, whereas almost $22 million is paid to Louisiana farmers who receive over $5,000 each in the farm subsidy program. Senator Strom Thurmond of South Carolina found the whole thing a "Democratic plot to get the Negro vote," but conditions were so bad in parts of South Carolina that his colleague from South Carolina, Senator Ernest Hollings, following a personal investigation, declared that "Congress is going to have to take the hunger problem and cross agency lines and come up with a solution." [57] The publicity was too glaring to permit the reduction of funds for investigation, however. In a voice vote—as a face-saving gesture to the Rules Committee—the Senate restored the funds. [58]

In the House of Representatives, opposition to the drive for alleviation of hunger was also concentrated among legislators who came from the affected areas. Of the thirty-four-member House Agriculture Committee nineteen represented districts with a quarter or more of its population below the poverty line. So powerful is Mississippi's Jamie L. Whitten (as Chairman of the Agriculture Appropriations Subcommittee) that reputedly he kept the Public Health Service from using Mississippi as one of its states for investigation, despite the fact that the state is one of the most critical hunger areas. (In Whitten's district 59 per cent of the population is impoverished.) House Agriculture Committee Chairman, W. R. Poage, repeatedly rose to the defense of the Agriculture Department in the course of the years of bickering, and did much to sabotage expansion of the program. When CBS cameras let the poor in Texas tell of their conditions, Congressman Whitten reportedly got the FBI to dispatch agents to question those who had appeared on the program. The reason, Whitten said, was "to determine the real extent of hunger in the country," but the investigators achieved little except to intimidate those who had spoken up. [59] Poage also attempted to controvert the evidence on hunger by writing to the health officers of the counties designated as extremely poor. Not surprisingly the loaded questions brought the expected response: the doctors in charge of the health of the people of those counties found nothing wrong. But because he asked "have you stopped beating your wife" questions, the responses were not surprising. [60]

57. "Hollings Assails U.S. over Hunger," *The New York Times*, Feb. 2, 1969.
58. Warren Weaver "Senate Rescinds Hunger Study Cut," *The New York Times*, Feb. 19, 1969.
59. See Robert Cole and Harry Huge, "FBI on the Trail of the Hunger-Mongers," *New Republic*, Dec. 21, 1968, pp. 11–13, quotation at p. 12.
60. See the Senate Document cited in footnote 51 above for Poage's letter and selected replies, and also the critical evaluation of those replies in a paper from the University of Iowa, pp. 160–80.

At the time this is being written legislation is pending to double the allocation of funds for feeding the starving, raising the amount to $750 million for fiscal year 1970 and doubling it for the next year. But the rural block still prevents giving free food stamps to the very poor, and resists a provision to force action to feed the poor in some four hundred counties where local administrators simply do nothing. And this is done simultaneously with a Senate refusal to concur with a *House limitation of $20,000 on the amount that can be paid to the Farmer for not growing crops!* We pay $3.3 billion annually in farm price supports, including as much as $3 million to a few individual farmers—indeed 16,430 farmers got over $20,000 in 1968. The strategy is to tie the problem of alleviating hunger to the price support program, which is a peculiar association to say the least because one part induces starvation and the other seeks to alleviate it.

If the Congress of the United States has not in the period of two years of relatively intensive effort been able to get action to alleviate hunger when it is obviously widespread, what is one to conclude about the "representativeness" of Congress? Particularly what is one to conclude when the chief opponents to action appear to be elected from the precise areas where the hunger is most prevalent? Perhaps the answers will be clearer if one conjures up a different situation and speculates on what Congress would do if it became clear that owing to inadequate action by the United States government there were thousands of children dying and in misery in Scarsdale, Santa Barbara, and Grosse Pointe? Would it take more than two years to attack the problems of those thousands as it has in the case of the twenty millions who still are hungry in affluent America today?

Which Minorities?

As we have argued, the Congress is preeminently a place where minorities clash. But some minorities, in Orwell's phrase, are more equal than others. They have opportunities to turn back much larger minorities if they feel intensely about an issue because Congress is so well suited to the nay-game. Or else the intense minority can charge a price —sometimes an utterly destructive one—for permitting legislation to pass. The proposing minority must be satisfied with a symbolic response to its needs, for a substantial answer is unobtainable. Thus the conservatively oriented minorities use the Congressional catch points to preserve the status quo. All of which raises a theoretical problem about democracy—a theoretical problem of great practical importance.

The theoretical question is whether a small minority that feels very strongly on an issue should be permitted to prevail in the face of a more apathetic but larger minority or even a majority. Robert Dahl argues that for practical reasons it is wiser to permit the intense minority to prevail, even though that does deny a majority its opportunity.[61] For those who feel very intensely about a matter may go to extreme lengths to prevent the application of the disliked policy because they do feel so strongly about it. In theory those defeated by an intense minority, being more apathetic, will react more calmly. Thus for the sake of stability it is wiser to permit an intense minority to prevail.

That, however, does not answer all the critical questions. Suppose that one intense minority opposes another intense minority? In that case the negative minority will almost certainly prevail, which inevitably will result in instability. But not necessarily. Negroes were for about a century refused when they petitioned for action, often being defeated by the racist minority even when potential majorities had been mustered for the cause. How does one explain their failure over those long years to create instability when faced with defeat? As a relatively small minority, and a thoroughly suppressed one, they did not for a long time resort to violence or other antidemocratic steps, but is it not clear that antagonism was growing? Congress assuredly played a significant role in leading nearly all socially conscious blacks to believe (or at least to reasonably suspect) that American government is fundamentally anti-Negro. The rejection of democratic norms among the most militant followed, QED.

So we are now, in fact, experiencing the consequences of the racist minority's having stopped another intense minority again and again. Can we ignore the fact that racists blocked antilynching laws for decades? What if it takes until 1964 and a martyred President to force enactment of the first civil rights bill of any consequence? What if business-oriented minorities, who surely feel intensely about their prerogatives, turn back consumer-oriented demands year after year? What if those demanding food for the hungry get the runaround for years? What if some symbolic action is all that remains when the minority system has squeezed the life out of a proposed program?

Is it too much to say that what is going on in the society today is in some degree integrally related to the incapacity of certain intense minorities to achieve their goals over decades? There is no opinion survey evidence to indicate precisely how black Americans felt about antilynching laws, but one has only to see what Negroes said on the subject to learn that they felt as deeply about this as any people could about a piece of legislation. They struggled for antilynch laws not just to save

61. *A Preface to Democratic Theory* (Chicago: University of Chicago Press, 1956), Ch. 4.

their brothers from the rope or the torch, but to gain some assurance that the society did not count them as subhuman beings whose death did not matter. How can one visualize legislation about which one could feel more intense?

Riots, civil disobedience, protest, antiwar demonstrations and other unusual political moves admittedly threaten the stability that is prerequisite for democracy. But the practice of permitting some minorities to turn others back time after time has done much to promote the rejection of democratic norms.

One may readily admit that altering the rules of Congress to permit majority rule to prevail more readily would be a very difficult process. For historical and practical political reasons certain minorities have much to gain by retaining the present system. Political parties are not and, given the diversity of the nation, will not soon be sufficiently internally unified to permit easy development of a set of majoritarian rules in Congress. Lewis Froman goes so far as to argue that the majority party, if it were unified and powerful as a party, could control operations without a single change in the rules.[62] This is an exaggeration perhaps—the seniority system and the filibuster, for example, would still empower reluctant minorities, unless Froman means that if one had rigid discipline and practically no deviation from party norms then minority resistance would not exist. But that kind of party unity is inconceivable in American practice, and therefore the rules, formal and informal, do constitute barriers to action that have demonstrably prevented many intense minorities from achieving their legitimate goals again and again. In the supposed pursuit of stability by permitting intense minorities to say no, we have contributed greatly to the most devastating instability that American society has experienced in at least a century. Which is a pretty poor result for a stabilizer to induce.

62. Op. cit., pp. 215–17.

CHAPTER SIX

Law, Courts, and Justice

Robert Nichols, a black man from Harlem, was in trouble, facing an indictment on nine counts, including robbery, assault, possession of a dangerous weapon, and felonious assault on two policemen. It all began, according to a white man who owned a bar, when Nichols attempted to hold him up with a gun. As the two grappled, the bar owner got shot in the shoulder. Two policemen came by in a patrol car while the two men were fighting, and after Nichols allegedly fired at the policemen, they reported that they fired warning shots at Nichols, disarmed him, and placed him under arrest. Nichols claimed that he was beaten up in the station house, and he further denied completely the account of the events given above. Instead he claimed that the bar owner and he got into an argument in the street, that the white man drew a gun on him, and that as he tried to fend off the gun wielder the shot was fired, and he claimed, as did other witnesses, that the police fired no shots. Nichols was to spend seven months in jail before he was cleared, but in the end the case evaporated, having been based upon lies by both the bar owner and the police.[1]

What motivates such distortion? For one thing the policemen escalated their role in order to win a departmental commendation for having disarmed a dangerous man—that being a route to promotion. Nichols's case illustrates more than police exaggeration, however. In Nichols's case one of the patrolmen was a devout Catholic who became distraught over his own behavior and confessed to his priest, who successfully urged him to report it to his superior officer. The system of justice does not always run true, however, especially where "outcasts" (like blacks, Puerto Ricans, hippies, antiwar demonstrators, as examples) are involved. Then the policeman becomes an agent of "The Law" and, quite apart from any duty to arrest violators of the law per se, he becomes an agent of suppression and regimentation on behalf of a comfortable

---

1. Paul Chevigny, *Police Power* (New York: Pantheon, 1969), pp. 153ff., recounts Nichols's story as he does many others in the course of this book, which is based upon his experience in running a project concerned with police abuse for the New York Civil Liberties Union in 1966 and 1967. It is more than a factual account of abuses, however; it is also a calmly and closely reasoned analysis of the causes and character of police abuse.

society alarmed over crime in the streets. The policeman is often ignored by his superior officers, prosecutors, judges, and others when he takes the law into his own hands and denies the civil liberties of distrusted and disliked persons. He may conduct illegal searches, make harrassing mass arrests, club the "enemy" senseless without any need or real cause, and at the extreme execute the enemy in gunfights as police have in numerous shoot-outs with the Black Panthers. As improper as these acts are and as nominally subject to discipline as theoretically a policeman would be for these acts, they commonly go unpunished or even unnoticed. The discretionary power of the man in the patrol car decides the law enforcement question in a broad range of situations and never involves judges, prosecutors, or juries. As Paul Cheviny aptly says, "For legislators and judges the police are a godsend, because all the acts of oppression that must be performed in this society to keep it running smoothly are pushed upon the police. The police get the blame, and the officials stay free of the stigma of approving high-handed acts. . . ." [2]

Criminal law and its enforcement are but a small part of the judicial business of the nation. However, it is important, as I shall try to demonstrate—important because it is a key aspect of the relationships between races and classes in this society. The police become the focal point of much of the dissension and division in the society today. But justice and the courts have far wider implications for the allocation of values in the society. The United States is no doubt the most litigious nation in the world; indeed the volume of cases heard annually is not even recorded, although it runs into the millions, even excluding minor matters like traffic violations. Along with the criminal cases, serious and petty, and the innumerable civil suits between private parties, there are important questions of public policy regularly decided by the judiciary in cases involving challenges to or interpretations of public law. All of which means that the courts in this country are critically important agents of government. Not only are they involved in providing the elements of some kind of justice to a vast public participating in court cases, they are also powerful determiners of public policy. Courts everywhere have a role in providing or abridging what we may call "procedural justice" in the sense of fair and impartial treatment for all parties to lawsuits of any kind. But American courts have an additional large role to play in determining "distributive justice" as well—that is, reasonable equity in the distribution of the goods and values of the society. For example, courts may be called upon to test the validity of a rule concerning the discriminatory hiring practices of a corporation or the exclusionary rules of a labor union. Or they may have to decide the

2. Ibid., p. 280.

allocation of tax burdens, as for example whether national banks must pay state and local sales taxes, or whether bulk mailers may be forced to assist the post office by sorting its mail according to zip code numbers—and a thousand other similar problems.[3]

Furthermore American courts are commonly involved in what one may call personal freedom cases, where challenges concerning political, social, or religious freedoms are raised. The Bill of Rights enunciates these various freedoms where the national government is concerned and the Fourteenth Amendment extends these freedoms to cover the states as well. If, as will be argued later, the public has tended to place greater emphasis on the capacity and willingness of the courts to defend these personal freedoms than the facts warrant, it may nevertheless be said that in American government the courts, for better or worse, have a significant role in determining the limits of personal freedom.

Accordingly we shall take up in turn problems of procedural justice, distributive justice, and the protection of freedoms. I readily admit that the real judicial world does not divide so neatly into the three categories as this suggests; there is overlapping. Providing fair procedures to a person accused of some political crime may also assist in protecting his political freedom. A court decision on a matter of discriminatory employment practices may involve a matter of proper procedure and distributive justice as well. But the three divisions are sufficiently distinct to facilitate an assessment of the functioning of the judicial system.

Procedural Justice

Concern for justice in human relationships has been a preoccupation of social philosophers from the earliest time, and for an obvious reason: the possession of discretionary power to punish or reward others allows for abuse. Although social theorists have struggled over the millennia to establish precise criteria and a rationale for justice, they have not even arrived at a commonly accepted definition of it. Almost any set of criteria can be shown to be flawed when applied with rigor. For example, consider justice as a requirement for equity of treatment. If equity is carried too far it crumbles, for mercy, humaneness, and rational considerations will insist on distinctions being made between cases. If Adam, a first offender, steals a car, shall he receive the same treatment

3. A New York Court appeared to levy a considerable tax on national banks when it held in late 1967 that these banks did have to pay state and local sales taxes, but that was not the last of the matter, because appeals could be taken. Accordingly the banks got back the moneys held in escrow for the taxes when the U.S. Supreme Court reversed a similar state ruling in 1968. See *Agricultural Bank* v. *Tax Commissioner*, 39 *U.S.* 339 (1968).

as Ben who has stolen a dozen cars and is now found guilty of stealing one to pursue other crimes? If one rules out special considerations for hardship, motivation, or mental state and adheres strictly to equity of treatment, the law will seem more draconian than just.

And so men have found it with other ways of prescribing justice. To mete out retribution equal to the offense—an "eye for an eye"—provided equity after a fashion but the more horrible the crime the more disgusting the retribution. When justice is called the impartial and consistent application of known rules, the question is whether *any and all* rules can be considered just if they meet these conditions. Could it be just to require that convicted pickpockets have their hands lopped off, providing the rule against it were well publicized and applied impartially and consistently? Indeed many would call any irretrievable penalty— such as death—inherently unjust.[4]

If philosophers have not produced a fully defensible concept of justice, there is no dearth of superficial generalizations about what justice is. Most men, for example, would readily agree that it would be unjust for an innocent person to go to jail for another's crime. On the face of it few would defend a criminal law system that regularly favored one racial group and abused another. But the trouble comes in the translation of these generalizations into practice. No one would contend that as a rule the innocent should be punished for acts of the guilty, but many are unwilling to accept the restraints on the police and prosecution intended to assure that the innocent are not convicted. Although most men reject the general idea of a judicial system favoring one race over another, many would and do object to steps that seek to remove those restraints, such as Negroes' being placed on jury panels in numbers proportionate to their population. In American traditional thought there is general condemnation of jailing a person for his political beliefs, but there was no lack of support for the idea of sending to jail those held in contempt of the Un-American Activities Committee.

In order to minimize abuse of discretion and promote the ends of justice it is necessary somehow to establish concepts of justice and to win their acceptance by officials and citizens alike. One thing that has helped convey the sense of justice to the American public is the vague but tenaciously held idea of "due process of law." Edmond Cahn rightly says that justice is more than an abstraction. It is also a matter of due process of law as that term has evolved over the centuries of use and misuse of the phrase. Cahn's requirements for procedural justice bear

4. Edmond Cahn presented an excellent introduction to the tangled evolution of the concept of justice in his article "Justice" in *International Encyclopedia of the Social Sciences* (New York: Crowell, Collier and Macmillan, 1968), Vol. 8, pp. 341–47.

quotation at length for they state succinctly the idea of procedural justice:

> No one must be accused of violating a rule of behavior unless he could have ascertained the existence and meaning of the rule before he committed the challenged act. When accused, a person is entitled to know the charge against him, to know the evidence adduced in support of the charge, and to have a fair opportunity to collect and present his own evidence. The judge or other arbiter must be disinterested, unbiased, and attentive. If the accusation is grave, the accused is entitled to the assistance of counsel. . . . Moreover, even if a person has been found guilty, procedural justice requires that some way be afforded to reconsider the case later and correct any serious error that comes to light.[5]

Criminal law safeguards are not the whole story, although they are a highly important part of it. The possibilities for using the criminal law for political purposes are so blatant that due process safeguards were developed not only to protect the citizen accused of criminal acts but also to protect the citizen from persecution for his beliefs. Thus, as a consequence of abuse of criminal law for political purposes in the seventeenth and eighteenth centuries, almost half the Bill of Rights is devoted to matters of the criminal procedure. The Bill of Rights does protect political activities (as in the First Amendment) but it is particularly noteworthy that Amendments IV, V, VI, and VII are primarily or entirely concerned with protection for those accused of crime.

Despite the constitutional safeguards of equity in criminal matters and notwithstanding the outcry at the Supreme Court's interpreting the rules so as to protect the defendant, there still remain grievous shortcomings in the law as it now operates. The innocent are convicted, and the odds against the poor when in conflict with the criminal code are decidedly different from those of the rich. As an introduction to these problems consider the travail of George Whitmore.

Whitmore at the time his legal troubles began in 1964 was nineteen years old, a resident of the Brownsville district of Brooklyn of which Mayor John Lindsay once said, "If there is a Hell, the people of Brownsville will take it in stride." He had left school in the eighth grade at the age of seventeen. His education had been limited because his vision was so impaired that he did not learn to read as a small child, and apparently he never caught up after he got glasses at age eleven. The police picked Whitmore up one morning at 7 A.M. and took him in for questioning concerning an assault on a Mrs. Elba Borrero that had occurred near the neighborhood where Whitmore lived. For the next twenty-five hours

5. Op. cit., p. 343.

Whitmore was in the station house, and most of it he spent answering questions. Without going into detail about the questioning tactics, the result of the process was three separate confessions. First he confessed to the assault about which he was originally questioned. Second he confessed to the murder of Mrs. Minnie Edmonds two weeks previously, and finally he confessed to being the murderer of two girls who had been brutally slain in their Manhattan apartment the summer before.

The latter murder had attracted wide publicity because the victims, Janice Wylie and Emily Hoffert, were young career girls working in the city and because one of them was the niece of a prominent writer. Thus when reporters heard about a major break in the Wylie-Hoffert murder case, they covered the television-spotlighted emergence of Whitmore from the station house. A crowd of reporters, anxious for a story, pressed around and shouted questions at him. "Why did you do it, George?" "Why did you kill the girls?" "Did they beat you, George?" "George, was it fun?" [6] Even *The New York Times* ran a front-page story on the confessions. No newspaper reserved much room for doubt about his guilt in the Wylie-Hoffert murders. But there was considerable room for it in reality, for it later became clear that the confession was entirely false. Yet the accusations of the press along with presentation of lurid details for the delectation of the community, had seriously abridged Whitmore's chances of getting a fair trial. As two prominent civil rights attorneys said in a letter to *The New York Times*,

> Not only have Whitmore's fundamental right to counsel and a fair trial been seriously—and perhaps hopelessly—abridged by the police and the press, but it is extremely likely that the public will have to bear the cost of multiple trials and appeals as a direct result of their unfortunate approach.[7]

Both predictions proved true.

It turned out that the murder of the two young women had been

6. This and all other direct quotations on this case are from Fred C. Shapiro, "The Annals of Jurisprudence, The Whitmore Confessions," a series of articles in the *New Yorker*, Jan. 8, 15, and 22, 1969. The quotation is taken from page 95 of the first article. The sketchy account provided here is drawn from the Shapiro articles, which are rich in revealing detail.

7. Ibid., p. 44. As Abraham S. Blumberg points out, the press can become a powerful force for conviction. Although news media may not so intend, they nevertheless may make it "virtually impossible for an accused to receive a fair trial by 'an impartial jury,' should he elect to do so, because an 'impartial jury' could never be constituted if the press, radio, and television have established for weeks in advance of the 'trial' that a defendant is guilty," *Criminal Justice* (Chicago: Quadrangle Books, 1967), p. 69. Blumberg, a lawyer-sociologist, presents an empirical analysis of a large city's criminal law system; the result, although stated in low key, is a searing indictment.

perpetrated by another person, who subsequently was tried and convicted for the crime, but in the meantime the publicity given the confession burdened Whitmore in the two other trials he had to face, for unfortunately for him there was not the same amount of controverting evidence to shake the other two confessions. In the case of the Wylie-Hoffert murders, it was evident that the detective had led Whitmore to his confession, step by careful step. Frightened, and, he claimed, slapped around by the detectives, and weary from relentless (if occasionally interrupted) questioning, and perhaps for psychological reasons that would be hard to explain, Whitmore told the detectives a version of the Manhattan murders very like what the police had deduced it must have been. (The detectives denied having hit him, said they had given him cigarettes when he wanted them, and had fed him sandwiches periodically.) The transcript of the questioning shows how the officers asked suggestive questions and provided him with "details" of the murder that he "could not have known" unless he did the crime. Later it was to be shown that a picture in his possession at the time of his arrest that had led to the original questioning about these then eight-month-old murders had nothing to do with the girls in question. And Whitmore could prove that he had been in Wildwood, New Jersey, on the day of the murder. (It happened August 28, 1963, the day of the "March on Washington," and witnesses were ready to testify he had watched the March on television in their presence—150 miles from New York City.)

The Edmonds murder and the assault cases still were to be prosecuted, and his lawyers pressed for the dropping of the indictment against him in Manhattan, because clearly he was not the Wylie-Hoffert murderer. But because the Manhattan prosecutor did not want to arouse the attention of the suspect who ultimately was to be convicted for the crime, he refused to move to dismiss the indictment. That meant that Whitmore had to go to trial with the Manhattan case nominally still being held over him. Because he was clearly innocent and was not even going to be tried, the refusal to dismiss was a critical consideration, for it was impossible to impanel a jury in the New York region who had not heard of George Whitmore and of his confession to one of the most bloody and gruesome murders in recent years. Furthermore he went on trial on the assault charge first, in itself an odd procedure because if he were convicted of the Edmonds murder (also to be tried in Brooklyn), then a mere assault charge would be scarcely worth trying. The logical assumption is that the prosecutor felt it would be easier to get a murder conviction *after* he had won a conviction in the assault case, particularly because there was nothing except the confession to base the murder trial upon. In the assault case, however, the victim, Mrs. Borrero, identified Whitmore as the man who had accosted her on her way home from work late at night, attempted to assault her, and was frightened off by a policeman when she screamed for help. She had, however, not identified him in a lineup of persons from whom she picked Whitmore, but rather had peeped at him through a hole in the wall during his session with the detectives in the course of the twenty-five-hour original interrogation. She was never shaken in her assurance that it had been he who attacked her, although much doubt about it developed in the trial. One major aspect of the assault trial was the jury's awareness that he was under indictment for the Wylie-Hoffert murders; another was evidence concerning a button that Mrs. Borrero claimed to have torn from the assailant's coat. The prosecution *had but did not reveal in court* a report from the FBI laboratory indicating there was no evidence that the button in question was similar to others on Whitmore's coat, but great emphasis was placed on the button as incriminating evidence. The verdict was guilty. So shaky was the evidence, however, that the prosecutor raised no objection to retrial of the case when a reporter and Whitmore's attorney found out about the FBI report and found that some jurors had been greatly influenced by the impending Manhattan trial, and by the fact that Whitmore was a Negro.

With the assault conviction on the record Whitmore was tried in the spring of 1965 for the murder of Mrs. Edmonds, who also had been attacked on the street late at night. Here the confession was all important, and it was inevitably attacked by the defense. A *New York Times* reporter got a story from two members of the Manhattan prosecutor's office concerning the confessions. One of the two attorneys told the *Times* reporter, "Call it what you want—brainwashing, hypnosis, fright—they made him give an untrue confession." The second lawyer said, "Let's face it, we've had executions in the past based on nothing more than a dead body and a confession." [8] And in the Edmonds case that was all the prosecution had: a confession and a body. After a hearing on the validity of the confession, a judge ruled it was admissible. In the course of the trial defense counsel stressed that the Manhattan confession had been clearly false, which therefore cast doubt on the validity of all three confessions given during that long interrogation. But the prosecutor responded by asking the jury if they knew the Manhattan murder confession was in fact groundless? He went on:

> Do you have the impression that the defendant has been cleared in the Wylie-Hoffert case? As a matter of fact, isn't the proof before you that the indictment is still pending . . . ? So far as we know, [the Manhattan prosecutor] is still in a position to move that indictment to trial.[9]

8. Ibid., second article, p. 82.
9. Ibid., second article, p. 83.

In fact the Manhattan prosecutor had no such intention and had already indicted a second person for the crime. But the Whitmore indictment remained legally in effect, some thought for the helpful effect it might have for the Brooklyn prosecutor. In the second day of its deliberation on the case the jury came back to the court to ask whether it was proper for certain members of the jury to continue to be influenced by the Whitmore confession to the Wylie-Hoffert murders and by the existence of a second indictment in that case. The judge replied it was not proper and the jury retired to continue its deliberations. Later, with the jury deadlocked, the judge declared a mistrial. Reporters questioned the jurors and found three for conviction, three for acquittal, and six confused about the Manhattan confession. Although legally that confession was not supposed to influence the jury, it was evident that the Wylie-Hoffert confession was influential. Four days *after* the Edmonds murder trial ended, the Manhattan prosecutor moved for dismissal of the indictment against Whitmore. The New York Civil Liberties Union issued a statement criticizing the District Attorney, saying the only plausible reason for the delay was to aid his fellow prosecutor in Brooklyn in trying to convict Whitmore. "We expect more of our public servants. They are charged with a public trust and must not place political loyalties on a higher plane than loyalty to justice." [10]

Whitmore was tried again on the assault charge and this time found guilty and sentenced to the maximum penalty: five to ten years in prison. After Whitmore had been in prison some months, an appeal was begun and about two years later Whitmore was at last free on bail while the appeal went forward. In due course the conviction was reversed, but a third trial for the assault was still possible. Although the Brooklyn prosecutor moved for dismissal of the Brooklyn murder charge after the hung jury failed to convict, he nevertheless decided to try the assault charge again. Once again the jury found Whitmore guilty of the assault and again the maximum sentence was levied, notwithstanding that Whitmore had since been married, had a job, and had never before or since had a police record. Once again defense counsel got an appeals court to issue a "certificate of reasonable doubt" about the trial, this time ordering reconsideration of the so-called showup identification, as opposed to a lineup. As of the time this is written a hearing on the identification procedure is scheduled, to decide whether once again Whitmore must be tried for a crime to which he once confessed and later recanted, had been found guilty of three times and two times won reversals.

What does the Whitmore case illustrate? Is it a case of injustice, of

10. Ibid., second article, p. 89.

persecution of a young man who got himself into years of trouble by answering questions compliantly, or is it a case of shackling the forces of law and order so that a malefactor cannot be punished and the people protected? As Herbert Packer says in his book *The Limits of The Criminal Sanction*, there are typically two views of problems of criminal procedure, the "Due Process Model" and the "Crime Control Model," and depending on which view of the criminal law process one holds the Whitmore case will take a different appearance. That in fundamental ways Whitmore was denied due process is evident, but it is also true that he was able to use available legal procedures to win review of his convictions. Euphoric acclaim for the availabilty of reconsideration is hardly merited, however, if one reflects on the chances Whitmore took in trial after trial, particularly in view of the continuing doubt about his guilt in any of the crimes. Thus the Whitmore story is a perfect illustration for Packer's dichotomous models. Packer's models, abstracted from the plethora of argument about the criminal process, are heuristically useful and can be summarized briefly.[11]

The Crime Control Model is based upon the proposition that the prime purpose of criminal law is after all to control crime. If crime runs rampant and the social order breaks down, the consequences are obviously so serious that some risk of injury to a given defendant may be the price required for civil orders. However, the fallibility of the criminal investigatory and prosecuting functions is greatly exaggerated. To place severe limitations on the apprehension and trial of those suspected of crime is to endanger the chances of protecting the public from the criminal element. Packer compares the Crime Control Model to an assembly line: the objective is high efficiency for maximum public safety. By contrast the Due Process Model is a factory with great concern for quality control, where efficiency is less vital than the prevention of error.

The Due Process Model springs from different values and reflects concern about the falliblity of the investigative and prosecutive processes. Because any failure in the process means someone's loss of liberty and the stigma of criminality, the Model stresses the importance of ample and continuing opportunities for questioning every phase of the criminal law operation. Although not oblivious of the need to control crime any more than the Crime Control Model is totally oblivious of the need to protect the innocent, the Due Process Model does involve constraints on the criminal law process to safeguard defendants. The Model also reflects concern about the fact that the defendant without money is at a severe disadvantage. Obviously the better the counsel in an ad-

11. See Packer (Stanford University Press, 1968), Ch. 8.

versary court proceeding the better the opportunity for success. Finally the Due Process Model expresses doubt about the morality as well as the utility of punishment for crime. The latter point is well made by Dr. Karl Menninger in his book *The Crime of Punishment*, which raises serious questions about the futility of imprisonment of persons convicted of crimes, particularly insofar as it is vengeance that motivates society to insist on punishment rather than treatment. The situation is suggested by these words spoken by a judge who had retired from the bench, "because I couldn't bear it any longer. The very best I could do was nowhere nearly good enough. . . . I found myself committed to a task not only inhuman but, as I came to feel it, more and more immoral." [12] Irving Ben Cooper, previously a judge of the Court of Special Sessions of the City of New York, went on to say

> During my fourteen years on the bench of the country's busiest criminal court, I have sentenced more than fifteen thousand young people for their first serious offenses against the law. . . . Three out of five of these, after serving the prison terms I was compelled to impose, went on from crime to more vicious crime. . . . Had my court possessed the proper tools of correction and rehabilitation, I believe we could have saved eighty percent. . . . And this is true of similar tribunals throughout the nation.

The skepticism about the morality and effectiveness of criminal sanctions is well summed up by Professor Paul Bator:

> In summary we are told that the criminal law's notion of just condemnation and punishment is a cruel hypocrisy visited by a smug society on the psychologically and economically crippled; that its premise of a morally autonomous will with at least some measure of choice whether to comply with the values expressed in a penal code is unscientific and outmoded; that its reliance on punishment as an educational and deterrent agent is misplaced, particularly in the case of the very members of society most likely to engage in criminal conduct; and that its failure to provide for individualized and humane rehabilitation of offenders is inhuman and wasteful. [13]

On each major aspect of the criminal process then the two models are in conflict. In the ensuing discussion of specific problems of procedural justice the different positions of the two models will be considered as we discuss in turn problems arising from the confessions, wiretapping,

12. Quoted by Menninger (New York: The Viking Press, 1968), p. 246. See also Blumberg, op. cit., Ch. 6, "The Judge as Bureaucrat."
13. Quoted by Packer, op. cit., p. 170.

preventive detention, the poverty-stricken defendant, the defects of judicial procedure, the content of the criminal code, and punishment as a deterrent to crime. These specific areas of procedural justice are meant to be illustrative rather than exhaustive of the possibilities, and the discussions are more suggestive than definitive, admittedly. But the purpose, as elsewhere in this volume, is to focus on the problems and to assess the manner in which the political system responds to them.

Confessions. Few decisions of the Supreme Court in recent decades have occasioned more furor than a series of cases in which the Court limited the conditions under which confessions could be taken from defendants and validly used in court. By restricting police and prosecutors in using the defendant to help convict himself, the Court brought down on itself a torrent of abuse. After all, they cried, are we not faced with a crime wave? Does it make sense to let a murderer go scot-free because his confession did not meet every jot and tittle of what the Supreme Court thinks necessary? Furthermore, if a man confesses to a crime does that not make a presumptive case for his guilt? Why else would anyone confess, now that the practice of the "third degree" (i.e., physical torture) confessions are by common consent rare? And the outcry is loud, for people are upset about "crime in the streets," demanding that the police get "tough" and courts really punish criminals. In February, 1969, the Gallup Poll reported that no less than 75 per cent of those questioned about crime replied that the courts should deal "more harshly" with criminals.[14] And 71 per cent would not permit parole to a person who had once been paroled but was subsequently convicted of a crime. The police themselves and a good number of judges have joined in the outcry and have contributed much to the sense of insecurity and fear of crime. In part this has been pique at the Supreme Court for forcing investigators to find other means than confessions for convicting the guilty, but it has also grown from the deepening antagonism between those who attempt to regulate police behavior and the police and their defenders.

But what about the crime wave? How crucial to prevention of crime, or even to findings of guilty, are confessions? From the records regularly released by the Federal Bureau of Investigation one would infer that crime statistics are kept with an accuracy similar to data gathered on meteorological conditions, but the validity of those statistics, in the view of many knowledgeable observers, might better be compared to meteorologists' predictions rather than their data. In the first place, a great many crimes are never reported to the police and thus never get into the records. In the second place, the concentration on police matters has recently resulted in improvements in the methods of reporting

14. See *The New York Times*, Feb. 16, 1969.

crimes, which can make the secular rate appear to be climbing much more rapidly than it actually is. Professor James Q. Wilson, a student of police practices and author of *Varieties of Police Behavior*, after commenting on the need for survey research data as a basis for judging the prevalence of crime, commented on the current "crime wave" in language that bears repeating at moderate length:

> If the causes of crime are so complex and hard to understand, the changes over time in the rates of crime are equally obscure. Most studies agree that during the period immediately after the Civil War the rate of violent crime in the big cities was higher than at any other time in our history. Murder is the crime which is counted most accurately (but not with perfect accuracy, since some murders will be mistakenly counted as accidents or suicides). The murder rate during the last several decades and until recently, has shown a generally downward trend in the nation as a whole but a sharp upward trend in many, but not all, big cities. Since murder is overwhelmingly a lower-class crime, and since cities have steadily lost their middle class and acquired, we suspect, a larger lower class, it is not surprising to learn that though murder may be less common in the nation, such murders as remain may be increasingly concentrated in the cities. (Why some big cities have *not* had an increase in the murder rate is puzzling.) [15]

Whatever the truth about the crime wave, there is enough crime and enough publicity focused on it to create public wrath. And the issue of forced confessions—and restrictions aimed at preventing them—has aroused even more public furor. There is mixed evidence about the utility of confessions for gaining convictions. Some hold that without confessions many criminals will go free, for there is no other way to convict them. Others argue that confessions are not that indispensable to the prosecution. For example, they point to the rash of spurious confessions that always come to the police when highly dramatized crimes occur. Apparently a pathological need for affirming guilt or perhaps psychological craving for publicity causes people to make such confessions. On investigation such cases are dismissed, but the borderline be-

15. "Crime and Law Enforcement," in *Agenda for the Nation*, Kermit Gordon, ed. (Washington: Brookings Institution, 1968), p. 183. See also Wilson's "Crime in the Streets," *The Public Interest* (Fall, 1966), pp. 26–35, which casts more doubt on the "crime wave." There has been, however, an apparent increase in violent crimes; that is the conclusion of the U.S. Crime Commission, which says that "The number of offenses—crimes of violence, crimes against property and most others as well—has been increasing." See *Challenge of Crime in a Free Society*, U.S. Government Printing Office (Washington: 1967), p. 30. The error is to assume that crime rates, relative to population, have ballooned in the exaggerated way that some observers report.

tween a psychopath confessing and a suspect under a certain amount of pressure confessing may not be as precise as some maintain. (At least the Whitmore case suggests that.) Moreover, it is pointed out that the hardened and experienced criminal will never confess to anything; he knows his rights from experience and will say nothing except that he wants to see his lawyer. But what about the person without a criminal record? What protections are appropriate for him? Gradually the Supreme Court has erected a set of safeguards to protect the rights of such persons.

The restrictions applied by the court on confessions began in 1936 when the Supreme Court held that Mississippi could not use physical torture to extort a confession of murder. In that instance the defendant was brought into court with the scars of rope burns around his neck from having been hoisted to force him to confess.[16] Over the intervening years the Court has narrowed the range of permissible police conduct in getting confessions. Long and relentless questioning under bright lights without further physical abuse was ruled out in 1944,[17] and the taking of evidence from a defendant by sticking a stomach pump down his throat when he had swallowed evidence was also held to be beyond the pale.[18] Two recent cases that aroused vigorous dissent were the *Escobedo* [19] and *Miranda* [20] rulings. In Escobedo's case during his interrogation as a suspect in a murder investigation, Escobedo requested permission to consult his lawyer, who was then in the station house, but the police refused and continued to question him and ultimately got a confession from him. The Supreme Court reversed the conviction on the grounds that this denied Escobedo counsel as guaranteed by the Sixth Amendment. More specifically the Court held that when an investigation had moved from a general inquiry to questioning of a particular person suspected of a crime the police should warn the suspect of his right not to have to answer questions. When the suspect requested and was refused the opportunity to see a lawyer his rights were further infringed. The decision divided the Court, five to four, with the minority holding that the traditional provision of counsel for the actual trial of serious crimes was as far as the protection need go.

The *Miranda* decision took the next logical step; it provided that investigators must warn a suspect that he has a right to be represented by counsel. The Court also held that an indigent suspect should have counsel provided by the state. Chief Justice Warren said this did not mean that a "station house lawyer" had to be present at all times;

16. *Brown* v. *Mississippi*, 297 U.S. 278 (1936).
17. *Ashcraft* v. *Tennessee*, 322 U.S. 143 (1944).
18. *Rochin* v. *California*, 342 U.S. 165 (1952).
19. *Escobedo* v. *Illinois*, 378 U.S. 478 (1964).
20. *Miranda* v. *Arizona*, 384 U.S. 436 (1966).

rather, he said it means that the police must tell the suspect of his right to have a lawyer and if they do not wish to provide one while the investigation is going on, they must cease to question him. The Chief Justice emphasized that in an adversary system of criminal law, the need for counsel included all phases of the process, for under certain conditions (like those in the Whitmore case, for example) the admission of guilt would create an insuperable barrier for counsel when the issue came to trial.

Have the *Escobedo* and *Miranda* decisions handcuffed the police? The evidence is as yet not conclusive, but the tentative indications are that they have not, the lamentations of the Crime Control adherents to the contrary notwithstanding. Research conducted by Yale Law School students in New Haven indicated that the restrictions were of relatively little significance. The police permitted the law students to sit in on some 127 investigations in the course of an eleven-week period, and their conclusions were that warning a suspect of his rights did not reduce his tendency to talk to investigators. None of those who were *not* warned confessed, whereas 21 suspects who were warned did confess. This is not the evidence it superficially appears to be, however, for the tendency of the police was apparently to warn those whom they expected to confess in order to assure the admissibility of the confession in court.[21] It is furthermore interesting, although of course it proves nothing, that Miranda and the three other persons whose similar cases were decided with his were all convicted subsequently in new trials where the confessions were excluded. It is also relevant that the FBI has long followed the practice of warning a defendant and telling him of his right to counsel, although not necessarily at the preliminary investigation stage. In some other nations, like Britain, the warning has also been traditional. In neither case has the practice appeared greatly to hamper police work. But some members of Congress did not wait for full evidence on the result of *Miranda;* they attempted unsuccessfully to repeal the ruling in the Crime Control Act of 1968 [22] (to be discussed later).

Electronic Surveillance.   For many decades now Crime Control advocates have pressed a simple and often persuasive argument to the

21. See "Interrogations in New Haven: The Impact of *Miranda*," 76 *Yale Law Journal* 1519 (1967). Other studies based on court records show little difference in confessions pre- and post-*Miranda*. Note also Professor Packer's judicious comments, op. cit., pp. 193–94.

22. In March, 1969, the Supreme Court took *Miranda* one step further by holding that police investigation prior to station-house questioning also required a warning to the defendant. The case involved statements made by a suspect while he was in bed surrounded by police officers. See *Orozco* v. *Texas*, 394 *U.S.* 324. See also Fred P. Graham, "High Court Widens Curbs on Questioning by Police," *The New York Times*, March 26. 1969.

effect that the criminal uses technologically advanced devices to pursue crime and therefore the law officer must be permitted to use equally sophisticated devices to counter the criminal. The contrary argument has been that such devices constitute an unconstitutional search (under the Fourth Amendment) and may seriously abuse the privacy of the individual. The judiciary has been caught squarely on the horns of this dilemma and has vacillated back and forth on the issue. In 1928 the Supreme Court considered the issue for the first time in *Olmstead* v. *U.S.*[23] In a 5 to 4 decision the Court determined that the use of a wiretap on the telephone of a bootlegger and the use in court of evidence gained from it did not constitute a violation of the Fourth Amendment. In a dissenting opinion Justice Holmes made his famous comment that "I think it less evil that some criminals should escape than that the government should play an ignoble part." A limited barrier to routine use of wiretapping came in the Federal Communications Act of 1934, which made it unlawful to intercept and divulge the contents of wire communications, and the Supreme Court held that this precluded the use of wiretapped evidence in court.[24] Wiretapping continued notwithstanding the prohibition. The Justice Department used wiretapping in various cases but did not attempt to bring the resulting evidence into court, nor did it prosecute state and local police who used wiretapping in flagrant violation of the Federal Communications Act. This left the Supreme Court with the peculiar role of deciding which acts of wiretapping it would sustain and which it would reject, notwithstanding that all such activity was theoretically illegal. It refused to overturn a conviction in Texas based in part on a wiretapped conversation,[25] and in 1954 the Court upheld a California conviction based upon a wiretap placed in the bedroom of a gambling suspect where all his telephone conversations were monitored.[26] In general the Federal Government was held to more rigorous standards in the use of wiretapping than were the states, but the practice went on nonetheless.[27]

23. 277 *U.S.* 438 (1928). See also Walter F. Murphy, *Wiretapping on Trial* (New York: Random House, 1965), which reviews the law on wiretapping, analyzes the Court's handling of the issue, and presents the background of the Olmstead case in some detail.

24. *Nardone* v. *U.S.*, 302 *U.S.* 379 (1937).

25. *Schwartz* v. *Texas*, 344 *U.S.* 199 (1952).

26. *Irvine* v. *California*, 347 *U.S.* 128 (1954). See also Alan Westin, "Bookies and Bugs in California," in Westin, ed., *The Uses of Power* (New York: Harcourt, 1963).

27. The Supreme Court ruled that federal agents were not permitted to use in federal court evidence found by state officials through wiretapping. See *Benanti* v. *U.S.*, 355 *U.S.* 96 (1957). In another instance federal agents tapped the wires of a suspected spy, one Miss Judith Coplin, but because the tap was discovered and because it was continued after her arrest during conversations with her defense counsel, the Court held that this constituted a denial of counsel. See reference to Coplin case in Murphy, op. cit., pp. 153–54.

The distinction made between the national and state governments rested upon an interpretation of the Fourteenth Amendment. As we have noted there is a distinction between the Federal and state governments where the Bill of Rights is concerned. The protections that are granted under it were not applicable to the states at all until the Fourteenth Amendment opened the possibility. The Court did little to implement the protection of personal rights against state action for nearly three quarters of a century, but late in the 1920's some movement in that direction began. Without tracing the tortuous path the Court took, suffice it to say that the states were held to far less rigorous standards in criminal matters, and in large measure the states were permitted to set their own standards so long as they did not outrage the sensibilities of the Supreme Court. Thus in 1949 in *Wolf* v. *Colorado* the Court permitted Colorado to use evidence based upon a search that under the Fourth Amendment would have been invalid in federal courts.[28] That rule was overturned in 1961 in *Mapp* v. *Ohio*, where state officers making a search of a private home without a warrant were held to have gone too far, making the seized evidence inadmissible in court.[29] Ultimately the Court came round to imposing stricter rules on state wiretapping, and in 1967 in *Berger* v. *New York* the Court invalidated a New York Statute that had permitted wiretapping even though a court warrant was required for the purpose.[30]

Advances in technology rendered the old-fashioned wiretap obsolete. Newer means of surveillance permit the concealment of transmitters of the size of a button, capable of transmitting conversations for great distances. Concerns manufacturing such gear advertise endless possibilities for overhearing nearly anything. Some supersensitive microphones can pick up sounds from hundreds of feet away. Thus the snooper can ply his trade from a distance and operate more secretively and more effectively than ever before. But snoopers not only become more efficient they also became more obnoxious, and from time to time disclosures of their activity threatened to produce legal restraints on their actions. But in attempting to control private bugging the hands of the government were if not tied, at least not free, for agents of the government continued to use electronic surveillance for their investigations. Thus it came to be something of a standoff—the proponents of regulation were countered by proponents of official surveillance and neither was capable of getting legislative action. That is, until late 1968, when Congress, in preelection fright and responsive to the hue and cry to

28. 388 *U.S.* 25 (1949).
29. 367 *U.S.* 643 (1961).
30. 384 *U.S.* 41 (1967).

stop coddling criminals, passed the Omnibus Crime Control and Safe Streets Act of 1968. Not only did that law permit bugging, it also reversed several decisions of the Supreme Court, which had attempted to grant some rights to the accused. The content and politics of that Act reveal much about contemporary problems of procedural justice.

The first part of the Act, Title I, establishes a Law Enforcement Assistance Administration. It provides funds for state and local law enforcement, with emphasis on riot control, a deemphasis on correction, probation, and parole work (by specifically limiting the amounts that may be expended for these activities). Title I proposes that the states create state law enforcement councils, which can be expected to keep the pressure on Congress to continue to provide the cash for more and more police work, although not necessarily for crime control. It is also significant and indicative of who was in control in this legislative fight that the Act is excluded from the provisions of Title VI of the Civil Rights Act of 1964—which forbids the granting of funds to any agency of state or local government that practices discrimination.[31]

Title II attempts to reverse three Supreme Court decisions, one of them the *Miranda* case.[32] The Senate rejected other parts of the original Title II, which would have removed the jurisdiction of the Supreme Court to review matters involving confessions from federal or state courts. It also removed a provision denying any federal court the power to consider a writ of habeas corpus from persons convicted in state courts. Even without these provisions Title II undercut some significant protections. The opponents of Title II in the Senate solicited opinions from legal scholars and received 212 replies from 43 different law schools—all opposed to Title II. Joseph O'Meara, Dean of the Law School of Notre Dame University, said,

> The effort to legislatively overrule *Miranda* is unfortunate and illegal. Unfortunate because Miranda . . . does no more than

31. See Section 518 (b) of the Law, formally designated Public Law 90–351 (1968). On the general politics of the passage of this legislation see an excellent article by Richard Harris, "Annals of Legislation," *New Yorker*, Dec. 14, 1968, pp. 68–179.

32. Besides the Miranda case others were *Mallory v. United States*, 354 U.S. 449 (1957), which held that in federal cases no suspect could be detained for questioning longer than it took to bring him before a magistrate for arraignment "without unnecessary delay," and *United States v. Wade*, 388 U.S. 218 (1967), which ruled that the lineup of a suspect along with others for possible identification by witnesses would be admissible evidence only if the suspect had been offered the opportunity to have counsel represent him at the lineup. This was intended to prevent situations such as a tall suspect being lined up with three short persons, one black among whites, one young among old, or other "aids" to identification.

extend to the poor and stupid what the wealthy and sophisticated
have had all along. Illegal because it attempts to amend the Constitution by statute.[33]

The Judicial Conference, headed by the U.S. Chief Justice and composed of the chief justices of the states opposed Title II, as did the
American Bar Association, but to no avail. The cry of crime in the
streets took precedence over the rights of "the poor and the stupid."

Title III authorized electronic eavesdropping. It permitted police to
plant listening devices for thirty days by showing a federal, state, or
local judge whom they wished to investigate and for what reason. The
permission can be renewed for subsequent thirty-day periods. In addition, and more ominously, any police official is permitted to undertake
surveillance for any forty-eight-hour period when he deems an "emergency" to exist. All this is supplemented by the general authority to
eavesdrop on matters of national security that had been going on anyhow. The uses to which Title III will be put remain to be seen. Attorney
General Ramsey Clark, who left office with the Johnson Administration, refused to expand federal snooping under the new law, but his
successor showed no such reluctance. John Mitchell, the new Attorney
General for the Nixon Administration, authorized wiretaps on racketeering operations within a few weeks after taking offiice. And state
police stepped up their surveillance work; one report indicated that the
New York State prosecutors had installed some seventy listening devices in roughly the first six months of the life of the new law—more
than all other jurisdictions combined, including the United States government. But the lag of the federal agents was soon corrected once the
reluctance of Clark was replaced by the eagerness of Mitchell; no fewer
than fifty federally planted listening devices were said to be in operation by mid-February, 1969.[34]

The last part of the Act, Title IV, provided limited gun controls.
That Title was politically important because the bill was under consideration during the simultaneous effort to enact federal gun control
laws, a campaign that is revived by each major assassination. Legislators anxious to crack down on crime played their cards expertly in
combining the elements of the Act as they did. The Johnson Administration wanted Title I because that let it appear that something was
being done to aid state and local police forces in combating the crime
wave; accordingly the get-tough element bargained to keep down Ad-

33. Harris, op. cit., pp. 144–45.
34. See Fred P. Graham, "Wiretapping and Bugging Rise Under New Federal
Law," *The New York Times*, Feb. 16, 1969.

ministration opposition to Titles II and III and kept Title I as a hostage to seal the deal by bringing Title I up for Senate debate *after* the other Titles had been approved. And Title IV (gun controls) was put to a vote first. Then with Title IV accepted and Title I as a hostage to keep the Administration from lobbying against the anti-Supreme Court Title II and the bugging authorization of Title III, the "crime busters" prevailed. What the cost of this will be, and what the Supreme Court will do in the face of a challenge as to the meaning of the Fourth Amendment remain to be seen.

Preventive Detention. Closely related to the 1968 Crime Act is the campaign that followed it in 1969. This is the effort by the Nixon Administration to get a statute denying bail to persons who are considered likely to commit crimes while on bail. Outraged by the fact that some persons who had been released on bail were charged with crimes prior to coming to trial on the original charge, the Crime Control contingent won the support of the President for the proposition that the Eighth Amendment should be suspended where, as Nixon put it, "dangerous hardcore recidivists" are concerned.[35]

There are innumerable flaws in the proposal. Although one study in Washington, D.C., indicated that 7.5 per cent of the defendants released in one year were charged with offenses while on bail, only 4.5 per cent were charged with crimes of "actual or potential violence," which is the main rallying cry of proponents of the measure. Even so there is no evidence whatever to show who, among those arrested, is likely and who is not likely to commit crime while on bail. In the absence of any reasonable guidelines for determining who should have and who should be denied bail, the potential for prejudicial use of this discretionary power is awesome. Moreover, one should recall that the defendant is *charged* with a crime at this point, not convicted of it. And as Professor Abraham S. Goldstein says, "The person denied release risks loss of employment, with all that that may mean to his family and to the public welfare rolls; he is less able to locate witnesses and generally to assist in his defense; the pressure of detention may have an unduly coercive effect upon him, leading to waivers of preliminary hearing, pleas of guilty and waivers of jury trial; and, in the end, he is likely to draw a heavier sentence than his released counterpart."[36] About all the proponents have been able to say in behalf of the measure is that

35. The Eighth Amendment says "Excessive bail shall not be required, nor excessive fines imposed, nor cruel and unusual punishments inflicted." Bail is not normally granted in capital cases, but refusal to grant it in lesser cases would seem to conflict directly with the Eighth Amendment.

36. Abraham S. Goldstein, "Jail Before Trial," *The New Republic*, March 8, 1969, p. 16.

sometimes crime is committed by the released, citing lurid examples. But isolated cases do not make an empirical showing in favor of a change in constitutional practice. Preventive detention is used, it is true, in some other countries, often to save the embarrassment of trials of the politically dangerous or bothersome, but this is hardly a strong recommendation for the practice. Nor is it irrelevant that many of the examples paraded as evidence of our need for such a law involve Washington, D.C., where the black population is proportionally higher than in any other large city in the country. Preventive detention has overtones of control for black suspects by frightened whites. That unfortunately is one reason why the law may pass.

The Indigent Defendant.   It is commonly assumed that the reason the poor and the black, who compose such a high proportion of the prison population, is that, for whatever reasons, the poor and the black commit the most crimes. The assumption may not be as well founded as it appears, however, because the kinds of crime committed by the underclass are those most easily detected—theft, assault, and intoxication, for example. In 1966 FBI crime statistics show that 1.5 million of the 5 million arrests were for drunkenness, and that 86 per cent of all arrests for serious crimes (a total of 872,000 arrests) were for various forms of theft, not including fraud and embezzlement. In the meantime white-collar crimes costing many billions of dollars a year are either undiscovered, covered up, or at least given full defense by attorneys skilled in the arts of minimizing sentences or avoiding penalties altogether. A recent newspaper story illustrates the point. It discussed a company in New York City that specializes in the uncovering of white-collar crime, and it gave an estimate of $5 million lost daily by businesses through the peculation of their own employees. And it cited one company that found its top supervisory personnel had been running a kickback scheme that paid off about $1 million for the conspirators, but no arrests were made.[37] Incidents of undiscovered cheating on income tax returns and fraudulent insurance claims may equal or exceed the number of lower-class persons arrested each year for *their* forms of theft.

But the difference in types of crime committed is not the only reason the poor and the black go to jail in disproportionate numbers. They also go because criminal law procedures are rigged against them in many ways. Putting aside the inescapable fact that most police, prosecutors, judges, and juries are predominantly white and tend to be prejudiced toward Negroes, resulting in increased severity of penalties for the black

37. "White Collar Crime Costly," *Newark Sunday News*, Dec. 1, 1968. Blumberg, however, finds that white collar crime cases constituted 8 per cent of the probation investigation list in 1964, and he notes that $250,000 was collected as "restitution money," much of it paid to victims of white collar crime. Op. cit., pp. 40–41.

person, there are other economic reasons that disadvantage the poor, both black and white. One is the problem of providing counsel for the poor. Although it has always been the rule that in capital offenses some kind of counsel had to be provided for the indigent defendant, it has only recently been true that counsel was required for lesser offenses, including ones for which the penalty might be as much as five or ten years of imprisonment. In view of the adversary nature of judicial proceedings, the Supreme Court decision that required the states to provide counsel for indigent defendants (*Gideon* v. *Wainwright* [38] is probably one of the most significant steps taken toward procedural justice for the accused.

But that should lead no one to the conclusion that the poor are in any sense given the same kind of counsel that a person with ample means can afford. Nor should one be misled by the kind of counsel provided for the indigent in the celebrated cases such as those involving notorious assassins. On the contrary, the counsel often provided is nearly useless. Being assigned by the court as counsel to the poor is not usually a desirable task for a lawyer, for the pay is meager or nothing, and the result is sometimes half-hearted effort. It is common for such counsel to persuade the client to accept a lesser plea in order to escape a jail sentence, when the defendant perhaps claims his innocence and desires to take his chances on proving it in a trial. But the busy lawyer will claim superior knowledge of the intricacies of the law and prevail on the accused to take the easy route. This may, however, mean that the defendant gets a conviction for perhaps a felony on his record with dire consequences if in the future he is again accused. In some jurisdictions repeated felony convictions can mean life imprisonment on the commission of a specific number of crimes. The innocent client may be unaware that he is possibly signing on for a life sentence when he complies with the advice of a harried and unconcerned attorney.[39]

Another inadequacy of assigned counsel is that many lawyers know little about criminal law and are inept in handling such cases. Often such jobs go to younger counsel because, having little else to do, they are willing to take poorly compensated work to get the experience. Or a busy and preoccupied attorney with little experience in criminal law is called upon to do his duty and take his turn at helping the unfortunate. If the charge is serious the client may face a serious risk because his in-

38. 372 *U.S.* 335 (1963).

39. See Blumberg's indictment of counsel—and not just assigned counsel either —in his Ch. 5, "The Lawyer as Agent-Mediator." He makes the point that the criminal lawyer becomes part of the bureaucratic system bent on processing cases *without* trial. See especially Blumberg, pp. 114–15. The lawyer, he shows, is often a "double agent."

experienced lawyer may face a highly skilled prosecutor whose political future depends upon getting convictions.

Most larger cities have legal aid agencies, some of them working in conjunction with law schools. These tend to be manned by dedicated, poorly paid, or part-time unpaid lawyers who are swamped with more applications for help than they can meet. Moreover, legal aid agencies do not exist in many areas and are overextended where they do function.

One alternative to the assignment of counsel by the court or legal aid bureaus is the public defender system to which some states have turned. This, if it is adequately supported with funds and is well staffed, is better than the hit-or-miss assignment situation. But there are flaws in it, even so. For one thing the public defender often lacks the staff for independent investigation to aid in the preparation of his case. And where investigative facilities exist they rarely match the investigatory resources of the prosecutor. The public defender may also find it difficult to work with defendants because he is suspected as being part of the government team and not worthy of trust. The doubt may be ill-founded, but when it exists the barrier can reduce the effectiveness of the public defender.

This is not to say that public defenders do not often do remarkable jobs, nor to deny that assigned or volunteer counsel often are experienced and dedicated attorneys who throw themselves into a case and fight it as if they were earning a large fee instead of expenses and a nominal fee. Without intent to disparage the good work often done by such persons, it is still a reflection on the adequacy of criminal justice that those who are asked to serve the indigent are asked to do so at a cut-rate fee (or nothing) and are pressured into the work, at times, without much regard for their experience or competence in criminal law. Also with respect to the public defenders, able as many of them are, it is often a job with a modest salary that does not attract the ablest lawyers, and in most instances the defenders are so overworked and understaffed that some defendants' interests are jeopardized.

There are other problems for the poor facing criminal charges. If bail is set pending trial the poor may not be able to raise the funds to put up bail directly or to pay the fees of a bail bondsman. Pretrial incarceration may therefore be routine for the poor just as freedom is routine for the affluent. This is an unnecessary and unjust burden on the poor, but a common one. That it is not necessary has been amply demonstrated by an experiment in New York City conducted by the Vera Foundation. By persuading prosecutors and police to permit them to interview defendants to determine their reliability for bail purposes, the Vera staff proved that most persons can be depended upon to show up for trial without bail. At first the officials were dubious of the procedure, but it has proved itself amply and is saving the taxpayer jail costs as well as providing justice for all rather than only those who can afford it.[40]

In minor cases the poor normally go to court without counsel of any kind, which greatly increases their chances of being convicted. A study in Miami cited by Dr. Menninger indicates that two thirds of defendants who have counsel are not convicted, whereas three fourths of those *not* represented go to jail. Proportionally three times as many represented defendants won dismissal of charges and twice as many got suspended sentences as did those without counsel.[41] There has been some recent effort to provide counsel in major misdemeanor cases where the penalty can be relatively severe, but that protection is not generally provided now. Furthermore, the poor once they are in jail may have to pursue by whatever crude methods they can the reconsideration of their cases. Inmates of prisons draft complex writs to plead review of their cases and do so in great numbers. Indeed between 1940 and 1966 the number of "paper pleas" to the Supreme Court for review of cases increased from 120 to 1,319. (The number granted only increased from 19 to 56, however.) [42]

Problems of the poor at court are not restricted to criminal cases, however. They face disadvantages in civil matters of equal importance ultimately, if not so dramatic as criminal matters.[43] A society accustomed to litigating all kinds of issues never stops to think that the poor, lacking founds for lawyers, have little opportunity to bring suits or appeals in their own behalf to challenge a decision or even a law. A real estate operator when turned down on a zoning ruling has the cash to hire a lawyer and appeal the matter to the courts. A welfare applicant who thinks she is being denied food for her children by some invalid ruling has little recourse. A welfare applicant *may* be able to challenge

40. See the testimony of Herbert Sturz, executive director of Vera, before the U.S. Senate Subcommittee on Executive Reorganization, Dec. 13, 1966, published in the Subcommittee's Hearings, entitled "Federal Role in Urban Affairs" (Washington: U.S. Government Printing Office, 1967), part 13 at pp. 27–40.

41. Menninger, op. cit., pp. 52–53.

42. See *Statistical Abstract*, 1968, p. 151. Interestingly state prison authorities, annoyed with efforts of their inmates to get reconsideration of their causes, have attempted to prevent "jailhouse lawyers" from helping fellow inmates in preparing papers. Recently the Supreme Court told the State of Tennessee to stop penalizing an inmate for giving such advice, noting that if the state did not provide legal assistance the inmate could be expected to use whatever counsel he could find. See *Johnson v. Avery*, 31 *U.S. Law Week* 4128 (1969).

43. On law and the poor see the symposium on that subject edited by Jacobus tenBroek, *The Law of the Poor* (San Francisco: Chandler, 1966). But more telling than the legal scholar's prose is Judge J. Skelly Wright's outspoken article, "The Courts Have Failed the Poor," *The New York Times Magazine*, March 9, 1969, pp. 26ff.

such a ruling just as a real estate man may, but look at the differences in the welfare situation. She would have to be aware that there was a possibility of legally challenging the ruling, be aware that an appeal can be made to a legal aid agency (if one exists), and know how to get that agency to help. And the agency will have to have the time, resources, and personnel to pursue the matter.

Or consider the situation of a poor person whose paycheck is garnisheed by someone claiming that he owes a bill. In sixteen states such a garnishee can be ordered without even a hearing to demonstrate that the bill is owed. Because fast-talking salesmen often prey on the poor, selling them junk that they don't really want or that proves hopelessly faulty once bought, there may often be real disagreement about whether a bill is owed. And loan companies and installment credit houses charge incredible interest rates and sometimes the victim finds himself paying many hundreds of dollars more than the manageable sum that he thought he was bargaining for. Then the small claims court becomes a collection agency for the vultures, and the victim never even gets a chance to contest whether he really owes anything at all. The first he knows of the matter is the notice from his employer that part of his wages is being withheld for the garnishee. Many employers discharge employees in this situation claiming that they are unreliable or that it is too much trouble to do the necessary accounting. This lack of due process of law led the Supreme Court to grant certiorari to review such a case in February, 1969.[44]

Judge Skelly Wright of the Court of Appeals for the District of Columbia also points to other deficiencies in the law that face the poor. When forced from their houses by urban renewal or highway construction, they often have a case at law against the dispossessing agency because it has not met the stipulation that residents are not to be removed until safe and sanitary substitute quarters are found. But the courts have turned a deaf ear to the entreaties. Wright aptly quotes Yale Law Professor Charles Reich on treatment of welfare clients in contrast to others subsidized by government (e.g., farmers, airlines, shipping firms, and so on): "It is a double standard from the moral point of view and a double standard from the legal point of view. There is a law for the poor and a law for the rest of us. . . ."[45]

In recognition of the many problems that face the poor in the courts, the Office of Economic Opportunity inaugurated its Legal Services Program, which has projects in 263 communities. Financed at more than $50 million a year, the projects provide legal counsel in a broad spec-

44. *Snaidach v. Family Finance*, 393 U.S. 1078 (1969).
45. Wright, op. cit., p. 112.

trum of judicial matters ranging from misdemeanors to challenges of governmental actions. Sources in the OEO provided me with the following rough breakdown of the 600,000 cases accepted by all the projects in 1968. Consumer and employee relations accounted for 100,000 cases; welfare problems, 40,000; housing-landlord disputes, 70,000; family problems, 250,000; juvenile cases, 25,000; misdemeanors, 13,000. In a number of dramatic instances Project lawyers have won reversals of state or local governmental policies, infuriating local officials and stimulating a thus far unsuccessful attempt to prevent the project from handling such cases. Some lawyers have also objected to the project as "socialized practice of law," but so far the system has survived to help bring the poor nearer an equitable position before the bar.

Deficiencies in the Judicial System. Many operational aspects of the judicial system militate against justice. It is possible here to do no more than allude to these problems, which are the subject of many learned volumes of legal scholarship. To begin with, it is an adversary system and that has some advantages for seeking truth when both sides are reasonably matched, but even then it does not always serve truth and it definitely does not when the adversaries are grossly mismatched. We need not repeat the points made earlier about the provision of counsel for the poor, but one must stress that the inadequacy of counsel is only exaggerated by the fact that it is an adversary system. The judge tends to play the role of umpire between contestants rather than being an official in search of truth. Counsel as they oppose each other are duty-bound not to reveal information or ideas that might work to the disadvantage of their cause, whatever distortion of truth nondisclosure might involve.

Court dockets for criminal matters are often clogged with such long lists of cases that the defendant becomes another item trudging down the assembly line rather than a human being with a serious problem to be considered. In large cities this is a particularly difficult problem. Overlong dockets may mean months in jail awaiting trial for the person unable to raise bail. Those arrested in riots always pose a special problem because they are numerous and the information about the crime is usually limited. Instead of real trials, the defendants are handled in summary fashion—in Newark those arrested in the 1967 riot had their cases disposed of in an average of two to six minutes. But even without the logjam created by an uprising, the courts often handle cases in assembly-line fashion. In Newark six judges of the municipal court annually dispose of twenty-five thousand cases plus several thousand housing and traffic offenses. In one day's operations a single judge heard seventy-five cases and postponed sixty more. Here speaks an assistant county prosecutor about the muddle in Newark courts:

There is insufficient time to prepare a case. . . . The defendants don't realize [how the court operates] and are caught in the
middle. There is the physical set up. All around the area where the
trial is conducted, policemen talk to the clerk, probation people
consult, department store detectives come to get ready for a case,
cellblock prisoners walk in front of the bench in chain gangs to
another court. And we are trying a case.[46]

Other cities have equally disgusting spectacles in their minor courts.
One has the impression that if justice takes place under such circumstances it is by accident more than design.

It must also be said that judges and prosecutors are often so prejudiced toward some defendants—and not only black ones—that fair
trials are out of the question. Prosecutors will at times hide information
that might exonerate a defendant. (Recall the suppressed FBI report in
the Whitmore case; in that instance the issue was retried but most such
situations go undiscovered.) [47] Typically the office of prosecutor is a
stepping-stone in a political career, and the holder of the office does not
expect to advance his career by losing cases. If some corners have to be
cut to win cases, well that is justified by the fact that the defendants
are probably guilty anyhow. Note too that judges have to win reelection
in most states, and although that may not put quite as much pressure
on them as it does on prosecutors—the judge having some self-protection in the robes he wears—still the possibility of a newspaper attack on
judicial softness might make the difference between reelection and
defeat. Moreover judges, whatever their expertise and detachment in
the vast proportion of cases, are sometimes the victims of their prejudices and will exercise their discretionary authority to punish a young
man because he wears his hair disgustingly long, to crack down because
anyone who desecrates the flag needs no compassion, to lower the boom
on anyone who threatens law and order. . . .

Judges and prosecutors are drawn from the circle of political lawyers,
particularly in lower courts, and the opportunities this provides for
favoritism are innumerable. Although the presiding judge of the Newark Municipal Court denies the truth of the following allegation, it can
be heard from more than one observer of that court:

A leading attorney described the hold City Hall has on the
judges: "The City Hall officials are on the judge's back. If the judge
doesn't want to listen then he won't get reappointed."

46. Taken from a series on the Newark Municipal Courts in the Newark *Evening News*, Dec. 15, 16, and 17, 1968; quotation from Dec. 16.
47. For a particularly flagrant case of a prosecutor concealing and distorting
facts in a murder trial see *Alcorta* v. *Texas*, 355 *U.S.* 28 (1957).

Councilmen are occasional visitors to the municipal courts. "That's to remind the judges that certain cases are coming up," said the attorney.

Said another lawyer: "You can always tell when the fix is in. That's if the judge really yells and screams but does nothing to the defendant. That's because the defendant is a 'political person.' " [48]

Furthermore the police are not only fallible, but they are sometimes backed to the hilt even when they are wrong. And the reason is the belief that unless the forces of law and order are defended in all their activities then respect for all authority will be undercut. The natural tendency for superior police officers is to doubt that their own men have practiced brutality, arrested persons needlessly, or verbally abused persons so that a reaction followed. The evidence suggests strongly that police not only do these things but also cover themselves by charging their victims with some crime like resisting arrest so that any possible civil action by the victim against the police would be undercut by the criminal conviction. Chevigny in his New York study, previously cited, shows that it is standard for the police to charge a victim with resisting arrest if the policeman has used force; it simply stands as his protection against a charge. Indeed he further indicates that felony charges are sometimes made with the expectation that that charge will be dropped in exchange for a plea of guilty to a misdemeanor, which will then protect the officer from a charge of police abuse.[49]

It is also difficult to refuse to accept the policeman's word for what happened. After all the suspect and the policeman do not arrive before the judge's bench as equals. The suspect represents the problems the society faces in criminal behavior, whereas the policeman represents the society and its effort to keep the peace. Likewise the frequent physical attacks on policemen are hardly helpful. Society has ignored or aggravated social problems and left it to the police officer to deal with the consequences. One need not condone the "police riot" in Chicago during the Democratic Convention of 1968 to believe still that the problems of being a policeman need more mature consideration than they often receive from the intelligentsia, who should know better.

I have stressed many problems in the operation of the criminal law and have cited notable instances of glaring failure, but not only for the purpose of condemning. Most of the leading members of the bar and

48. "Municipal Courts," Newark *Evening News*, Dec. 16, 1968.
49. Paul Chevigny, *Police Power* (New York: Pantheon, 1969), pp. 143ff., gives evidence of this in New York, where he believes it may be commoner than elsewhere because it is harder to get away with abuse in New York. Jerome H. Skolnick also presents a very balanced assessment of police problems in his *Justice Without Trial: Law Enforcement in a Democratic Society* (New York: Wiley, 1966).

bench deplore these conditions and often do their best to correct them. Superior officers in police uniform know the problems of police brutality and try to suppress it. But the failures, biases, and favoritism must be stressed because they put into stark relief the reasoning that lies behind the "get-tough" policy. As I shall say later in discussion of crime and punishment—or in Menninger's words the "crime of punishment"—we would have to be a lot more certain of our capacity to apprehend, fairly try, and humanely consider the individual cases of law violation than we are at present to justify the present system of senseless incarceration.

Judicial Mission: Impossible. No small part of the problem of the criminal process is that the criminal code includes many offenses that should not be there. Every year judges see a million and a half persons arrested for drunkenness. What sense does it make to arrest a person for being intoxicated? Driving a car while drunk and endangering others is a legitimate offense, but the state of intoxication without further threat to others is a peculiar "crime." If he is a chronic alcoholic, what good does it do to put him in jail for ten days, a month, or six months? Are the problems that give rise to his alcoholism any different when he comes out than when he went in? What was done to treat those problems? The answers are too well known to repeat, yet the silly charade goes on year after year. Why arrest someone who is on an occasional spree of inebriation? It may be strange and disapproved behavior (although even that would take some proving today), but it hardly fits the category of "crime" in the eyes of most observers. To arrest anyone because he is disturbing the peace and threatening others with harm, or doing harm while intoxicated is one thing, but then of course the arrest should be for the offense, not for the drunkenness. Yet the dockets are clogged with those million and a half cases annually. Who gains from that?

The law also forbids prostitution, and the police are constantly trying to break it up by one ruse or another. But the oldest profession is never suppressed by a few months in jail for its practitioners. A nuisance to the public perhaps when the solicitation becomes too pressing, prostitution represents neither major crime in any meaningful sense, nor anything the criminal law can correct. It springs up like mushrooms however often the subjects are arrested, and it is an invitation to bribery and protection because it is illicit. It is no doubt worth a considerable sum to the underworld that prostitution and gambling, for example, are illegal, for that helps make them lucrative.

Equally futile is the outlawing of various morals offenses, such as homosexuality, fornication, and other sex offenses that take place between consenting individuals. Why place on the courts the hopeless task of trying to suppress an activity that people obviously do not greatly disapprove? Every weekend in the autumn millions bet on football games—all illegally—and occasionally someone is arrested for it. State courts attempt to suppress betting away from the racetrack, while the state treasuries profit from betting at the tracks, and then to top it all, New Hampshire and New York conduct lotteries, with which they officially *encourage* people to gamble. Every year upwards of 100,000 arrests are made for gambling, but that does little to control it. The police are more commonly corrupted by gamblers than by any other illegal practice, unless it be prostitution. Much the same kind of futility is involved in the suppression of marijuana and certain other drugs. The prohibition makes it lucrative for the racketeer and attractive to the nonconformist. Prohibition of alcohol was the original stimulus for organizing crime syndicates, and the narcotics traffic has sustained racketeering since Repeal. A large number of thefts are attributable to the high costs of drug habits, but instead of treating the addiction we turn to criminal sanctions.[50] Apparently we never learned the lesson that Prohibition taught.

Are there better ways for police to spend their time than in trying to trap homosexuals in public urinals, in encouraging solicitations from prostitutes, in chasing numbers players, in arresting drunks? Because the presence of police probably does inhibit the more public crimes, it would seem that releasing police for routine patrol duty would help stem the "crime wave." If that does not lighten the load of the courts, at least judges may be doing a task for which they are truly needed.

The Crimes of Punishment. The governments of the United States spend over $5 billion annually for police, judicial, and correctional activities. Over one billion of it is devoted to what are called "correctional" institutions, although the accuracy of the term is much to be doubted. It would be as accurate to call prisons training schools for crime, because the evidence strongly indicates that the young are so embittered by prison life and so schooled in the criminal operations by their fellow inmates that the odds are overwhelming that the first offender will return to prison—and often. Recidivism is common in the young offender; about 60 per cent of them are rearrested in a relatively short time. One study of some eighteen thousand persons arrested in 1963 showed that within three years 55 per cent were arrested again. Another study showed that of those imprisoned for robbery 38 per cent go back to jail again within two years.[51]

Prison is intended to deter crime, to redirect the lives of those who

50. See Professor Packer's cogently argued case on narcotics law, op. cit., pp. 332–42.

51. See James Q. Wilson, op. cit., pp. 190–91.

commit crimes, and in extreme cases to restrain those whose behavior is dangerously and uncontrollably antisocial. But mixed in with these sensible goals is the grim demand for vengeance. We seek punishment, not correction, and every effort to stop prison brutality, to provide sensible training programs and psychiatric care, or even to create prisons that are not fire traps must fight an uphill battle against a thousand other more highly valued ways to spend public money. To change the prison system is difficult, for the inevitable cry is that someone is seeking to coddle criminals by providing them with leisure rather than the punishment they richly deserve.

There is no space here to describe the kind of "leisure" represented by the typical county jail or state prison. Jails are the most cruel and dehumanizng institutions in the land. Men and women cut off from normal heterosexual relationships become degraded and bestial in their homosexuality. Prisoners' physical abuse of each other is exceeded only by the grim and often stupid behavior of the guards. Wardens and other officials of prisons are normally untrained and incompetent, and frequently the jobs are small-time political patronage, which almost guarantees ineptitude. Poorly paid and respected neither by their prisoners nor by anyone else, prison officials take revenge on the inmates. The cold brutality of the movie *Cool Hand Luke* was apparently no exaggeration; such hell holes exist.[52] And if the state prison with its boredom and brutality is evil, the county or city jail for short-term offenders or for those being held for trial are equally offensive or even worse.

A report on sexual assaults in a Philadelphia prison recently revealed conditions in short-term jails. After a nineteen-year-old victim reported that he had been assaulted in a police van even before arriving at a Philadelphia jail, the district attorney's office and the city police commissioner began an investigation of the three city jails. The findings were blunt:

> In brief, we found that sexual assaults in the Philadelphia prison system are epidemic. As [jail officials] admitted, virtually every slightly-built young man committed by the courts is sexually ap-

52. Walter Rugaber presented such a picture with full grisly detail in his article on the Arkansas prison system; see *The New York Times*, March 28, 1968. That article is reprinted in Lockard, *Governing the States and the Localities* (New York: Macmillan, 1969), pp. 173–85. To maintain control in that Arkansas prison, guards resorted to such devices as the "Tucker Telephone," which involved the attachment of wires to the testicles of prisoners and turning on electricity, but that is just the beginning; there is much worse, including wanton murder of inmates. Something of the odious quality of prison life comes through in a record by Johnny Cash, called "Johnny Cash at Folsom Prison," Columbia Records, Stereo CS 9639. The response of the inmates poignantly suggests the futility of it all.

proached within a day or two after his admission to prison. Many of these young men are repeatedly raped by gangs of inmates. Others, because of the threat of gang rape, seek protection by entering into a homosexual relationship with an individual tormentor. Only the tougher and more hardened young men, and those few so obviously frail that they are immediately locked up for their own protection, escape homosexual rape.[53]

Guards did nothing to stop the attacks, and, with the exception of a single guard, they refused to take polygraph tests during the inquiry.

> One victim screamed for over an hour while he was being gang-raped in his cell; the block guard ignored the screams and laughed at the victim when the rape was over. The inmates who reported this passed a polygraph examination. The guard who had been named refused to take the test.[54]

If this were an isolated incident it would be serious enough, but it is apparently by no means rare. On District of Columbia jail, built to hold 700, has an average population of 1,200; normally about 700 of the 1,200 prisoners have not been convicted of anything but are merely awaiting trial. Felons are put with those charged with minor misdemeanors. Dr. Menninger cites the case of a middle-class widow, the mother of nine children, who adamantly refused to accept the edict of a court in a law suit, was cited for contempt, and was placed in the Cook County, Illinois, jail. Without going into the horrors of what she found inside those walls, suffice it to say that only by buying off her attackers with candy and cigarettes did she manage to avoid sexual molestation. After seven days her family persuaded her to obey the court's edict and win her freedom. She left saying that she didn't see "how any person who has the slightest connection with the jail can be ignorant about all the hate, torture and terror there." [55]

If jails are terrible and prisons as bad or worse, then why does anyone commit crime a second time, once he has had the experience of prison life? The question harbors the fallacious assumption that prisons actually deter crime. For the general population, prison may hold enough terror to help dissuade them from committing crimes, but in the

53. Alan J. Davis, "Sexual Assaults in the Philadelphia Prison System and Sheriff's Vans," *Trans-action*, Dec. 1968, pp. 8–16, at p. 9.
54. Ibid., p. 11.
55. Menninger, op. cit., p. 43.

specific case of the crime-prone individual it obviously does not. As
Herbert Packer has put it,

> Perhaps the most cogent criticism of intimidation [as a preven-
> tive measure] derives from observation of the effect of inhumane
> punishment on offenders. The combination of the corrupting influ-
> ence of criminal associations in prison with the feelings of bitter-
> ness, hatred, and desire for revenge on society that are engendered
> by inhumane treatment in a backward prison may well produce a
> net loss in crime prevention. Whatever feelings of intimidation are
> produced in the prisoner by the severity of his punishment may be
> outweighed by the deterioration of his character in prison. His
> punishment may contribute to the effect of deterrence on others,
> but in the process he is lost to society.[56]

Thus we spend $3 billion a year for police protection and over $1 billion for jails and prisons, but we do not spend the money that would
be required to understand crime and to devise ways of preventing it.
As the psychiatrist Karl Menninger says, everyone has his urges to
excessive acts, to expression of rage, and to aggressive action toward
others, but most people have developed the inhibitions to keep their
destructive urges from harming others. We do know that loveless child-
hoods often have the most destructive impact on the personality. A good
case can be made for the proposition that the life of John Kennedy was
sacrificed because of the warped childhood that drove Lee Harvey Os-
wald to ever more desperate steps to achieve some kind of recognition
and inner satisfaction. It is equally likely that Robert Kennedy fell victim to the distorted, bitter, violent childhood of Sirhan Sirhan. But not
enough is known about wellsprings of crime and even less about the
treatment of those who commit serious crimes. Whatever our level of
comprehension of crime, there is no subtlety about our uses of the
criminal sanction. As Menninger says,

> No distinction is made in the degree of punishment for the dan-
> gerous, the docile, the stupid, the shrewd, the wistful, the confused,
> or the desperate on the basis of these characteristics. The man who
> has broken his baby's bones with a club, the man who has forced
> the door of a warehouse, the woman who has collected two hun-
> dred pairs of stockings from the department store, and the ado-
> lescent who has set fire to an outhouse—all receive the same
> treatment, the same "punishment," varying only in duration.[57]

56. Op. cit., p. 47.
57. Op. cit., p. 63.

It is nonsense to treat such disparate problems the same way, as if they were alike when patently they are not. It is also expensive. Why put a forger in prison for thirty years? If he has never attacked anyone physically or shown any other signs of dangerously antisocial conduct, what sense is there in putting him in jail, where none of his abilities can be used and rehabilitation may be impossible. Would it not, as Menninger argues, make more sense to order such an offender to take employment and repay the person who has been defrauded, rather than to lodge him at public expense for the next thirty years while any remaining reputation or character he has can be thoroughly demolished? Or consider two federal judges' ways of handling two embezzlers. In one case a bank teller was sentenced to thirty weekends in prison. Apparently insensed by this light sentence a second judge sentenced a second bank clerk embezzler to three years in prison. In the second case the defendant turned himself in, had already returned over half of what he had taken, was working at two jobs in order to maintain his family and repay fifty dollars a week to the bank. Outwardly, at least, this embezzler appears to have been well on the way to self-restoration. What three years in a prison will do to such a personality one can only guess. Who committed the greater crime here, the judge or the defendant? [58]

In short the punishment does not fit the crime, and the ideas that underlie the system are archaic and perverted by a passion for vengeance. In the meantime, the waste of public funds, the destruction of human lives, and the risks of being victims of criminal activity all continue. The injustice of it is capped by its stupidity, but how, in this system of political legerdemain does anyone find the necessary resources to change it?

There are ways, if the will to experiment existed, to get at some of the ancient problems of criminal justice. The most important is to rethink what objectives we seek and to assess the implications of the paths we have followed. There are legislative and administrative changes that might pay off in various ways. If jails by enforcing a rigid monosexual life on men and women lead them into homosexuality and criminal bestiality, why not then consider, as many societies do, the conjugal visit? If self-respect and employability are factors—as probably they are—in allowing men to escape criminality why not attempt meaningful and really relevant job-training programs in jail instead of making these men stamp out license plates, a job not likely to be in great demand outside? If psychiatric problems beset most criminals—as prob-

58. See John Sibley, "Embezzler Given Three Years . . .," *The New York Times*, March 7, 1969.

ably is true—why not spend the money to at least attempt rehabilitation?

Similarly—to give one example—it might be possible to do much to modify some of the less attractive aspects of police behavior by making administrative modifications that play down firearms and violence and raise the importance of sensible community relations. This is not to suggest that the way to deal with ghetto-police conflict is to sweet-talk our way out of it, but because respect and a sense of pride—on both sides—is obviously involved in this conflict, it makes sense to get across to the police the nature of the problems involved. To be sure, such education is hard to get across, but through such devices as the New York City experiment with the family-crisis-team approach there might be opportunities to move ahead. In New York an experiment for settling family disputes was attempted in which settlement by force, arrests, or nightstick authority gave way to a showing of respect, an attempt to mediate, and a willingness to listen. This paid off with fewer policemen assaulted, and fewer crimes of violence in the families where police were summoned. A conscious modification of reward patterns in police departments that rewarded men for settling disputes and giving assistance rather than rewarding the tough and trigger-happy might produce considerable improvement.

Similarly there ought to be reconsideration of the political foundation of our courts, especially the lower courts. As of now the lower courts in many jurisdictions are highly unprofessional, the refuges of political hacks. The tawdry condition of those courts, including their kangaroo court characteristics and bribery and favoritism, is not solely due to politics and an unprofessional staff, but neither are those unrelated factors. It might, for example, be worthwhile to examine the West German judiciary with the long training and bureaucratic apprenticeship required of their court personnel. Considerably more expertise and a little less patronage might do much to improve our courts.

For many of the problems that we have discussed an extended system of providing legal counsel to the poor would have salutary results. If the poor could avail themselves of something like the legal resources that others can afford, at least the inequities of the poor versus the rich as they face each other or the state would be reduced. Through class actions in court cases aimed at, for example, injunctions against certain kinds of police abuse, it might be possible to reduce the injustice that now characterizes the criminal law in operation.

Distributive Justice

The judicial systems of most nations have a role in determining distributive justice, as they interpret the law and decide that a governmental ruling means that obligations fall on businesses or on individuals in certain ways. Courts are also involved in disputes over economic interests—between insurance companies and claimants, between private parties and corporations asserting all manner of economic damage or interest. In the United States, the judiciary also have an extensive interpretative role, but because it has the power of judicial review, the American judiciary has an unusually significant role in distributive justice. This is for two basic reasons. In the first place the power of judicial review means that the judiciary is constantly the target of dissatisfied interest groups or individuals who believe that by pressing for the review of a law it may be possible to get it wiped away entirely as unconstitutional. And because American courts have the power to declare laws unconstitutional, they have therefore become powerful political agents, and highly respected ones at that. The consequence is that the political system tends to emphasize the judiciary's role and to permit judges a kind of discretionary political power that in other systems is simply not allowed to the courts. Inevitably therefore the discretionary power of courts is employed to make authoritative determinations in the economic realm.

Why do American courts have that broad range of discretionary power? The answer is historically rooted and complex. One can suggest the essence of the matter briefly by tracing those historical roots. The conservative elements in the Constitutional Convention who were apprehensive about the potential power of the people, especially as it might be exercised through the House of Representatives, welcomed some means of counterbalance beyond those provided in the specific restrictions of the Constitution itself. And although there is some vagueness in the resulting language covering judicial power, it is true nevertheless that an unusually broad role was established there for the courts, and clearly this was intended as a countervailing power. Article III, which establishes the judiciary, does not specifically grant any authority for the courts to invalidate Congressional legislation because it is inconsistent with the Constitution, but it does grant jurisdiction to the Supreme Court over all cases "arising under this Constitution, the laws of the United States, and treaties made . . . under their authority." Then in Article VI, Section2, comes the key position that was to become the basis of judicial review. It states:

> This Constitution, and the laws of the United States which shall be made in pursuance thereof; and all treaties made, or which shall be made under the authority of the United States, shall be *the supreme law of the land*; and judges in every State shall be bound thereby, anything in the constitution or laws of any State in the contrary notwithstanding.

It may well seem that this is directed more to federal-state relations than to national legislation, and from its history (the supremacy language came from the New Jersey–small state counterproposal to the large state–Virginia Resolution) it seems that this was the way many, perhaps most, members of the Convention read it. But it also could be read to mean that the Constitution being the supereme law of the land, no Congressional action in conflict with it could be valid. To contemporary Americans this will seem to be the obvious meaning of the supremacy clause, but to men of the eighteenth century that was by no means the universal interpretation of it. Although there was a kind of precedent for judicial review in the British colonial practice of reviewing all colonial legislative acts, the precedent was not a firm one. The British review was not, after all, judicial in nature. And in the states at this time the state legislatures tended to be the last word on the validity of state constitutions rather than the state courts. On the other hand, the Supreme Court in the years before it took its first case involving a clear challenge to the constitutionality of a Congressional act (that being in 1803 with *Marbury* v. *Madison*), had several times held state laws invalid for inconsistency with the Constitution. This the supremacy clause seems clearly to authorize, but review of national legislation was something else.

In the celebrated case of *Marbury* v. *Madison*,[59] the Supreme Court under the iron-willed leadership of John Marshall boldly asserted that the Court had the power of judicial review. With his powerful logic he built a firm rationale for review in a masterful opinion. His achievement was remarkable for two reasons: first the case involved a heated political battle between the Federalists and the Jeffersonian Democrats, and second, the case was basically a fraud. It involved a dispute about whether Marbury had a right to receive from the Secretary of State a commission authorizing him to be a justice of peace in Washington, D.C. He had been appointed to the office by the outgoing President John Adams during the waning hours of his administration, but through some error it was not delivered to him by the then Secretary of State (none other than John Marshall himself!). The Jeffersonians, annoyed at this attempt to leave behind Federalist officials and tie the hands of the new administration, simply refused to carry out the act that Marshall had overlooked before he ceased to be Secretary of State.

The proper legal remedy for this kind of situation is a writ of mandamus, which orders an official to do some act that law requires be done. So Marbury came to the Supreme Court and pleaded for a writ of mandamus. How he came to the highest Court in the land for this piddling matter is no accident. The purpose was to challenge the new

59. Cranch 137 (1803).

administration frontally. The pretext for bringing the case to the Supreme Court was a provision in the Judiciary Act of 1789. Marshall, giving the opinion for a unanimous Court, took up first the question of whether Marbury had a right to the office, and he delivered a scathing attack on the Jeffersonians for not giving Marbury what he was due. Then came the question of whether the Supreme Court had the jurisdiction to issue the writ of mandamus. In a clever maneuver, Marshall ruled that the Court did not have jurisdiction because the Judiciary Act of 1789 was unconstitutional in having conferred that power. He achieved a twofold objective: he told off the new administration and he announced that he would declare laws unconstitutional if necessary to respond to the Jeffersonians' control of the Congress and the Presidency. The clever part of it all is that it permitted Marshall to threaten noisily but not to run the chance of being made to appear powerless when Jefferson refused to hand out the commission of office as he probably would have done had Marshall ordered it.

But the case is also a fraud, for there is nothing unconstitutional about the Act of 1789 except that Marshall wanted to declare it so. Marshall's pretext for overturning the statute was that it purported to add *original* jurisdiction for the Supreme Court, whereas under the Constitution the Court's original jurisdiction was specified and only its appellate jurisdiction left open to Congressional alteration. The writ of mandamus, as Marshall interpreted the Constitution, was an aspect of original jurisdiction and therefore unconstitutional. But the language in question (Section 14 of the Judiciary Act of 1789) quite clearly is divided into two sections: one dealing with original jurisdiction (which merely repeats the Constitution) and one dealing with appellate jurisdiction. The provisions about the writ of mandamus fall within the part of the section concerned with appellate jurisdiction, and no reasonable reading can produce any other conclusion. (Significantly Marshall never quoted the Section and did not even attempt to show why his interpretation was the correct reading of the law.) Under any normal judicial proceeding Marshall would have told Marbury he was in the wrong court, that there was no jurisdiction in the matter for the Snpreme Court. But the case was meant to serve a political purpose, and the distortion served that end.

The importance of the case is therefore twofold. It demonstrated the flexibility of the Court in dealing with politically sensitive issues, and it established a powerful rationale for judicial review. In his opinion Marshall asked rhetorically what the Court should do if some patently unconstitutional act is passed. Suppose a tax was levied on an export, a bill of attainder passed, or an ex post facto law, he says, is the Court obliged to accept it? (Notice he picked black and white examples, not the spurious one with which he was dealing.) Why, of course the Court cannot uphold such an act, for have not judges taken an oath to uphold the Constitution of the United States? If he has so sworn he then has no alternative but to invalidate the law. Marshall did not consider the fact, however, that the Congress and the President took the same oath and that they presumably are seeking to act consistently with the Constitution no less than is the Supreme Court. The oath therefore is no conclusive reason why the Court must overrule two other branches of government whose members have taken the same oath of fidelity to the Constitution. It is not, that is, unless the reader is already so well conditioned by his acceptance of judicial review that he begins nodding his head in agreement when he reads Marshall's argument based on the oath. Once the rationale is established for judicial review, it tends to become self-reinforcing. Someone has to interpret the Constitution, that function falls to the Supreme Court, and its determinations once made sustain future exercise of the power.[60]

The reverence for the Supreme Court that has reinforced its strong legitimacy is not the only reason the judiciary has gained such sweeping power in American politics. It is also the simple consequence of the fact that the other forces in American politics are so loosely organized and incapable of creating a strong majority force that they cannot counter the Court. Not only that, the Court can always depend on the support of the political elements that it is favoring at any given time. This means that the Court trades friends and enemies from time to time, but like an unbeatable champion it never quite goes down. During the first third of this century, when the Supreme Court was the handmaiden of the robber barons busily plundering the nation, it was not difficult to get support for the Court among politicians and among the influential elements of the public who fully shared the laissez-faire opinions of the bench.[61] Today, when the Court is under attack by conservative forces, it wins support from the liberal elements who approve of the Court's actions.

60. There were contrary arguments, however, offered in Marshall's day. See, to the contrary, *Eakin* v. *Raub*, 12 Sergeant and Rawle (Pennsylvania Supreme Court) 330 (1825). Also the dubiousness of Marshall's position was demonstrated in a case he considered about a week after *Marbury*—*Stuart* v. *Laird* (1 Cranch 299 [1803]) in which the Court accepted the dismissal of Federalist-appointed judges from office (by way of having repealed the act creating the courts they held). Had Marshall claimed in this case that the true spirit and perhaps even the letter of the Constitution was being abrogated he could have made a good case, but that would have left him in a politically impossible situation and he therefore backed down.

61. At the depth of its unpopularity and the height of President Roosevelt's political power the Court staved off the 1937 Court packing proposal. Although it appeared to be a serious challenge at the time, in retrospect the Court was probably not in as dire straits as it seemed.

The year 1937, as we have noted, separates the old Court from the new; the old Court intervened on behalf of economic interests and the new on behalf of civil rights and civil liberties. Although this is essentially true, it obscures as much as it reveals. The new Court has not ceased to be important to business even though it may be less inclined to say no to Congressional regulatory initiatives than the old Court. The judiciary is a very important last resort for businesses that have lost in the Congress, and perhaps have not got their way in the administration of a law (or fear they will lose there). Appeal not only to federal courts but to all courts of general jurisdiction is the right of every significant economic interest, and it is an avenue of appeal that pays off handsomely in many instances. Though the whipsaw tactics of dual federalism are no more, that does not mean that an economic interest has no entrée to the judiciary. The opportunities are legion.

Suppose one of the independent regulatory agencies like the Federal Communications Commission hands down a ruling that, for example, threatens to terminate a license for a radio or television station. The obvious recourse is to hire a good law firm and try to get the ruling reversed in the courts. The same is true of all the other regulatory agencies, such as the Federal Trade Commission (on a question of cigaret advertising), the Federal Power Commission (on pipelines or utility rates), the Securities and Exchange Commission (on stockbroker practices). The tobacco industry appealed to the courts when the FCC ruled in 1967 that broadcasters who used cigaret advertising were obliged to carry some countermessages on dangers to health from cigarets. The companies claimed this abridged the "free speech" of the broadcasters.[62] Such challenges are not limited to the regulatory commissions, of course. An interest dissatisfied with a state law that protects consumer interests, for example, will challenge the way a vote was taken in the legislature if it finds no other handle to grab. The vendors of firearms resist gun control laws, corporations contest government contract decisions, the rich attack tax regulations in the tax court. The list is endless.

Each of these rules may involve millions of dollars, and the interested parties fight accordingly. The cost of the contest is subsidized through the tax laws as a "legitimate" business expense. The regulation involved may be an attempt to protect the public from misleading advertising on drugs, a ruling that seeks to reduce public utility rates, or a critical labor law determination, or a billion dollar antitrust suit. They all have one thing in common—they are decisions that affect the distribution of wealth and values in the society.

62. *The New York Times*, Feb. 14, 1969.

The judiciary is not limited to suits challenging the government, of course. The courts also consider a wide range of economically important civil suits—such as those for damages. One of the largest items of judicial business is the automobile damage claim. These cases contribute much to the clogging up of the calendar of every civil court in the land. In many jurisdictions, although the legislature has steadily increased the number of judges that handle damage cases, the backlog of auto accident cases grows longer and the delays before a case can be brought to trial may last as long as two or three years. There are a number of reasons for this delay, besides the sheer volume of the cases, but a chief one is that the insurance companies are in the main not interested in doing anything about them. The longer a company delays paying off the cheaper the settlement it may negotiate. For with their resources the companies can far more readily wait two or three years for a settlement than can an injured person who is perhaps unable to work because of injuries. Further the accumulated income from money not paid on thousands of delayed cases and otherwise invested is a tidy sum.

The needless delay and injustice caused by automobile insurance cases affect not only automobile victims but also those involved in all other kinds of litigation. The injustice does not persuade those responsible to alter the system. It appears that the logjam could be broken by making auto insurance similar to fire insurance. That is, the person who suffers damage, whatever the cause, places a claim for damages without any necessity to show who was responsible for the accident. At present, sometimes after the memory-dimming passage of years, the system require that a futile effort be made to show whether Arnold's car was following too closely after Bert's, or whether Bert was driving recklessly and pulled in front of Arnold. In any event the cars are smashed, lives are lost, hospital bills are incurred—damage clearly has been done. But one or the other of the two parties will get no compensation for damage suffered and the other will, after an interminable delay if the issue is disputed, get repaid (without interest for intervening time). Proving responsibility in these cases is extremely difficult, for very often the fault is mutually shared, or perhaps it is impossible to assign responsibility. (Consider a multiple rear-end smashing case that happens in a dense fog on a high-speed highway: whose "fault" is that?) Furthermore the problem of the uninsured driver persists; one buys insurance for protection against damage suits but remains utterly unprotected against the uninsured.[63]

63. See the proposal for correcting the auto insurance tangle presented by law professors Robert E. Keeton and Jeffrey O'Connell, *Basic Protection for the Traffic Victim: A Blueprint for Reforming Automobile Insurance* (Boston: Little, Brown, 1965).

If this kind of indictment can be made against the prevailing auto insurance system, why then is it not reformed? First, most of the insurance companies oppose it. They do not suffer but gain from the interminable delays that the lawsuits involve, for the longer the delay the greater the pressure on the plaintiff to accept a smaller award. Insurance officials also have uncertainties about the proposal; they fear that claims would be excessive and the rates prohibitive. Worse still, they are afraid that if the change did not correct the situation the government then might step in to do something about it, thus injuring or killing the goose that lays the huge golden eggs. Equally important in opposition are lawyers who specialize in negligence cases. They resist because negligence practice is highly profitable. Once a law firm gains a reputation for success in such trials, that brings in more cases, and the more that come the wider grows the reputation. (Successful negligence lawyers also contribute greatly to the delay because they are involved in so many cases in so many jurisdictions that assignment judges cannot find dates when all participating counsel will be available.) Negligence lawyers normally take cases on a contingency fee, assuming (but not always) some of the risk of the case in order to increase their percentage of the award if the case is won. (Some require both a retainer fee and a contingency percentage.) Taking auto insurance out of the courts to be supervised by an administrative agency would ruin the practice of many lawyers. Because they are sharp operators who can size up reality accurately (or they would never succeed at law), they tend to have political connections that can be used to stave off reform. It is not irrelevant that lawyers compose a large proportion of state legislatures; their own self-interest is something they readily recognize.

The injustice of the auto insurance situation may be obvious, and its expense, directly and indirectly for government and the public may be onerous, but with the economic power of the insurance industry and the political power of the legal fraternity in opposition, an early reform in the system seems unlikely.

What are the implications of the fact that the judiciary is involved in cases involving billions of dollars? At the very least it means that injustice is risked and very often perpetrated for the simple reason that the adversaries are unevenly matched. An ordinary person pitted against a giant corporation in a suit involving, say, a defective automobile that caused an accident will not necessarily lose because he faces the economic might of one of the big three of the automobile world, but the odds are against him. The individual's disadvantage is paralleled by that of a small businessman facing a huge corporation.

Justice is also endangered by the fact that there is meager public-interest representation in economic litigation. In theory the regulatory agencies protect the public and when challenged by the economic interests it would appear that public representation would come through the counsel for the regulatory bodies. But that does not take into account the character of many of the agencies that are supposed to do the regulating. In most instances the regulatory agencies are so beholden to the interests they are supposed to be regulating that if the public is to be represented someone else will have to do it. Distorted and misleading advertising is common and goes unregulated. Why do regulatory agencies refuse to reveal data on, for examples, the accident rates of bus lines? The U.S. Department of Transportation says the release of comparative records would serve no purpose. Ralph Nader's response to this is that it might at least help by telling the rider

> "which line he's less likely to be killed on—and rewarding the safer line for its incentive and responsibility by giving it business. It's quite obvious that the Bureau of Motor Carriers is covering up for Greyhound, as it has done for years." [64]

Over half a century ago Upton Sinclair produced the Pure Food and Drug Act with his shocking book *The Jungle*. But we still eat adulterated meat from diseased animals, processed in filthy packing houses. The flagrant nonenforcement of coal mines safety rules is a national scandal admitted even by the Director of the Bureau of Mines after the West Virginia explosion in November, 1968.[65] Public utility commissions at the state level regularly sell out the interests of the public for the profits of the corporations they are supposed to be regulating. In all these regulatory agencies it is commonplace for the members to be drawn from the industry that they are to regulate, or if not they often develop very friendly relations with those whom they regulate, resulting in lucrative employment in the industry affected on departure from government service.

A few states have created agencies for consumer protection and in some instances public counsel to take the public's cause in rate regulation disputes, for example. But the practice of "public law" in this sense is rare. A few attorneys devote a proportion of their time to such practice, and in a few rare instances all their time (Ralph Nader, for example), but the impact of this is as yet marginal. The typical law graduate

64. Ralph Nader, Interview in *Playboy*, Oct., 1968, p. 202.

65. The Director, following the West Virginia disaster, asked that the Bureau begin to "represent the public interest rather than the industry alone." Secretary of Interior Steward Udall called the Bureau of Mines "timorous and almost apologetic" in regulating the industry. See Ben A. Franklin, "U.S. Mine Director Will Be Replaced," *The New York Times*, Feb. 17, 1969.

of the past was more concerned about finding himself a place in the world of corporate law than in devoting his talents to public practice. Perhaps this is changing, judging from the activities of law students and young lawyers today. But as Justice Brennan once warned the legal profession, it has not taken its social responsibilities seriously and the consequence has been deterioration of respect for law, among other losses. Speaking of the inequities in the law—criminal law, consumer fraud, civil rights, landlord-tenant relations, public welfare regulations, and many more examples—Justice Brennan exhorted the profession not to leave the constructive work to men just out of law school.

> The mechanism by which society makes choices and accommo-dates conflicting social interests has always been pre-eminently the law, embracing by that amorphous term not simply the courts but more broadly all the ways in which man structures the relation-ships that constitute society. Thus, every lawyer, no matter how well-established and regardless of his specialty, can and must con-tribute to the elimination of inequities now under such vehement attack by the disaffected.[66]

Legal Defense of Freedoms

The Supreme Court is commonly considered the real bulwark against rash and unconstitutional laws in this country and the prime protector of the liberty of the individual. It has indeed stopped much state legis-lation and in some eighty-five instances has declared acts of Congress unconstitutional. But most of its decisions on national issues, as Robert Dahl has pointed out, come on relatively minor matters.[67] The Court was most important in reversing legislation and in holding off Congress for years in economic matters. It prevented child labor legislation, as we noted previously, for a quarter century. But never has a piece of national legislation been declared unconstitutional on the grounds that it violates the freedoms established in the First Amendment.[68] For every recent case where the Supreme Court struck down a state statute

66. Justice Williams J. Brennan, "Remarks at the Centennial Celebration of Notre Dame University," Feb. 8, 1969 (mimeo).

67. He originally made this point in an article, "Decision-Making in a Democ-racy: The Role of the Supreme Court as a National Policy-Maker," 6 *Journal of Public Law* 279–95 (1957). The essence of that argument, updated, is presented in his *Pluralist Democracy in the United States* (Chicago: Rand-McNally, 1967), pp. 154ff.

68. A possible exception is *Aptheker* v. *Secretary of State*, 378 U.S. 500 (1964), where the Court invalidated passport regulations as being too sweeping. The opinion of the Court stressed the Fifth Amendment rather than the First, however.

on grounds of the Fourteenth Amendment in behalf of blacks, there are several in which the Court earlier ruled against state law and in behalf of slave holders, factory owners, or property interests.

The Court does not often try to stop a determined national majority when one appears, even when that majority is denying liberties. When the Radical Congress challenged the Court over Reconstruction policy by removing a case from its jurisdiction after it had been argued before the Court, the justices meekly accepted the interference.[69] In 1944, obviously pained at having to do so, the Supreme Court nevertheless gave its sanction for the incarceration of 112,000 Japanese-Americans in concentration camps during World War II. Despite the flagrant abrogation of the basic rights of these citizens, the Court was able to find that military necessity demanded their "relocation," to use the euphemism of the time.[70] In short, although the judiciary plays a role in protecting personal liberty, ultimately that protection must depend upon the political process. We are inclined in the United States to think that the statement of rights in the Constitution and the role of the Court really constitute the basic protection of those rights. Reality does not sustain that view. Congress and the President have often combined to deny liberty to the individual—as in sedition acts, thought control acts, and the operations of the Senate Internal Security Committee and the House Un-American Activities Committee—but the courts have been very cautious about curtailing such infringements.

The role of courts in protecting the freedom of the individual can be examined through a look at some illustrative cases involving the First Amendment and at the judicial role in providing equal rights to black people.

First Amendment Freedoms. The Court takes a different view of national as opposed to state laws that infringe the First Amendment. Although it has never invalidated a Congressional act on that ground, it has overturned several state laws for that reason. In fact, despite numerous federal limitations on free expression, it was not until 1919 that the Supreme Court even considered such a case. At that time the Supreme Court upheld the use of the Espionage Act of 1917 and the Sedition Act of 1918 in the landmark case of *Schenck* v. *U.S.*[71] In a

---

69. *Ex parte McCardle,* 7 Wallace 506 (1869). Congress passed a statute denying the Supreme Court jurisdiction in cases involving writs of habeas corpus and made it retroactive so as to prevent the Court from ruling on the validity of the military occupation of the South. Faced with an adamant Congress, the Court accepted an action that was dubious on its face, despite the power of the Congress to modify the appellate jurisdiction of the Court.

70. *Korematsu* v. *U.S.,* 323 *U.S.* 214 (1944).

71. 249 *U.S.* 47 (1919).

unanimous opinion Mr. Justice Oliver Wendell Holmes broached the doctrine of "clear and present danger." That much tortured phrase was Holmes's test of whether an act was such that it could be forbidden despite the protection of free speech in the First Amendment. But *Holmes did not call into question the validity of the law.* He was testing, he said, the application of the law and not whether the government had the power to enact such limitations on freedom of the press. (The case involved the distribution of pamphlets urging resistance to the draft law.) The "character of every act," said the venerable justice,

"depends upon the circumstances in which it was done. . . . The most stringent protection of free speech would not protect a man in falsely shouting fire in a theater, and causing a panic. It does not even protect a man from an injunction against uttering words that may have all the effect of force. . . . The question in every case is whether the words used are used in such circumstances and are of such a nature as to create a clear and present danger that they will bring about the substantive evils that Congress has a right to prevent. It is a question of proximity and degree."

In brief the First Amendment freedom of the press was no protection when *what* was said was uttered under *conditions* that raised a *clear and present danger* of some *substantive evil* that Congress had a right to prevent.[72]

A thousand persons were jailed under these wartime statutes and the Supreme Court went further in each successive case in its permissiveness about the suppression of dissent. None of the appeals resulted in a reversal of conviction, but after the war ended a minority view emerged on the bench. Repeatedly Holmes and Brandeis dissented from the application of the clear-and-present-danger idea in a way that Holmes had never intended, as it became what was known as the "bad tendency" doctrine. That is, if there was a *possibility* that some adverse consequence might follow then the conviction could stand. In *Abrams v. U.S.*[73] the majority of the Court upheld a conviction for the act of distributing a leaflet, elaborately garnished with Communist slogans,

72. The speech aspect of the doctrine was established in *Debs* v. *U.S.*, 249 *U.S.* 211 (1919), which involved a speech made by Socialist party leader, Eugene Debs, to a workers' rally in Akron. A unanimous Court upheld Debs's conviction, following the Schenck rationale.

73. 250 *U.S.* 616 (1919). In at least four other similar cases during 1920 and 1921 Holmes and Brandeis dissented. See for a good summary of the development of law in this area, Thomas I. Emerson and David Haber, *Political and Civil Rights in the United States*, 2nd ed. (Buffalo, N.Y.: Dennis and Co., 1958), pp. 292ff.

denouncing United States intervention in Russia. Holmes in dissent said that what might be necessary to prevent wartime dangers was not necessary in peacetime.

> Nobody can suppose that the surreptitious publishing of a silly leaflet by an unknown man, without more, would present any immediate danger that its opinions would hinder the success of the government arms or have any appreciable tendency to do so.

In the post-World War I "Red Scare" many states passed laws against sedition and anarchy, with the key phrase being an "attempt to overthrow the government by force or violence." Quite apart from whether there exists any "right to revolution," as some eighteenth-century zealots believed and preached, there is not much chance that any organized society is going to permit it, however libertarian it may be. But the important question is not whether some theoretical right exists to rise up against tyranny, but whether government will consider actions aimed at changing government by changing minds to be conspiracy to overthrow the government. Advocacy of ideas was clearly the target of the United States in the cases cited where Brandeis and Holmes dissented, just as it was in a string of state prosecutions for "criminal syndicalism," another euphemism for dissident political activity.

The leading case at the state level was *Gitlow* v. *N.Y.*, in which the Supreme Court now applied the "bad tendency" doctrine at the state level.[74] (*Gitlow* is also important because the Court admitted *for the first time* that the First Amendment applied to the states via the requirements of due process in the Fourteenth.) The case involved not only a Member of the Socialist party, but a member of "The Left Wing" thereof, to quote the Court majority. The defendant had published something called the "Left Wing Manifesto," for which New York State convicted him of criminal anarchy. No evidence was presented to show that the pamphlet has had any effect whatsoever. Indeed Gitlow's counsel claimed that if nobody paid any attention then it was hardly incitement to revolution, but the majority didn't agree. For them the possible tendency to incite was sufficient. In a brief dissent Holmes commented:

> It is said that this manifesto was more than a theory, that it was an incitement. Every idea is an incitement. It offers itself for belief and if believed it is acted on unless some other belief outweighs it or some failure of energy stifles the movement at its birth. The only difference between the expression of an opinion and an in-

74. 268 *U.S.* 652 (1925).

citement in the narrower sense is the speaker's enthusiasm for the result. Eloquence may set fire to reason. But whatever may be thought of the redundant discourse before us [meaning the "Left Wing Manifesto"] it had no chance of starting a present conflagration. If in the long run the beliefs expressed in proletarian dictatorship are destined to be accepted by the dominant forces of the community, the only meaning of free speech is that they should be given their chance and have their way.

Holmes thus presented in capsule a persuasive rationale for the free speech idea, but his argument was rejected. Holmes's phrase, "clear and present danger," is still repeated, but his substantive argument has, in fact, never been accepted. Perhaps the best proof of this is *Dennis v. U.S.*, upholding the Alien Registration Act of 1940 (more commonly called the Smith Act).[75] That Act had made it unlawful for anyone to advocate the violent overthrow of the government or to conspire or organize for that purpose. Eleven Communist party leaders were convicted of violating the Act and the Supreme Court upheld the conviction in *Dennis*, abandoning Holmes's clear-and-present-danger doctrine entirely, although retaining the words. The rationale of the Court was that the "gravity of the 'evil,' discounted by its improbability, justifies such invasion of free speech as is necessary to avoid the danger." In a long discourse on the Communist threat to the world Chief Justice Vinson laid out reasons why the situation was grave, although he did not present any evidence that any danger was either imminent or likely to become imminent from the internal Communist movement. The Chief Justice's opinion cites the clear-and-present-danger doctrine in support of the decision, but the concurring opinion of Justice Jackson points out that "clear and present danger" refers to the adequacy of the evidence and the circumstances concerning specific acts, which was not what the majority was testing in *Dennis*. Justices Black and Douglas, taking the position that the First Amendment means what it says, dissented. Justice Black said,

> At the outset I want to emphasize what the crime involved is and what it is not. These petitioners were not charged with an attempt to overthrow the Government. They were not charged with overt acts of any kind designed to overthrow the Government. They were not even charged with saying anything or with writing anything designed to overthrow the Government. The charge was that they agreed to assemble and to talk and publish

75. 341 *U.S.* 494 (1951). That law is excerpted in Emerson and Haber, op. cit., pp. 343ff.

certain ideas at a later date: The indictment is that they conspired to organize the Communist party and to use speech or newspapers and other publications in the future to teach and advocate the forcible overthrow of the Government. No matter how it is worded, this is a virulent form of prior censorship of speech and press, which I believe the First Amendment forbids.

Subsequent decisions, without reversing *Dennis,* have narrowed the scope of the Smith Act. In *Yates* v. *U.S.* the Court said that advocacy of an abstract doctrine of the desirability of the overthrow of government by violence did not fall within the Smith Act.[76] Then later, in *Scales* v. *U.S.,* it held that the provision of the law prohibiting membership in any group advocating violent overthrow extended only to "active" and not "passive or nominal" membership.[77] Similarly the Court narrowed the scope of the McCarran Act of 1950 and the Communist Control Act of 1954, ruling in one case that it constituted self-incrimination to force Communist party officials to register the party as required by law, because the act of registration would proclaim their violation of the McCarran Act.[78] The Supreme Court has never overruled the attempts to suppress the Communist movement in the United States, but it has interpreted some of the attempts in such a way as to render the suppression difficult.

Likewise the Court has never invalidated laws and executive regulations aimed at excluding "subversives" from government service—the so-called loyalty-security programs. But it has at times held the programs to their own stated procedures. Similarly the Court has checkreined the Un-American Activities Committee in a few cases, particularly in *Watkins* v. *United States,* where the Committee was obviously trying to "expose" persons it thought to be subversive rather than pursuing any clearly defined legislative objective.[79] The Court, however, refused to accept the proposition that the political beliefs of a person were by reason of the First Amendment beyond the Committee's investigative authority, holding that an individual's rights to silence about his political beliefs had to be counterbalanced by the national need for "self preservation." [80]

It is unnecessary to elaborate further on such cases; the examples and the nuances of interpretation are endless, but the fundamental proposition remains true: the Court has been willing to insist on certain

76. 354 *U.S.* 398 (1957).

77. 367 *U.S.* 203 (1961).

78. *Albertson* v. *Subversive Activities Control Board,* 367 *U.S.* 1 (1961).

79. 354 *U.S.* 178 (1957). *Sweezy* v. *New Hampshire* is based on similar reasoning; 354 *U.S.* 234 (1957).

80. *Barenblatt* v. *U.S.,* 260 *U.S.* 109 (1959).

procedural rights but has steadfastly refused to deny governmental power to restrict liberty on grounds of national security, whatever the language of the Constitution.

In many other areas the Court has similarly picked a cautious path through the demands of suppressors on the one hand and the constitutional restraints emphasized by dissenters. On the whole the last thirty years have represented an advance for the opportunity to dissent, for freedom from forced religious exercises, for freedom to publish, and for the right to organize for political acivity. But none of these gains has been without some counterlosses, and none of them is clearly established beyond change—for better or worse. In religious matters, for example, the Court, in numerous cases brought by the Jehovah's Witnesses, has gradually expanded the liberty of those wholly committed religious zealots, who remind one of the Christians of the second century A.D. Disciplined, resourceful, and secure in their faith, they pursue their religion against all odds. And the odds have at times been heavy as states and local communities have attempted to force them into conformity. Thus for a brief time it was held constitutional to exclude the children of Jehovah's Witnesses from school for refusal to salute the flag, which they held to be homage to a graven image, forbidden by the Bible in their view. But the rule was reversed when the state of West Virginia added that unless the parents sent their children to school and forced them to salute the flag, then the parents were guilty of making truants of their children and were liable to prosecution.[81]

State and local efforts to compel prayers in public schools have also received rebuffs from the Supreme Court.[82] This produced much bitter denunciation of the Court, but the Court held to its position that the state should not in any sense prescribe religious exercises.[83] Whichever way it rules the Court reaps enmity in these cases, for the religious are no less zealous about their faith than are many who seek freedom from compulsory religion.

The Court has also had its difficulty about the limits of proper protest or expression of opinion by other than strictly conventional means, such as speeches and writing. As far back as 1940 it approved the notion that picketing was an expression of opinion within the meaning

81. The obligatory flag salute was upheld in *Minersville* v. *Gobitis*, 310 *U.S.* 586 (1940), but rejected in *West Virginia* v. *Barnette*, 319 *U.S.* 624 (1943).

82. In *Engel* v. *Vitale*, 370 *U.S.* 421 (1962), the Court forbade a practice that permitted students to be excused from a school prayer, just as, earlier, it had outlawed a state-prescribed school prayer in *Doremus* v. *Board of Education*, 343 *U.S.* 429 (1952).

83. And it continued this in 1963 with a ruling that schools could not require a daily reading from the Bible in school, *Abington School District* v. *Schempp*, 374 *U.S.* 203 (1963).

of the First Amendment, and it has continued to support that general proposition, but increasingly it has permitted state limitations on picketing when there was potential violence associated with it.[84]

Nor has the Supreme Court been willing to curb the punishment of those who demonstrate in unusual ways against the war in Vietnam. It sustained convictions for burning a flag, and it has refused to accept the plea that an individual was refusing to enter the armed services on grounds of moral objections to the specific war in Vietnam or on grounds that the person who participates in that war risks a situation parallel to that involved in the trial of war criminals in the famed Nuremburg international tribunal that tried the Nazis. It is true that in 1965 the Court reversed convictions of persons refusing the draft for reasons of conscientious objection to war in general, even in the absence of a specific religious commitment,[85] but in the meantime the Court has refused to interfere with the cases of hundreds of draft-card burners and those who refuse the draft and are being sentenced typically to three to five years in prison.

The Rights of Black Men. In the course of discussing criminal law and the problems of the poor in this chapter and in the discussion of race in the chapter on federalism, I made and illustrated the point that the courts have played a less than noble role toward nonwhites. Can this negative role be squared with the reputation that the Supreme Court has for helping Negroes—a reputation that it has with many Negroes as well as with white racists. However large the deficiencies of the Supreme Court may be, there is still something to be said in its behalf. It has taken the lead at times, as it did in the school desegregation case, and in some other desegregation issues (such as transportation, restrictive covenants in housing, and in some voting rights situations). On balance, however, is there justification for Lewis M. Steel's accusation that the Supreme Court amounts to "Nine Men in Black Who Think White"? [86] In my personal opinion there is, although Steel, being a lawyer, exaggerates in typical lawyerlike fashion. A résumé of

84. See *Thornhill* v. *Alabama*, 310 *U.S.* 88 (1940), which protected picketing for the first time, and *International Brotherhood of Teamsters* v. *Vogt*, 354 *U.S.* 284 (1957), which placed restrictions on picketing freedom where violence was associated with the picketing; the case also presents a lengthy review of the law on the matter in the scholarly style of Mr. Justice Frankfurter.

85. *U.S.* v. *Seeger*, 380 *U.S.* 163 (1965).

86. *The New York Times Magazine*, Oct. 13, 1968. On black lawyers, Loren Miller provides a more conventional defense of the Court than did Steel. See the able history of the Negro's appeals to the Supreme Court by Loren Miller, *The Petitioners, The Story of the Supreme Court of the United States and the Negro* (New York: World Publishing, 1966, Meridian paperback); see Miller's summary judgment on p. 433.

Steel's case and a brief assessment of it will provide a brief consideration of the role of the judiciary and the black person's rights.

Steel's article, it may be recalled, set off an explosion within the National Association for the Advancement of Colored People, for which he was associate counsel. The moderates on the NAACP's board were incensed at Steel's attack, largely because the NAACP has been so committed to the use of legal means for advancement; rejection of the Court seemed to blemish the NAACP's record too. Patiently over the years NAACP counsel carefully chose and meticulously prepared dozens of cases for presentation to the Court, and most of the time counsel for the NAACP prevailed, but partly this was because their demands were tailored to the possibilities of the moment, having compromised their demands as the circumstances seemed to dictate. Steel's attack, therefore, was in effect denigrating the efforts of the moderate leadership, and they dismissed him peremptorily. (Because Steel had not been given a hearing or any opportunity to defend himself, all the remaining counsel of the NAACP resigned.) That imbroglio serves to highlight the division in the black community, even though Steel himself is nonblack. The reverence for the Supreme Court that is common among moderates is roughly akin, in the minds of more radical blacks, to the traditional affinity for the Republican party among Negroes who dimly associated the Republican party with Abraham Lincoln and Emancipation long after the party even symbolized a pro-Negro point of view— if it ever did.

Steel's argument brings the issue out into the open. He says that the Court has historically been the enemy of black Americans. Although in the fifteen years of Chief Justice Earl Warren's tenure it reversed some of the more scandalous rulings of earlier courts, Steel concludes that the Court has never endorsed the principle of full equality. He says further:

> The Court has time and again taken the position that racial equality should be subordinated—or at least balanced against—white American's fear of rapid change, which would threaten its time-honored prerogatives. Only where racial barriers were overtly obnoxious—and therefore, openly contradictory to the American creed of equality—has the Court designed to move. Yet its decisions have allowed a confused, miseducated and prejudiced white public to believe that its black fellow citizens have been given their full rights.

Then, after tracing the most negative role of the Court before it began some twenty-five years ago to recognize the Negro as a human being, Steel's argument turns to contemporary issues. His indictment centers on the proposition that the Court takes the gradualist, reformist tack—move slowly and be wary of counterpressures from the racists. As Steel says, "In recent years, a cautious Supreme Court has waltzed in time to the music of the white majority—one step forward, on step backward and sidestep, sidestep." He uses as evidence four types of cases: school desegregation, civil rights demonstrations, juries in Southern courts, and urban renewal controversies about ejecting black people from their homes.

On the school cases he decries the Court's ruling that schools were to be integrated "with all deliberate speed." [87] Like Justice Black, who criticized the "all deliberate speed" idea in a television interview in 1968, Steel focuses on this as a cardinal aspect of the desegregation decision. He points out that in other cases the Court does not say that execution of orders may be delayed to suchc an indefinite future. His conclusion is that "public reasons—the offense to white sensibility—existed to justify the delay. . . ." He claims that the Court refrained from issuing a direct order for desegregation because of concern for "the potential damage to white Americans resulting from the diminution of privilege. . . ." One wonders how he can be sure of the motivations of the nine members of the Court in the spring of 1955; how could anyone know—even a member of the Supreme Court bench perhaps—with certainty what motivated the justices? It is hardly a balanced assessment to omit entirely the difficulty that the Court could expect to have in trying to enforce a desegregate-now order. Given the sense of political reality the Court has usually shown throughout its history it seems strange to omit from consideration entirely the question of the political feasibility. One need not deny the proposition that the members of the Court, being white Americans, would be especially sensitive about the need for social stability and that this might be placed above the needs of blacks, but that does not eliminate entirely the sense of political difficulty that was bound to accompany a do-it-now order.

For the Supreme Court is acutely aware of the limitations of their practical power. They had, even in 1955, dealt too often with infractious lower courts and with evasive politicians in racial disputes not to be aware of the available means of resistance. This, one might then say, should have persuaded them *not* to open the road to delay and confusion by using the fatal words "all deliberate speed." But that is a con-

87. *Brown* v. *Board of Education*, 349 U.S. 294 (1955). The original decision was handed down in May, 1954, but it gave a reprieve on enforcement and the decree to carry out the decision waited until 1955. The citation for the original case is 347 U.S. 483 (1954).

clusion more easily reached in the leisure of hindsight than it is in the thick of battle. One need not defend "all deliberate speed" to grant that there may have appeared compelling political reasons for making this compromise.

Steel also asserts the Supreme Court reacted in the typical white American way as Negroes upped their demands and conducted more and more insistent demonstrations. The Court, having at first protected peaceful picketing against Southern sheriffs and dismissed trumped up charges to prevent peaceful demonstrations, then backed down and limited even peaceful demonstrations when they were directed at court houses.[88] More seriously (because in my opinion the picketing of a court does not seem to me to be a right of the first magnitude) the Court stepped back from its earlier actions in defense of the NAACP in its running battle for the right to operate in Alabama and permitted a Georgia court to inflict a heavy fine on the NAACP for picketing.[89] In 1968 the Court in *Cameron* v. *Johnson* [90] refused to review a Mississippi prosecution of civil rights workers who had maintained an orderly and peaceful picket line. Nevertheless in 1969 the Supreme Court did reverse the convictions of Dick Gregory and Dr. Martin Luther King for peaceful picketing.[91] In the King case fifty-two persons were arrested for parading without a city permit, which city officials made clear they wouldn't have granted had it been requested. The Gregory case involved a peaceful protest outside the home of Chicago Mayor Richard Daley. An angry crowd of white gathered, causing the police to order the Negro picketers to leave. When they refused, the police arrested them for disorderly conduct. The evidence, said Chief Justice Warren, showed the demonstrators were orderly and tried to demonstrate peaceably, and the Court overturned the conviction.

There is some validity in Steel's charge concerning the Court's restraints on demonstrations and picketing; the Court has undoubtedly

---

88. *Cox* v. *Louisiana*, 379 *U.S.* 536 (1965), reversed convictions on technical grounds but accepted the propriety of limitation on the picketing of courts. It accepted the same notion again in *Adderly* v. *Florida*, 385 *U.S.* 39 (1966).

89. *Georgia* v. *Rachel*, 384 *U.S.* 780 (1966). In the Alabama case, *NAACP* v. *Alabama*, 357 *U.S.* 449 (1958), the Court struck down state barriers to its operation. Then for the next *six years* the Alabama courts played cat and mouse with the Supreme Court, and ultimately only when in 1964 the Supreme Court declared *on the fourth occasion that the same dispute had been before them* that if the Alabama courts would not order compliance with its order then the Supreme Court would. It may be an extreme example, but it does illustrate the opportunities for evasion.

90. 390 *U.S.* 611 (1968).

91. The case involving Dr. King was *Shuttlesworth* v. *Birmingham*, 394 *U.S.* 147 (1969), and the other was *Gregory* v. *Chicago*, 394 *U.S.* 111 (1969).

hardened its stand. Whether this is the result of the Court's ceasing to support the civil rights workers because they have ceased to be "humble supplicants" and have annoyed whites by making strident demands is a matter of motivations about which Mr. Steel feels far more confident in judging than I do. But at the least it can be said that the Court has, as always, tended to reflect the community concern for stability and order.

In the matter of permitting Negroes to be on juries in proportionate numbers, the Court has also turned in both directions. After opening up the issue in *Morris* v. *Alabama*,[92] where the exclusion of Negroes from jury panels resulted in one of the reversals of the convictions of the Scottsboro boys in the infamous case that ran throughout the 1930's, the Court dawdled and moved very hesitantly about assuring black defendants trial by their peers. Then in *Swain* v. *Alabama*[93] it took a step backward when it allowed Alabama prosecutors to challenge and remove all Negroes from a jury. The Court, as Steel says, "overlooked the fact that a Negro had never sat on a civil or criminal jury in the county in question and accepted at face value the prosecutor's declaration that he would allow Negroes to serve under certain circumstances." With respect to Negroes being on juries—in both North and South it might be added—the situation is far from equitable and the Court's record in promoting justice in this respect has been considerably less than perfect.

Finally there is the issue of "Negro removal" as it is often called. As urban renewal or highway construction rips out whole sections of ghetto neighborhoods, vast numbers of Negroes are dispossessed and left to fend for themselves in a housing market that is typically substandard in quality and equal in price to normal housing beyond the walls of the ghetto. (It is noteworthy that whites and blacks pay about the same median rent, but because of the compression of Negroes in ghettos and the resulting creation of a false scarcity the slum lord reaps a tidy reward, although there is some evidence that the payoff is no longer so lucrative as it once was.[94]) In 1967 the Supreme Court had an opportunity to do something about the practice of shoving Negroes around—in this case, Negro petitioners claimed, in order to create a

92. 294 *U.S.* 597 (1945). Much earlier in its distinctly anti-Negro period, the Court overruled a West Virginia statute that barred Negroes from juries: *Strauder* v. *West Virginia*, 100 *U.S.* 303 (1880). But it did not follow through. Typically Negroes were excluded from Southern juries, for the jury panels were drawn from the lists of registered voters, and Negroes were assuredly not on those lists.

93. 381 *U.S.* 921 (1965).

94. See George Sternlieb, *The Tenement Landlord* (New Brunswick, N.J.: Rutgers Urban Studies Center, 1966), which is an intensive analysis of housing economics in Newark.

no-Negro barrier around a shopping center. (*Green Street Association v. Daley.*[95]) The Court, however, refused to review the case. And as observed earlier in another context the act of turning Negroes out of their homes for redevelopment of a parcel of land is supposed to take place only when there is adequate replacement housing. If the courts held public agencies to the requirements of the law in these dispossession controversies, ghetto residents would gain some much-needed leverage for self-protection.

This is a very sketchy review of the Court's role in matters affecting the rights of the Negro—many broad areas have not even been discussed (like voting, for example). But it may be sufficient to permit us to assess Steel's charge: Is the Court as totally negligent of the interests of Negroes as he suggests? He has in some respect exaggerated, it seems, and he has taken unwarranted liberties in divining the motives of the Justices. But in the last analysis he has much evidence to support his position. The Court is part of a white governing system. It gives the expected priority to stability and compromises continually as it contemplates political practicality. Regardless, for the moment, of the motivations or backgrounds of the Supreme Court, it remains a valid assertion that the Court has moved, when it has moved at all, in a very gingerly fashion in matters of racial equality.

Courts and Rights

From the evidence it is apparent that the judiciary is at best an uncertain source of the protection of rights. Judges share community prejudices and inflict them on litigants of all kinds. Yet the common view of Americans is that courts, and especially the Supreme Court, are the prime protector of the rights of the individual. Yet here, as in any country, rights are integrally involved with politics and in the long run only those rights are secure that the political system will sustain. If the legislature and the executive are intent upon abridging the rights of the individual there is little in the end that judges can do to prevent it.

What good then are bills of rights and other constitutional restrictions? They serve primarily to make it more difficult for proclaimed rights to be violated, and they do so in more ways than by giving a court grounds for a declaration of unconstitutionality. In the first place, respect for rights must be created in a community, and bills of rights contribute much to that objective. James Madison in correspondence with Thomas Jefferson about the Constitution makes this point well.

95. 387 *U.S.* 932 (1967).

Jefferson was dismayed that the original Constitution lacked a bill of rights, which in his view "is what every people are entitled to against every government on earth." Madison was skeptical about the value of a bill of rights, but not unwilling to have one. He replied to Jefferson this way:

> What use then it may be asked can a bill of rights serve in popular Governments? I answer the two following which, though less essential than in other Governments, sufficiently recommend the precaution: 1. The political truths declared in that solemn manner acquire by degrees the character of fundamental axioms of free Government, and *as they become incorporated with the national sentiment, counteract the impulses of interest and passion.*
>
> 2. Altho. it be generally true as above stated that the danger of oppression lies in the interested majorities of the people rather than in usurped acts of Government, yet there may be occasions on which the evil may spring from the latter source; and on such, a *bill of rights will be a good ground for appeal to the sense of the Community.*[96]

There is much wisdom in Madison's brief comment: bills of rights are very important as educators of the public and they also form an indispensable basis for "appeal to the sense of the Community." It may take an unconscionable length of time for the concepts to get into the public domain, but once the ideas are firmly rooted they serve not only as standards for courts to use in interpreting the law but as bases for legislative action and appeals to society to live up to commitments made. But respect for rights—the difficult and important ones like the rights of the unpopular to a fair trial or to a chance to speak their piece —grows only very slowly and with great difficulty. It is in my judgment one of the most significant saving graces of the United States that there is still enough openness for dissent to occur, that the poorest can still appeal and challenge the unfairness of a procedure or assert his denial of some right. It has taken centuries to provide us all with the right not to have to testify against ourselves—and it is still a less than secure right. For there is always passionate dislike for the nonconforming ones, hatred for political malcontents, and fear of the criminal. It took almost a century to begin to respect the provisions of the Four-

---

96. Quoted by Edmond Cahn in "Can the Supreme Court Defend Civil Liberties," a pamphlet issued by the Sidney Hillman Foundation (undated), pp. 11–12. Italics added.

teenth Amendment, and against what odds that campaign continues one need not tell any American. But rights once formally established have a chance to win public respect. And only when that public support is generated will rights be given any protection. Only then will legislatures act, only then will prosecutors be curbed, only then will courts dare or succeed in defending rights.

CHAPTER SEVEN

The Executive

THE President of the United States can more effectively influence national priorities than any other person in the land. To be sure he has competitors in the process and he is anything but a free agent in exercising his preeminent power. Still no one else has the visibility, the wide-ranging formal authority, or the political power that the President possesses. By endorsing a proposal he can give it life; by ignoring or opposing it he can often kill it. President Truman committed American troops to Korea and told the nation and Congress about it after acting. President Kennedy committed the nation to the race for the moon and the money to finance the chase was forthcoming. President Johnson decided to enter the Vietnam war on a massive scale and entrapped a nation. In each case the initiative of the President was the decisive factor. Thus the office poses a crowning paradox; Presidents commit us irrevocably to madcap missions, just as the Presidency also is the point of greatest initiative to turn the nation toward more sensible policies. No other element of government can provide ways out of the impasses of our time. The Supreme Court has clearly demonstrated in its desegregation efforts that it cannot do much to heal the rifts in the society created by racial antagonism. Congress is unlikely to be able to assert real leadership in redirecting our foreign policy. Nor is it even remotely possible that the bureaucracy can direct our energies toward solution of the pollution crisis. And so on with the states, cities, parties, interest groups. Initiative for change, if it comes, will come from the White House.

Granted, of course, that the main impetus for change is unlikely to come from anywhere inside government. It is the specialty of government to resist change, not to inaugurate it. The extragovernmental forces promoting change and new directions inevitably turn toward the President, for his is the focal point of pressure. Convince the occupant of the White House that new ideas are possible, that new approaches are necessary, that for political reasons it is obligatory to go in any given direction, and the chances of success are immeasurably better than if any other convert is won over. In fact, this is so true it is frightening. The President has so much personal (indeed lonely) power that he alone can exercise that he can be dangerous in crisis situations on the one hand a depressant to progress in general. To facilitate later examination of some of the ways in which presidential power is used and abused, it is appropriate to look briefly at how the office of President has developed. How did it emerge from the sketchy provisions of Article II of the Constitution to become the institution it is today?

The eighteenth century was the age of the legislature, and the Constitutional Convention accordingly lavished its greatest attention on Congress and was far less specific about the executive and the judicial branches of government. They devoted some eighteen hundred words to Article I, being highly specific about Congress and its powers, but Article II consists of less than seven hundred words, most of which concern the method of choosing and the qualifications prerequisite to being President. His powers are vaguely sketched in contrast to the specificity of the delegation of powers to Congress. Besides his being made "Commander in Chief of the Army and Navy" and being given a veto, the authority to conduct foreign relations, and the power to appoint personnel for the executive and judicial branches, he is also admonished to "take care that the laws be faithfully executed." From those constitutional elements a powerful institution emerged over time.

In essence the Presidency has become an elective kingship with decisive power in a broad range of matters. The initiative is the President's to use or withhold; he can start a war or end one; he can breathe life into a domestic project or smother it. And these powers are singularly his. He necessarily delegates authority to others, and he must depend upon his subordinates for information and the execution of any decision, but in the end the responsibility rests with him. No institutional method exists by which his singular authority can be shared with others—not the Cabinet, the Congress, nor anyone. If he is, as all presidents are to a degree, the captive of his subordinates who provide information and ideas and who consult with him on important matters, it is nevertheless he alone who personally possesses the power to act. How has so much power come to be vested in one person?

The Evolution of the Presidency

With few exceptions, those who occupied the office in its first century were content to play a modest role as President. They saw themselves as obviously important functionaries of government, but they tended to defer to Congress and used their powers sparingly. Thus George Washington assumed a semimonarchical role and sought to avoid personal involvement in political controversy. A cool and aloof individual, the role fitted him well, partly because he was so eminent a personage and partly because this was the late eighteenth century, when the monarchical pattern was after all the common (if formally rejected) heritage of Americans. But it was an impossible role all the same, for he was not king and did not wish to be one. And therefore his effort to establish a government "of talents" and not of politics—a government that could embrace the conflicting views of men like Jefferson and Hamilton—was ill-fated. Jefferson quit the office of Secretary of State when it became obvious that Hamilton considered himself to be a quasi prime minister and that the President was willing to defer to Hamilton in foreign affairs as well as in treasury matters strictly speaking.[1]

The importance of Washington's aloof, magisterial role was that it set one of the images that presidents have turned to for models of behavior for themselves. And every president, including the most political of them, like Franklin Roosevelt, has claimed that on vital matters he was not acting as a partisan but as President of the United States. Though they undoubtedly knew that there was in reality no total severing of the two strands of the office, they nevertheless were ready either to pretend they were separable for whatever gain they could glean from it, or they honestly did believe that whatever they were proposing was so much in the "national interest" that it stood above the acrimony of political tumult. There is, in any event, a direct line of continuity between Washington's avoidance of politics and the solemnity of a present day presidential address to the nation on some crisis issue; they are not the same and they are probably based on different motives, but the posture and the presumably intended effect are strikingly similar. Moreover, Washington established a firm base for subsequent defense of executive prerogatives. In foreign affairs generally, in the Whiskey Rebellion, and in the matter of divulging executive documents to Congress he firmly set precedents for the future.

If Washington was aloof from partisan involvement, Thomas Jefferson as President embraced it fully. Having won the office by hard political effort, he took command of his party in Congress and dominated it thoroughly. John Marshall's worried prediction about Jefferson proved essentially accurate. The Chief Justice wrote to Hamilton:

> Mr. Jefferson appears to me to be a man, who will embody himself with the House of Representatives. By weakening the office of

1. See Leonard D. White, *The Federalists* (New York: Macmillan, 1959), pp. 213ff. On the Washington administration generally see this volume. White's subsequent volumes in the series, *The Jeffersonians, The Jacksonians,* and *The Republican Era, 1869–1901,* are excellent sources on the development of the executive in the nineteenth century.

President, he will increase his personal power. He will diminish his responsibility, sap the fundamental principles of government, and become the leader of that party which is about to constitute the majority of the legislature.[2]

Jefferson may not truly have diminished the office where he, Jefferson, was concerned (indeed the contrary is more nearly true), but he left the office a lesser place than he found it because his successors lacked the political leadership qualities that had been Jefferson's strength. And so the office languished in the hands of lesser men; indeed that was true for most of his successors during the next century. Most of them were men of Whiggish orientation, disinclined to assert the potential of the office and willing to defer to the leadership of Congress. Where Jefferson went into the Congressional caucus rooms to get what he wanted, his successors were incapable of or unwilling to make such gestures. Whereas Jefferson decided upon the Louisiana Purchase and set out to win political support for it, later it was Congress that decided the issue of war (in 1812), the bank, and other prime issues. Indeed one student of Madison's two terms in office said Madison "could hardly have played a less important part, during those eight uncomfortable years if he had remained in Virginia." [3] Leadership passed from the President to men like Henry Clay, John C. Calhoun, Daniel Webster, and other legislative luminaries. In this era Abraham Lincoln, as a Congressman, said that if he were President, "I should desire the legislation of the country to rest with Congress, uninfluenced in its origin or progress, and undisturbed by the veto unless in very special and clear cases." [4]

There were, however, exceptions to the Whiggish Presidency, and those exceptions stand out today as greater foundations of the office than do the long intervals of recessiveness. I refer, of course, to incumbents like Andrew Jackson and Abraham Lincoln. Both realized and began to exploit their position as a popularly elected monarch. Both exercised their powers forcefully and independently, acting as they thought conditions demanded and their conception of the office permitted. No president after Jackson was ever quite so out-of-it as his immediate predecessors, who had been much under the control of Congress. (Then, remember, the Congressional caucus chose presidential candidates.) But Jackson had come to power by another route—by his fame as a fighting man and through his populist appeals for support in election campaigns that did much to democratize American

---

2. Quoted by Wilfred E. Binkley, *President and Congress*, 3rd ed. (New York: Random House, Vintage Books, 1962), p. 63.
3. Binkley, quoting Professor Ralph V. Harlow, ibid., p. 73.
4. Ibid., p. 126.

politics. And when he won the office he proceeded to remake it. He made appeals directly to the people, symbolizing the new President as no longer merely the leader (at best) of cabals of politicians but as an official with a very direct association with the people. He thought of himself as a "tribune" of the people. He used the veto freely as a political weapon, not as a device resorted to only when he was convinced that a law was unconstitutional. He entered into open and public controversy with Congressional leaders and humbled them when he had the majorities with which to do it. In the long battle over the renewal of the charter of the national bank he refused Congressional demands for executive records, removed his Secretary of the Treasury in the face of Congressional demands that he not do so, refused to have public funds in the United States Bank as Congress demanded, and got the votes to expunge from the Senate record a resolution of censure passed to condemn him. Cried the shocked Henry Clay to the Senate, "Must we blot, deface, and mutilate the records of the country to punish the presumptuousness of expressing any opinion contrary to his?" [5] His colleagues' answer was yes, for they voted to have the censure resolution edged in black and to have written across it, "Expunged by order of the Senate. . . ."

As I have indicated, however, the Jacksonian performance was an example that not all could or would want to emulate. Yet national popularity was a potential source of influence in any controversy. Later a President whose image was that of total timidity and restraint said that "It is because in their hours of timidity the Congress becomes subservient to the importunities of organized minorities that the President comes more and more to stand as the champion of the rights of the whole country." [6] The words are those of Calvin Coolidge even if in practice he rarely fought for those "rights of the whole country." Most Presidents from Jackson to Hoover were of a Whiggish orientation, but the exceptions—Lincoln, Theodore Roosevelt, and Wilson—were the designers of the present-day Presidency. [7]

Like Jackson, Abraham Lincoln had an expansive, flexible view of Presidential prerogatives: he felt he was the chosen representative of the people, and he believed that as a tribune of the people he was not held to the strict letter of the Constitution when he faced a crisis. He resorted to hitherto unimaginable actions to cope with the secession

5. Ibid., p. 104.
6. Ibid., p. 381.
7. I am aware that James K. Polk is a candidate for citation as a strong president based upon his firm leadership, his iron will, and his aggressive policies toward Mexico. I might have cited still others too had I sought to catalogue the full development of the office, but my purpose is a more limited one.

crisis and he did it all on his own initiative. The Civil War broke out in April, 1861, and instead of calling Congress to get authorization for coping with the situation, he met it with his own decisions. He called for volunteers to bring the Army up to seventy-five thousand, a move that clearly was only within the power of Congress. He suspended the writ of habeas corpus, an act that the Constitution does not precisely assign to anyone, although discussion of its suspension appears in Article I, not Article II, presumably indicating it to be a Congressional responsibility. Lincoln declared a blockade of Southern ports to advance the Union cause, and he ordered the treasurer to pay out $2 million to three private individuals to finance the expansion of the military forces. (This he did because he did not trust those in official positions.) He seized telegraph lines on his own authority. *Then* with the war well entered and the basic decisions made, he called Congress into session on July 4!

With the simplicity and boldness characteristic of him, Lincoln explained why he felt justified in these actions:

> My oath to preserve the Constitution imposed on me the duty of preserving by every indispensable means that government, that nation, of which the Constitution was the organic law. Was it possible to lose the nation and yet preserve the Constitution? By general law life and limb must be protected, yet often a limb must be amputated to save a life, but a life is never wisely given to save a limb. I felt that measures, otherwise unconstitutional, might become lawful by becoming indispensable to the preservation of the Constitution through the preservation of the nation. Right or wrong, I assumed this ground and now avow it. I could not feel that, to the best of my ability, I had ever tried to preserve the Constitution, if to save slavery or any minor matter, I should permit the wreck of the government, country, and Constitution altogether.[8]

It is true that Congress subsequently ratified the steps Lincoln took to meet the crisis, but that does not, strictly speaking, justify the assumption of power by Lincoln, particularly in view of the fact that Congress was not called into session for almost three months after the outbreak of fighting. In truth the nature of the crisis defined the scope of power available: he did what he thought the situation demanded and did it on his own authority. And many of his successors have done likewise in crises great and small.

8. Ibid., pp. 154–55.

Indeed, not only in crisis situations, but in any situation where there seemed to be a demand for Presidential action, Theodore Roosevelt found justification for action. He took himself to be very much a tribune of the people. As he said in his *Autobiography* the only thing that limited the President's use of power was a specific constitutional prohibition of a contemplated act. He said the President was "a steward of the people" and was obliged to act when circumstances demanded it even when he failed to find "some specific authorization to do it." And, he went on,

> My belief was that it was not only his right but his duty to do anything that the needs of the Nation demanded unless such action was forbidden by the Constitution or by the laws. Under this interpretation of executive power I did and caused to be done many things not previously done by the President and the heads of departments. I did not usurp power, but I did greatly broaden the use of executive power.[9]

In office Roosevelt consistently practiced his theory. He found the Presidency a "bully pulpit" and was the first one to exploit fully the public relations potential of the office. His messages to Congress were consciously addressed to a wider public. He saw policy leadership as a necessary element of the President's task and did his best to persuade Congress to accept what he thought necessary. He was a conservationist and took it upon himself to withdraw Western lands from public acquisition because it was believed that they contained minerals, although the law called for withdrawal of the lands only when minerals had been found on land. In a dispute with Congress about whether to send the Navy around the world to demonstrate our naval might, he simply sent the Navy off and left it to Congress to appropriate the money to get it back home again.[10] He took unprecedented steps to cope with a difficult and lengthy coal strike in 1902. As the consequences of the five-month-long strike became more serious, Roosevelt began behind-the-scenes negotiations to force the owners to accept arbitration, and he rigged the membership of the arbitrating board so that the miners would not lose out entirely. And if arbitration had not worked he was prepared to send in the Army, seize the mines, and run them under federal authority. His Attorney General told Roosevelt that such steps would be unconstitutional, but in his account of

9. *An Autobiography* (New York: Scribner's, 1924), p. 357.

10. See Edward S. Corwin, *The President, Office and Powers* (New York: New York University Press, 1948), p. 168.

his intentions he does not mention that advice.[11] He connived to get control of the Panama Canal Zone. Later he arranged for the United States to assume operation of the customs houses of the Dominican Republic. Claiming the Monroe Doctrine as his excuse and asserting that this was no departure from past performance, Roosevelt presented the Senate a treaty authorizing what he was doing. The Senate did not ratify it, but Roosevelt continued operation of the customs. He explained that it would have been preferable for Congress to have concurred, but if it didn't, he would still do his duty and "administer the proposed treaty anyhow, considering it as a simple agreement on the part of the Executive which would be converted into a treaty whenever the Senate acted." [12]

Roosevelt, hotheaded and impulsive, used his personal authority in other dubious ways, as for example in the infamous Brownsville incident. Three companies of Negro soldiers were based near Brownsville, Texas, in 1906, and the sensitivities of white residents appear to have been riled by their mere presence. When a fight started between fifteen soldiers and some whites and one white person was shot, the town demanded punishment, although a grand jury failed to indict anyone for the killing. A general native to the South was dispatched to investigate, presented a report on the basis of which Roosevelt summarily—without any gesture toward fair procedure—ordered that all three companies of soldiers be discharged dishonorably and be barred from all future employment by government. Roosevelt waited until the day after the 1906 Congressional election to issue the order. Understandably he makes no reference to this episode in his *Autobiography*.[13]

Though Roosevelt stretched presidential power, his successor was not a mover and shaker like the Rough Rider; on the contrary William Howard Taft, corpulent and conservative, expressed almost precisely the opposite conception of presidential power. He expressed the view that

the President can exercise no power which cannot be reasonably and fairly traced to some specific grant of power or justly implied or included within such express grant as necessary and proper to its exercise. Such specific grant must be either in the Constitution or in an act of Congress passed in pursuance thereof. There is no

11. Ibid., pp. 190–91.

12. Ibid., p. 551. See also the discussion of the Dominican issue in Dexter Perkins, *A History of the Monroe Doctrine* (Boston: Little, Brown, 1955 [new ed.]), pp. 236ff. The Senate did ratify two years later.

13. See Kelly Miller, *Radicals and Conservatives* (New York: Schocken Books, 1968), pp. 307–13.

undefined residuum of power which he can exercise because it seems to him to be in the public interest." [14]

This latter-day formulation of the Whig conception of the Presidency, couched in legalisms characteristic of Taft, sounded the opposite note from Roosevelt's expansionist view. But there was more than legalism in the difference between the two men and their administrations. Where Roosevelt was a man of action and bombast, Taft was a man of deliberation and restraint. Instead of becoming deeply involved in legislative policy he withdrew and left leadership to the Congress; he was as inept in politics as he was qualified as a legal technician. Yet it suggests something about the development of the presidential office that a man who expressed this limited conception of the office was nevertheless willing to continue the Roosevelt policy of barring public lands from acquisition, doing so on shaky legal grounds. Characteristically too the Court sustained him in the *Midwest Oil* case.[15] When Congress got around to granting the President authority to withhold lands from public purchase for reasons of conservation of mineral resources, it made no reference to past acts of withdrawal of lands by Roosevelt and Taft. The Court nevertheless sustained Taft's action on the ground that Congress had had ample opportunity to correct the practice of presidential withdrawal of lands but had not done so. As Edward Corwin commented, "In short, the President was recognized as being able to acquire authority from the silences of Congress as well as from its positive enactments, provided only the silences were sufficiently prolonged." [16]

The *Midwest Oil* case was neither the first nor last time the Supreme Court has considered the question of the scope of presidential power in the absence of specific statutory authorization. With few exceptions the Court has found that the President has power that is roughly akin to a residual, inherent authority to meet emergencies or to act in unanticipated but "necessary" ways. A landmark statement on this came in 1890 when in *In re Neagle* the Court upheld the President's authority to assign a United States marshal to protect a threatened Supreme Court Justice. Briefly, the factual situation was that Justice Stephen Field had been threatened by a Californian who had lost out in an inheritance suit over which Justice Field had presided. Although no law specifically authorized it, a marshal was assigned to protect the Justice when he

14. William Howard Taft, *Our Chief Magistrate and His Powers* (New York: Columbia University Press, 1916), p. 139.

15. *U.S.* v. *Midwest Oil Co.*, 236 *U.S.* 459 (1915). Taft did, however, reverse Roosevelt on some of the lands the latter had withdrawn.

16. Corwin, op. cit., p. 148.

went to California to "ride circuit," which Supreme Court Justices then did. Upon encountering the person who had made the threat, the marshal, one Neagle, drew his gun and killed him. California arrested Neagle for murder (partly because of political disputes in California), and he sought a writ of habeas corpus, which he claimed on the ground that United States law provided for release of a prisoner held for "an act done or committed in pursuance of *a law* of the United States." [17] But there was no "law" stating that marshals could be assigned to protect judges. The Court nevertheless found that the broad authority of the President to "take care that the laws be faithfully executed" constituted a law. The opinion went on to state that the duty of the President was not limited to "the enforcement of acts of Congress or of treaties of the United States according to their express terms." Instead said the Court the President's power extends to "the rights, duties and obligations growing out of the Constitution itself, our international relations, and all the protection implied by the nature of the government under the Constitution."

Thus with a political basis established through Lincoln's acts in time of crisis, the acts of Theodore Roosevelt when faced with what he deemed threats to the public interest, and with the legal base of inherent presidential power established by *Neagle*, the use of presidential prerogatives went on expanding as this nation faced the complexities and crises of the twentieth century. To recount all the illustrations of this would demand a treatise of book length in itself—and in fact several such have been written. It will be sufficient to present a few more examples to illustrate the expansion of executive power and to show how these broad powers have become more and more accepted by the public, indeed even demanded.

Woodrow Wilson is a prime example of a President who both in crisis and in ordinary times broadened presidential authority. "The President," he prophetically said, "is at liberty, both at law and conscience, to be as big a man as he can." Following ample precedent, Wilson repeatedly invaded Central American nations, continuing the policies of his predecessors. He sent troops to Mexico in 1914 and seized Vera Cruz to follow up a demand of a United States admiral that the officials of that city not only apologize but "salute the American flag" in penance for the arrest of some naval officers who went to the city. Wilson invaded Mexico again in pursuit of Pancho Villa in 1916. He occupied Haiti in 1915 and the troops stayed there for fifteen years, and he did the same thing in the Dominican Republic, where the troops remained for eight years. He armed American merchant ships prior to

17. *In re Neagle*, 135 *U.S.* 1 (1890).

our entry into World War I, despite the fact that Congress had failed to pass legislation permitting it. He sent American soldiers to Siberia in 1918 to support the White Russians in opposition to the Communist Revolution. And in many ways he stretched his authority during the War, as executives always do under the pressure of war conditions.[18]

Franklin Roosevelt, faced with the crises of the Depression and World War II, went even further than Wilson, partly because the crises were more severe and partly because his political strength was greater. Again it is unnecessary to recapitulate all the acts he took on his own authority, but among them were the suspension of banking early in his first term under the "Bank Holiday Proclamation"; the various actions leading up to World War II, which are discussed later; the deal with Britain by which the United States traded overaged destroyers for long-term leases on military bases in the Western Hemisphere; the seizure of war plants; and his notorious executive order to remove all Japanese persons from the West Coast.[19] (After the fact, again, Congress concurred.)

Perhaps some of the discretionary sweep of the President's powers and the focus of responsibility in him alone can be conveyed by describing briefly the meeting that Roosevelt had with Winston Churchill in 1940 on the Atlantic Ocean, where they conferred aboard warships. Roosevelt took along Sumner Welles, Under Secretary of State, and some of his personal advisers (like Harry Hopkins), but his Secretary of State, Cordell Hull, was not present and he had no contact with other members of the Cabinet or Congressional leaders. Churchill by contrast was constantly in communication with London during the proceedings. In fact he sent some thirty messages to the Cabinet and on one occasion, late in the so-called Atlantic Conference, Churchill sent a tentative draft of the "Atlantic Charter" and the Cabinet met considering it until 4 A.M., responding with suggestions for minor changes. Roosevelt acted entirely on his own.[20] The Atlantic Charter was not an earthshaking document, and yet it stated postwar aims, and it tended to tighten the alliance between a warring nation and ourselves. The significant point,

18. For example, he issued a "loyalty order" that authorized the dismissal of federal employees whose retention was deemed to be "inimical to the public welfare." (See Corwin, op. cit., p. 122.) He created a War Labor Board on his own initiative and used it to coerce strikers in many ways, and he also seized industrial plants producing war needs. He seized railroads, an act that Congress later authorized.

19. See Morton Grodzins, *American Betrayed: Politics and the Japanese Evacuation* (Chicago: University of Chicago Press, 1949).

20. See Harry Hopkins's comment on the difference between Roosevelt's and Churchill's respective obligations to consult with others. See Robert E. Sherwood, *Roosevelt and Hopkins* (New York: Harper, 1948), p. 361.

however, is that Churchill could not arrive at his decisions about it personally. No doubt had he been challenged on any important facet of the Charter he would have prevailed, for politically he was in a strong position, but the point is that he was required by custom and by the understanding of the British Constitution to consult with his colleagues. Roosevelt, like other American Presidents, was on his own to decide as he chose and to consult or not consult as he determined.

In the case of the destroyer-bases deal, no authorization other than an "executive agreement" with Britain was deemed necessary. There were many who vehemently argued that the transfer of United States property to a foreign power and the acquisition of military bases should have had the consent of Congress, but there was even more widespread approval of the act, for which legal sanction was found by Attorney General Robert Jackson.[21] Similarly Roosevelt was sustained by Jackson when, faced with a strike at the North American Aviation plant in California, Roosevelt seized that installation six months before Pearl Harbor. Roosevelt cited his own proclamation of an "unlimited emergency" and the "shoot on sight" order concerning German submarines as one reason for the necessity of the takeover, and the Attorney General found authority for the seizure in the

duty constitutionally and inherently resting upon the President to exert his civil and military as well as his moral authority to keep the defense efforts of the United States a going concern [and] to obtain supplies for which Congress has appropriated money, and which it has directed the President to obtain.[22]

All of which leads to the situation in 1951, when, faced with a steel strike during the Korean War, President Harry Truman seized the nation's steel mills. In the district court where the steel owners challenged the seizure, an attorney for the United States bluntly stated that it was not necessary to show any dependence on a statute to justify he seizure. Resting his case on precedents in and out of court, he argued ". . . as to the President's power to seize: I think in the last analysis it is fair to say that the magnitude of the emergency itself is sufficient to create the power to seize under these circumstances." The trial judge pressed the United States attorney: "So you contend the Executive has unlimited power in time of an emergency?" To which the reply was, "He has the power to take such action as is necessary to meet the

21. His legal opinion is to be found in *The Presidency*, John P. Roche and Leonard W. Levy, eds. (New York: Harcourt, Brace and World, 1964), pp. 177–80.
22. Quoted by Corwin, op. cit., p. 297, who cites many other illustrations.

emergency." [23] There is much more of the same, with the Court pressing and the counsel responding with defenses of an undefined residuum of inherent presidential power to meet emergencies. Thus baldly put, it was too much for a majority of the Supreme Court, and Truman's seizure was rejected. But the opinion of the Court is a weak and confusing set of doctrines to rely upon if one were trying to build a case against broad presidential prerogatives. To begin with, it was a 6 to 3 decision, and it took no fewer than seven opinions to express the divided sentiments on the Court—a "majority opinion," five concurring ones, and a dissent! To be sure the majority said the President could not point to anything in the Constitution or in the laws to sanction his seizure, that only Congress could authorize such an act, and that therefore, this being a system of separated powers, the President could not "legislate" in this fashion. Mr. Justice Douglas in his concurring opinion, however, gave the true sentiment of the Court majority when he said,

> We pay a price for our system of checks and balances, for the distribution of power among the three branches of government. It is a price that today may seem exorbitant to many. Today a kindly President uses the seizure power to effect a wage increase and to keep the steel furnaces in production. Yet tomorrow another President might use the same power to prevent a wage increase, to curb trade unionists, to regiment labor as oppressively as industry thinks it has been regimented by this seizure.

At issue here was the fact that Truman had refused to apply the Taft-Hartley Act, through which he could have gained an eighty-day injunction to hold off the strike. Having gained even more time than that by persuading the steel union leaders not to strike, Truman chose his own route when the strike finally was called. From a close reading of the opinions one can infer that had he seized *after* using Taft-Hartley he would have been sustained by the Court. At least then the "crisis" would have been more unavoidable and one major line of judicial argument would have been weakened.

Even so a majority of the Court expressed agreement with the concept of inherent presidential power. Jackson said ". . . congressional inertia, indifference or quiescence may sometimes, at least as a practical

23. See Alan F. Westin, *The Anatomy of a Constitutional Law Case* (New York: Macmillan, 1958), p. 62. The case is *Youngstown Sheet and Tube* v. *Sawyer*, 343, U.S. 579 (1952).

matter, enable, if not invite, measures on independent presidential responsibility." Clark also concurred in the opinion but expressed the thought that in the absence of Congressional action, "the President's independent power to act depends on the gravity of the situation confronting the nation." And of course the three dissenting Justices found ample precedent for inherent powers; indeed as one reads these opinions one finds that the vast body of the law and precedent are with not the majority but the minority. The only cases cited in the leading majority opinion are, in fact, on a collateral issue unconcerned with the inherent power doctrine, whereas Chief Justice Vinson's dissent reads like a law clerk's research memorandum on every relevant case available, and there were many.

The length to which the claim of executive powers can go is suggested by a brief filed with a federal district court in a case involving persons charged with inciting riots at the 1968 Democratic Convention in Chicago. The Justice Department asserted that it had used wiretapping and electronic eavesdropping on the defendants without getting a judicial warrant to do so and without regard to the 1968 Crime Control Act that set up procedures for surveillance of that kind. Arguing that there "are in this country today organizations which intend to use force and other illegal means to attack and subvert the existing forms of government," the brief relied upon a general constitutional power to eavesdrop rather than any Congressional authorization. The brief further stated that, faced with riots and subversive threats,

> any President who takes seriously his oath to "preserve, protect, and defend the Constitution" will no doubt determine that it is not "unreasonable" to utilize electronic surveillance to gather intelligence information concerning those organizations which are committed to the use of illegal methods to bring about changes in our form of government and which may be seeking to foment violent disorders.[24]

Furthermore, the Justice Department asserted that the question of whether to conduct eavesdropping in such situations "in order to protect the nation against the possible danger which they present is one that properly comes within the competence of the executive and not the judicial branch."

Here the "subversives" were antiwar demonstrators, who in the judgment of many observers were less perpetrators of violence than the

24. The brief is quoted by Fred P. Graham, "U.S. Claims Right of Wiretapping in Security Case," *The New York Times,* June 14, 1969.

victims of innumerable assaults by the Chicago police in what was called in an official report a "police riot." Other "subversives," like Elijah Muhammad of the Black Muslims and the late Dr. Martin Luther King, Jr., have been subjected to similar electronic spying. Not only because this is a free-swinging interpretation of presidential power and not only because it involves invasions of privacy is this Justice Department presumption a monstrous action. It is, in a word, tyranny, for it amounts to the suppression of *political* opposition. And such harassment is claimed as *executive privilege beyond judicial interference*. The constitutional reliance is upon nothing more substantial than the oath of office, but of course the constitutional point is of marginal importance; the truth beneath the constitutional point is that there is political support for such suppression. Under the wraps of secrecy and with sweeping discretionary power, the oath of the President becomes an excuse for what, in other circumstances at least, would assuredly be labeled tyranny.

It has been the scholarly custom in recent years to discount the fears of critics of ever-rising presidential power—like Edward Corwin and Charles Hyneman.[25] Corwin in fact wondered whether "the Presidency is a potential matrix of dictatorship."[26] The standard response to this argument is that, yes, the President does have a great deal of power and it is highly personalized, but he is not without counterpressures and he certainly does not always achieve his goals. He must take Congress and the public's possible reactions into account; therefore, he is more powerful in appearance than he is in reality and much of the concern about his being excessively powerful in a dictatorial sense is a false apprehension. As Nelson Polsby has put it,

> Measured against the opportunities, the responsibilities, and the resources of others in our political system and in other nations, the powers of the Presidency are enormous. It is only when we measure these same powers against the problems of our age that they seem puny and inadequate.[27]

25. Edward Corwin's *The President: Office and Powers*, op. cit., and Charles Hyneman's *Bureaucracy in a Democracy* (New York: Harper and Row, 1950) are both critical of a superpowerful Presidency and both proposed ideas for limiting his authority by tying him closer to Congressional advisers, a point I shall consider later.

26. Ibid., p. 353.

27. Nelson W. Polsby, *Congress and the Presidency* (Englewood Cliffs, N.J.: Prentice-Hall, Inc., 1964), p. 30. Robert Dahl raises the question of excessive power and asks whether in this "age of Caesars" the Presidency should be "scaled down to more nearly human proportions." But he never answers his question (*Pluralist*

But is the office so puny? One grants that Congress must authorize presidential expenditures, but one must also recognize that it does so blindly in a considerable part of its appropriations process. Congress was surprised recently to learn that over half a billion dollars a year was being spent for chemical-biological warfare (CBW), a sum that was carefully scattered in the defense budget in order to prevent Congress from learning about it.[28] The CBW story began to emerge only when a test of nerve gas caused the death of six thousand sheep in Utah.[29] (Characteristically, the Army at first announced it had no responsibility for the mass death of the sheep.) In many areas secrecy shrouds sweeping powers being exercised without much restraint. Until the U-2 photographic spy plane was shot down by the Russians, knowledge of its operations, let alone of its flights over Russian territory, was a tightly held secret. Until the Koreans captured the spy ship *Pueblo* and later shot down a Constellation spy aircraft, Americans had been generally unaware that ships and planes could be used for electronic eavesdropping. The President is in command of all such operations, in theory at least, but the important point is that it all takes place in secrecy until some crisis brings it out in the open.

Likewise the President can make agreements with foreign nations that commit this country in unknown ways, and can do so without any obligation to report to anyone. In the past, commitments were made primarily through the treaty process, and indeed the Senate, at least in the late nineteenth and early twentieth centuries, frequently refused to ratify them. But today foreign relations are conducted more by executive agreements with other nations than through treaties, and there is no obligation to get approval of agreements, nor even to report that they have been made. Some indication of the trend of foreign policy de-

---

Democracy in the United States, p. 108). James McGregor Burns and Jack Peltason also raise the question but feel reassured by the fact that the President either has to run for office again or wants his own party to win after his second term. They are apprehensive, however, about the inadequacy of the political opposition, because they think a president needs a "strong and durable opposition. This is perhaps the weakest link in the American democratic structure. . . ." *Government by the People*, 6th ed. (Englewood Cliffs, N.J.: Prentice-Hall, Inc., 1966), p. 548. A review of other commentary on excessive power in the Presidency leads to the conclusion that most writers consider the issue marginal at best.

28. See John W. Finney, "Pentagon Bares Cost of Germ War Study," *The New York Times*, May 5, 1969.

29. Soon other revelations followed. One was that a poison had been developed that was so deadly that a drop of it on the skin caused instant death. Another was a plan to transport from Colorado a huge supply of poison gas to dispose of in the Atlantic Ocean. See Seymour M. Hersh, "Germs and Gas as Weapons," *New Republic*, June 7, 1969, pp. 13-16, for a brief introduction to the mad world of CBW.

velopment by executive agreement is suggested by the following table, which includes only *publicized* executive agreements.

	Treaties	Executive Agreements
1789–1939	800	1,200
1940–1960	300	2,000
1963–1967	47	1,136

In extenuation of this power it may be said that the President has to make every commitment in the light of the possible costs to himself and the nation. That is, if the commitment might involve the United States in a war or in a major dispute, he will need Congressional and public support. But that is a lesser restraint than it appears, particularly where military threat is involved. When President Johnson decided to escalate the Vietnam war and wanted a Tonkin resolution, it took only two days to get it; later that year, when he wished a $700-million supplemental appropriation to finance what he had done, the *House acted in less than forty-eight hours on his request and the Senate almost as speedily.* (Actually he proposed the supplemental budget on a Tuesday, the House Appropriations Committee approved it the same day, and the House passed it the next day by a vote of 408 to 7. On Thursday the Senate went along: 88 to 3.[30] To assess the President's power and the political limitations on it as though the same limits applied in foreign and military matters as in domestic ones is grossly to misconceve the problem. And it is surely not insignificant that foreign affairs are the major preoccupation of the executive; in terms of the time devoted to such matters, the money spent on them, and their seriousness for the peace and safety of the world, international affairs edge domestic matters into the corner. And thereby, because the President has such sweeping authority in foreign affairs and such unbridled opportunities to exercise it, his power has escalated enormously in the last two decades. Some further light will be shed on the fatefulness of the scope of that power by an examination of how presidential decisions led us into the morass that is Vietnam.

The Executive and Vietnam: Unlearned Lessons

Nothing in modern American history better illustrates the vital significance and fateful power of the Presidency than does the Vietnam war. From the time the United States became involved after France's withdrawal from its colonial empire in Indochina down to the present

30. See *The New York Times*, May 8, 1965.

(mid-1969), a nation has been ravaged and more than a million persons have been killed. And at each tortuous stage of the bitter war decisions (and nondecisions) of presidents of the United States have been critical determinants of life and death, not only for Americans in service there but for the thirty-five million Vietnamese, North and South. From the White House came the decisions that resulted in the deaths of over fifty thousand Americans, the grave injury of 280,000 others, and more than five hundred thousand enemy dead found in the endless "body counts" after battles, the million civilians slain in the South (by the estimate of two civilians dead for each enemy soldier killed), plus an unknown number of civilians dead in the North from the bombing raids there. Perhaps by looking at the evolution of American policy toward that blighted land we can reveal some of the critical aspects of executive decision-making, the sweeping discretionary power of the Chief Executive, and some of the political, constitutional, and moral problems involved.

American involvement in the Vietnamese trial by fire begins with a refusal to come to the aid of the French colonial regime that was doomed to defeat in the siege of Dienbienphu during the spring of 1954. Several members of the Eisenhower Administration (including John Foster Dulles, Richard Nixon, and Admiral Arthur Radford) [31] were anxious to have American airpower and, reportedly, three Army divisions [32] committed to the support of the beleaguered French garrison. President Eisenhower directed that several steps be taken before any commitment was made. First he wanted the French to agree to grant greater independence to the Vietnamese, concurrent action by Great Britain, and agreement from Congress on the commitment of United States forces. He got none of these. France resisted granting greater independence; Britain concluded that air action would be insufficient and ground action likely to lead to a general Asian war. Further, Anthony Eden told the House of Commons that to intervene would destroy any chance of getting a peaceful settlement for the area in the then impending Geneva Conference.[33] And in Congress the warm memory of the Korean War and a continuing dread of massive land war in Asia quashed hope of winning general support there. Accordingly the French went down to defeat without Americans fighting beside them.

Faced with a single decision to engage in a colonial war, Eisenhower

31. An excellent journalistic account of this decision is Chalmers M. Roberts's "The Day We Didn't Go To War," *The Reporter*, Sept. 14, 1954, pp. 31–35.

32. The source is Anthony Eden, *Full Circle* (London: Cassell, 1960), p. 143.

33. Quoted by George Kahin and John Lewis, *The United States in Vietnam* (New York: Delta, 1967), p. 39. This balanced and detailed account is an excellent source on the war down to 1966.

refused, but he and his successors in a series of small, less conspicuous decisions fully committed us to war. Shortly after Dienbienphu Eisenhower took the fatal first step by seeking to strengthen Ngo Dihn Diem, premier in the government of Emperor Bao Dai. The United States government granted economic assistance in return for promises to make "needed reforms." From 1955 onward the United States became the economic mainstay of South Vietnam, supplying an average of almost a quarter of a billion dollars a year in aid. In addition the United States supplied vast amounts of military equipment and sent military personnel to train and improve the South Vietnamese army. With United States support, Diem repudiated the Geneva agreements particularly with respect to internationally supervised elections for reunification of Vietnam; when Ho Chi Minh proposed negotiations on these elections, Diem, certain of defeat, refused to cooperate. Vietminh workers began soliciting popular support for the election, only to have many leaders of the organization arrested; indeed the future president of the National Liberation Front spent six years under arrest by Diem.[34]

Through 1956 North Vietnam continued, without success, to seek reunification elections. And as Diem sought to establish his regime more firmly he resorted increasingly to police state tactics, using the pretext of suppression of Communism. Even Diem's friends in the United States had to admit, as did *Life* magazine, that the regime existed on a system of "decrees, political prisons, concentration camps, milder 'reeducation' centers, secret police." A presidential decree of January, 1956, supposedly aimed at suppression of Communism, resulted in thousands of non-Communists being detained, and, *Life* went on, "The whole machinery of security has been used to discourage active opposition of any kind from any source." [35] The suppression helped intensify the opposition and by the time Eisenhower left office, the National Liberation Front had been organized. (Not, as official Washington claims, on orders from the government of Ho Chi Minh, but in fact in opposition to it.) [36]

Opposition to Diem grew and spread throughout the country, but generous American support of his regime helped it survive. Insurgency spread rapidly, however, and by the time John Kennedy became President, Saigon had lost control over much of the countryside. The resurrected Vietminh, which had borne the brunt of battle against the French, now became the Vietcong, and North Vietnam began providing support to it. Some infiltration into the South took place, but at this stage, even United States official claims about infiltrators were modest.

34. See Kahin and Lewis, op. cit., pp. 84–85.
35. Quoted by Kahin and Lewis, p. 101.
36. See the sources on this point in Kahin and Lewis, pp. 118–20.

Military activity increased, and the Kennedy Administration now had to make basic decisions about Vietnam. Kennedy at this point greatly increased American military involvement, making the third cardinal decision on Vietnam (the first being Dienbienphu and the second to back Diem). Between the time he took office and the middle of 1962 the number of American troops in Vietnam increased from two thousand to ten thousand. These troops were supposedly not directly involved but advised and trained troops and planned operations, but before the end of the year helicopters manned by Americans were firing at the Vietcong. It is said that the introduction of helicopters put the Vietcong at a considerable disadvantage, temporarily stabilizing the military situation for Diem. But Diem and his family continued to resist the pressures for reform from the United States and suppressed the opposition ruthlessly, and the tide of battle once again swung back to the insurgents. Said David Halberstam of *The New York Times* in 1963, "A year after the American build-up of weaponry and personnel had reached its peak, it was clear that the Government had lost the initiative, that the enemy had benefited more from the weapons than we had." [37]

As tension grew and political opposition deepened, Diem resorted to even more drastic measures, culminating in the use of his special force troops to attack several Buddhist pagodas and the arrest of large numbers of Buddhists. At that point President Kennedy voiced concern that Diem had got "out of touch" with the people. Kennedy put pressure on Diem, including a refusal to continue paying the cost of Diem's special force unless it was committed to battle in the field.[38] Then, in a coup, Diem and his brother were murdered and a new government was installed, headed by General Duong Van Minh. It was generally believed that Washington had something to do with the coup that ended the eight-year Diem regime. Max Frankel, writing for *The New York Times* observed that the Administration welcomed the coup, "assumes that its policies helped to bring it about and is confident of greater progress now in the war against the Communist guerrillas. . . ." [39] Reports were common that the United States government had done much more than merely "help bring about" the coup.

Whatever Washington's involvement in the downfall of Diem, the Minh government proved to be less resolute about pressing the war and more neutralist in spirit than Washington liked. President Lyndon Johnson told General Minh in a 1964 New Year's message that "Neu-

37. David Halberstam, *The Making of a Quagmire* (New York: Random House, 1965), p. 189.
38. See Kahin and Lewis, op. cit., p. 144.
39. Nov. 2, 1963.

tralization of South Vietnam would only be another name for a Communist takeover. . . ." [40] The Minh government lasted only three months, falling to another coup, this one led by General Nguyen Khanh. Khanh offered as justification for the coup the necessity to halt the drift toward neutralism. Stop that drift he did, but the military situation continued to deteriorate. In April, 1964, a United States report "stated that only 34 per cent of Vietnam's villages were government controlled, 24 per cent were 'neutral,' and 42 per cent were outright Vietcong." [41] The inability of the South Vietnamese to make headway against the Vietcong was disturbing to Washington, and during the spring of 1964 there were signs that Washington was moving toward an expansion of the American role in the war. Whereas it had been the stated intention of the Kennedy Administration to withdraw most American troops from Vietnam by the end of 1965, the policy now became one of increasing rather than decreasing American involvement.[42]

Apparently encouraged by support from Washington General Khanh began to talk about carrying the war to North Vietnam, and Nguyen Cao Ky, then Commander of South Vietnam's air force and later to become premier, announced the readiness of his command to bomb the North. "We are ready," he said. "We could go this afternoon. I cannot assure that all of North Vietnam would be destroyed, but Hanoi would certainly be destroyed." [43] In response to the rumors and threats of escalation of the war, several international efforts were made to seek peace negotiations. U Thant, Secretary General of the United Nations, attempted in early July to get agreement to reconvene the Geneva Conference. Later that month General Charles de Gaulle called for a meeting similar to the Geneva Conference, and the Soviet Union communicated directly with the fourteen nations that had participated in the Geneva Conference, asking urgently that they meet once again. South Vietnam promptly and angrily rejected the de Gaulle proposal; North Vietnam replied favorably to the Soviet Union's suggestion. President Johnson told a news conference on July 25, 1964, that, "We do not believe in conferences called to ratify terror, so our policy is unchanged." [44] The next day it was announced in Washington that five

40. Quoted by Kahin and Lewis, op. cit., p. 152.
41. Ibid., p. 153.
42. See Franz Schurmann, Peter Scott, and Reginald Zelnik, *The Politics of Escalation in Vietnam* (New York: Fawcett, 1966), p. 32.
43. Quoted from the *New York Times* of July 23, 1964, by Kahin and Lewis, op. cit., p. 154.
44. Schurmann et al., op. cit., p. 37. Schurmann and his colleagues speculate that the stepping up of military pressure by the United States and South Vietnam were negative responses to the peace overtures. See pp. 35–39.

thousand to six thousand more United States troops would be committed in South Vietnam.

Meanwhile American domestic politics began to focus on the Vietnam war. On July 15 Barry Goldwater overwhelmingly won the Republican nomination for the Presidency. Goldwater was so military-minded that he became the butt of endless grim jokes and pitiless denunciation, including vague allegations of insanity in one national journal, against which Goldwater won a libel judgment. Still, he was the author of *Why Not Victory?*, he had an apparently childishly simple conception of Communism, and he had said, while campaigning in New Hampshire, that he advocated "carrying the war to North Vietnam—ten years ago we should have bombed North Vietnam, destroyed the only access they had to North Vietnam, with no risk to our lives." [45] He was a weak opponent as it turned out in November, but in the course of the summer of 1964, when riots broke out in many cities across the land (New York, Rochester, Paterson, Elizabeth, Philadelphia), when there was adverse reaction to the passage of a civil rights act, and when a frenzy of patriotic enthusiasm was engendered by the Goldwater candidacy, the backlash phenomenon stirred considerable interest among politicians. In the opinion of many observers the adamant demand by Goldwater for carrying the war to North Vietnam represented a potential loss of votes for Democratic candidates.

Three developments then set the stage for another decisive step for the United States in Vietnam. First there was the failure of the South Vietnamese army combined with the weakness of the government; second, the developing international peace moves; and third, the domestic political challenge: all set the stage for the Tonkin Gulf affair.

The public first heard of it at an unusual hour—11:36 P.M.—when the President spoke on television. He spoke of a North Vietnamese attack on two American destroyers that were on routine patrols in international waters, and he announced he had ordered a retaliatory air strike on the bases in North Vietnam from which the attacking patrol boats had come. He said that he would go to Congress the next day and ask that it show the unity of the nation "in its determination to take all necessary measures in support of freedom and in defense of peace in Southeast Asia." His message promptly did go forward to Congress the next day; hearings were held the following day; and the third day the joint resolution that came to be called the "Tonkin Gulf Resolution" was enacted: 88 to 2 in the Senate and 416 to 0 in the House of Repre-

45. T. H. White, *The Making of the President 1964* (New York: Signet, 1965), p. 132.

sentatives. It is appropriate to quote the Resolution in full in order to demonstrate what it was Congress agreed to on short notice and to set the stage for further analysis of this decisive presidential action.

JOINT RESOLUTION, U.S. CONGRESS

August 7, 1964

To Promote the Maintenance of International Peace and Security in Southeast Asia.

WHEREAS naval units of the Communist regime in Vietnam, in violation of the principles of the Charter of the United Nations and of the principles of the Charter of the United Nations and of international law, have deliberately and repeatedly attacked United States naval vessels lawfully present in international waters, and have thereby created a serious threat to international peace; and

WHERAS these attacks are part of a deliberate and systematic campaign of aggression that the Communist regime in North Vietnam has been waging against its neighbors and the nations joined with them in the collective defense of their freedom; and

WHERAS the United States is assisting the peoples of southeast Asia to protect their freedom and has no territorial, military or political ambitions in that area, but desires only that these peoples should be left in peace to work out their own destinies in their own way; Now, therefore, be it

Resolved by the Senate and House of Representatives of the United States of America in Congress assembled.

SEC. 1. That the Congress approves and supports the determination of the President, as Commander in Chief, to take all necessary measures to repel any armed attack against the forces of the United States and to prevent further aggression.

SEC. 2. The United States regards as vital to its national interest and to world peace the maintenance of international peace and security in southeast Asia. Consonant with the Constitution of the United States and the Charter of the United Nations and in accordance with its obligations under the Southeast Asia Collective Defense Treaty, the United States is, therefore, prepared, as the President determines, to take necessary steps, including the use of armed force, to assist any member or protocol state of the Southeast Asia Collective Defense Treaty requesting assistance in defense of its freedom.

SEC. 3. This resolution shall expire when the President shall determine that the peace and security of that area is reasonably assured by international conditions created by action of the United

Nations or otherwise, except that it may be terminated earlier by concurrent resolution of Congress.[46]

The attack on American vessels, the reprisal air strikes on the North Vietnamese mainland, and the enactment of the joint resolution raised a host of questions about presidential power, American policy, and constitutional law. But they were not raised immediately. At the time of the incident, Congress accepted the President's assertion of necessity to respond to an aggressive act in order to prevent expansion of the war. Voices, such as those of Senator Wayne Morse and Senator Ernest Gruening—the only two members in either house of Congress who dared vote against the Resolution—went unheard. Morse on August 6, 1964, made a general attack on the war and on the Resolution in particular, but he was not believed when he said that although "the resolution will pass, Senators who vote for it will live to regret it." Later he said,

> "Unpopular as it is, I am perfectly willing to make the statement for history that if we follow a course of action that bogs down thousands of American boys in Asia, the administration responsible for it will be rejected and repudiated by the American people. It should be." [47]

(As it turned out Senators Morse and Gruening were "repudiated" along with the Johnson Administration—at least Morse and Gruening, persisting in their opposition to the war, were defeated for reelection in 1968, and if the Johnson Administration was not repudiated it surely was not buoyed up by its Vietnam policies.)

In the five years following the Tonkin Gulf incident a flood of accusations, rationalizations, investigations, and reconsiderations has raised a number of fundamental questions that cleave to the heart of the issue of presidential leadership. Among others the following questions

46. Department of State *Bulletin*, Aug. 24, 1964.
47. *Congressional Record*, Aug. 6, 1964, pp. 18425, 18427, and repeated in the *Congressional Record* for Feb. 21, 1968, pp. S1591, S1601. On February 21, 28, and 29, Senator Morse placed in the *Record* some materials not otherwise available on the Tonkin Gulf Incident, including a number of hitherto secret communications that reveal much of the background of the issue. See *Congressional Record* (daily edition), Feb. 21, 1968, pp. S1589–1604; Feb. 28, 1968, pp. S1885–91; Feb. 29, 1968, pp. S1947–52. After this chapter was written a book on the incident was published, Joseph Goulden, *Truth Is the First Casualty* (Chicago: Rand-McNally, 1969). Mr. Goulden's account is detailed and penetrating, raising even more doubt about the affair than my own more limited investigation revealed. On all important issues, however, I find no inconsistency between Goulden's account and my own.

either arise directly from the Tonkin affair or are collaterally rooted in it:

1. Why did North Vietnam send patrol boats out to attack United States destroyers on the high seas?

2. Were the destroyers on "routine missions" as claimed?

3. Did the attacks actually take place?

4. Why did the United States respond so massively (with sixty-four sorties flown) and so rapidly (within less than twelve hours)?

5. Why was the issue not taken to the UN Security Council?

6. What are the implications of the fact that the Resolution had been drafted long before the incident took place?

7. Was the reprisal intended to shore up the sagging Khanh regime?

8. What are the implications of the acquiescence and speed of Congress in enacting the Tonkin Resolution?

9. Who, today, has the authority to "declare war"?

10. Does the United States have an obligation to be "policeman to the world," or is it "neo-isolationist" to raise such a question?

11. Why has the Senate Foreign Relations Committee not pursued its investigation of the Tonkin Gulf incident to its logical conclusions?

Let us take up these questions in order and assess some of their implications.

1. *Why did North Vietnam send patrol boats out to attack United States destroyers on the high seas?*

An attack by patrol boats on a destroyer, especially when the destroyers have air support, is at best an uneven match. What could have induced the North Vietnamese to make such an attack? One possible (I believe, likely) reason is that the North Vietnamese assumed the presence of the destroyers was more than casually connected with naval attacks being made by the South Vietnamese on two North Vietnamese islands. On the night of Friday, July 31, 1964, several South Vietnamese patrol boats, supplied by the United States and with American-trained crews, made a raid on the islands of Hon Me and Hon Ngu. On August 1, the next day, the United States destroyer *Maddox* patroled within four miles of Hon Me island. Then on Sunday, August 2, during daylight hours three North Vietnamese torpedo boats attacked the *Maddox*, firing some torpedoes and machine guns. The *Maddox* suffered no damage, but American aircraft reportedly sank two of the three attacking boats. In what may have been a crossed-signals situation, the Pentagon said the next day that the raid did not constitute a "major crisis"—that the situation was "unwelcome, but not especially serious." [48] On the same day the President dispatched a note of protest to North Vietnam saying,

> The U.S. Government expects that the authorities of the regime in North Vietnam will be under no misapprehension as to the grave consequences which would inevitably result from any further unprovoked offensive military action against U.S. forces. [49]

In any event North Vietnam claimed the *Maddox* had invaded its territorial waters, that it had acted as a cover for the raids carried out by the South Vietnamese boats, and that their attack had been in retaliation for those actions.

The Administration stressed repeatedly that the destroyers were attacked while in international waters far off the North Vietnam coast, and the North Vietnamese emphasized that the destroyers did enter her territorial waters shortly after the South Vietnamese raids. The United States says that the *Maddox* went no closer than four miles from Vietnam and held this not to be within Vietnam's territorial limits, maintaining that a claim to a twelve-mile territorial limit was not asserted by North Vietnam until a month after the Tonkin incident—which North Vietnam denies. Whatever the validity of this, one hardly needs to ponder long about what the United States reaction would be if an apparently hostile destroyer steamed by four miles off Florida following gunboat raids from, say, Cuba a few days before. [50]

During the night of August 3–4, another South Vietnamese patrol boat attack took place, and during the following night the *Maddox* and a destroyer that had joined her, the *Turner Joy*, reported further attacks, lasting for over an hour. Both destroyers returned fire, and some men aboard the *Turner Joy* reported seeing attacking vessels; aircraft called to further the search for the attackers were unable, however, to locate the attackers. The night had been unusually dark and visual sightings were difficult. Claims that North Vietnamese attacking patrol boats were hit and perhaps had been sunk were unconfirmed by any debris found on the water when daylight came, although a search was made.

48. See Schurmann et al., op. cit., p. 40.
49. Quoted by Secretary McNamara in his testimony before the Senate Committee on Foreign Relations, "The Gulf of Tonkin, The 1964 Incidents," Hearings, Ninetieth Congress (Washington: U.S. Government Printing Office), Feb. 20, 1968, p. 10.
50. The territorial waters issue is discussed by Robert McNamara in his February 20, 1968, testimony before the Senate Committee on Foreign Relations, "The Gulf of Tonkin, The 1964 Incidents," pp. 37–38, 48–49, 104–105.

North Vietnam denied that the raid ever took place, and a captured North Vietnamese naval officer gave evidence that he knew of the first attack but stoutly denied that the second one happened. Nevertheless, some nine hours after the second attack (assuming it actually occurred), Secretary of Defense McNamara released the President's order for the retaliatory air strike.[51]

2. Were the destroyers on "routine missions" as claimed?

When the President told the public of the attacks and when Secretary McNamara presented evidence to a joint session of the Senate Foreign Relations Committee and the Senate Armed Services Committee the next day, the destroyers were reported to have been "carrying out a routine patrol of the type we carry out all over the world at all times." [52] This was evasive language at best, for the *Maddox* appears to have had at least two other roles to play. One was to use its electronic equipment to spy on North Vietnamese communications. (The spy operation was called the "DeSoto Patrol.") There is a dispute as to whether the *Maddox* had the capacity to "stimulate" North Vietnamese radar and thereby get readings on it, or whether it had "passive" gear that allowed listening in only; Secretary McNamara flatly stated later that the *Maddox* could and did "stimulate," but the Commander of the *Maddox* operation denied that the ship was so equipped. At the minimum it had some spy function.[53]

The second function of the *Maddox* related to the South Vietnamese raids on the North Vietnamese islands, called "34-A ops" in Navy parlance. The official United States claim was that the destroyer *Maddox* had absolutely nothing whatever to do with the raids. Secretary McNamara on August 6, 1964, told the Senate Committees that the *Maddox*

> was not informed of, was not aware of, had no evidence of, and so far as I know today has no knowledge of any South Vietnamese

51. The Secretary discussed the timing of his actions in his February 20 testimony cited above; pp. 57–59. He also claimed that a second captured North Vietnamese sailor affirmed the second attack. The clearest brief account of the attacks was an Associated Press recapitulation written three years later and placed in the *Congressional Record* for February 28, 1968 (pp. S1888–90). By contrast—to illustrate Pentagon "managed" news—see the *Life* magazine story that follows (pp. S1890–91).

52. Quoted by Senator Morse on the Senate floor, Feb. 21, 1968, *Congressional Record*, p. S1590. (Subsequently cited as "Morse speeches" with appropriate dates and pages.)

53. See *The New York Times*, Feb. 24, 1969; note, however, that Secretary McNamara was then a week short of departing the office of Secretary of Defense; contradicting him then doubtless seemed easier to do than previously.

actions in connection with the two islands that Senator Morse referred to [meaning Hon Me and Hon Ngu].[54]

However, on August 4 the Commander in Chief of the Pacific Fleet sent a message to the *Maddox* saying that its patrol

will (a) clearly demonstrate our determination to continue these operations; (b) possibly draw North Vietnamese Navy patrol boats to northward away from the areas of 34-A ops; (3) eliminate De-Soto patrol interference with 34-A ops.[55]

Furthermore, on the day after the first attack, the commander of the DeSoto patrol, Captain John J. Herrick, sent the following message to the commander of the Seventh Fleet:

Evaluation of info from various sources indicates that North Vietnam considers patrol directly involved with 34-A operations. North Vietnam considers U.S. ships present as enemies because of these operations and have already indicated readiness to treat us in that category. (b) North Vietnam is very sensitive about Hon Me. Believes this is PT operating base and the cove there presently contains numerous patrol and PT craft which have been repositioned from northerly bases." [56]

Not only that, the commander of the DeSoto patrol *ten hours before the first attack* sent the following message to the Commander, Seventh Fleet: "Consider continuance of patrol presents an unacceptable risk." [57] It is not apparent from the available evidence exactly what basis of Captain Herrick's message concerning the danger was (he was never called upon by the Senate Foreign Relations Committee to testify), but presumably his electronic eavesdropping had indicated the North Vietnamese were thoroughly stirred up and ready to respond.

Secretary McNamara's reply when questioned about the above indication of danger was that Captain Herrick later said he could recall no basis for issuing such a warning. The sending of the message was not denied, but Herrick merely asserted to a *New York Times* reporter that

54. Morse speech, Feb. 21, p. 1590. Indeed the Secretary even more sweepingly at one point denied that the Navy knew anything about the "South Vietnam actions, if there were any," ibid., p. 1589. The South Vietnamese proudly proclaimed their attacks on the islands.
55. Morse speech, Feb. 21, p. 1590.
56. "Gulf of Tonkin, The 1964 Incidents," Senate Foreign Relations Committee Hearings, p. 33.
57. Morse speech, Feb. 29, 1968, p. S1949.

the message was based "mostly on conjecture on my part." This arose, he said, from the fact that the North Vietnamese "had turned hostile" on August 2 (first raid).[58] That may be an answer of sorts for the second more detailed message mentioning the attacks on the island, but it gives no explanation whatsoever for the message on August 1, which spoke of continuing the mission as an "unacceptable risk." At that time the North Vietnamese had attacked no American ships.

Consequently, for the Secretary of Defense to come before the Congress on August 6, 1964, and say that the two destroyers were on a "routine mission" and to assert that they knew nothing of the parallel South Vietnamese attacks at the very least raises serious questions about the way the executive "led" Congress by selective divulgence of information to put the most charitable name on it.

3. *Did the attacks actually take place?*

Of the first attack there was no question: North Vietnam admitted it and gave reasons for it. But they called the second one a fabrication and denied ever making it. From reading the available published evidence and debates, I have serious doubts that any attack occurred and certainly not a massive one. A flotilla of torpedo boats would have been necessary for such an encounter because each PT boat carried two torpedoes, and there is speculation that some of the attacking vessels did not even carry torpedoes and were equipped with no more than machine guns. If the sea had been dotted with such attack craft, it seems strange that flares revealed no boats to the aircraft that quickly sought the enemy. There is much testimony about a searchlight that shone for some time, and there are reports of explosions in the direction from which the attacks were thought to be coming. The firing of hundreds of shells at nonexistent attackers is hardly unprecedented, and if that happened here it would not be the first time that an unseen "enemy" produced a barrage of "return" fire in a combat situation. There was a heavy cloud cover at the time and there was speculation that the radar sightings of enemy craft were the result of atmospheric disturbances and an "overeager [sonarman]." First reports said that from neither the *Maddox* nor the *Turner Joy* were there any "actual visual sightings or wakes." Four hours before the United States retaliatory attack Captain Herrick sent the following message:

> Maddox scored no known hits and never positively identified a boat as such. Furthermore, weather was overcast with limited visibility . . . air support not successful in locating targets. There were no stars or moon resulting in almost total darkness through-

58. *The New York Times*, Feb. 25, 1968.

out the action. . . . No known damage or personal casualties to either ship. *Turner Joy* claims sinking one craft and damaging another.[59]

Sufficient doubt existed in the Pentagon about the attack to produce a call for verification. Hence the Pacific Fleet Commander asked, "1. Can you confirm absolutely that you were attacked? 2. Can you confirm sinking of PT boats? 3. Desire reply directly supporting evidence." Shortly before McNamara gave the order to make the air strikes on the mainland the destroyers were asked to make a search for debris to serve as evidence that an attack took place; the search showed nothing, but that report came in long after the United States air strike hit Vietnam.

No official inquiry board was established to investigate whether the two destroyers had used their ammunition against phantom enemies, although a month later two other destroyers made similar radar sightings, fired against them, and a court of inquiry found that no actual attack had taken place.[60] Whatever else may be said about the question of whether the second attack took place, the following comment about the impression left with the Congress at the time seems to me justified. Senator Morse said on February 21, 1968,

> As for the second incident itself, Mr. McNamara told the committee [on August 6, 1964] that there was no doubt that the attack on the *Maddox* and the *Turner Joy* had taken place as described. He even told the committee that two North Vietnamese PT boats had been destroyed. His testimony gave no indication that there was any doubt as to what had occurred. The reports, however, show that as the hours went by after the second incident there was increasing concern that the attack may not have taken place at all. I think it did, but there was such little objective evidence immediately available that there was doubt.[61]

4. *Why did the United States respond so massively (with sixty-four sorties flown) and so rapidly (within less than twelve hours)?*
No one other than those directly involved in deciding to strike back at North Vietnam can answer this question, and they have not, to the best of my knowledge, given a direct answer to the question, except to suggest that once they were convinced that a second attack on the destroyers had been made they wanted a "prompt and firm military

59. Morse speech, Feb. 29, 1968, p. S1950.
60. See Morse speech, Feb. 28, 1968, p. S1951.
61. Morse speech, Feb. 21, 1968, p. S1592.

response." For hours on February 20, 1968, Mr. McNamara was under relatively hostile inquisition by the Committee on Foreign Relations and repeatedly he was asked why such a sudden response, but he gave no explicit answer as to why the retaliation could not have been held up until it was more certain that an attack had taken place. Further inquiry a week and again two weeks after the August 4 incident seemed to make it appear more likely that an attack had occurred. (Yet to a skeptic the fact that we had already retaliated might make it seem rather difficult at that stage to discover that no attack had occurred.) But the early doubt about the attack certainly makes the haste seem strange. It has suggested to many that there was in effect a conspiracy to induce an attack on the basis of which retaliatory action could be taken. Such an assertion Secretary McNamara, not surprisingly, found "monstrous," and indeed Chairman of the Foreign Relations Committee, J. W. Fulbright, agreed that he did not think any conspiracy was involved. The point is, however, Senator Fulbright continued,

> whether the decision making process, with all these conflicting reports coming in, is sufficiently accurate and reliable to justify taking such a decision to declare war on another country, which was the immediate outgrowth of this particular series of events.[62]

Shortly after this exchange Senator Fulbright referred to a message that Captain Herrick had sent to his superiors some four hours after the attack, in which he said:

> Review of action makes many recorded contacts and torpedoes fired appear doubtful. Freak weather effects and overeager sonarman may have accounted for many reports. No actual visual sightings by *Maddox*. Suggest complete evaluation before any further action.[63]

Senator Fulbright told Secretary McNamara that that message alone, had he been told of it on August 6, would have kept him from urging the Senate to pass the Tonkin Gulf Resolution. Mr. McNamara replied that Captain Herrick had made up his mind before the retaliation that the attack had been real. To which Fulbright replied that Herrick had suggested a "complete evaluation before any further action," and that, said Fulbright, "is a very strong recommendation from a man on the scene in charge of the operation." [64]

62. "The Gulf of Tonkin: The 1964 Incidents," op. cit., p. 79.
63. Ibid., p. 57.
64. Ibid., pp. 80–81.

In neither of the attacks was any damage sustained by the destroyers nor were there casualties among American personnel. Navy reports stated, however, that two to four North Vietnamese patrol boats were sunk. That sounds like a small naval victory for the United States, so why the massive retaliation? When that question was put to Mr. McNamara his response was that the attack was not a massive one (sixty-four aircraft struck the Vietnamese mainland in two waves) because "we attacked such low-value targets as the bases of the PT boats instead of the much more important military targets that lay within reach of those 64 flight paths." [65] This order of response to attacks in which the United States apparently suffered no damage, especially in view of the doubt about the reality of the second attack, may not be unusual when compared with other American military activity in Vietnam, but it was scarcely a mild response. Moreover, it is important to recall that the attack was made entirely on presidential authority and without anyone except military advisers being consulted.

5. *Why was the issue not taken to the UN Security Council?*

Secretary McNamara, when asked that question, replied simply, "We had no reason to believe the United Nations could have acted in any effective manner." And in response to a question from Senator Frank Lausche of Ohio, McNamara agreed the reason was that "Russia would not permit it to do" anything in the situation.[66] Senator Morse, however, offered a radically different explanation. That the United Nations might not have acted

> does not excuse ignoring our obligations under international law. The fact is that with the history we had already made in the case, with the constructive aggression we had already made in the case, the last thing we should have done was to have ordered the bombing of those PT boat bases. We should have called upon the United Nations Security Council to assume jurisdiction." [67]

Beyond the legal issue and beyond the likelihood of effective United Nations action, there is another excellent reason the Johnson Administration did not take the issue to the Security Council. To present for United Nations scrutiny the kind of record that developed even in the limited Senate investigation would have compromised the United States' position disastrously.

6. *What are the implications of the fact that the Resolution had been drafted long before the incident took place?*

65. Ibid., p. 70.
66. Ibid., p. 71.
67. Morse speech, Feb. 28, 1968, p. S1887.

Months before the Tonkin affair William Bundy, Assistant Secretary of State for Far Eastern Affairs, drafted a paper intended for presentation to Congress to get its concurrence with Administration Vietnamese policy. This apparently was received and revised to fit the Tonkin Gulf incident and presented to Congress the day following the United States air strike. To some this also suggested the possibility of a conspiracy—that the incident was purposely provoked as an excuse for the retaliatory blows. Such a conspiracy, McNamara felt, no one "familiar with our society and system of Government could suspect" for it would have had to

> include almost, if not all, the entire chain of military command in the Pacific, the Chairman of the Joint Chiefs of Staff, the Joint Chiefs, the Secretary of Defense, and his chief Civilian Assistants, the Secretary of State and the President of the United States.

This McNamara called "monstrous" and as he put it, it is. But as I. F. Stone read the evidence, a less preposterous conspiracy did seem plausible—and the predrafted Resolution is a very relevant part of the evidence. Stone said that

> the more one studies the evidence so far available the more one does see the outlines of a conspiracy, not to fabricate the incident of August 4, but to plan and to put into motion a sharp escalation of the Vietnamese war in the very year Johnson was campaigning for election as a man of peace. The aerial deployments necessary, not for one retaliatory strike . . . but for the continuous bombing of North Vietnam which began in February 1965, were ordered and accomplished—as was the alerting of combat troops—in the very year Johnson was promising *not* to widen the war. This was the conspiracy and this *was* monstrous and this is what will fully appear if the Senate Foreign Relations Committee finishes its job.[68]

Although McNamara and General Earl Wheeler, Chairman of the Joint Chiefs of Staff, who accompanied the Secretary of Defense at the hearing on February 20, evaded Chairman Fulbright's questions about a planned buildup of American forces in Vietnam, it appears almost an inescapable conclusion that the troop buildup and the bombing were planned ahead and that the drafted resolution was aimed at getting

68. I. F. Stone, "McNamara and Tonkin Bay: The Unanswered Questions," *New York Review of Books*, March 28, 1968, p. 6. This article is an incisive review of the Committee's Record, "The Gulf of Tonkin, The 1964 Incidents."

Congressional approval of those steps. If, therefore, the Tonkin incidents were fortuitous, they were also "convenient."

7. *Was the reprisal intended to shore up the sagging Khanh regime?*

Again that is a question about motives and necessarily a speculative matter. The common belief was, however, that one result of the raid was to strengthen Khanh politically. A British reporter in Saigon wrote the day following the bombing that Khanh's position "now appears to have been consolidated." [69] Shortly thereafter Khanh made himself Chief of State and assumed emergency powers and became quasi dictator, indicating he was granting greater scope to the Americans in setting military strategy.[70] Whatever short-run gain the American retaliation brought Khanh, it did not resolve his problem of political instability. Despite Washington's warning that "it would take an extremely serious and negative view of any move to oust the regime of President Nguyen Khanh," [71] his situation continued to deteriorate and a civilian-dominated government took over in October—but only until the next coup in December. In brief there is no available evidence to show that the retaliatory air strike was motivated by expectations that it would stabilize South Vietnam's politics. Much more likely is the simple proposition that the air strike was, preplanned or not, an important part of the process of Americanizing the war. As the often embarrassingly candid Senator Richard B. Russell said shortly after the November, 1964, election, following a conference with President Johnson, "We either have to get out or take some action to help the Vietnamese. They won't help themselves. We made a big mistake in going in there, but I can't figure out any way to get out without scaring the rest of the world." [72] Whatever may be said of his logic, the Senator's blunt candor came nearer reality than the pious affirmations that came from more guarded spokesmen for the Administration.

8. *What are the implications of the acquiescence and speed of Congress in enacting the Tonkin Resolution?*

It certainly is not normal for Congress to do anything in forty-eight hours, so why did this "functional equivalent" of a declaration of war (as Under Secretary of State Nicholas Katzenbach called it) get such speedy action? One reason was that President Johnson stressed that quick action would demonstrate national unity on the war and thereby reduce the danger of North Vietnam's misapprehending the American

69. Schurmann et al., op. cit., p. 41.

70. See Kahin and Lewis, op. cit., p. 159.

71. Quoted from *The New York Times* of August 25, 1964 by Kahin and Lewis, op. cit., p. 160.

72. Quoted by Kahin and Lewis, op. cit., p. 163.

resolve to pursue its ends in Asia. Equally important, probably, was the fact that an attack on American forces had taken place, which (especially when there appeared to be no provocation) inclined Congress to back the President. The Senate Foreign Relations Committee also saw—in retrospect—the Resolution as further evidence of the erosion of Congress's role in international affairs, an erosion that left not only the initiative but the decisive power in the executive. The Committee in a report on "National Commitments" said that "in the course of two decades of cold war the country and its leaders became so preoccupied with questions of national security as to have relatively little time or thought for constitutional matters." [73] Not only broad constitutional questions were submerged, however. Equally obscure was the fundamental issue of what the country was doing and intended to do. Senator Fulbright and others *later* said they were under misapprehensions when they helped to rush the Resolution on its way. Discussing his promotion of it on the floor of the Senate, Fulbright said all his comments derived from the brief meeting with McNamara.

> I had no independent evidence, and I now think I did a great disservice to the Senate. I feel guilty for not having enough sense at that time to have raised these questions and asked for evidence. I regret it. I have publicly apologized to my constituents and the country for the unwise action I took, without at least inquiring into the basis. It never occurred to me that there was the slightest doubt, certainly not on the part of Commander Herrick who was in charge of the task force that this attack took place.[74]

But apart from the doubts about what happened, there is the supineness of the Senate and House in granting this blank check for future use as the President saw fit. They went along because of a "crisis" atmosphere, the cold war, nationalism, anti-Communist fervor, and (for many) bellicosity in general. One hopes the experience may make Congress more skeptical in future "crises," but it is no simple matter to refuse to back a President when he claims the enemy has attacked. The herd instinct makes objectors into scapegoats when the times are (or can be made to appear) dangerous to the country.

9. *Who, today, has the authority to "declare war"?*

The precipitate action in the Tonkin incident sharply illustrates the transfer of the war power to the executive branch. The constitutional authority to declare war is unmistakably clear: Congress alone has that

73. Committee on Foreign Relations, U.S. Senate, Report, "National Commitments Report," 90th Congress, 1st Session (Washington: U.S. Government Printing Office, Nov. 20, 1967), p. 20.
74. "Gulf of Tonkin, The 1964 Incidents," op. cit., p. 80.

power, both by express language of the document and the clear intent of the framers. In the Constitutional Convention, Article I was amended to strike out a power of Congress to "make" war and to substitute "declare" war. The intent was to place in the executive the power to conduct war and to repel sudden attacks on the United States while leaving to Congress to determine whether to commit the nation to a state of war. Thomas Jefferson thought this a wise course and said in a letter to James Madison, "We have already given . . . one effectual check to the Dog of war by transferring the power of letting him loose from the Executive to the Legislative body, from those who are to spend to those who are to pay." [75] And for the most part during the nineteenth century the war power remained in Congressional hands; with the coming of the twentieth century, however, the executive repeatedly committed the nation's military forces and thereby determined the issue of war or peace.

Simply put, the expansion of the executive prerogatives in the use of military power was born of rising American imperialism. The Monroe Doctrine of 1823 had warned European nations not to expand their colonial empires in the Western world, but the American expansionist ardor from the late nineteenth century onward converted Monroe's anti-European doctrine to a manifesto of United States superiority in the Americas. When our investments or interests in Latin America were threatened, or appeared to be, the standard remedy was to "send the Marines"—indeed it became so commonplace that the phrase became a household term for the use of mayhem. Theodore Roosevelt precipitated and protected a phony revolution in Panama to permit our acquisition of the isthmus for the Canal, and he intervened in Cuba and the Dominican Republic. Presidents Taft, Wilson, and Coolidge followed Roosevelt's lead. "Dollar diplomacy" in the Caribbean nations made the residents of many nations familiar with sight of the U.S. Navy and Army. Wilson seized Vera Cruz to "enforce respect" by Mexico for the United States, and he sent an American army into Mexico to pursue Pancho Villa. Again and again presidents—with and without Congressional concurrence—took over the governments of such countries as the Dominican Republic, Haiti, and Nicaragua.

Franklin Roosevelt put the nation on a collision course with Hitler prior to the American entry into World War II. Between March and November, 1941, Roosevelt took the following steps more or less on his own initiative. He ordered the seizure of sixty-five Axis-nation vessels in United States ports, made an executive agreement with Denmark for the United States to defend Greenland, and appealed to the French people not to support the Vichy government, a puppet regime

75. Quoted in "National Commitments," op. cit., p. 9.

installed by Hitler. On May 21, with German U-boat warfare increasing, the United States merchant ship *Robin Moor* was sunk by a German submarine off the Brazilian coast, and on May 27 Roosevelt proclaimed a state of emergency, ordering the U.S. Navy to "shoot on sight" any Axis submarines found west of the twenty-sixth meridian (a line running roughly from Iceland through the Azores and more than two thousand miles from the east coast of the United States). This Roosevelt proclaimed as our "defensive waters." Then he announced an agreement with Iceland whereby the United States assumed responsibility for the defense of that small nation. On August 14 Roosevelt and Winston Churchill met in the Atlantic where they set common postwar policy objectives and produced the famed "Four Freedoms" pronouncement. The Atlantic Ocean became a naval battleground as German submarines sought British convoys; the American Navy was heavily involved. On October 17 a United States destroyer, *Kearney*, was hit by submarines off Iceland and two weeks later the destroyer *Reuben James* was sunk off Iceland with one hundred men lost. An undeclared war moved inexorably toward a declared one.

Nor has the post-World War II era diminished the prerogatives of the executive in committing the United States through military actions. When the invasion of South Korea began President Harry S Truman threw American forces into the battle and informed the leaders of Congress after the fact. Six months later Senator Robert Taft asserted that Truman had no authority to take such a step, calling it a usurpation of authority "in violation of the laws and the Constitution" to send troops to fight in an undeclared war.[76] Later in 1951 Secretary of State Dean Acheson, defending the President's proposal to send American soldiers to Europe, said,

> Not only has the President the authority to use the Armed Forces in carrying out the broad foreign policy of the United States and implementing treaties, but it is equally clear that this authority may not be interfered with by the Congress in the exercise of powers which it has under the Constitution.[77]

Acheson added, petulantly,

> We are in a position in the world today where the argument as to who has the power to do this, that, or the other thing, is not exactly what is called for from America in this very critical hour.[78]

76. "National Commitments," op. cit., p. 16.
77. Ibid., p. 17.
78. Loc. cit.

As the cold war progressed. Presidents sought, more for political than for constitutional reasons, to get Congress to go along with major new ventures in foreign policy. Part of this has been aimed at disarming the political opposition, for it is worth remembering that between 1947 and 1971 different parties controlled Congress and the Presidency for ten of those twenty-four years. Presidents have also wanted broad public support for their policies and Congressional concurrence was a means to that end. Apart from the regional compacts in which the United States has become a signatory—and involving treaties in each case—there have been a number of other ventures similar in general to the Tonkin Gulf Resolution.

The first of these was Eisenhower's request in 1955 for Congressional *authorization* for presidential action to defend the Pescadores Islands and Formosa. He indicated that he felt no lack of authority to meet any emergency situation by deploying the armed forces as he saw fit, but he added:

> However, a suitable congressional resolution would clearly and publicly establish the authority of the President as Commander in Chief to employ the Armed Forces of this Nation promptly and effectively for the purposes indicated if in his judgment it became necessary.[79]

No subsequent resolution asked for "authorization" for presidential action, for increasingly this was taken for granted. When Eisenhower sought the Middle East Resolution of 1957 the authority was more or less assumed to exist and the Congress was asked for support and a show of national unity. So too with the Cuba Resolution, which President Kennedy requested in the summer of 1962, just a month before the Cuban nuclear weapons crisis, and with the Tonkin Gulf Resolution. As the Committee on Foreign Relations observed, the prevailing attitude was in each case "one of concern not with constitutional questions but with the problem at hand and with the need for a method of dealing with it, heightened in all three cases by a sense of urgency. Nonetheless, precedents were set." [80]

A miasma of confusion surrounds the question of presidential authority to commit the forces of the United States in such a way as perhaps to involve war. Congress has not insisted on clarification of the issue, and at the time of the Middle East Resolution in 1957 seemed pleased to have left the issue ambiguous, and in fact when Eisenhower

79. Quoted in "National Commitments," p. 17.
80. Ibid., p. 18.

in 1958 committed fourteen thousand troops in Lebanon, no reference was made to the Middle East Resolution whatever. In 1962 Kennedy wanted from Congress blanket authorization to use "whatever means may be necessary, including the use of arms" to prevent Cuba "from exporting its purposes" elsewhere in the hemisphere, to prevent the establishment of foreign military bases in Cuba, and to support Cuban aspirations toward self-determination. But Senator Richard Russell thought this amounted to granting the President the power to declare war, and the substitute form of the Resolution expressed United States determination to achieve goals expressed in the original Resolution and omitted the authorization. The Gulf of Tonkin Resolution was the ultimate in such pronouncements: it gave the President endorsement, as he understood it, to do nearly anything he desired in Southeast Asia. It was, as his Under Secretary of State said, the "functional equivalent" of a declaration of war. Indeed Mr. Katzenbach called the formal declaration of war something "outmoded in the international arena" now. "What," he asked, "could a declaration of war have done that would have given the President more authority and a clearer voice of the Congress of the United States than that [the Tonkin Resolution] did?" [81]

The essence of the matter appears to be that the President asks the Congress to come along when he feels there is some political advantage in doing so, and he does not when he feels it would be useless or heavily debated or refused. It is assuredly nonsense to say, as it is by some, that after all the Congress always has the power to withdraw the resolutions, as in the Tonkin Gulf instance Congress reserves to itself to do. Reversing such a statement of agreement during wartime or even when some sense of emergency, real or feigned, exists, is next to impossible politically—for obvious reasons. Note, too, that when Presidents Eisenhower (in the Middle East) and Kennedy (in Cuba) got ready to act they acted on their own general authority, not on the resolutions given by Congress. And when Johnson went to war, in effect, to quash the uprising in the Dominican Republic in April, 1965, he referred to no Congressional actions. He did what Presidents have been doing now for over half a century in Central America—invading now and providing rationalizations later.

Patently the real, whatever the constitutional, power to "declare war" is now in the hands of the President. Later we shall consider some proposed methods of tempering that power, but there does not seem to be much doubt about where it now resides.

81. "U.S. Commitments to Foreign Powers," *Hearings* before the Committee on Foreign Relations, U.S. Senate, 90th Congress, 1st Session (Washington: U.S. Government Printing Office, 1967), pp. 82, 83.

10. *Does the United States have an obligation to be "policeman to the world," or is it "neo-isolationist" to raise such a question?*

The Tonkin Gulf incident and the ensuing retaliation were decisive points in the American involvement in Vietnam; they were also steps that revealed—for the first time to many—the changed character of the United States mission in world affairs. The bombing of the North, the Tonkin Gulf Resolution, and the increasing of United State troop strength in the South all heralded the Americanization of the war and demonstrated the vulnerability of the United State as a result of our worldwide commitments. Before the Tonkin Gulf incident the United States had only 16,500 servicemen in Vietnam, but within a year the number had grown by over 300 per cent and within two years more than 250,000 troops were engaged there—a figure that itself was again to be doubled. Retaliatory air strikes on the North continued sporadically for about six months after the Tonkin affair, but in February, 1965, the pretense of retaliation for specific enemy actions was dropped and a ferocious air onslaught was released upon the North, dumping an incredible tonnage of high explosives on that small nation. As of late 1968 almost 3,000,000 tons of bombs had been used in Vietnam, North and South, whereas the total amount used by the United States in World War II in all Europe and Asia was just over 2,000,000! About one fifth of the bombing was done in the North, which means some 600,000 tons of bombs, at a cost estimated by I. F. Stone at $2 billion (and perhaps as much as $4 billion), including the loss of nearly a thousand aircraft.[82] In short the Tonkin Gulf incident and the following air and ground campaigns altered the Vietnam War from a local affair to an American war on a massive scale.

This escalation produced a response from North Vietnam and the National Liberation Front. The number of troops coming south to aid the Vietcong was modest prior to the Tonkin affair. Official figures on the estimated number of infiltrators range from something over 500 per month to over 1,000 per month between 1961 and 1964, and prior to 1964 there were no reports of regular North Vietnamese army units operating in the South. Once the United States escalated its operations, the rate of infiltration per month went up from about 1,000 to about 5,000, and by 1966 five North Vietnamese regiments were operating in the South (30,000 troops).[83] And by the time the United States had committed 500,000 men the northern infiltration had increased; in January, 1968, there was an estimated influx of 20,000 North Vietna-

82. Stone made these calculations from information he got from the Pentagon at the time the bombing of the North stopped. See *I. F. Stone's Weekly*, Nov. 18, 1968, p. 3.

83. See Kahin and Lewis, op. cit., p. 185.

mese.[84] (This despite the heavy bombing supposedly intended to halt such traffic.) The Administration constantly emphasized that the United States was involved in Vietnam because of "aggression" by North Vietnam, while overlooking the civil war background of the conflict and while ignoring the timing of our acts and the North's responses.

Consequently as the Vietnam war stagnated, as the number of American dead passed thirty-six thousand, and no end seemed in sight, three lines of thought about the impasse developed. Some merely advocated more of the same, the apparent thesis being that only by massive battlefield victories would it be possible for the United States to extricate itself. This is the standard military argument. Others advocated keeping the pressure on the enemy while moving toward negotiations, while urging the South Vietnamese government to do likewise. Those advocating this position appeared not to doubt the validity of the American presence in Vietnam nor to derive from that experience any "lesson" except that perhaps in this case an overcommitment had been made, a commitment that must be honored even if compromised. In essence this was the last position of the Johnson Administration and it remained Nixon's in the first six months of his tenure. A third position holds that the United States should gradually withdraw from Vietnam and that similar involvements should be avoided in the future. The argument is essentially that the nation has overcommitted itself on the one hand and has committed itself too often to regimes that represent the opposite of our traditional values of democracy and personal freedom. To go on trying to bolster sagging dictatorships not only places the United States in an untenable position but in a morally and politically indefensible position as well.

Despite this divergence of views on Vietnam in particular, there has been an unbroken commitment to the "free world leadership" role. Why? Part of the reason is the prodding of Americans who invest abroad and want their interests protected. From the time American investment abroad became economically important, those with interests to defend have successfully persuaded presidents of the virtue of varying forms of "dollar diplomacy." And foreign investments are lucrative. The prime reason for exorbitant profits from this investment has been low labor costs abroad, and the invitation to exploit foreign opportunities has been irresistible to many large corporations—leading to large dollar outflows in investment and to the negative-balance-of-payments problem that has plagued the United States economy in recent

84. See the questioning of Secretary of State Dean Rusk by Senator Mike Mansfield reported in *The New York Times* of March 12, 1968, for the source of more recent infiltration data.

years.[85] Some critics argue that *the* explanation for the new imperialist policy of the United States is found in these economic facts. That is, they contend that we have driven blindly on in Vietnam to save American investments there and in adjacent countries. Powerful as some of the interests with investments in Asia are and significant as those investments are to the American economy, the net consequence of our Vietnam war policy has been decidedly negative to American economic concerns. At least a partial refutation to the exaggerated economic determinism argument about the Vietnam war is that Wall Street's reactions to peace overtures have become bullish and to escalations bearish. Only a fool would overlook the role of oil interests in our Middle East policy or of sugar, oil, and metal ore concerns in our Latin American policy, but factors beyond economic interests also have propelled the expansion of the United States policeman role.[86]

It seems to me that two other important elements in the new imperialist role are anti-Communism and nationalism. Fear of Communism is hardly a new political phenomenon, but in the cold war era it became a force that blinded men to the implications of policies and offered them rationalizations for practically any policy that could be made to appear anti-Communist. Combined with this cold war fever was both nationalistic fervor and a pervading fear for the security of the nation. All kinds of policy became "defense"-oriented; when the $75 billion interstate highway system was begun in Eisenhower's Administration it was called the "National Defense Highway Act"; decisions to provide federal aid to education and to finance space explorations and many other policies were rationalized in the sacred name of defense.

Hence the vast expenditures on defense, the posture taken by this country around the world, and hence the gradual slipping into the quagmire of Vietnam. Where challenges arise from Communist forces—or what may or may not be Communist groups in reality—the United States has again and again taken the side of oppressive dictatorships rather than with the people of those nations, who are seeking to throw off the yoke. We have shored up such regimes as those of notorious dictators like François Duvalier of Haiti, Fulgencio Batista of Cuba, Chiang Kai-shek in Taiwan, Diem in Vietnam, Rafael Trujillo in the Dominican Republic, Francisco Franco of Spain, and the cruel military dictatorship in Greece—among many others. The following news story

85. Investment has been a prime source of this problem, but war and cold war expenditures also account for a major share of it.

86. See the remarkable analysis of United States-Peruvian relations involving the seizure of Standard Oil's Peruvian subsidiary by Richard Goodwin, "Letter from Peru," *The New Yorker*, May 17, 1969, pp. 41–109. The relative importance of economic interest and political maneuver are well illustrated by Goodwin.

about our military forces in Spain illustrates the kind of ridiculous situation into which the world police role puts us.

> Washington, June 14, 1969 (UPI). The State Department acknowledged today that United States forces had conducted joint maneuvers in Spain recently to practice putting down a theoretical rebellion against the Spanish government. Officials said a review was under way to prohibit such practices in the future. They refused comment on the present nature of the U.S. commitment to the government of Generalissimo Francisco Franco. . . . A State Department spokesman declined to say today whether the U.S. is committed to help defend Spain. While confirming that the maneuvers took place he indicated that they had been undertaken without the department's knowledge.[87]

Similarly we have plotted against or openly attacked such regimes as Fidel Castro's, Juan Bosch's in the Dominican Republic, Jacob Arbenz Guzman's in Guatemala, and many others. As Senator Claiborne Pell said in 1967,

> When a government is brought down by force, the United States usually sits on its hands when a coup is staged by forces of the right, but when the overthrow is carried out by the left we condemn the action and occasionally commit our power to reverse it. The reason for this difference in our reaction is clear enough. Rightist or conservative forces usually represent the status quo, and we tend to be more tolerant of their political activities, even when a constitutional government is the victim.
> Since 1960, for example, the United States has given at least tacit approval, and in most cases quick recognition, to seven new regimes in El Salvador, Korea, Burma, Guatemala, Ecuador, Ghana, and Indonesia. During the same period we supported only one left wing coup and that was in Yemen.[88]

Political instability is endemic in the less developed nations, and rebellion often results, sometimes with significant Communist support and sometimes without it. When there is, or appears to be, a chance of Communist success this seems to sanctify American involvement. Then we preach about the values we seek to protect in such circumstances:

87. *The New York Times*, June 15, 1969. See also Richard J. Barnet, *Intervention and Revolution, America's Confrontation with Insurgent Movements Around the World* (New York: New American Library, 1968).
88. *Congressional Record*, Aug. 21, 1967, p. S11866.

self-determination(!), freedom, democracy. Invariably we explain that we intervene not for any territorial aggrandizement or other material gains, and there is some pretense that we have been invited to come to the rescue of some local ruling clique—or challenging group as the case may be. Consider the case of the Dominican Republic in the spring of 1965. That tragic land, having got rid of Trujillo and elected a civilian government under a democratic leader, Juan Bosch, experienced a coup by the military (in September, 1962) which removed Bosch on the supposed grounds that Cuban Communists were taking over the nation. When the coup took place, President Kennedy withdrew American recognition of the Dominican government and suspended economic aid, but a month after Kennedy's death the Johnson Administration changed course and the military junta was again recognized. Then in April of 1965 backers of Bosch attempted to wrest control from the junta. Four days after the uprising began, President Johnson ordered the Marines to move in, consistent with our standing practice in the Caribbean. The uprising began on April 24; by the beginning of May, sixty-two hundred United States troops were either in Santo Domingo, capital of the Republic, or on their way there. President Johnson told the American people that he had ordered the troops in to protect the lives of American civilians. Later in his address he gave another reason for intervening:

> The revolutionary movement took a tragic turn. Communist leaders, many of them trained in Cuba, seeing a chance to increase disorder, to gain a foothold, joined the revolution. They took increasing control. And what began as a popular democratic revolution, committed to democracy and social justice, very shortly moved and was taken over and really seized and placed into the hands of a band of Communist conspirators.[89]

The contention that the revolution had become Communist-dominated raises several questions. In the first place many on the scene deny the truth of the claim, including Juan Bosch himself. Second, it is interesting that the Johnson Administration was able within a few days to determine the exact leadership developments in a nation as turbulent and confusing as the Dominican Republic at that point. Third, even if true, would the presence of Cuban-trained leaders justify American intervention? By what legal authority or moral right may the President commit troops to the support of a military junta? If one accepts the Communist conspiracy doctrine as justification, that places the United

89. Quoted by Marvin E. Gettleman and David Mermelstein, *The Great Society Reader* (New York: Vintage Books, 1967), p. 386. The best source on the Dominican affair is Tad Szulc's *Dominican Diary* (New York: Delacorte Press, 1965).

States in exactly the same position as Russia when it invaded Czecho-slovakia in 1968. The Russians asserted an obligation to invade their neighbor because socialism was in danger; i.e., the liberalizing moves of Alexander Dubcek's government seemed a threat to the Kremlin's control and thus justified removal of that government by force and its replacement by a more pliable regime. *Pravda*, in its inimitable style, explained why this was necessary:

> Marxist-Leninists believe that whenever there is a threat to the revolutionary gains of the people in any country, and hence a threat to the fraternal community, it is the internationalist duty of socialist states to do everything in their power to remove that threat and strengthen the sovereignty of all socialist countries.[90]

The rhetoric is different from Johnson's but the message is identical.

Such are the paradoxes of empire, and an empire the United States has become. In thirty nations around the world the United States military is located in 429 major and nearly 3,000 minor bases. Stationed at those bases are a million military personnel and a half million dependents; the net cost of the operation is between $4 billion and $5 billion a year.[91] To withdraw from those bases, it is said, would "detract from the credibility of our deterrent." To abandon our positions abroad would diminish our role as a world leader and would be a denial of the "responsibilities of power" to use Senator Fulbright's term. A great power, says Fulbright, has no alternative but to expand and exercise power beyond its borders. Or at least that is the excuse offered by those who see a kind of inflexible determinism about the role of large and powerful nations. But is the imperial role so involuntary as that? Fulbright says that

> Nations, like individuals, have some freedom of choice, and America of all nations is equipped to exercise it. . . . If ever a nation was free to break the cycle of empires, America is that nation. If we do not, it will not be because history assigned to us an imperial role. It will be because we *chose* to believe such pompous nonsense, because power went to our heads.[92]

President Nixon gave a scathing reply to such "new isolationists" as Fulbright in an address to the Air Force Academy cadets in 1969. He

90. *The New York Times*, Apr. 7, 1969.
91. See the story by Benjamin Welles, "U.S. Bases Abroad Stir a New Debate," *The New York Times*, Apr. 9, 1969. The story is based upon a classified report on our strategic alternatives and the role of foreign bases in those strategies.
92. J. W. Fulbright, "The United States and 'Responsibilities of Power,'" *The New York Times*, Jan. 27, 1968.

condemned those who "have grown weary of the weight of free world leadership that fell upon us in the wake of World War II." To take the new isolationist course, he said, "would be disastrous for our nation and the world." Then he went on:

> Imagine for a moment . . . what would happen to this world if America were to become a dropout in assuming the responsibility for defending peace and freedom in the world. As every world leader knows and as even the outspoken critics of America would admit, the rest of the world would live in terror. Because if America would turn its back on the world, there would be a peace that would settle over this planet, but it would be the kind of peace that suffocated freedom in Czechoslovakia.[93]

Nixon's comments place him in an unbroken line of succession with his predecessors; the rhetoric is identical and the same clichés adorn his catechisms on virtue and evil. He says the rest of the world would tremble in fear if we ceased our imperial role, but if we take Vietnam as an illustration, it might well be asked who did the greater terrorizing? Could the Communists under Ho Chi Minh have wrought more death and destruction in South Vietnam than has the United States? Town after town destroyed, innocent and uninvolved people killed by the tens of thousands, a rigid military dictatorship supported by the United States, losing presidential candidates jailed by the winners: "free world leadership"?

This is the kind of "democracy" we are defending in Vietnam. It is a government that conducted a rigged election in 1967—an election that excluded candidates who advocated neutrality or negotiations with the Vietcong, and in which threats and pressures were put on the people to vote for the ruling clique. Yet the government garnered only 35 per cent of the vote. Shortly after the election one of the candidates, Truong Din Dzu, was arrested for advocating a coalition government with the Vietcong, and he is still in jail. At a time when the possibiliy of coalition government at the end of the war was being discussed all over the world, President Nguyen Van Thieu laid down the law, "pounding his fist for emphasis," said *The New York Times*.

> From now on, those who spread rumors that there will be a coalition government in this country, whoever they be, whether in the executive or the legislature, will be severely punished on

93. The speech was excerpted in *The New York Times*, June 5, 1969.

charges of collusion with the enemy and demoralizing the army and the people. I will punish them in the name of the Constitution.[94]

Besides supporting a dictatorship in South Vietnam, we have killed so many civilians that Vietnamese hatred of the United States will live a long time. When the enemy in Vietnam wants to turn the populace against the United States, according to a captured document, said to be the remarks of a Vietcong general, the easiest way to do it is to raise the Vietcong flag over a town, and let the Air Force do the job. "The Americans cannot resist bombing our flag," he said, "no matter where it flies, from the public school or the church steeple." Said a U.S. Army major, "We can reconstruct the hamlets. There will be very few scars to show for it all. But the mental impact on the people—how long will it take to remove those scars? Maybe these people just want to be left alone." [95]

War always brings suffering, however, and the argument is that resistance to Communism now is better than allowing the situation to develop into a more ghastly war. We had better not, they say, repeat the blunder of Munich, when we appeased Hitler and the world paid an ultimately unbelievable price for it. Dean Rusk at the time he was leaving office put the case this way:

> [We] are now 23 years beyond the end of World War II. With the passage of time, some of us may have become careless or forgetful about the great central issues which were in front of us in the forties, when the world was thinking long and hard about how to prevent another catastrophe. . . . If we are in the opening stages of a great debate on the subject of how to organize a durable peace, I myself welcome it. If the idea of collective security is not a satisfactory answer, by all means let us find a better one. But this time, let us be sure that we do not stumble on a worse one.[96]

The shaky Munich analogy calls into question the adequacy of the assumptions on which the present policies are founded. Is the confrontation with Communism today really comparable with the rise of Hitler in the 1930's? Is it isolationist to be unwilling to defend regimes like

94. Terence Smith, "Four of Opposition Group in Saigon Are Summoned to Police Inquiry," *The New York Times*, June 18, 1969.

95. See Peter Arnett's story "Decisions in Vietnam: Death of a Hamlet," *The New York Times*, June 1, 1969, which recounts the destruction of 380 homes in the town of Bokinh: nineteen civilians dead and fifty seriously wounded.

96. *The New York Times*, Dec. 1, 1968.

those of Chiang Kai-shek and Franco? The hollowness of the Munich argument has been demonstrated so often that one hesitates to tread that ground again, but because it recurs so often some comment may be necessary. Perhaps a good approach would be to compare Hitler's Germany and Mao Tse-tung's China with respect to their aggressiveness and threat to the peace of the world. Any reading of the history of the Hitler regime must stress its military aggressiveness and its territorial ambitions: Munich represented but one stage in a series of aggressive moves. Hitler announced his intention of making Germany the ruler of Europe and set about to achieve that end at any cost. Whatever the ultimate reasons for World War II, this much can be said: Hitler repeatedly and aggressively attacked his neighbors, kept them under incredible oppression, and systematically murdered tens of millions of persons. A good case can, therefore, be made that failure to perceive the threat that Hitler represented and to prepare to counter his thrusts were serious flaws in the diplomacy of the thirties.

How apt is this as an analogy to the threat of China today? In the years since the Communists took control of China it has certainly not threatened its neighbors the way Hitler did. Indeed its one major military engagement was in defense of their Korean allies who were threatened with defeat by the United States. The United States assumed that China would not enter the Korean War and when General Douglas MacArthur led American troops over the border into North Korea, the Chinese entered the War on a limited basis—but sufficiently to push the American-South Korean forces back in a devastating defeat. The Chinese have talked a fierce fight against Taiwan and have often shelled small islands just off their coast still held by Chiang's forces, and the mainland Chinese have been involved in border disputes with India and Russia. Their one action that clearly qualifies them as an aggressor is their seizure of Tibet—an action to which the United States did not respond, there being no easy way to do so. In short the Chinese, although hostile in word are less so in deed, preoccupied as they are with economic and political developments within their borders. To be sure, China has aided movements friendly to them in other countries, but if we are to brand nations as aggressors on that ground, we will have to wear that nametag too.

Perhaps the reason the Chinese have not invaded and threatened more is because the United States constitutes a barrier to it? But for United States intervention Mao probably would have taken Formosa and the off-shore islands, but it does not follow that China would have been an aggressor in Asia had the United States been absent. They were not so frightened of our force that they refrained from attacking us in North Korea when they felt threatened; furthermore there is no evidence that they want to take Indochina, nor is there anything that would convince a skeptic of their success in subverting regimes by nonmilitary means. Their failure to subvert Indonesia was impressive. Although one cannot "prove" what might have been had the United States not been ominously present, there is little reason to believe that China represents the kind of threat that calls for the expenditure of tens of billions of dollars a year to stave it off. And if China does constitute such a threat, will it be possible forever to stave it off with purely military means? Is it the course of wisdom, assuming such a threat is real, to refuse even to recognize the legal existence of China? It seems incredible to me that anyone seriously believing that China is such a threat would fail to make contact with China and continue to exclude it from the councils of the world. Instead we offer insult and refuse to recognize the fact that Mao rather firmly occupies the Chinese mainland, and we use every stratagem available to keep China out of the United Nations.

If the ground is shifted from China to the world "Communist conspiracy" that in some mastermind fashion forments the rebellions of the world, then the argument is no more impressive. The disunity of the Communist world is strikingly apparent; indeed it has become so obvious that the old argument for a unified conspiracy has finally declined, and reliance is placed on such notions as the "domino" theory—that if one regime becomes Communist so will its neighbors. There are, it seems to me, two sound answers to that. First, it just has not happened that way elsewhere in the world. Even the Middle East nations on the border of Russia have not resembled each other in their varying degrees of sympathy with Communism—nor have the African nations. The other argument is really a question: If another nation desires to adopt Communism, is it our function to stop them? Indeed, more realistically, if a Communist-supported rebellion develops in an underdeveloped country, why is it automatically our duty to suppress it? If our professed belief in "self-determination" has any meaning, why does it not apply here? How, after all, did this nation gain its independence and reject monarchy?

Finally, consider the argument that the proponents of retrenchment of our commitments are isolationists. In part this is a specious accusation, for the protagonists are not men who wish to withdraw the country from world affairs—as the use of the term suggests in the American context arising as it does from pre-World War II isolationism. On the contrary, the proponents of anti-imperialism (to bring the pejorative terminology to play on the other side) are well aware and stress the importance of recognizing the political and moral implications of the fact that we represent 5 per cent of the world's population and possess half its wealth. To wish to keep the United States from suppressing revolutions and bolstering dictatorships is not necessarily to reject foreign trade, or international cooperation, as the term "new isolationist" seems to suggest.

11. *Why has the Senate Foreign Relations Committee not pursued its investigation of the Tonkin Gulf incident to its logical conclusion?*

Five days before Christmas of 1968, at a time presumably calculated to produce the least publicity, Senator Fulbright released the final report on the Tonkin Gulf affair. It consisted of an exchange of letters between the Committee and the Pentagon, providing answers of a sort to some questions, no answers at all to others, and not even raising some very crucial issues that had been left hanging at earlier investigations. There were three hearings on the Tonkin incident: first, the speedy session of August 6, 1964, just prior to passage of the Tonkin Resolution; second, a secret hearing in 1966, the content of which has not been released; third, the all-day hearing with Secretary McNamara and General Wheeler on February 20, 1968. At none of the hearings were critics of the Tonkin incident called, nor were those who were on duty at the Pentagon in August, 1964, nor anyone from the destroyers. An anonymous letter to the Committee from someone in the Pentagon spoke of a "Command Study" that had been done on the incident, and a desultory request for it from the Committee produced no results. Possibly Senator Fulbright *meant* for no result to follow for he asked not *for* the study but about "the *status* of the command and control report evaluating the Tonkin Bay incidents." [97] The Pentagon replied that it was an internal study and "not appropriate for dissemination outside the Department." [98] As I. F. Stone has pointed out, had the Senate wanted to see the report it could have subpoenaed it from the Rand Corporation, where there were copies, as Senator Gore commented. Likewise the Senate Committee knew the name of the author of the report and did not call him to testify.[99] The writer of the anonymous letter advised the Foreign Relations Committee to get the Command Study, although he warned that it was tightly guarded. He went on to say that

> it is based in part on the tape recordings of conversations over the phone of the President, the Secretary of Defense, Admiral Sharp and others during the period when the critical decisions were being made. Very probably an effort will be made to have all copies of

97. See "Gulf of Tonkin, The 1964 Incidents, Part II," op. cit., p. 1. Italics added.
98. Ibid., p. 2.
99. Stone gives considerable detail on the Senate's disinterest in pursuing the matter in his article, "The Supineness of the Senate," *New York Review of Books*, Feb. 13, 1969, pp. 3–6.

the study destroyed when and if there is any intimation that you know of [its] existence. . . . The study will not disclose that the incident was a put-up job. It will disclose several embarrassing things, however. [He lists several, all of which have been considered in the previous discussion of the incidents.] . . . It was clearly a case of making a definite decision when operational circumstances dictated haste but the facts suggested caution. . . . I am sure that if I signed this I would lose my job, but if you proceed wisely, you should be able for the good of the country to learn the truth of all I have suggested here and much more.[100]

An anonymous letter constitues thin evidence perhaps, but its writer had apparently read the Command Study, and if the Senate Committee had wanted to get to the roots of the issue, that Command Study would certainly have been a crucial piece of evidence. To stop the inquiry without even a serious effort to dig deeper raises serious questions.

Obviously the Senators did not want to find out. Why? Was it a decision to let President Johnson alone now that he had retired, now that the bombing of the North had ended and negotiations were under way in Paris? These factors may partially explain the reluctance to pursue the issue further, but the feeling persists that more may have been involved. The Tonkin Gulf incident is perhaps all too revealing of the American role in today's world because it suggests too much about the way the military manipulates civilian leaders, too much about the shaky grounds for intervention in other nations by American presidents. If the Senators were sufficiently concerned about the implications of this kind of power and its use, it would appear that considerations about personal embarrassment for Johnson would be less important than shedding some light on the way such decisions get made. For certainly there has been no change in the executive's assumptions about the world, no alternation of the role of the military since late 1968, when the Committee smothered the Tonkin issue. President Nixon made that amply clear in his address to the Air Force cadets. He said the military had been subjected to unwarranted attacks; American "responsibility in the world is derided as a form of militarism," he said. He defended huge military expenditures as necessary to national security: ". . . if I have made a mistake, I pray that it is on the side of too much and not too little. If we do too much, it will cost us our money. If we do too little, it may cost us our lives."

In short the Tonkin Gulf incident and its larger context reveal the sweep of presidential prerogatives, the enormous power of the military, the pervasiveness of dubious assumptions about the world that are the

---

100. Senator Morse entered the letter in the February 20 *Hearings* at pp. 84–85.

basis of decision making. Any analysis of the Presidency demands that this cold war-interventionist set of attitudes and practices be taken into prior account—before attempting to analyze the way priorities are determined and decisions made in the White House, before assessing the historical, constitutional, political, and institutional aspects of the office. For the military and international elements of presidential decision-making are so critical and so costly that all other concerns must take second place or worse.

The fixing of priorities in the proposed federal budget for fiscal year 1970 illustrates the point. President Johnson proposed a budget of $195 billion, which included approximately $106 billion for defense and defense-related spending. (That is, $81 billion directly attributed to defense, $16 billion in interest, most of it incurred by war expenditures, nearly $8 billion for veterans' services, and $1.5 billion to cover a military pay increase.) If one exempts from the total budget the $43 billion allocated to the Social Insurance Trust Funds—which until recently was not included in the budget—then *military and military-related expenditures accounted for 70 per cent of proposed federal expenditures.* (Or, by leaving the Social Insurance Trust Funds in the calculations, the percentage is still 54.5.) Nor have I taken account of other spending that has military implications, such as an incalculable part of the space budget and funds for military foreign aid. Patently, therefore, the opportunity is severely limited for the President to recommend funds for dealing with decaying cities, curbing pollution, providing health services, or for myriad other domestic needs.

President Nixon, however, revised the budget, reducing it by some $4 billion. He took $1 billion of the reduction from the military, largely through cuts in munitions for use in Vietnam and a reduction in first year outlay for the Anti-Ballistic Missile program. The real bites came in the Department of Health, Education and Welfare and in Social Security disbursements, which suffered cuts of about $1 billion each. Thus the Head Start Program for disadvantaged preschool children was trimmed, and most of the Job Corps camps were abruptly closed to provide further savings, and a proposed increase of 10 per cent in Social Security payments to the aged was reduced to 7 per cent. As President Nixon said while he was campaigning in 1968, "The Presidency is a place where priorities are set." Indeed.

The President and the Bureaucracy

If, as I believe, the President exercises a dangerously personalized power, that should not obscure the concurrent problems that any incumbent in the office faces in trying to make the United States government respond to his will. In its sprawling size and the complexity of its undertakings, it can become immobilized and dangerously arterio-sclerotic. President after president has discovered that the bureaucracy has a life of its own, a capacity for capturing the President's carefully picked men and making them serve the bureaucracy's interest first and the President's second. Richard Neustadt quotes Truman contemplating Eisenhower in the White House and saying, "He'll sit here, and he'll say, 'Do this! Do that.' *And nothing will happen.* Poor Ike—it won't be a bit like the Army. He'll find it very frustrating." [101] Such bureaucratic immobilism is not restricted to government. The late Pope John XIII on hearing an Easter prayer referring to "perfidious Jews" ordered the words excised from the prayer. The following year he heard the prayer again—without change. He repeated his order and this time it was obeyed.

The bureaucracy knows how to avoid responsibility or at least how to spread it around to minimize damage in case of attack. Hence the red tape that gets wound in the gears and soon turns any agency into a self-protection association as much concerned with the survival and success of the agency per se as with the mission on which it is sent. This has been demonstrated endlessly in the literature on administration, and it continues to be illustrated in the news columns of every newspaper. The office of Economic Opportunity expressed a desire early in its life that its leaders would not remain in the job too long, believing that the innovative aspect of the program would work only if it had both a temporary outlook while on the job and having new men to blast away the encrustations that would develop in the organization. For all its effort to encourage new programs and innovative ideas about the difficult task of rescuing people from poverty, the overwhelming proportion of the OEO's money ended up being spent for "more of the same"—that is, more service-oriented programs like ones that already existed in communities.[102] Proposals that came to the OEO for "head start" projects (for preschool children) were usually cast in the typical educational bureaucratic mold; few were innovative and community-oriented in reality—as had been planned.[103]

101. Richard Neustadt, *Presidential Power* (New York: Wiley, 1960), p. 9. Neustadt's book is a seminal work that analyzes presidential power with detached empiricism. I find this analysis persuasive but I think Neustadt brings us to the point where the moral aspects of presidential power emerge—and stops. Presidential power, in my view, is more than a matter of technique.

102. For commentary on OEO operations see Sar Levitan, *The Great Society's Poor Law* (Baltimore: Johns Hopkins University Pess, 1969), and the Metropolitan Applied Research Center, *A Relevant War Against Poverty* (New York: Metropolitan Applied Research Center, 1969).

103. A brief and somewhat embittered commentary on this can be found in Polly Greenberg's excellent book on the Child Development Group of Mississippi, *The Devil Has Slippery Shoes* (New York: Macmillan, 1969).

Not only do bureaucrats find it difficult to be innovative and to take chances of failure in order to aim for higher goals, they also resent controls over them. No more telling example of this can be found than the military's bitter hatred of Secretary of Defense McNamara for his partially successful attempt to assert civilian control over the Defense Department. Accustomed to taking command of their civilian superiors, the military brass was galled at McNamara for bringing with him a group of young intellectuals (soon called the "Whiz Kids") who sought to put greater rationality and control into military operations and especially into spending. McNamara, however, is a special case; most cabinet members are unequal to the task of riding herd on their subordinates in that fashion. The State Department, for example, has a way of wrapping any Secretary of State or Under Secretary (whose job is to administer the operations of the Department) into the cocoon of career-club control that has long been characteristic of the Department. When President John Kennedy put Chester Bowles in the Under Secretary's job, it was not long before the career diplomats got rid of him by various forms of sabotage. Nicholas Katzenbach, as Under Secretary, found the same difficulties; he tried manfully to run the Department but it was, according to some observers, simply not possible. Secretary of State Dean Rusk

> believes the Secretary of State is more the President's adviser on foreign affairs than the executive head of a major operating agency. His critics say this monopolizes Mr. Rusk's attention on a few key issues while he leaves the State Department to run itself.[104]

Not all the ineffectiveness of bureaucracy is to be blamed on the bureaucrats, however, for to some extent the laws that establish programs often build in confusion and delay, and indeed undercut operations before they begin. As Murray Edelman has so well demonstrated in *The Symbolic Uses of Politics*,[105] many regulatory programs were never intended to do in fact that they seem to propose. Laws stand as symbols that "something" is being done, but reality is different. Consider, for example, the civil rights law with respect to discriminatory hiring practices. Instead of providing the federal agency with powers to issue cease-and-desist orders, the agency was permitted to confer with the parties and attempt conciliation but was not given the teeth with which to do its job.

104. See Benjamin Welles, "Katzenbach Finds State Department Bureaucracy an Impediment to Reform," *The New York Times*, Nov. 12, 1967.
105. (Urbana: University of Illinois Press, 1964), especially Ch. 3.

Symbolic support and covert sabotage of a program can also be achieved by placing the "right" personnel in administrative positions. Thus, in the spring of 1969, the American Medical Association and Senator Everett Dirksen fought to prevent the appointment of Dr. John H. Knowles to be Assistant Secretary of Health, Education and Welfare. Dr. Knowles is a supporter of health programs, which makes him the "wrong" man to be Assistant Secretary for Health and Scientific Affairs, so far as the AMA is concerned. For over six months the appointment was held off and then suddenly the White House conceded to the AMA and its legislative allies. Similarly Secretary of the Interior Walter J. Hickel appointed as deputy assistant secretary for water and power development a man who previously had served the Chamber of Commerce as a lobbyist aginst water pollution legislation. The appointee was at first made a temporary consultant (at $98 per day), but later he was given the permanent post; when the press questioned his appointment, it was explained that he was not being placed "in a policy-making position." [106]

Politically sensitive matters frighten bureaucrats and they often equivocate endlessly rather than pursue the matter with vigor. Take the case of the "truth in packaging" program established to protect the consumer. Partly because the Act had loopholes in it to permit sellers to delay meeting the provision of the law and partly because the persons enforcing the law equivocated, the law, as one observer put it, "has borne meager fruit" during its first two years and four months of existence. Enforcement was assigned to three different agencies, the Food and Drug Administration, the Fair Trade Commission, and the Commerce Department. The FDA promulgated its regulations on food one year after the effective date of the law, and its regulations on "drugs, devices, and cosmetics" came a year later. Fair-packaging rules for other consumer goods were made by the FTC a year and a half after the effective date of the law. But "the most optimistic forecasts are that labels of packages on retail shelves will be in general compliance with the law some time in 1970 or 1971." [107] And the law was passed in 1966!

One could go on recounting the examples of bureaucratic bumbling. Waste is endemic, particularly in the military, where any expenditure can be justified on the grounds that after all it is for "defense" and therefore necessary. Richard A. Stubbing, a Bureau of the Budget analyst, made a study of the performance of complex weapons systems and said, among other things: "The low over-all performance of elec-

106. An Associated Press story in the *Newark News*, June 4, 1969.

107. See John D. Morris, "Little Aid to Consumer Found in Labeling Law," *The New York Times*, March 9, 1969.

tronics in major weapons systems developed and produced in the last decade should give pause to even the most outspoken advocates of military hardware programs." He noted that in thirteen aircraft and missile projects developed since 1955, costing $40 billion, only four had electronic systems that proved adequate in operation. Another four programs worth $12 billion were canceled or phased out after a few years because of low reliability. Only four programs (worth $15 billion of the $40 billion) proved satisfactory.[108] Needless to say these failures were anything but financial failures for the areospace industry that produced them.

But when investigating officials point to such messes they often get disciplined, not rewarded, for their efforts. In one instance an inspector found huge thefts of military fuel in Thailand—losses amounting to over $5 million—but instead of being rewarded he was demoted to an insignificant job, avoided by his colleagues as though he had the plague, and later informed that the job to which he had been transferred was about to be abolished.[109] In another case an Air Force inspector disclosed to high civilian officials the excessive costs above estimates for the huge jet transport plane called the C-5A. His $2-billion discovery was not appreciated and discipline was planned. The employee, A. E. Fitzgerald, got senatorial support because at the time of the affair Senator William Proxmire's subcommittee was conducting an investigation into defense waste. An Assistant Secretary of the Air Force told Senator Proxmire's group that no action was planned against Fitzgerald, and then Proxmire read an Air Force memorandum that outlined three ways in which Fitzgerald could be dismissed from his civil service post. He was not fired, but he was demoted and assigned to oversight of the building of a twenty-lane bowling alley in Thailand.[110]

108. When Mr. Stubbing's research was publicized, Secretary of Defense Melvin Laird sought to discount it on the ground that it was a "graduate thesis" and therefore not really reliable. But Mr. Stubbing was hardly a typical graduate student. He was so well respected in the Bureau of the Budget that he was awarded a "midcareer" year of graduate study at the Woodrow Wilson School of Public and International Affairs at Princeton University. During that year he wrote the controversial analysis of defense spending, and he had very good qualifications for the job. He is a graduate of the Harvard Business School, spent four years as a cost engineer in industry, and several years as an analyst in the Bureau of the Budget. He was a member of a seminar I offered during his year at Princeton and I had occasion to observe his work. He is by no means what Laird presumably meant to imply in referring to this as graduate student work. See "Improving the Acquisition Process for High Risk Electronics Systems," mimeographed paper dated May 3, 1968. A capsule comment on the report and its receipt by the brass is in *I. F. Stone's Weekly*, Feb. 10, 1969.

109. See *Boston Globe*, Jan. 2, 1969 (United Press International story).
110. For details see *The New York Times*, June 18, 1969.

Having said this about the intractable bureaucracy, one must face the other side of the matter—which introduces, I submit, a sublime irony. That is, the bureaucracy of today is one of the marvels of the world for getting things done. As a method of organizing incredible numbers of people to do complex tasks in reasonable coordination, as a way of communicating and commanding, it is without parallel in the history of the world. It is worth recalling that the feat of landing men on the moon was not only a scientific achievement but a bureaucratic one as well. The coordination of so vast an effort would have been inconceivable in pre-bureaucratic times. Bureaucracy's distinguishing characteristic, as Max Weber saw in the early days of its emergence as the key feature of modern government, is that it systematizes and impersonalizes its procedures. That is, it makes rules to cover all possible contingencies and it lives by, with, and for those rules. The purpose is to get the job done and not to question why or to apply the rule in such a way as to humanize it. If the system is devoted to the shipment of human beings to death chambers and it works well, then those responsible for it take pride in the operation—as Adolph Eichmann did at his trial. As Weber saw it, bureaucracy was a system of relationships between superior and subordinate officials that involved strictly defined rights and duties, standard treatment for all persons in similar categories, uniform compensation, and standardized promotion procedures, all of which were part of a greater governmental system that had won legitimacy for its operations, thus justifying the uniform application of bureaucratic rules.[111] And, he observed, the system works best when "love, hatred, and every purely personal, especially irrational and incalculable, feeling" is excluded from official tasks.[112] An absurd but revealing illustration of this is the order by a Florida policeman to an incapacitated person to get a driver's license to operate his motorized wheelchair. An official who examined drivers said the applicant would have to pass both written and road tests before he could drive his wheelchair again. "A little observance of the manipulation of the chair is all we'll require—as ridiculous as it seems, it's the law and it has to be done."[113]

It is the success of bureaucracy that leads Hannah Arendt to equate it with tyranny. From Greek antiquity to today, she notes, we have classified government as the rule of one or the few over others (mon-

111. See *From Max Weber*, H. H. Gerth and C. Wright Mills, eds. (New York: Oxford University Press, 1946), pp. 196–244. Also see the excellent article on "Bureaucracy" by Reinhard Bendix in the *International Encyclopedia of the Social Sciences* (New York: Macmillan, 1968), Vol. 2, pp. 206–17.

112. Quoted by Reinhard Bendix, op. cit., p. 207.

113. Newark *Evening News*, June 21, 1969 (Associated Press story).

archy or oligarchy), or the rule of the best or the many (aristocracy or democracy), and then she adds:

> to which today we ought to add the latest and perhaps the most formidable form of such dominion, bureaucracy, or the rule by an intricate system of bureaux in which no men, neither the one nor the best, neither the few nor the many, can be held responsible, and which could properly be called the rule by Nobody. Indeed, if we identify tyranny as the government that is not held to give account of itself, rule by Nobody is clearly the most tyrannical of all, since there is no one left who could even be asked to answer for what is being done. It is this state of affairs which is among the most potent causes for the current world-wide rebellious unrest.[114]

Does this amount to a contradiction of what I previously argued about the intractable and independent bureaucracy? On the contrary it is a confirmation of the argument. Precisely its independence, its internal controls, its systematic self-aggrandizement and self-protectiveness make it difficult to control and at times seemingly inexorable in its plodding way. Consider, for example, the wiretapping and electronic eavesdropping done by the Federal Bureau of Investigation. Theoretically illegal until recently, the process nevertheless became a commonplace activity in pursuit of, first, information on national security threats; then it was extended to cover the world of mobsters; and by easy progression it came to the bugging of the telephone of the late Martin Luther King. J. Edgar Hoover, the utterly independent and serene ruler of the FBI world, claims that Robert Kennedy, when he was Attorney General, authorized the King wiretap, a point disputed by two succeeding Attorneys General, Nicholas Katzenbach and Ramsey Clark. Said Mr. Clark, "Mr. Hoover repeatedly requested me to authorize FBI wiretaps on Dr. King while I was Attorney General. The last of these requests, none of which was granted, came two days before the murder of Dr. King." [115] Hoover, who has been unusually clever and effective in building up the image of the FBI as an heroic, efficient, and lovable institution, has been untouchable by presidents, even when they disagreed with him. Who has been the victim of FBI taps and for what ostensible purposes it is impossible to know, and indeed we would not have known that King's phone had been tapped but for evidence of it that came out in a rehearing of a case against Muhammed Ali

114. Hannah Arendt, "Reflections on Violence," *New York Review of Books*, Feb. 27, 1969, pp. 19–31, at p. 23.

115. John Herbers, "Clark Suggests That Hoover Quit," *The New York Times*, June 21, 1969.

(Cassius Clay, World Champion boxer). The FBI is not, however, the only freewheeling agency of government, as I shall demonstrate further in analysis of presidential decision-making.

So the control of bureaucracy is an enormously important and difficult task. And that raises another point of ironic paradox. The President has frighteningly great power in some important areas—like foreign and military policy—but at the same time he is captive to the bureaucracy and if he is not personally resourceful and capable the bureaucracy will constitute a threat because of his weakness. I can illustrate the paradox of weakness and strength by turning to Warren Gamaliel Harding for a moment, for his brief tenure in the White House illustrates the ultimate dangers of an ineffective president.

No man who ever occupied the office was less fitted for it than Harding. A small-town newspaper editor and convivial poker player, his career was boosted by an ambitious wife and an Ohio politician who directed his political ascent. After a dull and uneventful term in the U.S. Senate, he emerged from the deadlocked Republican National Convention of 1920 as the dark horse candidate. He is reported to have said privately about his nomination, "I feel like a man who goes in on a pair of eights and comes out with aces full." [116] He had no notion of of how to run the government. "I listen to one side," he said, "and they seem right, and then . . . I talk to the other side and they seem just as right, and there I am where I started. . . . God, what a job!" On another occasion he lamented, "I can't make a damn thing out of this tax problem. . . . I know somewhere there is a book that will give me the truth, but hell! I couldn't read the book." The subtlety of Harding's mind is suggested by a speech of his concerning "progressivism," which he wanted to fuse with "progress" to coin a political slogan. "Progression," he said, "is not proclamation nor palaver. It is not pretense nor play on prejudice. It is not of personal pronouns, nor perennial pronouncement. It is not the perturbation of a people passion-wrought nor a promise proposed." [117] And around him, probably without his being aware of it, was a gang of thieves who were by bribery and deceit enriching themselves. In time—after Harding's death—the scandals, prosecutions, and suicides followed. Before the fall, however, the public admired him and was impressed with the excellence of his appointments; his death came as a shock and the public mourned a fallen leader, unaware that he was totally incompetent to occupy the office. There have been others—Franklin Pierce, James Buchanan,

116. See Andrew Sinclair, *The Available Man, The Life Behind the Masks of Warren Gamaliel Harding* (New York: Macmillan, 1965), p. 154.
117. Ibid., p. 50.

Ulysses Grant, and Chester Arthur, for example—but in this age the appearance of a genuine incompetent in the Presidency is doubly depressing to contemplate. And not just because he would be unable to lead the nation effectively toward any set of goals, but worse because he could so easily become the captive of the bureaucracy, and especially of the military, as I shall demonstrate in the course of assessing the way decisions are made at the top.

Decision Making at the White House

There are few easy decisions in the White House. The easy matters are resolved before they are shunted up the ladder of command to the President for his ultimate decision, or a crisis converts an apparently simple problem into a complex one, therefore involving the President. Or a President will convert a nonissue into a problem because he decides it merits attention. Whatever the source, the multiplicity of issues that arrive at his desk is incredible and the pressure for their resoluion can be enormous. The difficulty in deciding (for many reasons) is matched only by the difficulty in getting the decision carried through. As Harry Truman once said, "I sit here all day trying to persuade people to do the things they ought to have sense enough to do without my persuading them." [118]

As Richard Neustadt has demonstrated, whether the President will be successful in seeing to it that he "persuades" people to do things depends on several conditions and also on the way the President himself approaches his task. Neustadt points to "assurance that the President has spoken" as a factor "favoring compliance with a presidential order." [119] Because the President's power is great it is not uncommon for others to impute their objectives to the President, and furthermore it is not always clear that the President does in fact want what it appears he is asking for. Therefore making crystal clear what he means is one means of reaching his objectives. Thus in effect General Douglas MacArthur defied President Truman when MacArthur publicly called for the surrender of North Korea at a time when the President was moving toward a negotiated settlement of the war. MacArthur knew what Truman really wanted, but it had not been said unequivocally to him, and MacArthur knew, furthermore, that it would put great pressure on the President if he did defy him in this fashion. Such open defiance is rare; more covert defiance is commonplace. In this case the action brought a sharp response: Truman considered it insubordination and removed

118. Quoted by Neustadt, op. cit., p. 10.
119. Ibid., p. 19.

MacArthur from his command, fully realizing that the act would cost him heavily in political support, which it did. Hence another important aspect of the superior-subordinate relationship is, that it is rarely a one way relationship: the subordinate may have fewer resources than the superior, but a threat of resignation, the possibility of airing an issue in open controversy, or an insubordinate act to force either dismissal or backing down—all these are important resources in the hands of the subordinate. For no president wants to be placed in the position of appearing to be unable to control his own house, or to give the impression that there is bitter controversy in his administration. Many public letters of resignation and acceptance are poor reflectors of the actual controversies that preceded the forced resignation or the resignation in disagreement.

Much also depends, as Neustadt rightly says, on the professional and the public reputation of the President.[120] If he has a reputation in Washington among the "pros" for following through on his demands, and if he is known as a man not lightly to be crossed, he is the more likely to get what he wants. On the other hand, if he wavers and is vague and has a reputation for deferring to others, he may find it increasingly difficult to achieve his goals. For example, President Eisenhower's Secretary of the Treasury, George Humphrey, completely undercut the proposed budget for fiscal 1958 by issuing a press statement on the day of the announcement of the budget that predicted a "depression that will curl your hair" because of high tax burdens. "There are a lot of places in this budget that can be cut," Humphrey said, and he added he would be glad to see Congress cut it.[121] The President could have stopped Humphrey's comment but declined to do so. Once the attack on the budget had been made the budget cutters concluded that Eisenhower was of two minds about the budget (which he was) and thereby they deduced they need have no fear of retaliation if they pared the budget. Eisenhower's later attempts to regain control of the situation had little effect.

The President's capacity for getting his way also depends upon his reputation in the community at large; a popular president with the country behind him can get away with things that a president in poor repute would never even attempt. Thus Franklin Roosevelt sent a message to Congress on September 7, 1942, stating bluntly that unless Congress passed a proposed price control amendment he would act on his own.

I ask the Congress to take this action by the first of October.

120. Ibid., Ch. 4 and 5.
121. Quoted ibid., p. 66.

Inaction on your part by that date will leave me with an inescapable responsibility to the people of this country to see to it that the war effort is no longer imperiled by threat of economic chaos.[122]

The blunt warning was credible: Congress complied with his demand. The wartime situation and his reputation combined to get results. This is a rare situation but an illustrative one—at least as compared with Eisenhower in his budget battle.

Perhaps by considering the steps that Theodore Sorenson identifies as "theoretically" part of an "ideal" decision-making process for the President we can see not only some of the problems inherent in making those decisions, but something about the critical nature of the process itself. Sorenson says the ideal decision would involve

first: agreement on the facts;
second: agreement on the overall policy objective;
third: a precise definition of the problem;
fourth: a canvassing of all possible solutions . . . ;
fifth: a list of all possible consequences that would flow from each
solution;
sixth: a recommendation and a final choice of one alternative;
seventh: the communication of that selection; and
eighth: provision for its execution.[123]

Having been a White House staff man, Sorenson knows better than most that such tempered and rational steps are not always possible; the ideal case, he says, is the exception, not the rule. But if these are "ideals" to be sought, it is worth noting how difficult—at times next to impossible—it is to meet them in the real world.

1. *Knowing the facts.* Because the President is the key initiator of all policy and ultimately the sole decider of great issues in foreign affairs, his sources of information are obviously important. Whoever provides—or even who sifts and culls—information may go a long way toward making a decision. As a result presidents sometimes (often with good reason) suspect the information they get from certain sources. Some of his advisers, as previously noted, are captives of their subordinates and become such stanch partisans of a parochial view that they are special pleaders before the President and not his "neutral"

---

122. Quoted by Corwin, op. cit., p. 304. Roosevelt also asked his staff for "something I can veto" to demonstrate to Congress what he could and would do (Neustadt, op. cit., p. 84).

123. *Decision-Making in the White House* (New York: Columbia University Press, 1963), pp. 18–19.

aides. Therefore over the years presidents have built up the Executive Office of the President in the search for greater and greater control over information and closer relations between the President and those who advise him directly.[124] Gradually the Executive Office has become institutionalized itself, and only a few close advisers function as the eyes-and-ears extension of the President. The Council of Economic Advisers, the Bureau of the Budget, the Office of Science and Technology, the National Security Council, the Office of Emergency Planning, and so on are all part of the official White House establishment at least in the sense that they are not "of" any other department of government, but the closeness that any one of them (or its top leaders) has to the President himself is dependent upon a relationship that develops between the President and the adviser. The President obviously needs expert advice, but he also needs objectivity and personal loyalty—and therein lies a problem. The expert may lack a wide perspective precisely because he sees deeply into his realm of expertise, and the fully loyal aide may lack expertise. The usual resolution of the paradox is to find a number of bright, loyal staff men who become intermediaries between the President and the experts or the captured cabinet member.

Consider the problem from the perspective of a new President facing a decision on the invasion of Cuba in the spring of 1961 as John Kennedy did. Kennedy first learned that the escapade was being planned on November 17, 1960, shortly after his election. The CIA had established a camp in Guatemala where Cuban refugees were being trained for a landing at the Bay of Pigs in Cuba; President Eisenhower had allocated $13 million for the project in August, 1960, and the men were trained and ready to go shortly after Kennedy took office. United States troops were not to be directly involved, but the supplying and training of the guerrillas was completely an American undertaking. A series of meetings was held in the White House to determine the course of action to take. There were three key questions to answer: Would there be an uprising in Cuba against Castro to support the landing? Should the United States directly engage in the attack? And what would be done with the trained Cubans if the mission was called off?

The CIA stated flatly that there would be an uprising against Castro if the landing were made. Military planners gave an apparently unanimous recommendation that the raid be carried out and that was based on the validity of the CIA's predicted uprising, which proved utterly

---

124. I make no attempt here to describe, much less to evaluate, the machinery (or the voluminous literature about it) that has been created to aid the President.

false in practice. This was a matter of prediction more than "fact," of course, but it was a prediction based upon knowledge gleaned from supposedly reliable intelligence sources. In all probability it was based upon the feverish enthusiasm of anti-Castro exiles.[125]

Should the United States directly become involved? Here, there was considerably more disagreement, but the conclusion was that the United States should not become more directly involved than it was through training and supplying the guerrillas. Some contend that there was an implicit agreement for the United States to provide air cover for the operation, but whatever the understanding, President Kennedy firmly decided against it. What was the basis in fact for his decision? In part it turned back to the question of the expectation of an uprising by Cubans once the raiders were there. No one had seriously expected that fourteen hundred men alone would be able to withstand all that Castro could bring against them, and therefore the decision to keep the United States out of direct miiltary engagement in the escapade was based not only on some sensitivity about world opinion, but also on the warped assumption that the whole affair was an "internal" Cuban affair.

The decision had its political implications, too. Kennedy had denounced Castro in his campaign, and he feared the consequences of revelation that he had refused to permit a raid that Eisenhower had set up. And the chief of the CIA, Allen Dulles, made it abundantly clear what the factual situation was in that respect. He told the President, "Don't forget that we have a disposal problem. If we have to take these men out of Guatemala, we will have to transfer them to the United States, and we can't have them wandering around telling everyone what they have been doing." [126]

So, on April 17, 1961, the landing went on its bungled way. A pretense was made that the bombers dispatched from Nicaragua to bomb Cuban airfields were supposedly bombers flown by Castro defectors who had taken off from the very fields they bombed. This lie was reported at the United Nations by Adlai Stevenson, believing he was telling the truth. The bombing had little effect and the Cuban planes

125. A former high-ranking CIA official claims the Bay of Pigs was a disastrous failure because of the poor intelligence work, attributable to the fact that those directly involved in the project also predicted the uprising rather than relying on independent intelligence sources. See Lyman B. Kirkpatrick, *The Real CIA* (New York: Macmillan, 1968), pp. 184–204. Note also that Roger Hilsman suggested that his State Department intelligence analysts make an independent estimate of the chances of an uprising, which Secretary Rusk refused. See Hilsman's *To Move a Nation* (Garden City, N.Y.: Doubleday, 1967), p. 31.

126. Arthur Schlesinger, *A Thousand Days* (Boston: Houghton-Mifflin, 1965), p. 242.

mercilessly strafed the attackers. Castro's militia fought well, and the invaders who survived the slaughter were rounded up and imprisoned. The lesson of the affair, Kennedy later said, was that the President should not rely on experts. Arthur Schlesinger explained that Kennedy decided to go ahead with the invasion partly because he had been in office only seventy-seven days at the time, and partly because the feasibility of the project had been widely endorsed and almost no voices were raised against it.[127] No doubt there were many reasons behind the President's decision to go through with the landing, but a cardinally important reason was the factual assessment of the situation by the CIA. And as is often true—and not just in matters of military intelligence—the acquisition of a sound grasp of a factual situation is a difficult matter. Kennedy asked Ted Sorenson in the bitter aftermath, "How could I have been so far off base? All my life I've known better than to depend on experts. How could I have been so stupid, to let them go ahead?" [128] But overdependence on expertise and shortness of time only partially explain. The feared political repercussions of preventing any blow against Communism were also deeply involved.

2. *Clarification of policy goals.* It is obviously significant to determine what the goals of a given policy truly are, but it is more difficult to do than it would appear on the surface. For example, President Johnson and many of his advisers were not of the same mind about what the War on Poverty was to do. Daniel P. Moynihan, one of the President's advisers in the matter, states that the "war on poverty was not declared at the behest of the poor: it was declared in their interest by persons confident of their own judgment in such matters." [129] President Johnson saw the program as a way of helping people who were in need of help. His declaration of "unconditional" war on poverty was window dressing and he had no intention of fighting poverty the way he meant to (or did at least) fight the Vietnamese, but he *had* willed a program to combat poverty. It was certainly not clear what kind of program had been intended, however. For soon after the law went into effect some of those who were carrying it out saw as one of their goals the "arousing" of the poor to defend themselves rather than just providing "help" as, according to Moynihan, Johnson intended. The following words of the then Attorney General, Robert Kennedy, to the House Labor and

127. Schlesinger says that he and Senator Fulbright were alone among those who openly opposed it; Chester Bowles, who attended one discussion in place of Dean Rusk, was appalled and wrote a memorandum against it to Secretary of State Rusk, but apparently it was never shown to the President (ibid., pp. 250–51).

128. Theodore Sorenson, *Kennedy* (New York: Harper and Row, 1965), p. 309.

129. Daniel P. Moynihan, *Maximum Feasible Misunderstanding* (New York: Macmillan, 1969), p. 25.

Education Committee, testifying in behalf of the original Economic Opportunity Act, show an entirely different set of goals:

> [Welfare workers] plan programs for the poor, not with them. Part of the sense of helplessness and futility comes from the feeling of powerlessness to affect the operations of these organizations. The community action programs must basically change these organizations by building into the program real representation for the poor. This bill calls for "maximum feasible participation of the residents." This means the involvement of the poor in planning and implementing programs: giving them a real voice in their institutions.[130]

Moynihan says that neither the White House nor Capitol Hill really comprehended what was meant by the "maximum feasible participation" of the poor, but the unclarity of its goals was to plague the program for years. The innocent-sounding phrase permitted an interpretation of the law that invited the poor to be more than passive recipients of help. And it is important to recognize that any statement like that in a statute can be the basis of action that, intended or not, now has at least an appearance of authorization. For those few who were of an experimental and radical frame of mind in the program, "maximum feasible participation" was such an authorization.

3. *Defining the problem.* Over and over again, it seems to me, occupants of the White House—both superiors and subordinates—have utterly failed to define the nature of the problem in Vietnam. Enough has been said about that tragedy already and I shall not repeat myself, except to stress the fact that at no time, apparently, did high level personnel achieve a clear analysis of the situation in Vietnam. For example, John T. MacAlister, Jr. told the Senate Foreign Relations Committee in March of 1968 that half a million American troops had been unable to master the situation in Vietnam because an internal revolution has been going on in that nation for two decades. He continued:

> Our . . . difficulties have arisen because when we went into Vietnam we did not realize that the country was in the midst of an unresolved political conflict, nor did we understand what the underlying nature of this conflict really was. We are not merely fighting against an external invader that is attempting to gain control over a culturally distinct foreign country by force, nor are we fighting in a civil war that is a purely internal matter among south-

130. Ibid., pp. 90–91.

ern Vietnamese, but, instead, we have become engaged in a revolutionary war involving all of the Vietnamese people. . . . The war now raging in Vietnam is a continuation of the pattern of conflict launched by the Communist-led independence movement, the Viet Minh, against France and the non-Communist Vietnamese during the First Indochina War of 1947–54; it is not a war being fought between two separate nations but it is a revolutionary struggle involving two competitor governments within one nation. More conspicuously than in wars between nations, revolutionary war is a "continuation of politics by other means." It is a competition between two or more governments, each of which wants to become the sole legitimate government of a people.[131]

Is it hindsight to say that had the situation in Vietnam been better understood the entrapping military-political commitment might have been avoided, and both nations would have been spared the grim toll that has been taken? Although MacAlister's analysis comes years after the nation made the fateful commitments, he is not the first observer to point to the continuing revolution inside that nation—he is rather the most thorough and successful one in demonstrating the reality. Warnings that we were getting into a more and more impossible situation came from many authoritative sources, but they were ignored. The problem was never accurately defined nor were the true goals of the United States clarified; instead there was continuing dependence on such things as the domino theory, the obsession with Munich, and the propagandistic repetition of the charge of aggression from the North. And the realities were consciously warped to match these preconceptions. These were sad substitutes for clear analysis, as history abundantly illustrates and as many former proponents of the tough military policy have one by one admitted.[132]

4. *Considering alternative solutions.* The second Cuban crisis is a useful illustration of the difficulty in choosing among alternative strate

131. John T. MacAlister, Jr., "The Nature of Revolution," *Hearings Before the Senate Committee on Foreign Relations* (Washington: U.S. Government Printing Office, 1968), p. 154. See also MacAlister's *Vietnam, The Origins of Revolution* (New York: Alfred A. Knopf, 1969). See also James C. Thompson, Jr., "How Could Vietnam Happen: An Autopsy," *Atlantic Monthly*, Apr., 1968, pp. 47–53. Thompson makes clear how difficult it is to oppose a dominant idea from within government.

132. McGeorge Bundy proposed a troop withdrawal and cessation of bombing in October of 1968; see *The New York Times*, Oct. 13, 1968. Former Defense Secretary Clark Clifford reversed his position in an article in the June, 1969, issue of *Foreign Affairs*, which is excerpted in *The New York Times* of June 19, 1969. See also the hindsight observations of Townsend Hoopes, former Under Secretary of the Air Force: *The Limits of Intervention*, (New York: David McKay, 1969).

gies. The crisis was brought about by the discovery in October, 1962, that the Soviet Union was placing missiles in Cuba. The crisis, in the opinion of Robert Kennedy, "brought the world to the abyss of nuclear destruction and the end of mankind." [133] That it was a grim confrontation, Kennedy makes appallingly clear in his personal memoir of those tense thirteen days between October 16, when photographs taken by U-2 reconnaissance planes revealed the missile sites, and October 28, when word was received from the Russians that they would withdraw. During those agonizing days not only were alternatives debated endlessly; they were revised as developments changed the situation, and rejected alternatives were revived for new consideration.

The gravity of the situation is suggested by the fact that an estimated 40 per cent of Russia's nuclear strike force had been committed in Cuba, according to Harold Macmillan, who at that time was Prime Minister of Britain.[134] That meant that Russian missiles were within killing range of 80 million Americans. At the White House, there was a traumatic sense that speed was of the essence, for once the missiles were installed, they could not be removed without grave risk of atomic war. And all this took place in the atmosphere of an ongoing Congressional election in which some Republican candidates were calling for military action against Cuba. The Russians consistently assured American officials that the only armaments being given to the Cubans were "defensive" and denied that missiles were being sent there.

The process of choosing alternatives, under such enormous pressure, revealed many things. One was that the President had learned something from the Bay of Pigs incident, even if some others had not. Another was that full consideration of every alternative had to be given, and accordingly there were running discussions and debates on all aspects of the crisis constantly in progress during the thirteen days. At times the President sat in on the sessions involving White House staff men; the secretaries of State, Justice, Defense, and Treasury, and some of their higher-ranking subordinates; the Chairman of the Joint Chiefs of Staff; some specialists on Russian and Latin American affairs; the Chief of the CIA; and occasionally Vice President Lyndon Johnson and UN Ambassador, Adlai Stevenson. But more often the President did not attend the meetings, feeling that his presence inhibited discussion and tended to induce men to take the position that they believed the President favored. Said Robert Kennedy, "Personalities change when the President is present, and frequently strong men make recommendations

133. Robert F. Kennedy, *Thirteen Days, The Story About How the World Almost Ended* (New York: W. W. Norton, 1968), p. 23.

134. Associated Press report of a Macmillan television comment, *Boston Globe*, Jan. 30, 1969.

on the basis of what they believe the President wishes to hear." The group was instructed to canvass alternative courses of action and make recommendations. And at several stages the group convened with the President and he heard their arguments, put sharp questions to them, and urged consideration of various courses of action.

The main alternatives were the following. The first was to accept the fact that the missiles were there and do nothing. This had little support, even though it represented the same situation that we had put the Russians in when we installed missiles in places like Turkey and Italy. A second alternative, one that remained alive until near the end of the crisis, was bombing the Cuban sites to destroy the weapons. A variant on that involved bombing first and a follow-up invasion with as many as a quarter million troops. (Orders actually went out and troops were moved to the southeast for the assault, and one hundred ships were ordered for their transportation.) Another alternative was to blockade the Caribbean to stop further shipment of missiles to Cuba and to demand the withdrawal of those already there. This was the alternative chosen. A variant on that (later suggested by Adlai Stevenson) was to offer to withdraw our missiles from Turkey and Italy and to agree to abandon our naval base in Guantanamo, Cuba, as a token of good faith, and to insist on removal of the missiles in Cuba; this proposal of Stevenson's was rejected.

In the early stages of the crisis there appears to have been a great inclination to resort to air strikes or a land invasion to remove the missiles. General Curtis LeMay of the Air Force argued with the President that military attack was essential. The President asked what the Russians would do then. LeMay assured the President the Russian would do nothing. Hearing such arguments, Robert Kennedy commented that the military took positions "which, if wrong, had the advantage that no one would be around at the end to know." [135] The argument for United States military action followed this line of reasoning: the President, being responsible for the security of the American people, was obliged to take actions necessary to provide that security; if that meant bombing to destroy the missiles, then bombing was manifestly necessary. Robert Kennedy says he rejected that stand on the moral ground that a massive surprise attack by a large nation on a small one was wrong. He therefore concurred with Robert McNamara in holding out for a blockade.

The argument for the blockade was that it permitted the Russians time to reconsider, and that it was an act short of war and would be less likely to trigger a tragic response. A legal basis (of sorts) could be gained for the blockade by getting the Organization of American States

135. Kennedy, op. cit., p. 36.

to call for it. But the important thing was that it stopped further missiles from reaching Cuba and gave both the United States and Russia time to maneuver without overt military strikes. One thing that apparently helped the President decide in favor of the blockade was the statement to him by the Commanding General of the Tactical Air Force that there would be no assurance that air attacks would in fact eliminate all the missiles.

The blockade forced further choices of alternatives, some of them with incredible risks. On Wednesday, October 22, came the confrontation at sea when Soviet vessels reached the line of the blockade. (Previously, to allow the Kremlin a little more time, the line had been moved to within five hundred miles of Cuba instead of eight hundred, although the closer range brought our Navy within range of land-based Russian aircraft in Cuba.) At the White House the President and his advisers awaited the confrontation that would come between 10:30 and 11 A.M. Then a Russian submarine was located between a United States aircraft carrier and the closest Soviet merchantmen. Said Robert Kennedy,

> I think these few minutes were the time of gravest concern for the President. Was the world on the brink of a holocaust? Was it our error? A mistake? Was there something further that should have been done? Or not done? His hand went up to his face and covered his mouth. He opened and closed his fist. His face seemed drawn, his eyes pained, almost gray. We stared at each other across the table. For a few fleeting seconds, it was almost as though no one else was there and he was no longer President. . . . The voices droned on, but I didn't seem to hear anything until I heard the President say: "Isn't there some way we can avoid having our first exchange with a Russian submarine—almost anything but that?" "No, there's too much danger to our ships. There is no alternative," said McNamara. "Our commanders have been instructed to avoid hostilities if at all possible, but this is what we must be prepared for, and this is what we must expect." [136]

Of this situation, Robert Kennedy said, "President Kennedy had initiated the course of events, but he no longer had control over them. He would have to wait. . . . What could we say now—what could we do?" The answer came from the Kremlin: an order for the Soviet ships to stop. With that the U.S. Navy was ordered not to interfere. "For a moment," said Robert Kennedy, "the world had stood still, and now it was going around again."

A few days later, the blockade still in effect, Adlai Stevenson made his proposal about the removal of our missiles in Turkey and Italy and

136. Ibid., pp. 69–70.

our withdrawal from the naval base we maintain in Cuba. As it turned out, the missiles we had in Turkey and Italy were superseded by our submarine-borne Polaris missiles in the Mediterranean, and in fact the President had suggested an approach to Turkey about removing the missiles. When Turkish officials resisted this, the State Department let the matter drop, although the President thought he had made it clear the missiles were to be removed whether the Turks liked it or not. And, according to his brother, he was angry when he discovered that being President and having made his wishes clear had not resulted in action. But on the other hand, he refused to remove the missiles from the Turkish and Italian bases because they would amount to giving in under the threat of the Russians. The President stated that he did not want to risk a catastrophic war over missiles in Turkey that were "antiquated and useless," but he did just that, nevertheless, for the Russians in their communications urged their removal as a reciprocal act.

A first exchange of letters between the President and Khrushchev indicated that there must have been as much tense and confused debate going on in Moscow as there was in Washington. (The hawks in Russia apparently were as sure we were bluffing and would do nothing as were American hawks sure Russia would not act.[137]) By the time the second weekend came around after the original discovery of the missiles on Tuesday, October 16, and the work on the missile sites was being accelerated, the blockade was in effect, but Russia had not agreed to remove the missiles. The military were pressing for an air strike the following Monday, October 28. The President's decision was not to attack but to resort to another letter. The letter called for removal of the missiles under UN supervision, gave assurances that we had no intention of invading Cuba, but simply neglected to mention the Russian demand for the reciprocal removal of our missiles. It worked; the Kremlin backed down and the missiles were eventually removed. The President had risked nuclear war to achieve his goals, but he had chosen among the alternative courses of action those that allowed the opposition some way of reversing its course, allowed time to maneuver and consider. The essence of the nearly two weeks of playing with the fate of mankind had been the choice of alternatives; if the "right" ones had not been chosen in some long-run sense of objective history—if such a thing is imaginable—at least that time the choices were ones that were not "terminal," although clearly they could have been. But is there any doubting that one day hawks will preside on both sides and different alternatives will be chosen?

5. *Weighing consequences.* Having just discussed the choice of alternatives, it is apparent that we have simultaneously been discussing

137. See Michel Tatu, *Power in the Kremlin* (New York: Viking Press, 1969).

the assessment of possible consequences of decisions. Patently the probable consequences of actions—as both Cuban crises and our Vietnam policy amply demonstrate—are at best risky guesses. There is no way of knowing what the outcome of a decision will be, for it depends upon actions over which the original actors have no control. Thus General MacArthur and his intelligence officers assured Washington that an invasion of North Korea could be executed without danger of Red China's becoming involved. The ensuing Inchon landing was a disastrous miscalculation leading to the bitter defeat of American soldiers, who became pawns in an international guessing game. After the event Richard Neustadt asked Truman about that decision. He replied that the United States should not have invaded the northern part of Korea.

> We knew the Chinese had close to a million men on the border and all that. . . . But [MacArthur] was commander in the field. You pick your man, you've got to back him up. That's the only way a military organization can work. I got the best advice I could and the man on the spot said this was the thing to do. . . . That was my decision—no matter what hindsight shows.[138]

Hindsight often shows that the calculation of consequences is a frighteningly fallible process.

6. *Choice of a course of action.* In major matters, as previously noted, the choice of alternatives is ultimately in the hands of the President. One must stress, however, the importance of his subordinates in that process, and the procedural problems involved in the relationships between the President and those subordinates. But it is not a problem of institutional and personal relationship alone. It is also a matter of *ideas.* President Truman accepted the responsibility for the Inchon error because that is the way the military system has to operate. President Johnson accepted the advice of his military counsel again and again to increase the American involvement, believing that more military power could not fail. President Kennedy refused to remove our missiles from Turkey because it would seem like backing down in the face of Soviet pressure.[139]

138. Neustadt, op. cit., p. 128.

139. Nationalistic fervor leads to international games of "chicken" to see who will bend first, as in childish fashion, leaders play silly games for the sake of "national honor." The front page of *The New York Times* once carried a large photograph showing American and North Korean officials sitting, staring at each other across a table at an Armistice Commission meeting. After seven and a half hours in conference, it was the North Korean's turn to call an adjournment. When he failed to do so the two sides sat mute, facing each other, for four more hours before the American representative got up and left (*The New York Times*, Apr. 13, 1969).

In short the pressures of nationalism and the commitment to force determine presidential choices as much as the institutional context does. And the military system is an embodiment of the literal opposite of Immanuel Kant's corollary to his categorical imperative: namely "Act so that you treat humanity, whether in your own person or in that of another, always as an end, never as a means only." [140] Nationalism "justifies" taking great risks because of the absolute priority of the security of the United States, and it rules out some alternatives because they would seem to diminish the prestige of or indicate some lack of independence or power of the United States. How else explain a decision not to give up missiles in Turkey that were useless and, indeed, that Kennedy had thought he had already ordered removed? Similarly nothing but a military mentality could explain how half a million men could be committed to the Vietnam war and fifty thousand of them killed.[141] The essence of the policy is that men are indeed nothing but means and never ends in themselves. When a mountain is held by the enemy, as "Hamburger Hill" was in Vietnam, the military mentality says, "Clear it." If that costs the lives of 113 American soldiers, the price has to be paid. For what? To get and hold a mountain? On the contrary, the victors left the hill and it was reoccupied and a new attack was called for by military men. To what end? "Keeping on the pressure" to force a peace settlement at the Paris negotiations presumably. And by that process have more than ten thousand Americans died since the Paris negotiations began.[142] Similar in theory to the generals who calculate that "even if it takes a whole division" they will retake "Hamburger Hill" (so called by the soldiers because of the butchery involved) but different in scope was President Nixon's decision to build what he, characteristically, chose to call the "Safeguard" ABM system to protect the safety of the United States. Some scientific observers have stated the risk of all-out nuclear attack to be no less than 2 per cent per year, which in fifty years makes the odds for annihilation impressive.[143] Yet rather than take the chance of the enemy's getting some advantage while both sides negotiate a deescalation of the arms race, the Presi-

140. *Foundations of the Metaphysics of Morals* (Indianapolis: Bobbs-Merrill, 1959), p. 47.

141. David Halberstam trenchantly portrays this mentality in operation in his article, "The Very Expensive Education of McGeorge Bundy," *Harpers Magazine,* July 1969, pp. 21–42.

142. See *The New York Times* editorial, "Maximum Military Pressure," May 28, 1969.

143. One prominent physicist who has often been a consultant to the Defense Department on matters of nuclear policy told me the only trouble with the 2 per cent chance prediction is that it is too conservative, especially as more nations gain the technical capacity to develop the bomb.

dent made the choice that a military mentality dictates. Each major weapons system of the past two decades has been rendered obsolete or has been countered in some fashion by other more drastic killing devices. But the growing threat seems only to cause the military mentality to make greater demands for "security" expenditures rather than to consider deescalation.

7. *Communicating the decision.* As earlier examples have demonstrated, the communication of presidential wishes or even orders is not an automatic process. That is one reason why the President has to depend heavily on his own trusted staff men—to see to it that what he has proposed is indeed done. For many reasons the bureaucracy may prefer to slide over a presidential directive unless it is unequivocally clear. Thus the State Department, when it got a negative response from the Turks about removing our missiles from their country, let the matter ride rather than pressing or insisting that they were going to be removed. MacArthur resisted the President's initiative for a negotiated settlement in Korea because he wanted a clear "victory" rather than a compromise. In countless other situations similar evasions or subtle defiance of presidential decisions takes place, and in a government so large and complex that is probably to be expected.

8. *Execution of orders.* Presidents adopt different styles of putting their decisions into execution, depending on the temperament of various presidents and on the situation involved. President Eisenhowever, following his military experience, tended to rely on his staff men to carry through for him, resulting in a situation where his top aide, Sherman Adams, became a kind of assistant president rather than assistant to the President. President Kennedy, instructed in the complexities of presidential politics by his reading of history and his association with Richard Neustadt, distrusted experts and wanted loyal men of many talents for his immediate subordinates. They were assigned areas in a loose way and were expected to cover matters on assignment and to be capable of following through on a wide range of issues. Kennedy thought little of the elaborate centralization of staff work and especially distrusted the ad hoc interdepartmental committees for special purposes established by Eisenhower, and he abolished them by the dozen when he took over the Presidency. In his frustration with the State Department, however, Kennedy tended to create his own State Department in the White House, much as Franklin Roosevelt had done when he ceased to rely on Cordell Hull but found it politically impossible to dismiss him. President Nixon, on the other hand, leans toward President Eisenhower's methods and assigns an important role to the National Security Council—unlike his two immediate predecessors, who relied more heavily on their personal staff than on the Council, which consists of

the Vice President, the Secretary of Defense, the Director of the Office of Emergency Planning, and two advisory members (the Director of the CIA and the chairman of the Joint Chiefs of Staff). Nixon has also established other committees—such as the ones on Urban Affairs and on Environmental Quality Control—to coordinate activities and follow through on programs. Nixon emphasizes the necessity of getting the widest advice he can from within the government, but decides personally which courses to take. He also depends heavily on his White House staff, but apparently he relies on formal groups—Cabinet, National Security Council, and his special councils—more than his two immediate predecessors.

Limiting Presidential Power

What are the chances of restraining the power of the President, if indeed it has become a center of too highly personalized power and too much discretionary power? Let me review the major alternative ideas suggested for shielding great presidential power in some fashion, by looking first at the Supreme Court and then Congress as possible sources of limitation.

Although the Court has from time to time vetoed things Presidents did or wanted to do, the judiciary is not a particularly promising source of limitation. Despite *Youngstown* v. *Sawyer*, the Court has rarely reversed the President; when challenged the President has usually found the Court on his side. It is true that in some after-the-fact cases, the Court has said the President should not have done something. The Court held in *Ex parte Milligan* and *Duncan* v. *Kohonamoku* that the executive does not have the authority to try persons in military courts when the civil courts are open and in operation, but these cases came up just *after* the Civil War and World war II respectively.[144] In limited ways the Court has trimmed the presidential power to remove subordinates from office; permitting certain legislative limitations on the removal power, but on balance these do not stand as significant restraints.[145]

More commonly the Court has gone along with presidential authority, as it did in the *Neagle* and *Midwest Oil* cases, previously cited. And in international affairs the Court is even more lenient. In the *Curtiss-Wright* case an extremely conservative Justice who repeatedly joined anti-Roosevelt majorities on the Court in the New Deal days,

144. *Milligan*, 4 Wallace 2 (1866), and *Duncan*, 327 *U.S.* 324 (1946).

145. *Myers* v. *U.S.*, 272 *U.S.* 52 (1926); *Humphrey's Executor* v. *U.S.*, 295 *U.S.* 602 (1935); *Wiener* v. *U.S.*, 357 *U.S.* 345 (1958).

nevertheless rendered an opinion that gave the broadest scope to presidential power in international affairs. Justice Sutherland, in a case involving an unusual grant of delegated authority by Congress (it had permitted the President to determine when a policy of neutrality should be declared in the Chaco War in the 1930's and to declare an arms embargo pursuant to his declaration), said that executive power in foreign affairs was in a wholly different category of constitutional law from domestic law. For the power to act in external affairs comes not via the delegated powers assigned to Congress, but through the sovereignty of the nation inherited, in effect, from kings. And said Sutherland, the President is "the sole organ of external relations and the sole representative with foreign nations," and he has a "very delicate, plenary and exclusive power . . . as sole organ of the U.S. in international relationships." [146]

Nor does the Court interfere much in military matters. We have previously cited the Court's reluctant agreement to the incarceration of Japanese Americans during World War II on the orders of President Roosevelt. In the *Korematsu* case, which authorized the evacuation of all Japanese persons from the West Coast, Mr. Justice Jackson commented:

> I would not lead people to rely on this Court for a review that seems to me wholly delusive. . . . If the people ever let command of the war power fall into irresponsible and unscrupulous hands, the courts wield no power equal to its restraint. The chief restraint upon those who command the physical forces of the country, in the future as in the past, must be their responsibility to the political judgements of their contemporaries and to the moral judgments of history.[147]

What are the possibilities of using Congress to dampen the power of the Presidency? Edward Corwin once proposed that the Cabinet be drawn from a "legislative council," drawn in turn from the two houses of Congress. This body would "advise" the President but would not have the power to veto his actions; in their refusal to condone his actions they might restrain him somewhat. As Corwin put it,

> The proposed Cabinet would comprise men whose daily political salt did not come from the presidential table, whose political fortunes were not identical with his, who could bring presidential

146. *U.S. v. Curtiss-Wright Export Corp.,* 299 *U.S.* 304 (1936).
147. *Korematsu v. U.S.,* 323 *U.S.* 214 (1944).

whim under an independent scrutiny which today is lacking, and yet who, by putting the stamp of their approval on his proposals, would be able to facilitate their enactment into law. It would be a body both capable of *controlling* the President and of *supporting* him.[148]

As noted previously, Charles Hyneman offered a similar proposal except that he would have permitted the President to select his cabinet from among Congress rather than having Congress choose them for the President. Neither Corwin nor Hyneman see any bar to their proposals in the language of the Constitution, Article I, Section 6, which says that "no person holding any office under the United States shall be a member of either house." Their subterfuge would be that the Congressional cabinet men would have executive subordinates who would be administratively responsible for running the government, but the Congressional cabinet member would be the true leader of the department while technically only a member of Congress.

The real problems with the Corwin-Hyneman idea, however, are not constitutional but political. In the first place there is no root system for such a structure to be grafted onto. If we had developed a parliamentary style of government, such a grafting job would be unnecessary because collective responsibility would already exist, but to suggest the essence of the prime minister role for a president whose traditions and practices are utterly alien to that role would be not only unlikely to be acceptable as a reform but unpredictable in consequences. It might restrain where restraint would be undesirable and not restrain where restraint was needed. It might, for example, place a damper on the domestic leadership of the President at a time when the President's visibility and persuasiveness may save the system from falling into a damaging *immobilism*.

Nor does the experience of consultation with Congressional leaders on foreign policy indicate that they urge restraint on the President. In the second Cuban crisis, when Kennedy called in legislative leaders they were appalled that he was not going to use the Air Force to blast the missiles out of Cuba. When Johnson went to them with the Tonkin Gulf incident they acted with indecent speed. Perhaps, however, this is unfair to Congress. In both these instances the Congress was called in for the crash landing rather than being consulted at the takeoff; in hurried conferences they were presented with startling facts and gave quick responses. Indeed Robert Kennedy notes that the immediate Congressional reaction in the Cuban crisis was the same as that of the ad-

148. Corwin, op. cit., p. 362. Italics in original

ministration personnel when they first got the news. It was only after further reflection and much deliberation that the more deliberation that the more sane alternatives were chosen. Furthermore, there is a chance that many members of Congress have learned their lesson from Vietnam and related ventures.

That Congress has changed is indicated by the fact that on June 25, 1969, the Senate passed the Fulbright Resolution, which states the "sense of the Senate" that national commitments to foreign countries should be made only with the concurrence of Congress. It binds a President to nothing in legal terms, but politically it is significant that the Resolution was passed by a vote of 70 to 16. President Nixon had expressed his disapproval of the Resolution, fearing it would "tie the hands" of the executive, but only a handful of Senators agreed with him. The Resolution, originally reported out of the Senate Foreign Relations Committee in late 1967, was not brought to a vote sooner, partly in deference to the political muscle of Lyndon Johnson. But, with repeated expressions of assurance that the Resolution was not aimed specifically at Mr. Nixon, Senator after emphasized the need for redressing a constitutional balance that the Senate felt had given undue discretion to the executive. The Resolution says,

> Whereas accurate definition of the term "national commitment" in recent years has become obscured: now, therefore, be it
>
> Resolved, that a national commitment for the purpose of this resolution means the use of the armed forces on foreign territory, or a promise to assist a foreign country, government or people by the use of the armed forces or financial resources of the United States, either immediately or upon the happening of certain events, and
>
> That it is the sense of the Senate that a national commitment by the United States results only from affirmative action taken by the legislative and executive branches of the United States Government by means of a treaty, statute, or concurrent resolution of both houses of Congress specifically providing for such commitment.[149]

How significant is the Resolution? So far as the sweeping discretion of the President's legal powers are concerned, I think the Resolution has affected it not at all. In emergency situations, as the President defines them, he will still have the "authority" to proceed—or doubt-

---

149. The rationale for the resolution is presented in the Committee Report, "National Commitments," loc. cit.

less will so claim if he wants to act fast. If Presidents can stampede Congress into writing blank checks like the Tonkin Gulf one, the Resolution will have scant potential. Therefore, perhaps the greatest significance of the Fulbright Resolution is to be found, literally, in the fact that the Senate saw fit to pass it. That is, the Senate has become apprehensive about some commitments and that apprehension in itself may act as a minor depressant for the future. But in my judgment the passing of the Resolution does not suggest that the ideas that have led us into our world position have been widely abandoned. The vagueness of the Resolution drew a wide spectrum of support because it allows a broad interpretation. As I said at the outset of this book, what we appear to have learned from Vietnam is not that we are playing a dubious world role, but that we got too deeply into a particular situation. It appears to me that the real reason for the Fulbright Resolution is Vietnam, and therefore the future importance of the Resolution will depend on what we learn from that blunder.

Resistance to foolhardy ventures that by hindsight appear to be such is not the same thing, however, as providing an ongoing restraint on presidential initiatives in general. The Corwin-Hyneman institutional device seems to me to offer little hope of success and to raise many doubts about its net consequences. It is, alas, but another example of the Constitutional Convention fixation that pervades so much of American political thought. If there is something wrong, then back to the drawing board for a new institutional remedy. But I suggest that the problem is not only or primarily institutional. We can debate about new ways of choosing the President, bemoan the lack of a politically responsible cabinet, and conjure up new devices to meet the problems, but in the end the problem is political. And the President is not wholly without a sense of political restraint after all—he is not only culturally adapted to responsiveness but he is induced to it as well by his need for political support. Therefore, no small part of the problem is that mad ideas captivate both the public and the officials. At root is our quasi-imperialist mentality. For the primary source of restraint on the truly dangerous aspects of presidential authority remains the attitudes of the people. That is, if there is widespread belief in the divine role of the United States as world policeman, if there is acceptance of playing the game of nuclear chicken, if anti-Communism continues to be a matter of devout conviction, then Presidents will be dangerous in domestic and international affairs because they know where their support comes from. Robert Kennedy tells of talking with his brother during the hours before the confrontation in the Caribbean Sea when they both realized the course they had taken could lead to a world catastrophe. The President said,

"It looks really mean doesn't it? But then, really there was no other choice. If they get this mean on this one in our part of the world, what will they do next?" "I just don't think there was any choice [Robert Kennedy answered], and not only that, if you hadn't acted, you would have been impeached." The President thought for a moment and said "That's what I think—I would have been impeached." [150]

Without doubt the impeachment thought was a bit of therapeutic rationalization at a moment of tension and uncertainty, but given the mood of the nation and the fever pitch of antagonism that existed toward Castro and toward Khrushchev and all that Communism represented, is it not patently clear that the President would have had the most severe political opposition if he had not acted? And the fact is that his popularity rose, as the polls measured it, after the incident took place.

What then is the importance of the Presidency for setting national priorities? Clearly on the one hand it is part of the part of the process by which examination of true priorities is evaded and obscured, but at the same time it is an instrument that often commits the nation irrevocably to particular policies. Despite the fact that he has much potential initiative, the President remains the captive of the ideas and of the political forces that prevail in this society. In truth, as the final chapter will argue about the whole of American politics, the decisive change will not be a modification of the executive institution but a change in the paradigms we use to explain and to justify social, economic, and political reality.

150. Kennedy, op. cit., p. 67.

CHAPTER EIGHT

Morality and
Setting Priorities

ETTING priorities in a society is not only a matter of power and competition among interests but also a matter of surpassing moral importance. And contemporary conditions make the moral facet of the problem more important as society grows larger, more complex, and more impersonal. In a simpler society all manner of discriminatory and abusive treatment of one group by another certainly took place, but life in a complex society is even worse; there are innumerable ways in which the human element is eliminated from the setting of priorities because human beings do not need to be considered. Modern technology makes possible the modern metropolis with its incredibly complex economy and its impersonal community. The perfect illustration of the point is the cybernetic revolution, which can reduce the human element to zero. For the computer is the essence of impersonality as well as symbolic of the speed of action and the hugeness of society. One commentator on technological change has pointed to a computer used in Vietnam to select bombing targets for the Air Force. The computer is fed intelligence data on the *probability* that enemy troops will occupy given spots on the map, then on the chance that the enemy will in fact be where it "ought" to be as the computer "reasons," the Air Force drops tons of bombs. That may make more military sense than to drop bombs on targets selected by throwing darts at a map, but it utterly forgets the villagers who happen to occupy the target areas. Indeed, in the very process of determining who shall die it eliminates the personal elements! [1]

Impersonal treatment is characteristic of massive operations whether in business, education, industry, or government: one becomes an element in a process, not a human being producing or receiving some good or service. So we calculate the "overkill" of millions of persons and, further, insist that such "reasoning" is indispensable. Population ex-

1. See John McDermott, "Technology and the Intellectuals," *New York Review of Books*, July 31, 1969.

pands exponentially but the world's food supply expands only arith-
metically, and people therefore starve. The masses abroad and those
caught in our slums or left behind in decaying rural areas of America
are quite invisible to the affluent commuters to suburbia. As resentment
grows among the denied ones and they disrupt society, the result is
anxiety on the part of those who are or feel threatened, and from that
anxiety and fear comes the demand for repression—and more neglect
of the human element as the clubs swing and the weapons blast away.

Nor is the diminution of the human factor restricted to the sup-
pressers. Radicals, in their antagonism toward the "system," its impersonality, and the manifest injustices associated with it, also lose sight
of the dignity of the individual in their certainty that they are right and
that the system and all its representatives must be wrong. Verbal abuse
and denigration of the opposition not only deny respect for human
beings but declare persons physically dispensable in pursuit of the
sanctified goals, whatever they may be. "Up against the wall" is not
coincidentally a common radical phrase. And the more fervent the belief
the greater the willingness to sacrifice human beings in the defense or
pursuit of it; the agents of the Inquisition who burned heretics at the
stake no doubt thought their commission of murder was completely
justified.

Thus the overwhelming importance of somehow regaining a moral
view of the establishment of priorities: only in respect for the dignity
of man is there hope for curtailing the grossness of a system that is blind
to the human being. Only by making the moral consequences of decisions about the allocation of resources as important as the "efficiency"
factor can a morally acceptable society be created. A system that pays
farmers for not producing while others starve, a system that sacrifices
miners for the sake of low production costs, a system that provides
medical care for the wealthy but not for the poor, a system in short
that perpetrates the kinds of evil described in these pages is morally
intolerable.

Apart from its moral deficiencies, the system has to be reexamined
because it threatens human existence. It is true that technology and
contemporary social organization have produced great wealth and
have made it possible to feed and keep physically alive millions of
people who in the past would have died in infancy, but, ironically, in
its very success the system poses a grim threat. If technologically it is
possible to feed and care for ever greater numbers, the very existence
of those numbers poses dangers of many kinds. The existence of all
those billions of persons is causing a severe drain on resources, for
example. Already we are unable to feed our present population adequately, and the competition between the poor half of the world and

the rich half becomes more serious year by year. Not only will this competition be an invitation to war, but contemporary war with its technological horrors for the first time can possibly exterminate life from the planet. Concentrations of persons and industrial operations threaten to pollute the world so as to threaten life. Thus war, pollution, overpopulation, and resource depletion, all the products of blind actions, raise dangers of self-extinction for humankind.

We do not take the steps necessary to prevent these catastrophes for many reasons. For one thing they do not seem really believable. The individual feels uninvolved in the problem, helpless to prevent the wrong actions, or self-concerned and unwilling to sacrifice immediate gratification to achieve future social objectives. And what is true of individuals is even more so for organizations, which make decisions by bargaining, by compromise, and in competition—that is to say, which make decisions irresponsibly so far as consequences are concerned. A company that dumps wastes in a river, killing the living things in it and altering the ecology of an area, does not consider this as a moral issue: the problem is how to compete in the production of paper or chemicals. If waste can be disposed of without direct cost it obviously will be. By and large the costs of air and water pollution have been hidden costs paid for by the individual who suffers the results and not by the polluter.

But one does not have to turn to pollution to see the consequences of blind decision-making. Equally guilty are the economists who have long held that the important thing for national economic well-being was an ever-increasing Gross National Product. Economic growth and development would inevitably benefit all, for the benefits would "trickle down" to those lowest in the social and economic hierarchy. And in fact there has been a slow decline in the number of families living under conditions of poverty—defining that by a baseline of approximately a $3,000 income. The "full employment" of the 1960's did result in the improvement of the position of the vast proportion of the population; some sixteen million Americans have departed the poverty category since 1961. But that does not mean there are no moral issues involved in raising the GNP in the way it was raised. Part of the economic growth was due to technological advances that disemployed many persons by increasing productivity immensely. The introduction of machinery for the mining of coal resulted in forced idleness for hundreds of thousands of miners, and for some it meant permanent unemployment. The introduction of new technology in the culture of cotton threw onto the human scrap heap hundreds of thousands of Negro farmhands. Another illustration is the throwaway bottle. When it was found that new bottles could be produced more cheaply than old ones could be collected and reused, the unskilled manpower involved in the reuse process was abandoned, and the more highly skilled workers who make bottles (cheaply) gained. Technological innovation results in the improved status of educated and skilled persons, who can add to the total wealth by his greater productivity, but this happens at the cost of the uneducated and unskilled, whose only sources of employment are drying up.

Nor is this simply a matter of relative economic deprivation for the twenty-five million Americans caught at the bottom of the pile. The ramifications of that poverty sweep widely. Hunger, disease, disgrace, death are regular company for those whom the whirl of economic success sifts out as irrelevant. Of hunger we have said enough previously; it is more pervasive and damaging than was realized until recently. Health and medical attention are the privileges of the affluent; the poor take what they can get—often nothing. Although it is true that public expenditures for health have grown greatly in the last five years, this is not as much gain as it appears because the costs of medical care have skyrocketed. My colleague Herman Somers comments that "An old and popular saw has it that the rich and the poor get the best medical care while the middle class has the roughest time. This has never been true. The poor generally get bad care and relatively little of that." [2] That the poor get inferior medical care is shown by unbelievable health statistics. This, the richest nation in the world, ranks fifteenth among all nations in its infant mortality rates, but the sadness of infant death does not affect all mothers equally. In Detroit's more affluent neighborhoods the infant mortality rate per 1,000 live births in 1967 was 12.1 (the United States rate is 23.4), but in the poorest area of Detroit the rate was 61.1.[3] Negro mothers die in childbirth at four times the rate for white mothers. The same is true for other health problems: the poor see a doctor far less often than do the middle class, suffer greater losses of time from work for disability, and more often suffer from tuberculosis, influenza, pneumonia, and cancer of the cervix (curable when found early and treated), all of which take a heavy toll among the poor but not the affluent.

This is what occurs when the moral implications of the operation of a hugely productive machine are ignored; in pursuit of maximum productivity or profit, social costs are obscured. It is not that any given corporate official or legislator or administrator *wills* a miserable education to the poor child, unemployment for the unskilled, air pollution,

---

2. "Health Services: Problems of Cost and Distribution," in *Social Security in International Perspective*, Shirley Jenkins, ed. (New York: Columbia University Press 1969), p. 91.

3. "T. R. B.," *The New Republic*, May 5, 1969, p. 4.

hunger, or any of these other scourges. It is rather that by nonaction, by the simple refusal to take the social consequences into account the evil is perpetrated. The blindness of the productive engine, the obliviousness of public officials have nevertheless bred a grim set of threatening problems. It now becomes conceivable that the disadvantaged will so disrupt the operations of the society as to bring upon themselves a kind of repressiveness that will produce a fascist regime. It now looks possible for mankind to eliminate itself from the earth through nuclear holocaust. That civilization can be destroyed one knows from even a slight knowledge of history; that mankind can now be destroyed in several ways in this technologically "advanced" age has for the first time become a possibility. The explosive growth of population if it continues unabated will soon be adding 1 billion persons to world population every five years; the population of the United States will double by the end of the century. If such growth occurs in the United States we will need to build a city of 250,000 every month between now and the year 2000 to accommodate the new Americans. If such growth continues in the world, wars and rebellions over poverty and territory are bound to ensue. As nuclear capacity is achieved in more nations, why assume that nuclear disaster is avoidable?

Thus for reasons of compelling practicality and for compelling moral reasons it is mandatory that we consider these issues and seek answers. Why have we not addressed ourselves to these questions in the past?

Why the Perverted Priorities?

There is no dearth of explanations of why we set the kinds of priorities that we do. Power structure theorists, Marxists, pluralists, and others provide conflicting reasons why the system works as it does. I maintain none of these is a wholly satisfactory explanation, although there is some truth in all of them. Social causation is incredibly complex and too often the explainers hit on some significant determinant, which becomes for them the root of the matter—the key that unlocks the puzzle. Thus Karl Marx spent a lifetime in studying the capitalist system and worked out an elaborate explanation of the primacy of economic considerations in all historical development. His intellectual successors often employ his ideas in overly simplistic, not to say dogmatic, ways to explain all the shortcomings of a capitalist society. If similar difficulties occur in Communist nations, the reason is that those states are imperfect because they are threatened by the capitalist world. If it be argued that since World War II the Communist nations have matched the West in expenditures for military purposes and have apparently been no more willing to take risks for the sake of disarmament, the reason is that the West was threatening. Or if one points to the continuity of Soviet and czarist foreign policy where neighboring nations are concerned, the response is again that the problem is not one of "imperialism" such as the West practices, but of danger from the West.

There is no gainsaying such argument, of course. One cannot prove or disprove such contentions. But the similarities of United States and Soviet concerns with military might, the similar diversion of resources for military ventures or participation in the race to the moon, the similar refusal to take the risk of disarmament in order to avoid a disastrous conclusion to the bluff and counterbluff—such similarities make the Marxist explanation dubious to me. It has not been convincingly shown that there has been a singularity of American or Western concern with armaments and aggressiveness. Even if that were demonstrable, it does not seem logically necessary to take the next step and conclude that *the decisive difference has been the alternative kinds of ownership of capital in the two societies.* No doubt much of the American incapacity to plan is attributable to not only the economic fact of private capital but also the ideologically reinforced restraints upon public involvement in economic life that accompanies capitalism. But central planning, some of which in my view is mandatory, is not necessarily the touchstone of success that some American Marxists believe.[4] Huge bureaucracies and bureaucratic inflexibility also take a toll in centrally planned economies.

Closely related to the Marxist argument, although distinct from it, is the power structure theory, which holds that a small elite governs the nation. The elite consists essentially of corporate, military, and political leaders. The military-industrial complex is a good illustration of the power structure argument. At the end of World War II the United States emerged as the strongest power in the world by a wide margin, having lost little and grown enormously in weaponry and power during the War. We alone possessed atomic weapons. At about that time the drums began to beat about the dangers Russia posed to the United States, and since that time no less than a trillion dollars have been spent in beating off that threat. As three members of the Senate Armed Services Committee said in a minority report against the ABM:

> The American people have lived with fears of a Soviet attack for some quarter of a century, ever since World War II, and have expended a thousand billion dollars on defense in recognition of

4. For discussion of incremental as opposed to centralized policy making and planning, see David Braybrooke and Charles E. Lindblom, *A Strategy of Decision* (New York: The Free Press, 1963).

this possible danger. These gigantic expenditures have been detri-
mental to many other plans, programs and policies which now also
appear vitally important to the security and well-being of this Nation. The American people now know that many billions of these
dollars spent on defense have been wasted.[5]

It is the power elitists' contention that these expenditures were determined by the elite in its own best interests, not in the interest of actual
defense or anything else.

    As the reader will recall, I take a very serious view of the power
of the military-industrial complex; its power and success command
respect even if it be the respect one gives a rattlesnake. But that does
not mean that the only factor determining our military expenditure
policy has been the greed of those who profit from it. The Russians
helped produce the policy by giving ground for the fears by, for example, their policies in Eastern Europe, and particularly in Czechoslovakia
and Hungary. And as I shall argue momentarily, the nationalistic fervor
of the American people needed little encourageemnt to make them
approve ever more expensive and destructive military weaponry. The
elite who benefited from the military construction had fast allies not
only in the American Legion but also among workers who gained employment from the armaments industry. Every munitions factory, aircraft plant, or military base in the United States enlisted a strong base
of local support when the economic contributions of such establish-
ments became apparent.

    Thus in an area of public policy where the power elite argument is
at its strongest, it can be shown that other factors were included. It
might be argued, however, that jingoistic propaganda, masterminded
by the elite, whipped up a feverish mood in the society and made the
masses the tool of the military-industrial elite. Without doubt military
and corporate leaders did resort to propaganda of all kinds to get the
public to hate and fear the Russians and to love military expenditures.
Nationalistic fervor, however, does not need to be generated by a
conscious policy; it is independently rooted. Moreover the Russians
played a cooperative role. News media have played the anti-Communist
game, but not necessarily at the behest of a group of conspirators who
pulled strings to get the desired reactions. Thus it is common for
small-town newspapers to have headlines about what the "Commies"
are doing, and enemy soldiers in Vietnam become in the news media
"Communist soldiers," although I have yet to hear Americans referred

    5. Quoted in *I. F. Stone's Weekly*, July 28, 1969, p. 1. See also Richard Barnet,
The Economy of Death (New York: Atheneum, 1961), Ch. 1.

to by their political orientation. Nationalistic fervor and xenophobia serve the ends of the elite but are not necessarily created by it.

In short, in this as in other areas the power structure analysis is oversimplified. The power elite has competitors; it does not "control" on many issues, and even where it is extremely powerful, as in military matters, to attribute full authority to the elite is to reduce to insignificance such forces as ideology, nationalism, foreign nations' actions, and even Congressional resistance to military spending, as demonstrated on the ABM issue in August of 1969. The ABM issue aroused much opposition in the nation, presumably in part because of the attention focused on military matters by the Vietnam war, but whatever the reason it was possible to muster forty-nine Senate votes in opposition to the deployment of ABM despite all the arm twisting the Nixon Administration could apply, all the self-promotion of the Pentagon, and an advertising and distortion campaign conducted by the defense industry itself. (Thus, in a grossly distorted statement in a newspaper advertisement, falsely suggesting that an overwhelming proportion of the public favored the ABM system, it was discovered that 55 of the 344 signatories of the ad were connected with companies holding defense contracts.[6])

The pluralists take an opposite tack and find such a wide distribution of authority that supposedly all groups have an opportunity to influence the policy process. Again, the evidence adduced in the preceding chapters raises doubts about the validity of pluralism. There are nearly impossible barriers for some elements of society, which may not mean that an elite exists, but it does suggest a much greater degree of inequality among participants than the pluralists perceive.[7] But the point scarcely needs to be elaborated further here. If the reader has not been persuaded by the preceding chapters concerning inequalities of power among groups, then no argument in summation is likely to alter his opinion.

On the general question of the distribution of power in this society, I take a position different from those of the Marxists, the elitists, or the pluralists. I have argued that reality contains some elements of all

6. In fact fourteen signers were in businesses then doing work on ABM. See *The New York Times*, Aug. 4, 1969. The ad reported that 85 per cent of the public favored ABM, but in reality the Gallup Poll found that 60 per cent had no opinion on it or were unaware it was an issue, while 25 per cent favored it and 15.per cent opposed.

7. See the excellent critique of pluralism and elitism in Theodore J. Lowi's *The End of Liberalism* (New York: Norton, 1969). Lowi's book became available to me when all but this concluding chapter had been written; I find that we share many fundamental positions, although his argument is more ideologically oriented than mine.

three theories. The private ownership of industry and the private control over resources are enormously important political forces, but they are not all determinative. There are elites and some of them are inordinately powerful, although none of them assumes the kind of exclusive control that the elitists perceive. There is dispersion of authority as the pluralists claim; there are counterforces that influence the economic lords and the more powerful elites, and any attempt to comprehend power in this society without taking that counterforce into account is bound to go awry. But to posit these elements of truth in the Marxist and the elitist interpretations is to undercut the pluralist case.

Therefore what appears to me to come closer to reality is the kind of concentration-dispersal that I have argued for previously. That is, inequalities of power are patently great and have significant impact on the lives of us all, and especially on the lives of those with little money and not much political leverage. But those elites are not all powerful by any means. And there is much dispersal of authority, much opportunity to counter what elites want to achieve, or what reformers try to do when they seek to alleviate problems. Thus the concentrations of power and the dispersal both have an impact on policy making, for the elites use both their concentrated power and the dispersal of authority in the veto system to achieve their ends.

The elitists fail to see the uses to which dispersal of power can be put in achieving the ends of those with great power. Because the goals of those with the greatest economic stakes in public policy can usually be served by the preventing of action, the veto system becomes a critically important facet of the governing process. It becomes a prime source of authority, for it can be the means to deciding whether action will be taken or in what form if action is to be permitted. In Congress, for example, power is widely dispersed and tollgates are accordingly set up through which all legislation must pass—often only after a fatal levy has been paid. Power, far from being structured, is variable, scattered, and applied in competitive, bargaining situations that alter with the time and the issues involved. But there is one constant in the power utilization process: the have-not's either cannot get in the bargaining room or they enter with meager resources. *Minority elements face just as much difficulty from the dispersal of power as they do from the unequal power held by the elites, for both serve to create the priorities that exclude the poor or racial minorities from consideration.*

Thus an historic bias against governmental action in general, a system of dispersed power in the legislature that inhibits or distorts policy making, a very powerful judiciary that delays and further distorts policy, an independent bureaucracy that often obfuscates and modifies policies, and a federal system that disperses power to the scattered states (and, in effect, localities too)—all serve to constrain the effectuation of policies that would aid the have-not's. Because dispersal invites negotiation and bargaining, the poor or the racial minorities are denied, for they have the least opportunity to be represented in bargaining and the least leverage even when they are there. The dispersal process spreads beyond government, taking certain matters of vital importance to the poor out of the public arena entirely. For example, the racially discriminatory policies of labor unions and employers are beyond the reach of ghetto dwellers; they may try to force the employment question into the public arena but getting or keeping it there is difficult. Thus in Newark black leaders held up the decision to build a new state medical school in the city until they won assurance of fair employment practices in the construction force. They won a signed agreement but still failed to get a significant number of black construction workers hired—partly because the unions and the employers see their policies as *private* not public.

The issue of relocation of residents in urban renewal will illustrate how this works. Elite groups in cities became gradually aware, following World War II, that the cities were decaying and that the economic base of the city was threatened. If the deterioration became bad enough it would endanger an enormous investment in center-city real estate, therefore the Urban Renewal Program won elite approval. In the bargaining process by which the legislation was created, the poor who lived in the path of the intended bulldozers were only nominally and indirectly represented. A demand was made for relocation of the victims in alternative housing that was not substandard and such a provision went into the law, but that did not mean it went into effect. Cities had to agree formally that they would provide decent alternative housing, but finding it proved difficult and therefore the vast majority of those who were displaced by the new business buildings or roads or high-cost housing were never provided what the law said they must have. Slum residents still find it impossible to force the system to do what the law requires. Riots, demonstrations, orderly protest, in addition to all the channels of "normal" political activity, have not made available safe standard housing for the residents of renewed areas.

Why? Because an elite systematically denies it to them? On the contrary, the elites that benefit most from most renewal programs are scarcely aware that the poor are forced into worse housing by renewal. To be sure, the power of elites is one factor in making the policy that results in the disadvantage to the displaced residents, but it is a dispersal of power in the political and the administrative system that keeps the victims from getting redress for their grievance. In Newark, for example, the construction of a highway, a medical school, and numerous urban renewal projects have kept families moving about like nomads—sometimes twice a year. Alternative housing is scarce and in the last five years the vacancy rate in Newark has declined from 3 to one per cent. The city itself has very limited funds with which to provide decent housing, and neither New Jersey nor national political leaders are willing to appropriate money with which to create decent housing, even on land that has already been cleared. Said one group demanding action from the U.S. Department of Housing and Urban Development:

> The fact is there is no vacant housing . . . and hundreds of families have been relocated in substandard . . . housing without any effective means of protesting what now appears to be an obviously grossly unfair system of dislocation without effective community participation, supported by federal money granted on the basis of artificial figures, and monitored only superficially by any federal officials.[8]

Another factor tends to make it difficult for renewal victims to get remedial action, and that is the process of submerging issues before they even get on the agenda. By isolating those who attempt to bring an issue to the attention of decision makers, elites may manage to "decide" the issue by keeping it from ever being considered. Or sanctions—both negative and positive—can be used to prevent leaders from raising issues. That is, by cooptation, leaders of the ghetto may be bought off and prevented from raising troublesome issues, or a threat of denial (such as patronage or a political nomination) may quash an issue before it is a public matter. Peter Bachrach has spelled out the ways in which such suppression of issues has taken place in Baltimore on a broad range of matters of vital concern to the black community.[9] But he also shows that the coming of greater militancy on the part of black leaders and the organization of black slum dwellers through the War on Poverty undercut the power of the elites to suppress issues. In Newark militancy and new forms of ghetto organization likewise have increased the capacity of black leaders to force issues onto the agenda, but forcing an issue to be considered and publicly debated is not to force its favorable resolution. Black leaders have succeeded often in raising the relocation issue, have even managed to get signed agreements with public authorities about relocation, but the problem per-

8. Letter from Junius Williams and Charles Bell to George Romney, Secretary of HUD, quoted in the *Newark News*, Aug. 1, 1969.

9. "Nondecision Making and the Urban Racial Crisis," paper delivered at the 1969 Convention of the American Political Science Association, mimeo.

sists. The evasiveness of the system has outdistanced the capacity of the black leadership to force action.

Is this an elite dominating **the** poor in Newark with a conscious policy of denying decent housing? Is it pluralism with open access for all to participate equally? Rather it is a situation in which power serves the ends of elites through both concentration and dispersal—concentration in determining broad policy objectives and setting the main priorities, and dispersal to legislatures, administrators, states, cities, and courts, which frustrates the efforts of the victims seeking remedies.

An alternative notion must be considered, however, and that is the proposition that the denial of the minorities is a consequence of the fact that they are a minority—that the denials are the simple product of majority rule. Herbert J. Gans, for example, has argued that the only way to end the "urban crisis" is to "end majority rule." [10] He says that most voters and their representatives are unwilling to give cities the necessary funds and authority to deal with poverty, segregation, and municipal decay. Voters may support defense spending or shooting the moon, but are unwilling to support governmental ventures to help persons other than themselves, said Gans. The poor are powerless to prevent this because they are a minority, are the victims of gerrymanders, and are not a homogeneous group capable of organizing for self-defense. He contends that majority rule is unusually prevalent in American politics; anyone may propose policy but only "the majority" can decide. Gans has an oversimplified view of majoritarian democracy, but his general point is valid: the minority's minority status is one of its most serious difficulties.

But the problem is not only the functioning of the majority principle; it is also a matter of the successful manipulation of the system by certain minorities to provide their benefits, whereas others cannot accomplish this. Being in minority status has not hindered the leaders of corporations in pursuit of their goals; producers of goods are far fewer than the consumers of them, but the latter have far less capacity to demand protection than the former have in avoiding it. In fact, as I tried to show in my discussion of Congress, the system is more properly described as a system of "minorities rule," where many minority elements are in conflict and where no permanent majority exists. The problem is to improve opportunities for impoverished minorities to achieve programs appropriate to their needs rather than beating down a permanent denying majority.

There is, nevertheless, validity in the proposition that legislators and

10. "We Won't End the Urban Crisis Until We End 'Majority Rule,'" *The New York Times Magazine*, Aug. 3, 1969, pp. 12ff.

elective officials do respond to the attitudes of the mass of the voters. They build massive highway systems and fail to create tenable mass transit systems because voters obviously prefer to drive. But it would be a gross error to conclude that the reasons we build highways and not mass transit systems is solely a matter of responding to voter wishes. Demonstrably there are also powerful interests that have reason to want highways—the automobile makers, the truckers, the highway builders, the oil industry, to name the more obvious ones. Moreover, legislators need not respond to voter wishes—insofar as they are ascertainable—in anything like the automatic way that the enunciation of the majoritarian idea suggests. There is in fact a wide leeway for discretion on the part of policy makers. If the mass of people were as selfish as the Gans argument suggests we would not be spending $9 billion in public funds for health services, nor $16 billion from the federal treasury for income maintenance alone in fiscal 1970. What therefore must be found is not necessarily an alternative to the majority principle but ways of improving the leverage of the denied minorities.

I shall argue in the concluding section of this chapter that this is not a hopeless undertaking, although it is certainly a difficult one. I have some hope that it can be done, because of one other important policy-shaping force: the power of ideas. I am not so naïve as to say that if we change the notions in the minds of leaders and the public we can readily override the power of elites who want no change in the status quo—certainly not change that will cost them money. But it can be reasonably argued that among the most powerful sources of de-termination of policy are the ideas that men accept. No better proof of that can be found than the fact that so many people support the war in Vietnam practically without thinking about it despite the devastating refutation that can be and often has been made. If one spreads the simplistic Communist threat notion widely enough it can be sold, and a wasteful, dangerous, and destructive policy can be based upon it.

Perhaps we can make a better case, however, by referring to past events, thus removing the emotional overtones of current controversy. In the first years of the Great Depression, followers of the laissez-faire doctrines believed that the less government interfered with business the sooner the economic dislocation would be righted. If anything was learned from those disastrous years, it was precisely the opposite—that governmental noninterference was ruinous. Yet so firm was the grip of those ideas on the minds of President Herbert Hoover and his entourage that direct governmental action to feed the jobless seemed like rank heresy. An even more drastic example of men's causing suffer-ing because they were enthralled with mad ideas is the case of the laissez-faire politicians of England during the Irish potato famine. When a blight killed the potato crop in Ireland in 1845, the British government at first provided direct relief measures, like the importation of food from the United States and Europe, but a new government met the worse crisis of hunger in 1846 by deciding it was wrong for the government to interfere. Though people were starving in droves, and were being carted away for mass burial by the barely surviving, the government refused to give in. The ministers in London convinced themselves that it would be utterly wrong for government to interfere with the laws of economics by feeding the dying Irish. One may grant that the Irish were the British equivalent of American "niggers," but the leaders of the government persisted in their refusal to meddle, despite their expressions of horror at what was happening. They were so utterly sure that remedial action would bring more harm than good that they permitted a million people to die without turning a hand to help.[11]

One could go on citing endless examples of mad policies based upon equally mad ideas. It is depressing to reflect on what people will believe and what they will do on the basis of their beliefs. In World War I a carnage of such incredible proportions took place that it is retrospectively almost impossible to understand how governments could go on supporting generals who showed nothing but a willingness to throw more and more millions of bodies into the maw of war. But there was little in the way of rebellion against the policy, and much public support for it. If this is a depressing observation, there may be hope in it too; *for if such stupidity and sacrifice can be acceptable, then other kinds of sacrifice in demonstrable ultimate self-interest may be acceptable too.*

11. See Cecil Woodham-Smith, *The Great Hunger* (London: Hamish, Hamilton, 1963).

CHAPTER NINE

What Is to Be Done?

I HAVE attempted to describe some of the crises the nation and the world face, and I have pointed to the complexity of the reasons why those crises exist. There is no simple explanation, no key that provides *the* answer to the riddles of social causation. Nor is there any panacea that will magically solve the problems. Americans suffer from twin illusions that not only must there be a "solution" to every problem, but very likely the solution will be some change in governmental structure—the Constitutional Convention syndrome. There is scant reason to hold either of these ideas. Our more chronic social problems rarely can be solved in the way poliomyelitis was eliminated. Poverty, interpersonal conflict, inequality, and injustices of various kinds will never be removed. Nor is there much reason to hope that tinkering with the structure of government will provide the answers either. Power will still be in the hands of someone and power can always be misused as well as rightly employed. Society is inconceivable in the absence of politics (in the sense of competition for values and the exercise of influence), and therefore, given the inequalities among men that are inevitable also, there will be injustices no matter how government is structured.

Thus a healthy skepticism about gimmicks for structural change is warranted. But that does not mean that modification of institutions and political practices is unimportant. Obviously the institutional structure gives advantages and disadvantages to participants in the political process, and major alterations in the structure can redistribute power. But we are by no means certain always what the consequence of changes will be. Predicting the resulting redistribution of power through modification of political parties, for example, or the method of electing the President is far from being a simple task; experts and practitioners seem to misjudge about as often as they are accurate. Moreover, some kinds of basic modifications are so impossible of attainment, because of the roadblocks already in the system, that seeking the changes would be a waste of time. Thus some reformers have called for remapping the country and arranging state boundaries in some more rational fashion—thus accommodating the need for greater urban power and independence from suburban or small-town control. Without going into the complexity of deciding how to separate the inseparable (you might take the city out of the metropolitan area only to find it was still there with a new set of complications and artificial boundaries producing different but enduring disputes), one should remember that such a change can come about only with the consent of the people who would be removed, or else through constitutional amendments, which require the assent of two thirds of Congress and three fourths of the states.

So it is with many of the gimmicks often proposed; they are often impossible of achievement, unpredictable, or self-defeating. Herbert Gans, for example, would provide in legislative bodies that any proposal could be kept alive and brought up for reconsideration if a quarter of the representatives voted for it. A more expeditious method of preventing action would be difficult to conceive; simply keeping issues on the agenda does not make them law, it merely clogs the agenda. Gans would also "cure" the disease of too much reliance on majority power by making "administrative agencies and their bureaucracies more accountable, perhaps by replacing appointive officers with elective ones, or by requiring such bodies to be run by elected boards of directors." [1] This sounds to me like the hair-of-the-dog remedy for a hangover: to cure an overdose of liquor, drink some more! Why assume that making the bureaucracy more responsive to the majority will would make it more sympathetic to the minority, whose problem is partly animosity of the majority? Raising the Office of Economic Opportunity to cabinet status or creating a Department of Minorities, which Gans also suggests, might do no harm, but neither—without other policies and other commitments—would that do much good. Creating a Department of Housing and Urban Development has certainly not solved the housing shortage for the poor.

Others contend that only through a revolutionary change in the ownership of the means of production—socialism—will it be possible to achieve justice. Leaving aside for the moment the validity of the argument that socialism is a necessary precondition to significant change, the more immediate question is whether we have time to wait for the millennium to provide us with such a drastic change. Socialism, even in the moderate Scandinavian or British versions, is bound to be doubly difficult to introduce in the United States; a more hostile soil for growing that commodity would be hard to imagine. If it is not going to be achieved by Fabian persuasion neither is it coming via revolution. The chances for a successful uprising on the part of the small minority that feels a revolution is necessary are so miniscule as to be negligible. The consequence of the attempt will be brutal suppression, as the sym-

1. Op. cit., p. 26.

pathetic student of revolution, Barrington Moore, rightly says. Moore argues persuasively that it is unlikely that black and white radicals could collaborate adequately or get the necessary support from workers in key industries. "There is even smaller likelihood that they could neutralize the police and the army." If major disruption were attempted, it would not be long before the mass of the population would demand that the electricity be turned back on, whatever the cost.

> By and large [Moore comments] it seems safe to predict that the groups interested in disruption would be on opposite sides of the barricades: police and other city employees on one side, blacks, student radicals and a few intellectuals on the other. Hence any such major disruption would very likely result in martial law or worse." [2]

The fact is, like it or not, it will be necessary to work within the existing system, making such modifications as possible with whatever political power can be mustered and whatever means of persuasion can be developed. To wait for utopian changes or to function as though we had generations of time in which to modify iron-bound institutional structures before attacking the problems is to ask for disaster. For the threat of nuclear war, population pressures, disruption from racial discrimination, starvation, and fascist repression are not remote possibilities but present dangers. It may well be too late to stave off these catastrophes; it may already be too late to undo the consequences of a racist history or to halt the drift toward a nuclear holocaust, and clearly millions will die around the world and in the United States before sensible policies are developed for feeding the hungry.

In the face of the intractable interests that have so much to gain from the status quo, does it then make sense to contend that we must begin by publicizing the nonsense basis of the priorities we now have? It can be said that some changes, at least, have come about by that route. President Lyndon Johnson dared not run for reelection because of the unpopularity of the war in Vietnam, and much of that unpopularity was the direct result of demonstrations and other dissent aimed at publicizing the stupidity and immorality of that war. Although defense budgets have in the past been accepted with little scrutiny and each new weapons system approved with barely a ripple of dissent, Pentagon spending is beginning to receive the critical examination it deserves. Opponents of military waste prevailed in the Senate in August, 1969,

2. See Moore's article "Revolution in America?" *New York Review of Books,* Jan. 30, 1969.

by insisting on a closer accounting of military spending. The Chairman of the Armed Services Committee called the proposal "unAmerican" but it passed 47 to 46.[3] In fact, during six weeks of debate on the 1969 Armed Forces Appropriation Bill the Senate accepted eleven and rejected five proposed amendments. Some of the modifications were minor; others were significant. Opponents of the ABM came within one vote of preventing the deploying of that dubious venture. Considerable revision of the inequitable income tax law seems inevitable. Legislation has been enacted for automobile safety, and tighter drug controls have also been passed, both actions following publicity that stressed the dangers involved. We have awakened to the nature of black life in America because black leaders and especially black youth dared to resist the system, rejected the pleas to wait another generation, and publicized their acts by every means possible in order to get public support. Slowly, public policy concerning birth control assistance for the poor, both in this country and abroad, has changed, action has at last been inaugurated to curb pollution, and aid for the hungry has been increased. And much more.

Of course, not enough has happened. The killing continues in Vietnam, we are going to have the ABM, and people go hungry. But change is possible—it has happened and more can be done. The necessity to act is clear; the question is can we? To do it we shall have to accomplish four acts of persuasion. First, it will have to be shown that it is economically feasible to deal with our social problems. Second, we must demonstrate the dangers inherent in the priorities we presently tolerate. Third, the inhuman consequences of the present bargaining process must be stressed. Fourth, the deeply traditional American fear of public authority must be broken.

Economic Feasibility. In view of the resources the United States puts into military programs, especially during wars, there does not seem to be much question that resources would be available to meet our needs for decent housing, job training, educational facilities, pollution abatement, new and sensible programs for handling criminal behavior, and other programs. During World War II the economy boomed while fifteen million men were sustained in the military, most of them doing nothing useful, and countless other millions labored to produce and deliver an incredible amount of war matériel. In fact, at that time the federal budget reached nearly $100 billion from a Gross National Product of $212 billion; today all public expenditures account for less than

3. See Warren Weaver, Jr., "Senate, 47 to 46, Asks for Review of Defense Costs," *The New York Times,* Aug. 8, 1969. See also the optimistic but perhaps not unrealistic argument of John Kenneth Galbraith, *How to Control the Military* (New York: New American Library, Signet edn., 1969).

a quarter of the GNP. Thus even with present expenditures of $30 billion a year for Vietnam there is opportunity for spending much greater sums on constructive programs, even though it would necessitate tax levies that assuredly would be resisted. With a significant cutback in military expenditures, however, great amounts would be available for domestic programs. And the programs themselves would generate still more economic activity. If the billions that are going into the ABM system had instead been devoted to rebuilding the slums of the nation, we could invigorate the economies of the cities by providing vitally necessary employment to the slum dwellers and the inevitable impact on other business activity would be enormous. And there is almost no end to the demand for development of decent housing, not only to replace the hovels of today but to meet the population growth of tomorrow. The Senate Committee on Nutrition and Human Needs asserts that $4 billion a year would be needed to bring the diets of twenty-five million Americans up to adequate levels.[4] That sounds like a lot of money, but there are also countless thousands of unemployed farm workers who could be employed in producing that food. The "bargaining" way to feed the poor would be merely to buy the food from farmers, getting it at the lowest price. But it might make more sense to assist the rural poor to produce the food and to finance the program in part by ending subsidies to farmers for not growing food. Surely it must be possible to devise ways of "profitably" feeding the poor by assisting the poor in gaining employment while providing needed food. If some small part of the ingenuity that went into putting men on the moon went into feeding the hungry and employing the idle, is there any reason to believe it could not be done?

We now spend billions to provide minimal income levels for those on welfare, and we shall have to continue to do so, because most of those who are helped are either children, aged or handicapped persons, or mothers of small children. But others are unemployed or underemployed because they are black, are poorly educated, or live in economically depressed areas. Systematic programs to train the physically capable would produce an enormous payoff. The Job Corps, which the Nixon Administration sharply curtailed, was a promising venture precisely because it did equip young men to take jobs rather than to face lives of futility. The complaint that the Job Corps training cost several thousands of dollars per trainee is a ridiculous objection. The productivity of the individual would compensate for the investment, and to provide

4. Senate Select Committee on Nutrition and Human Needs, *Interim Report*, "The Food Gap: Poverty and Malnutrition in the U.S." (Washington: U.S. Government Printing Office, August, 1969).

a person with an alternative to crime or public support for lack of employment opportunities might save the public far more than expended. Nor does it make much sense to close the camps because drugs, drinking, and fighting had been found there. Who were these young men and women but fugitives from slums that are rife with drugs, drink, violence, and worse? The purpose of saving men from death at an immature age—from a police bullet, an overdose of heroin, or tuberculosis —is worth the investment in a society that cares about human values.

The $4 billion we spend annually for jails and police protection is another example of inhuman economics. Because jails are a prime training ground for crime, and because recidivism is common, does it make sense to go on fighting crime with more and more repression when the repression only invites more crime? We do not even know accurately what crime actually costs, because not all crime is reported to the police, but we are aware of many billions in losses annually. Because we know that jails do not stop crime, except when the prisoner is behind bars (and not always then), would it not seem appropriate to try something other than the most degrading life imaginable for persons found guilty of crime? It would cost large sums of money to provide imaginative psychiatric treatment for the criminal, but if an accurate accounting were made the sums expended might be more than repaid, not only in lives saved but also in property spared.

The common belief that the expenditure of public funds is "waste" and not productive of economic good must be attacked, and the public must be shown that investment in education, for example, is one of the most productive expenditures a society can make. It must be made clear that building new towns or reconstructing center cities as decent places to live is no more "waste" than to create a steel mill or drill an oil well. The economic system of the nation is enormously productive and it will continue to grow and expand further. Therefore the resources for achieving a decent life for everyone are within reach if we decide to do it. If we cut our military expenditures to a proportion of the GNP comparable to the pre-Korean War level and thus reduce our military outlays to about one half of present levels, we would free about $40 billion a year for useful as opposed to destructive purposes. (In 1950 we spent $14.1 billion for defense or about 5 per cent of the GNP; now we spend about $80 billion and about 10 per cent of the GNP.) But even without deep cuts in defense it is possible—if admittedly politically difficult— to begin to appropriate the moneys necessary to build a decent society for all.

Our Dangerous Present Priorities.   These pages have stressed (again and again, I fear) the dangers generated by the priorities we now hold. It is necessary to get across to the American people the gravity of the dangers and to make them realize the necessity for different policies. For example, the price black people have paid because of white racism is gradually beginning to be realized, but a far more intensive campaign is necessary, using every medium of communication available, to get across to white Americans the implications of racism and the potential risks of not acting. So long as whites do not realize that Negroes are not just white people with black skins, so long as they have no appreciation of the historic deprivations suffered by black people, there will be no willingness to act in rational ways to overcome the deficits accruing to Negroes. I am under no illusions about the difficulty of such a campaign; the ingrained distrust and/or hatred of Negroes is too deep to be eradicated in less than centuries. Poor whites (or working-class whites) who feel threatened by Negro advances are not going to be readily won over by any educational process. A more modest but important goal would be merely to convince liberal whites of the necessity of at least comprehending the position and problems of the black community. Even persons who have attended parochial schools, lived in ethnic neighborhoods, participated in intense ethnic politics, and belonged to churches and organizations with emphasis on ethnicity still react with horror to Negroes' emphasizing their ethnic pride. A demand for black-oriented schools is seen as dangerous separatism and self-segregation; the nation has not perished as a result of parochial education, nor will black teachers and principals in our unfortunately segregated school system be ruinous. After decades of failure to achieve integrated schools, insistence on community control over the existing schools may be at least an understandable demand. If those who have felt themselves to be friends of the Negro but who are becoming increasingly hostile to such confrontations as those over school decentralization and union hiring practices can be made to realize the nature of the black community, the possibility of progress will be greater. For, as I shall argue later, we shall make progress only if some real authority is asserted in such matters as upgrading slum schools and permitting minority groups to ply skilled trades from which they have been excluded. To gain support in contests with teachers, educational bureaucrats, and labor unions a broader base of comprehension must be created.

It hardly seems necessary tc repeat what has been said about the creeping dangers of pollution, resource depletion, and population growth, or the imminent threat to us all of nuclear annihilation. But if we are to stave off these threats we shall have to convince people that there are ways of thinking about problems other than in nationalistic terms. My colleague Richard Falk, warning of threats of the kind just cited, sees a need for a "transnational consciousness" and a world order with the power to "define community interests and to impose them on a global basis. This kind of solution is essentially political and moral rather than technical," he says. Recognizing that there would be intense opposition to such a movement, Falk says there will be evidence of its becoming a serious part of our political life if its proponents are willing to be jailed by the people who fear the challenge. What the chances are for the creation of such a world order, one cannot be sure, although it certainly would seem highly doubtful. But surely a precondition of any possibility for it would have to be the spreading of a much fuller awareness of the costs of not moving in some such directions.[5]

The Inhuman Consequences of Aimless Bargaining. Hardly anyone in this society can be completely oblivious of the fact that the bargaining process operates in amoral ways. But I do not believe that most people realize the full impact of that process, nor do they realize that in other nations some of the negative consequences of the bargaining game have been eliminated. In Britain, for example, the provision of medical services for all has made first-rate medical care available to all, improving the health of a whole society. In the United States profit-motive medical care has skyrocketed in price, and the inevitable consequence is that those with money can afford excellent medical care, but the poor get wretched care. The blindness of the American medical system has also resulted in a critical shortage of doctors, often resulting in the total absence of them from center-city areas or depressed rural sections. Indeed, so critical has our neglect to train doctors become that we now import thousands of doctors from other countries, including the underdeveloped ones where the need for doctors is even more imperative than it is here. The pages of British medical journals ran over four thousand advertisements for doctors to come to the United States in 1966; it costs over $20,000 to train a doctor, and the wealthy United States takes from less wealthy countries to supply our needs.[6] Likewise, by attempting in the United States to make a commercial venture of supplying human blood, we have not only failed to provide a supply sufficient to meet needs but have also boosted the price of blood to confiscatory levels for the average person who needs a large amount for some critical illness. One student of the situation says the American consumer is far from sovereign in the matter of blood transfusions. The consumer risks contracting diseases because much of the blood is often taken from addicts who sell their blood to support their habit, whether

5. See Israel Shenker's interview with Falk, "Man's Extinction Held Real Peril," *The New York Times*, Apr. 7, 1969.

6. See Richard M. Titmus on this problem in his *Commitment to Welfare* (New York: Random House, 1968), p. 126.

or not they have hepatitis or other diseases. Our system is judged to be wasteful and expensive with an

> immense and swollen bureaucracy required to administer a complex banking system of credits, deposits, charges, transfers, and so forth. Above all it is a system which neglects and punishes the indigent, the colored, the dispossessed and the deviant.

By contrast in Britain,

> There is no shortage of blood. It is freely donated by the community for the community. It is a free gift from the healthy to the sick irrespective of income, class, ethnic group, religion, private patient or public patient. Since the National Health Service was established the quantity of blood issued to hospitals has risen by 265 per cent.[7]

I have cited many other examples of the crude ways in which the pluralist system sifts the disadvantaged ones out onto the scrap heap. The disemployment of miners and cotton-field hands through technological advances is a perfect example. No provision for their futures was made, because they simply did not matter. In the short run it has no doubt proved cheaper to ignore these victims than to take them into account, even if we have to spend billions for their relief. In the long run it may not be so profitable, however, if all the consequences are taken into account. If the divisions in the society become ruinous, and as the drag on the economy from unemployed and unemployable persons becomes more extensive, it will be bound to cause major losses. Thus, for economic as well as moral reasons we need to make it tellingly clear to all what the costs of the human scrap heap approach really are. In other words we must emphasize the importance of providing every able-bodied person with the opportunity to contribute to his own maintenance and to the community good through providing the dignity that purposeful employment involves. What we owe every man is not just sustenance to keep him and his family alive, but the chance to work in some meaningful job to provide self-respect as well as income.

Breaking Down the American Fear of Public Authority. It has been deemed the genius of American government that it was so constrained that it could not effectively govern. Our historic fear of excessive power originated in colonial resistance to London's exercise of power over the colonies even before we were a nation. The Revolution reinforced that

7. Ibid., pp. 150–51.

dread and made the curtailing of public authority a virtue; subsequent political leaders reified the doctrine and conservative political interests benefited handsomely from it. I hardly need repeat now the innumerable ways in which power is restrained. Nor am I so naïve as to believe it will be possible to strip away most of those restraints. But I am convinced that it is imperative to begin to show some of the consequences of overconcern with tyranny of the majority and begin to permit policy to be enacted and to be effectively enforced in realms where heretofore it never has been.

For one prime example, it is necessary to do something about the independent regulatory agencies, which become singularly important in the absence of public ownership of the means of production. If we cannot alter ownership and control over production, the next best thing is to equip the government to ride herd on the uncontrolled forces of industry. It certainly is not so equipped now. The regulatory agencies were outfitted with rubber teeth from the day of their conception; they cannot and do not protect the public. Thus a special panel, drawn from inside the Food and Drug Administration, gave a devastating critique of the FDA's operations. The group said it believed the public thought it was being guarded against hazardous products, but that, they said, was a misconception. "This misconception should be dispelled to the greatest extent possible. The consumer must be exposed to the realities of what the F.D.A. can and cannot do—both from the standpoint of legal authority and resource allocation." There is neither manpower nor statutory authorization to deal with the $130 billion in annual sales of the industries supposedly covered by the agency.[8] The FDA, like other regulatory agencies, was given independent status on creation to prevent the line departments from exercising controlling authority, but this also converted the regulatory process into a bargaining, legalistic process. Regulatory powers were delegated to the agencies, as Theodore Lowi points out, but for various reasons they simply are not exercised. One problem is that agency personnel tend to share the viewpoint of the regulated industries. Presumably the agencies are highly specialized bodies, but more often the commissioners are selected for their political reliability, or they come from the industry being regulated. And when a vigorous regulator is proposed for appointment the industry usually manages to defeat his appointment or reappointment if he gets by and makes trouble. What it amounts to is a situation in which a wealthy industry battles for its interest in an arena where the public interest is weakly represented or not represented at all.[9]

8. See Harold Schmeck, "Food-Drug Panel Criticizes Agency," *The New York Times,* Aug. 8, 1969.
    9. Lowi, op. cit., Ch. 5.

What we should do with the regulatory agencies is abolish them one and all, transfer their authority to the line departments, and make a set of determinations about what policy is to be and enforce it rather than leave the law vague, and thus permit the law to evolve in the course of bargaining between the timid bureaucrats of the regulatory agencies and the powerful regulated interests. This is the argument of both Professor Lowi and another recent commentator on the agencies, a *Wall Street Journal* reporter, Louis M. Kohlmeier. Kohlmeier in a devastating analysis of the regulatory agencies shows how the Federal Communications Commission fails to regulate the radio and television industries, over which it supposedly has charge; how the Interstate Commerce Commission has never regulated the railroads in any rational way— how indeed all the agencies soon forgot their original charge: the protection of the consumer.[10] It does not follow axiomatically that transfer of the regulatory authority to the line departments would result in speedy, appropriate controls, but there is at least a chance for action with the breaking through of the encrusted bureaucracy of the agencies and the necessary reconsideration of the intent and methods of regulating. At least it would end some of the legalism that the independent status created; it would put power where it could more easily be used if a will to use it existed.

One could cite other examples of the necessity for the exercise of power in the public interest. Perhaps the public can be aroused sufficiently over drug safety, filthy food, poisoned air, polluted streams, dangerous cars, and the like to make such regulation feasible. Even so, it will be doubly difficult to tackle the problems of racial discrimination in hiring and the educational bureaucracy, as examples of places where power is needed but will be hard to muster. Yet only if real authority exists to penalize unions and employers that discriminate and only if that authority is vigorously exercised will we get equal opportunity entrance into skilled trades and get the kind of revision of the school system that will make it, particularly in the ghetto, the kind of system that will turn out employable persons.

A potentially important contribution to providing some of the backing necessary for the exertion of greater authority in some of these critical areas is the greater participation of the poor and the black in the political process. To be sure, that is a difficult task, particularly because the lack of governmental action in their behalf tends to discourage the poor and the black from taking the effort to participate in politics. But for many reasons there may be new developments on this front. For one

10. *The Regulators* (New York: Harper and Row, 1969). See also Murray Edelman's *The Symbolic Uses of Politics* (Urbana: University of Illinois Press, 1964).

thing, the greatest impact of the antipoverty program may prove to have been the Community Action Program, which stimulated the poor to participate. Some of them acquired skills in political action from the CAP experience, and some leaders emerged who may be able to advance the cause of their people in many ways before cooptation tames them. Furthermore the Civil Rights Act of 1964 opened the door to black voter registration in the South, with the result that hundreds of thousands of previously disenfranchised Negroes now go to the polls. Because the South with its constrained one-party system, based fundamentally on exclusion of the Negro from politics, produces the most conservative phalanx in national politics, there may be some ground for hoping that even more extensive black participation in Southern politics may remove from the scene some of the more impossible nineteenth-century types who decorate Congress. Fourteen of the twenty-one Democratic votes in favor of ABM came from Southern Senators, which shows the size of the problem; but on the other hand a more liberal Democrat a few years ago did unseat Judge Howard Smith from the House Rules Committee by beating him in a primary, and a few of the mossback Southern Senators came out in favor of feeding the hungry, which most of them still do not favor. A shift of half a dozen votes in the Senate and twenty or thirty House seats to men with more modern views of life could have a considerable impact on the potential policy outcomes in Congress. Recognition of the potential impact of the poor brought to the polls in registration drives can be seen in the 1969 tax reform legislation, which forbids foundations to use funds for voter registration drives—a truly dangerous activity from the conservative viewpoint.

We may, however, be moving toward a new conservatism, as apparently President Nixon believes and with which he intends to be reelected in 1972. Certainly the rising radical right, as manifested in the George Wallace movement and in many right-wing organizations that thrive not only in rural and small-town America but in urban areas where residents feel threatened by Negroes, is ominous. If the society is tending to the right and if no action can be taken to make this a more human-oriented society, the consequences may be unpleasant. And it may be a puny response to the crises I have noted to say that they can be tackled by publicizing the stupidity of the policies we now follow. But other alternatives seem to offer no greater hope, therefore let us see whether men can be persuaded to reexamine the perverted priorities of American politics.

Index